Women, Migration & the Cashew Economy in Southern Mozambique

Women, Migration
& the Cashew Economy
in Southern Mozambique
1945–1975

Jeanne Marie Penvenne

Department of History
Tufts University

JC JAMES CURREY

James Currey
is an imprint of Boydell & Brewer Ltd
PO Box 9, Woodbridge, Suffolk IP12 3DF (GB)
www.jamescurrey.com

and of

Boydell & Brewer Inc.
668 Mt Hope Avenue, Rochester, NY 14620-2731 (US)
www.boydellandbrewer.com

British Library Cataloguing in Publication Data

A catalogue record for this book is available from the British Library

ISBN 978-1-84701-128-2 (James Currey cloth)

This publication is printed on acid-free paper

Typeset in 11 on 12pt Photina MT by Avocet Typeset, Somerton, Somerset

Até que enfim

to

The cashew shellers of Tarana
with admiration and in solidarity

to

Norman Robert Bennett
John Norman Bennett
& Louis Penvenne Bennett
for your patience and loving support

Contents

2 **Tarana**
History from the Factory Floor   80

3 **Migration**
Pathways from Poverty to Tarana   121

4 **Lives around Livelihoods**
'Children Are Not Like Chickens'   155

5 African Urban Families in the Late Colonial Era
Agency   180

Conclusions
Gendered Perspectives on Work, Households and Authority   210

Epilogue
Mozambique's Cashew Economy, 1975 to 2014   217

Sources and Bibliography

List of Illustrations

Maps

Graphs

Figures

Acknowledgements

I am deeply embarrassed that it has taken so long for this book to appear in print. I postponed writing up this research in order to diversify my dossier for a tenure and promotion review at Tufts University. It worked. Transcription, translation and analysis of oral narratives in three languages take a lot of time. Research, writing, and rewriting at a glacial pace is unfortunately what I do. Thank you for your patience. I have accrued a great many debts. I hope that the people who helped me a great deal and whose names I forget to include below will forgive me.

The first and most important acknowledgment is to the workers, staff and administration of Cajú Industrial de Moçambique. More than a hundred people from throughout the Chamanculo and Machava cashew shelling factories took this project seriously. They shared their own thoughts and memories, and listened intently to others. Their words and faces have lived with me throughout this process, helping me refocus and try to get it right. I obviously do not pretend to speak for the women and men of Cajú Industrial. They spoke for themselves and their taped words are available in the *Arquivo Histórico de Moçambique*. They taught me a great deal. I tried to share that in this book. I am also sure I misunderstood things they tried to convey, and I am grateful for their patience. I hope this effort honors their time and words.

The generous funding I received from the Fulbright Regional Research Award (1992–1993), Fulbright Scholar-Lecturer Award (2004–2005), U.S. Speaker and Specialist Award (1998), Gulbenkian Foundation International Fellowship (1993), and Tufts Faculty Research Awards (1995, 1996, 2008) was thanks to the efforts of wonderful colleagues who wrote endless references and authorized funds to support my research program: Sara Berry, Frederick Cooper, Allen Isaacman, James McCann, Jean Hay, the late Gerald R. Gill, Howard Malchow, Leila Fawaz, Sugata Bose, David Northrup, Kevin Dunn, and Laura Walters. Thank you for believing that my efforts might amount to something. The late Leroy Vail was one of my sharpest critics and most loyal supporters. His ability to draw connections among archival, text, song and interview perspectives, and to keep competing narratives in play provides a high standard for us all.

All of the Fulbright and USIA grants were awarded through the Council for International Exchange of Scholars and administered through the United States Information Agency and the Public Affairs Office of the United States Embassy in Maputo. Special thanks to Harriet McGuire, David Ballard, Edward Kemp, their families and the truly wonderful professional staff at the Public Affairs Office.

Many people made the oral research project at the core of this book possible, beginning with my Portuguese, Zulu, Changana and Ronga language teachers: Katherine Demuth at Boston University, Aurélio Simango and Bento Sitoe of the Department of Modern Letters at UEM. Bento Sitoe has unfailingly responded to queries about Changana and Ronga words. I secured research authorization for both the cashew shelling and tobacco processing industries with help from José Mateus Katupha, and Arlindo Lopes. They introduced me to the then Secretary of State for Cashews, Juliano Saranga, who authorized the project. Filipe Guambe guided me through the Chamanculo and Machava plants, providing introductions to the factory administration. They all made the cashew factory oral history project possible. Devica Nystedt provided an introduction to George Tsilhakis, proprietor of Sociedade Agrícola de Tabacos [SAT], who generously hosted an interview session with a group of SAT retirees.

Bento Sitoe introduced me to Joaquina Boane Machava who worked with me from January to August 1993 as a research assistant, interpreter and transcriber in Changana and Ronga. I discuss our working relationship in more detail in the introduction. Joaquina Machava's sunny spirit, quick wit, transparency and deep humanity set the tone for our relationships with everyone we encountered. We laughed a lot, cried sometimes, and truly enjoyed working as a team.

My archival work was shaped by the generosity and competence of the staff of the Arquivo Histórico de Moçambique [AHM]. The late Director Maria Inêz Nogueira da Costa, graciously allowed me access to the archive's largely un-cataloged warehouse in the lower city. António Sopa guided me through published newspapers, periodicals, business journals, archival correspondence, documents and especially photographs. He is simply a national treasure. Since Joel das Neves Tembe succeeded as Archive Director, he and his team have unfailingly supported my work. I appreciate the professionalism and warmth I always associate with AHM leadership and staff.

Manuel Araújo, then Director of the Faculty of Letters, and the staff and colleagues at the Department of History and Centro de Estudos Africanos [CEA] at Universidade Eduardo Mondlane [UEM], Arquivo de Património Cultural and Universidade Pedigógica all shared their work and gave critical consideration to my research proposal and incremental publications. Thanks to Bento Sitoe, Arlindo Lopes, Joel das Neves Tembe, David Hedges, Amélia Neves de Souto, Carlos Serra, Arlindo Chilundo, Aurélio Rocha, Luís Covane, Benigna Zimba,

Gerhard Liesegang, João Paulo Borges Coelho, Mário Chitaúte Cumbe, Adriana Cândida Biosse de Caifaz, Vitorino Sambo, Olga Iglesias das Neves, Denise Malauene, Fatima Mendonça, Matteu Angius, Sidney Bliss, José Fialho Feliciano, Ana Maria Gentili, Yussuf Adam and Alexandrino José. Women's history has been pioneered at the CEA, Núcleo de Género and the Women and the Law in Southern African Project [WLSA], Muleide and Forum Mulher. I am especially grateful to Teresa Cruz e Silva, Ana Maria Loforte, Isabel Casimiro, Valdemir Zamparoni, Eulália Tembe and Terezinha da Silva for sharing sources and discussions about their work on gender. Alpheus Manghezi generously encouraged me to use his unpublished work. David Hedges, Alda Saúte Saide and Joaquim Saide repeatedly and generously critiqued my work, made difficult translations and shared sources.

Scores of colleagues have supported me with materials, critical discussions and friendship. Kathleen Sheldon's critiques and materials were essential as were Signe Arnfred's unpublished materials. I thank David Morton for sharing an unpublished report that he painstakingly photographed. Tufts University students, staff and colleagues from History, Women's Studies, International Relations, and Africa in the New World, the African Studies Center, Boston University, and the Lusophone African Studies Organization of the African Studies Association all supported my work. It is a pleasure to thank colleagues for their enduring support: Joseph Miller, David Birmingham, Landeg and Alice White, Sherilynn Young, Anne Pitcher, Derek Peterson, Rosemary Galli, Ayesha Jalal, Randall Packard, Eric Allina, Maurine Flanagan, James Armstrong, Heidi Gengenbach, Pauline Peters, Kenneth Wilson, William Minter, Michel Cahen, Didier Péclard, Eric Morier-Genoud, Patrick Harries, Joana Pereira Leite, Hermínia Manuense, Nuno Miguel Rodrigues Domingos, Edward Alpers, Steven Lubkemann, Nazneen Kanji, the late José Soares Martins, Modhumita Roy, Rosalind Shaw, Pearl Robinson, Ina Baghdiantz McCabe, Sol Gittleman, Angela Raven-Roberts, Astier Almedom, Karen Jacobsen, Leila Fawaz, Sonia Hofkosh, Elizabeth Remick, Laura Walters, Regina Raboin, the staff at Tisch Digital Design Studio, Annette Lazzara, Lori Piracini and my wonderful new cohort of young historians at Tufts.

The late Mucove Joaquim Cossa took care of our family for fifteen months. We loved him and miss him. Many people, including those already mentioned, extended themselves on our behalf during every trip, and it is all too little to thank them: J. Michael Turner, George and Susan Jenkins, João Paulo Borges Coelho, Maria Manuel Rodrigues Seno, Teresa and Jacinto Veloso, Bento Sitoe, Alzira Machanga, and the late Gabriela Mukavele, Rita and Arlindo Lopes, Joaquina Ferreira da Silva, the late José Soares Martins, Mateu and Fernanda Angius, Manoela and Joel das Neves Tembe, Benigna Zimba and Gilberto Cossa, Lara and Renato Carilho, Patrocinio and Lucia da Silva, António Sopa, Amélia and Luis Souto, Nadja and Alpheus Manghezi, the Katupha family. When we had a crisis in Maputo many people came to our rescue. Alda Saúte, Joaquim Saide, Teresa Cruz e Silva, Humberto Coimbra, Manuel Araújo, Terezinha da Silva, David Hedges and Sophia Beal were excellent friends, neighbours and colleagues. I especially miss the jingling of keys and fresh-caught fish cooked amidst laughter!

Nancy Warner, Eileen Penvenne, Perry Penvenne and their families supported my work always. My aunt and uncle, Eileen Shugg and the late Tillar Shugg, took excellent care of our sons John and Louis. That enormous gift can have no adequate thanks. Our sons have since added wonderful people to our lives: Shauna Sadowski, Simrin Parmar, Mika Sage Sadowski Bennett and Kavi Norman-Singh Bennett. I shared this project from the start with Norman Robert Bennett, John Norman Bennett, and Louis Penvenne Bennett. We learned together, laughed a lot, argued loudly when necessary and inspired one another always. Of all the miracles I count on, the most important is having my beloved family in my life.

Finally, the publishers and I are grateful to all the institutions and individuals listed for permission to reproduce the materials in which they hold copyright. Every effort has been made to trace the copyright holders; apologies are offered for any omission, and the publishers will be pleased to add any necessary acknowledgement in subsequent editions.

Jeanne Marie Penvenne
Tufts University & Duxbury MA

Abbreviations

ACLM	Administração de Concelho de Lourenço Marques
AHM	Arquivo Histórico de Moçambique
AHR	American Historical Review
AIA	Agribusiness Industries Association
AICAJU	Associação de Industria de Cajú
ASR	African Studies Review
BNU	Banco Nacional Ultramarino
BSEM	Boletim da Sociedade de Estudos de Moçambique
CEA	Centro de Estudos Africanos, Universidade Eduardo Mondlane
CEP	Centro de Estudos de População
CIM/M	Cajú Industrial de Moçambique in Machava
CJAS	Canadian Journal of African Studies
CMM	Câmara Municipal de Maputo
CNCDP	Comissão Nacional para as Comemorações dos Descobrimentos Portugueses.
CNSL	Cashew Nut Shell Liquid
Cx	Caixa – Box
DGS	Direcção Geral de Segurança, formerly PIDE
DPAC	Direcção Provincial de Administração Civil
DPCCN	Departamento de Prevenção e Combate as Calamidades Naturais
FGG	Fundo do Governor Geral
IIED	International Institute for Environment and Development
IJAHS	International Journal of African Historical Studies
ILO	International Labour Office
INCAJU	Instituto de Fomento do Cajú
Inh	Inhambane
ISANI	Inspecção dos Serviços Administrativos e dos Negócios Indígenas
JAH	Journal of African History
JAPA	Junta Autónomo do Povoamento de Baixo Limpopo
JSAS	Journal of Southern African Studies
LM	Lourenço Marques

MRLS	Mozambique Rural Labour Market Survey
NGO	Non-Government Organization
OMM	Organização da Mulher Moçambicana
OT	Oral Testimony
PAM	Posto Administrativo de Munhuana
PIDE	Polícia Internacional e de Defesa do Estado, later DGS
PNG	Personal Narratives Group
R/ Cx	Uncatalogued Red Box
RCNI	Repartição Central de Negócios Indígenas
RIEA	Revista Internacional de Estudos Africanos
ROAPE	Review of African Political Economy
RTE	Repartição Técnica de Estatística
SAT	Sociedade Agrícola e Tabacos
SINTIC	Sindicato Nacional dos Trabalhadores da Indústria do Cajú
SPSS	Soft Programming for the Social Sciences
UEM	Universidade Eduardo Mondlane
USACLM	American Consul General, Lourenço Marques, Mozambique
USAID	United States Agency for International Development
WLSA	Women and the Law in Southern Africa
WNLA	Witwatersrand Native Labour Association

Glossary

Acção Social	Colonial era social work agency in Mozambique
Amancebado	Living as lovers or in common law marriage
Amêndoa	Cashew almond or kernel
Arrumar	Literally to clean up, commonly to set aside the day's shelling efforts to fulfill a daily quota the next day
Assimilado / a	People of African heritage considered citizens in colonial era
Bairro / bairros (pl)	Neighbourhoods
Bairros de caniço	Urban neighbourhoods where housing had to be built from impermanent materials
Bebidas cafreais	Literally kaffir drinks, home brewed or distilled alcoholic drinks
Biscate	Odd jobs, petty sales and services
Brincadeira / Brincadeiras	Literally 'little games' but generically foolishness, also sexual intrigues or harassment
Cajú	Literally cashew, vernacular for the cashew industry and factory
Cajueiro	Cashew tree, *anacardium occidentale*
Caniço	Reeds used in home construction, vernacular for bairros de caniço
Cantina	Small dry goods shop often combination bar / shop / rooms
Cantinheiro	Shopkeeper / Barkeeper
Capulana	Multi-use length of cloth worn by women as a skirt wrap or shoulder shawl or used to secure a child on one's back
Castanha	Whole unshelled cashew nut
Chitiki	Rotating savings system
Colono	Portuguese settler in Mozambique
Criado / a Djamangwana	Person working general domestic service Literally 'difficult', vernacular for shelling and peeling sections of the industry and for

	political prisoners and prison where they were held in Machava
Dono / a da casa	Literally 'master' or 'mistress' of the house, husband or wife'
Épocha de Ucanhé	Season of ritual first fruits and accompanying drinking
Escudo / Escudos	Portuguese currency in Mozambique from 1911 to 1980
Haháni	Paternal aunt, the father's sister whose bridewealth accrued to his marriage in patrilineal southern Mozambique
Indígena	Literally native, colonial subject, non-citizen
Indigenato	Body of laws that applied to persons considered indígenas and subjected them to special taxes and controls
Ku thekela	To call in social debt for food in time of famine / difficulty
Kwakwanana	Literally 'rush rush', vernacular for brusque, undignified treatment by Native Affairs personnel
Lar	Hearth, conjugal home
Lobolo	Bridewealth paid by husband's family to wife's family
Machamba	Garden plot
Magaiça	Mozambican man who returns to Mozambique from employment in South Africa, historically in the mines
Malalanyana	Literally 'skinny one', nickname for A. H. Ferraz de Freitas
Mamamele	One who walks quietly like a cat, nickname for Roquette
Mamana	Mother, polite form of address for adult woman
Mamparra magaiça	Alternatively mambarha gayisa, magaiça who squandered wages before returning home
Marcar	To mark a cashew shelling quota sheet as complete for payment
Mathlothlomana	Unending chaos, vernacular for brothels and the areas of town with brothels
Matrikin	People related through one's mother
Mestiço / a	People born of multiple heritages
Metical / meticais (pl)	Mozambican currency, replaced Escudo in 1980
Milando	Disputes, often around bridewealth or claims on women and children

Monhés	Vernacular for South Asians especially Muslims
Mudahomu	A ritual herb necessary to settle disputes
Mugwaza	Volunteer paid labour, but could elide into forced labour if employers were short of labour, especially for women and children
Mulher sem dono	Woman living outside the authorization / care of a man
N'wamafasitela	Literally 'the man who wears glasses', nickname for Duarte Eduardo da Silva
N'wamagange	Literally 'the man who wears blue jeans', nickname for Bardin da Silva
N'wamacholo	Literally 'old boys', vernacular for men who were repeatedly seized for forced labour
N'wasalela	Literally 'person who remains behind', vernacular for a man wealthy enough not to have to migrate for wages
Palmatório	Portuguese instrument for punishment, paddle with holes used to beat the palms of hands, buttocks, breasts
Pancada de graça	Literally 'a gratuitous beating', vernacular for domestic violence
Pombe	Home brewed maize beer
Quintal	Backyard, enclosed area around home
Sul do Save	Southern Mozambique, South of Save River
Tarana	Vernacular for Jiva Jamal Tharani and his factory
Tinumerini	Vernacular for people who could count
Uputsu	Home brewed maize beer
Vale	A debt chit from a shopkeeper
Wusiwana	Ordinary poverty
Xaniseká	Poverty that creates great suffering
Xawani vamamana	Respectful greeting of adult women
Xibalu	Alternative spellings, forced labour, poorly paid labour
Xicaju	Cashew based alcoholic drinks
Xicalamidade	Used clothing, used goods, divorcee or widow
Xiculungo	Socially isolated, very poor person
Xidanguane	One who lives by the sale of home made cashew alcohol
Xilunguine	Lourenço Marques, place of the whites
Xipswahla	Native Affairs Office in Munhuana
Xungwa	Woman who lives alone, suggests promiscuity / prostitution
Zaunzwanas	Gossips and rumour-mongers

Introduction

Mozambican women and the cashew economy

In the early 1970s at the close of its colonial era, Mozambique was a global leader in cashew production. The Portuguese colony's cashew processing industry was inaugurated in the 1950s and by the 1970s it accounted for the largest share of the world's production of raw cashew nuts and the country's foreign exchange earnings. The cashew economy was big and important. At almost every stage, from planting to exporting cashews, the industry rested fundamentally on the work of Mozambican women. The women who sustained the factories of the emergent cashew industry put aside their usual work implement, the hoe they used to till their family fields, to embrace what they called 'the hoe of the city'. Celeste Mpandane explained: '*Axikomu xa lomu i kutihra* – The hoe of the city is a job.'[1] Jobs for women in Mozambique's cashew shelling factories became a beacon; fueling urban migration by Southern Mozambican women who wanted or needed to turn in their field hoe for a job. Although it is irrefutably true that the entire cashew processing industry depended upon the labour of African women, the raft of colonial era press, scientific and business literature about the promising industry made virtually no mention of the labour force in this labour intensive industry, and the handful of articles that mentioned the women portrayed them as a constraint on production rather than the backbone of the industry. This is the history of the most successful industry in the late colonial era. It was reconstructed through an extensive oral history project anchored among three generations of women who comprised the great majority of the cashew industry's workforce from the late 1940s through to independence in 1975. It also draws touchstone concepts from four popular songs performed by women of Southern Mozambique. Each song captures themes and images that run through narratives and the following chapters.

The colonial era's print media may have failed to acknowledge Mozambican women when charting the spectacular growth of the era's signature cashew industry, but the women whose narratives

---

[1] OT, Celeste Marcos Mpandane, 26 May 1993.

comprise the basis of this study claimed their due. Rosa Joaquim Tembe was among the original cohort of workers at what became the colony's largest cashew processing factory, Cajú Industrial de Moçambique, in the Chamanculo neighbourhood of Mozambique's capital city, Lourenço Marques. After independence the city was renamed Maputo.[2] Tembe spoke for her cohort and subsequent generations of cashew shellers when she claimed: 'We worked hard for this factory. It grew from our strength.'[3] In one way or another the women's narratives highlighted their contribution to the founding, growth and endurance of Mozambique's cashew economy. Their oral testimony revealed a great deal about the industry, the people and power relationships of life on the Chamanculo factory floor and also about migration and life in the African neighbourhoods of the late colonial capital city. They recounted the many paths that led women from the countryside to the cashew shelling factories. They explained their determination to make a life and livelihood in Lourenço Marques, and in so doing provided nuanced understandings of urban family formations, quotidian rhythms and women's strategies around housing, subsistence, partnerships and children. Their narratives and songs insist that women's perspectives are co-normative with men's. They comprise a treasury of complex and contrasting stories, and a window into the quite different ways women and men experienced and explained migration, factory labour, and urban living in the late colonial era.[4] They fill a big gap.

The oral history narratives at the heart of the study capture a great deal of important information, but they also have a very important bias – they are the stories of those who survived working in the toxic and dangerous cashew shelling industry. The people who shared their recollections with this project included those who were barely surviving, those who were flourishing and many in-between, but if the historical actors here seem disproportionately strong, it is because they were. We did not hear from the thousands of women who 'couldn't take it,' and left.[5]

Mozambican women played an integral role in all aspects of the colony's developing cashew economy. Women planted, tended and harvested cashew trees to sell the fruit and nuts to wholesalers. They

---

[2] This study retains the colonial era name, Lourenço Marques.

[3] OT, Rosa Joaquim Tembe, 2 June 1993.

[4] As detailed below, many scholars highlight the different ways women and men explain the past. Jan Bender Shetler, *Imagining Serengeti: A History of Landscape Memory in Tanzania from Earliest Times to the Present* (Athens: Ohio University Press, 2007); Jan Bender Shetler, 'The Gendered Spaces of Historical Knowledge: Women's Knowledge and Extraordinary Women in the Serengeti District, Tanzania', *International Journal of African Historical Studies [IJAHS]*, Vol. 36, No. 2 (2003): 283–307; Nancy Rose Hunt, 'Introduction', *Gender & History*, 8, 3 (Nov. 1996): 323–37; Nancy Rose Hunt, 'Placing Women's History and Locating Gender,' *Social History*, 14 (1989): 359–79.

[5] As detailed in Chapter 2, 'Couldn't take it' was the phrase most women used to explain why some left their jobs in the cashew factory and others did not. OT, group of retirees, 2 June 1993; OT, Ester Tafula, 3 June 1993.

processed the fruits and nuts into food and drink for consumption in the household and gift economies and sold them in the informal economy. Finally, they were the core labour force for industrial cashew processing. Although the women's narratives focus on the industrialization of cashew shelling and life on the factory floor, they also shed light on the broader economy of cashew alcohol and food, on regional migration patterns and urban African social and economic history. The introduction sketches the appropriate historical context, explains the research methods and suggests how these findings and interpretations enhance contemporary scholarly literature. It seeds the main arguments and previews their location in the subsequent chapter order.

Women's knowledge and core concerns about factory production and urban life de-centre the essentially androcentric narrative of colonial labour history. That narrative inadequately embraces the pervasive and foundational contributions of women, and reproduces analyses that obscure women's historical contributions.[6] Women's experiences and explanations explicitly conflated their participation, social claims and obligations across the home, gift, informal, and formal economies, highlighting the need for an analysis that allows historians to see connectivity and overcome artificial divisions that weight male dominated sectors of the economy over those populated by women and children. The discourses of first and second-generation migrants delightfully imbricated images from rural and urban, formal and informal, household and factory.[7]

Women ordinarily developed resources, invested and staked claims in multiple family lineages and social networks in ways that scholars still neglect and misinterpret rather than anticipate and assess. Although the great majority of women who shared their experiences lived in societies accurately described as patrilineal, patriarchal and virilocal and upon marriage, most women moved from the lands and from the control of the appropriate people in their father's home to the lands and the control of the appropriate people in their husband's home, they did not then relinquish or cease making claims on resources in their father's or mother's lineages and lands upon marriage. The great range of urban and rural household and family forms that women developed suggests the need to test embedded assumptions about the superiority of and preference for some household and family forms over others. Scholarly literature often portrays women headed households, common-law marriage and polygyny as disadvantageous for women, but many women explained the advantages and disadvantages they experienced in these and other forms.

---

[6] That was certainly true of my earlier work, Jeanne Marie Penvenne, *African Workers and Colonial Racism: Mozambican Strategies for Survival in Lourenço Marques, Mozambique, 1877–1962* (Portsmouth: Heinemann, 1995); Jeanne Marie Penvenne, *Trabalhadores de Lourenço Marques, 1870–1974* (Maputo: AHM, 1993).
[7] OT, Celeste Marcos Mpandane, 26 May 1993; OT, Rabeca Notiço, 24 May 1993.

Finally, historical analysis of labour migration and urban labour that is grounded in the wholeness and connectivity of women's experiences and explanations, must open the field for women's agency and interrogate the utility of the gendered and hierarchical distinctions drawn among formal, informal, gift and household economies.[8] This is particularly important for the cashew economy. The formal sector industrialization of cashew shelling and cashew by-products and the export of unprocessed cashew nuts generated foreign exchange and were charted in government statistics, but throughout Mozambique, cashews and cashew based drinks were important seasonal staples in the household, gift and informal economy, but were not understood or valued in the same way. These components were an integral part of the overall cashew economy. Women's broad and important contributions are only fully revealed when Mozambique's economy and society are treated as whole cloth. The important work women do is eclipsed if the focus is limited to the formal economy, or even the formal and informal economies. This is an effort to broaden the lens.

Historical context

This section provides the briefest historical context for Mozambique in Southern Africa, and as a colony of Portugal.[9] Portugal and its African colonies (Mozambique, Angola, Guinea Bissau, São Tomé, Príncipe and Cabo Verde) were broadly engaged in colonial, regional and international relationships and tensions in the twentieth century. Mozambique's late colonial era, 1945 to 1975, was shaped by many factors, but four were particularly important: Portugal's authoritarian New State regime and its strategy of sponsored white settlement of her mainland African colonies; neighbouring South Africa's capacity to draw migrant labour from the southern African region into employment in its mining, agricultural and manufacturing sectors; South Africa's engineering of white minority rule at home and its support for white minority regimes in the region, including Mozambique, Southern Rhodesia, Angola and Namibia; and finally, the Cold War's shadow over this strategically and economically important southern African region. Although political control, economic domination, mineral and resource wealth were quite uneven, the southern African region clearly featured authoritarian white rule and the development of resources to profit colonial and minority populations at the expense of the majority African population.

[8] Paul Tiyambe Zeleza brought attention to many of these dynamics in 'Gender Biases in African Historiography', in Ayesha M. Imam, Amina Mama, Fatou Sow, eds, *Engendering African Social Sciences* (Dakar: CODESRIA Book Series, 1997): 81–115.
[9] Malyn Newitt, *A History of Mozambique* (Bloomington: Indiana University Press, 1995); Malyn Newitt, 'The Late Colonial State in Portuguese Africa,' *Itinerário*, 23, 3/4 (1999): 110–22.

Map 1 Southern Africa, 1974
(Based on maps-africa.blogspot.com)

Map 2 Late Colonial Mozambique
(Based on David Birmingham and Phyllis Martin *History of Central Africa: The Contemporary Years* (Longman, 1998), 230)

In the wake of World War Two, when Britain, France and Belgium began to transition away from colonial over-rule, Portugal's so-called New State regime (1930s to 1974), under António Salazar (to 1968) and Marcello Caetano (1968–1974), perversely committed itself to state-sponsored white settlement in Angola and Mozambique.[10] Despite the intransigence of Portugal's political exclusion and economic exploitation of the African majority, her investment in Mozambique's economic growth and diversification in the closing decades of the colonial era provided increasing employment for Africans and white Portuguese alike. State and private investment in import substitution industries for the growing settler market and agricultural processing for the national and export markets opened more and better jobs. When the New State opened investment to international companies in the 1960s, in part to court support for Portugal's continuing colonial rule in Africa, some of those companies pushed for a more settled, better qualified, higher paid majority workforce.[11] The New State's bureaucracy aspired to place white Portuguese in the most attractive positions, and thereby antagonized educated and skilled black Mozambicans.[12] Africans comprised the rank and file workforce in the new processing and manufacturing jobs in Lourenço Marques and its suburbs.

Portugal's investment in Mozambique's infrastructure and opening to international and national expansion of processing industries took place in tandem with South Africa's reconfiguration of migrant to local labour in its mining and other employment sectors. From 1900 to 1970 between 60 to 80 per cent of South Africa's mine labour force was comprised of international migrants. In the early twentieth century men from Southern Mozambique made up as much as 70 per cent of the

---

[10] Cláudia Castelo, *Passagens para a África Portuguesa: O Povoamento de Angola e Moçambique com Naturais da Metrópole (c. 1920–1974).* PhD thesis (Lisbon: Universidade de Lisboa, Instituto de Ciências Sociais, 2005); Eric Morier-Genoud and Michel Cahen, eds, *Imperial Migrations: Colonial Communities and Diaspora in the Portuguese World* (New York: Palgrave Macmillan, 2012); Valentim Alexandre, 'The Colonial Empire,' in António Costa Pinto, ed. *Modern Portugal* (Palo Alto, CA: The Society for the Promotion of Science and Scholarship, 1998): 41–59; Jeanne Marie Penvenne, 'Settling against the Tide: The Layered Contradictions of Twentieth Century Portuguese Settlement in Mozambique', in Caroline Elkins and Susan Pederson, eds, *Settler Colonialism in the Twentieth Century: Projects, Practices and Legacies* (New York: Routledge, 2005): 79–94.

[11] Newitt, 'The Late Colonial State,' 110–22; Michel Cahen, 'Corporatisme et Colonialisme – Approche du Cas Mozambicain, 1933 –1979,' [Part I, 'Une Genése difficile, um Mouvement Squelettique,' Part II, 'Crise et Survivance du Corporatisme Colonial 1960–1979,'] *Cahiers d'Etudes Africaines,* 92 (1983): 383–417 and 93 (1984): 5–24; 'Annual Economic Report' and 'Annual Labor Report' [titles vary] from the US Consular Office in Lourenço Marques from the 1940s to the early 1970s make this clear. Many are available in the collections 'Documents concerning Labor and Economic Conditions in Mozambique from 1951 to 1963,' and 'Documents concerning Labor and Economic Conditions in Mozambique from 1964 to 1974' obtained from the Department of State through the Freedom of Information Staff, Bureau of Public Affairs, US Department of State, bound and held at Boston University's African Studies Library.

[12] The implications of white settlement on black workers is discussed in Jeanne Penvenne, 'Here Everyone Walked with Fear': The Mozambican Labor System and the Workers of Lourenço Marques, 1945–1962', in Frederick Cooper, ed. *Struggle for the City: Migrant Labor, Capital and the State* (Berkeley: Sage, 1983): 131–66 and 'Settling against the Tide'.

total. By the late 1920s the percentage of Mozambicans had dropped to the forties, and after World War Two, they were around a quarter of the total, but even at that percentage we are still talking about over 100,000 men. South Africa increasingly recruited from Lesotho and eventually more South African men took jobs in the mines. As opportunities for employment in South Africa diminished in the 1960s and 1970s, Mozambican men looked to jobs in Lourenço Marques. Women had never been recruited for jobs in South Africa, but Mozambican women also increasingly sought waged labour in the capital city's newly diversified manufacturing and processing plants, particularly in agricultural processing, textiles and garments. These economic shifts fueled and were fueled by the drive for political change.

Portugal's authoritarian New State did not tolerate political contestation in the metropole or colonies. Mozambicans and Portuguese ultimately mobilized political and military support to challenge colonial rule. In 1962 the group of Mozambican insurgents who emerged from contestation for leadership named themselves the Front for the Liberation of Mozambique, Frente de Libertação de Moçambique, and became known by the acronym FRELIMO.[13] FRELIMO organized bases in Tanzania and launched an armed insurgency into Northern Mozambique in 1964. Portugal's counter-insurgency strategy required greatly expanding the transportation and communication infrastructure. As was the case with Portugal's economic investments, most new infrastructure was designed to benefit Portuguese settlers, and support the colonial state. The press and archives revealed that most colonial administrators continued to view the African majority as either implements for or impediments to settler driven development. Nonetheless, these changes and Portugal's push to Africanize the colonial military and court some level of elite African collaboration in light of the FRELIMO insurgency, provided a window particularly for men to move into more secure, better-paid jobs and even some positions of authority in the civil service and military.[14]

Although infrastructural and economic investment and relatively stable currency characterized late colonialism in Mozambique, growth was regionally and racially uneven. In the southern regions and Lourenço Marques investment and economic growth were strongest and white settlement was most dense.[15] These regions did not directly

[13] Walter Opello, 'Pluralism and Elite Conflict in an Independence Movement: FRELIMO in the 1960s,' *Journal of Southern African Studies [JSAS]* Vol. 2, 1 (1975): 66–82; Georgi Derluguian, 'The Social Origins of Good and Bad Governance: Re-Interpreting the 1968 Schism in Frelimo', in Eric Morier-Genoud, ed. *Sure Road? Nationalisms in Angola, Guinea-Bissau and Mozambique* (Leiden: Brill, 2012): 90–98.

[14] John P. Cann, *Counterinsurgency in Africa: The Portuguese Way of War, 1961–1974* (Westport: Greenwood Press, 1997).

[15] During the 1950s the capital's share of the nation's installed industrial capacity increased from around 10 per cent to 62 per cent, and by 1970 was nearly 89 per cent. Maria Clara Mendes, 'A rede urbana em Moçambique', *Livro de Homenagem a Orlando Ribeiro*, Vol. 2 (Lisbon: Centro de Estudos Geográficos, 1988): 609–17; Penvenne, 'Settling Against the Tide,' 79–94.

experience the violence of the anti-colonial insurgency by the time the Portuguese military coup of 25 April 1974 signalled the beginning of the end of the New State and its commitment to continued colonial rule.[16] In the wake of the coup, FRELIMO forcefully negotiated Mozambican independence with Portugal, claiming to be the sole legitimate representative of the Mozambican people and rebuffing attempts by competing groups to contend for political power. When FRELIMO transitioned from a military insurgency to political leadership it retained the name Frelimo, but no longer as an acronym.[17] On 25 June 1975 Mozambique became independent. Within two years Frelimo declared itself a Marxist-Leninist Vanguard Party, signaling its alignment with the Soviet Union and Eastern Block countries who helped train and support Frelimo's military and political cadres.

The rush tide of Portuguese white settlement in Mozambique had diminished throughout the 1960s and in 1971 it actually turned. Thousands of Portuguese whites left in the early 1970s, particularly after the coup in 1974.[18] After independence, the nationalization of some properties and businesses, in combination with the Eastern block alignment encouraged a further exodus of both Portuguese and South Asians from Mozambique. Portuguese whites dominated management and skilled labour in industry, manufacturing, transportation and civil service, and South Asians were key to commerce, particularly rural trade. Their flight meant economic disruption was widespread and quickly resulted in a scarcity of basic goods.

The situation of economic scarcity, communication and transportation breakdowns was exacerbated by the late 1970s when a new insurgency emerged. Resistência Nacional Moçambicana, Mozambican National Resistance Movement, known by its Portuguese acronym, RENAMO (usually written as Renamo), was recruited, trained, funded, and fielded by the intelligence branch of the white minority government in Rhodesia. When Rhodesia was about to transition to majority rule in 1980 as Zimbabwe, the South African security and intelligence forces took over support of Renamo from the Rhodesians.

Renamo also picked up support from Mozambicans who had either never embraced Frelimo or had become disillusioned. By the mid to late 1980s Renamo's insurgents were widespread and had inflicted horrific violence and destruction, particularly in the centre and south of the country.[19] With the political transformations in the early 1990s,

---

[16] Norrie MacQueen, *The Decolonization of Portuguese Africa: Metropolitan Revolution and the Dissolution of Empire* (New York: Longman, 1997).

[17] John Saul, *Recolonization and Resistance in Southern Africa in the 1990s* (Trenton, NJ: African World Press, 1993): p. xiii, n. 1. From this point I use Frelimo, rather than the upper case acronym, FRELIMO, to refer to this group regardless of the period.

[18] Castelo, *Passagens para a África*, p. 178 fig. 3, p. 179 Quadro 17.

[19] William Finnegan, *A Complicated War: The Harrowing of Mozambique* (Berkeley: University of California Press, 1992) Lina Magaia, *Dumba Nengue, Run for Your Life: Peasant Tales of Tragedy in Mozambique* (Trenton, N.J.: Africa World Press, 1988); Karl Maier, *Conspicuous Destruction, War, Famine and the Reform Process in Mozambique* (New York: Human Rights Watch, 1992); David

Renamo could no longer count on South African logistical and arms support. Regional, international and Mozambican attempts to forge agreement between Renamo and Frelimo were many and protracted. They eventually produced the Rome Peace Accord in October 1992.[20] By that time, more than a third of Mozambicans were refugees, internally displaced or affected by the war. Hundreds of thousands had been maimed or killed, many more thousands died of disease and starvation. Mozambique's economy and infrastructure were in complete ruin. Poorly mapped or unmapped land mines were planted all around the countryside. The capital city was under daily curfew. Travel everywhere was dangerous even if by military convoy.[21] The decade 1982 to 1992 was a time of starvation, insecurity, dislocation and disillusion for hundreds of thousands of Mozambicans. It should never be forgotten that the country's industries, infrastructure, and plantations were neither simply neglected nor mismanaged, they were intentionally wrecked.

Despite continuing tensions and occasional violent flare-ups between Frelimo and Renamo in the decades since the Rome Peace Accord, Mozambique has maintained peace. The country has held elections and incrementally rebuilt its infrastructure and economy. Foreign and state investment is more regionally balanced than in the colonial era, but the southern capital city is still the power centre. Some parts of the colonial era economy recovered but others did not. Completely new sectors were built, changing the country and region's overall economic profile.[22]

(contd) Birmingham, *Nationalism in Angola and Mozambique* (Trenton: Africa World Press, 1992); Phyllis Johnson and David Martin eds, *Frontline Southern Africa: Destructive Engagement* (New York: Four Walls Eight Windows, 1988).

[20] Alex Vines, 'Renamo's Rise and Decline: The Politics of Reintegration in Mozambique,' *International Peacekeeping*, Vol.20, No.3 (June 2013): 375–93; Margaret Hall and Tom Young, *Confronting Leviathan: Mozambique Since Independence* (Athens: Ohio University Press, 1997); Cameron Hume, *Ending Mozambique's War; The Role of Mediation and Good Offices* (Washington: United States Institute of Peace Press, 1994).

[21] Jeanne Marie Penvenne, 'A Tapestry of Conflict: Mozambique 1960–1995', in David Birmingham and Phyllis Martin, eds, *History of Central Africa; The Contemporary Years* (London: Longman, 1998): 230–66.

[22] Numerous scholars have assessed Mozambique's economy since independence. Carlos Nuno Castel-Branco and colleagues at Instituto de Estudos Sociais e Económicos http://www.iese. ac.mz/?__target__=home, Fernando Lima and colleagues weekly paper, *Savana*, http://www. savana.co.mz/and Joseph Hanlon all provide regular posts, http://www.open.ac.uk/technology/mozambique/. Hanlon also published a series of monographs on Mozambican economic and political changes, for example, Hanlon and Teresa Smart, *Do Bicycles Equal Development?* (Woodbridge, Rochester, NY: James Currey, 2008); Kathleen Sheldon, *Pounders of Grain: a History of Women, Work and Politics in* Mozambique (Portsmouth, NH: Heinemann, 2002); Anne Pitcher, *Transforming Mozambique: the Business of Politics, 1975–2000* (New York: Cambridge University Press, 2002); Merle Bowen, *The State against the Peasantry; Rural Struggles in Colonial and Postcolonial Mozambique* (Charlottesville: University Press of Virginia, 2000); Chris Alden, *Mozambique and Construction of the New African State: from Negotiations to Nation Building* (New York: Palgrave Macmillan, 2001); Carrie Manning, *Politics of Peace in Mozambique's Post Conflict Democratization, 1992–2000* (Westport: Praeger, 2002).

The Cashew economy and the cashew shellers

Chapter 1 introduces Mozambique's cashew economy in detail. Again, cashews and cashew by-products became Mozambique's leading export by value, edging out familiar colonial staples like sugar and cotton. Cashew exports had historically been of most interest to South Asians: the merchants who bartered for or purchased cashews from small-scale rural producers and the exporters who shipped unshelled cashews to India – the world's largest processor of shelled cashews. As the promise of the industry began to soar in the 1950s several entrepreneurs in Mozambique experimented with domestic cashew shelling and processing cashew bi-products. One such entrepreneur, South Asian merchant Jiva Jamal Tharani, transformed cashew shelling in Lourenço Marques from a widely dispersed urban cottage industry to an industrial enterprise. The Mozambicans who worked with him called him Tarana, the vernacular rendering of Tharani.[23] In a familiar pattern of name conflation, local people used Tarana to name the man, his Chamanculo cashew factory and the overall cashew industry.

Soon the colonial state and the banks and businesses closely associated with it became involved in all aspects of the industry, from agronomy and technical innovation to export taxes and production regulations. Between 1953 and 1970 the quantity of cashew nuts shelled in Mozambique increased 2,495 percent, from 5,897 tons in 1953 to 14,700 in 1970.[24] Economic competition between Portuguese and South Asians in Mozambique was both keen and longstanding. It spiked in December 1961, thanks to India's annexation of Damão, Diu and Goa, the coastal enclaves on the Indian subcontinent long claimed by Portugal. The flight of Portuguese and South Asians at independence badly disrupted every stage of the cashew economy. By the 1980s Renamo attacks eclipsed efforts to sustain and further develop agricultural processing industries. Cashew processing barely limped along through the war years. After the Rome Peace Accord, state support and private innovation within the industry increased. It would have been difficult to recover the wartime loss of market share to Brazil, India and Southeast Asia in any case, but in the mid-1990s Mozambicans felt sabotaged by World Bank interference in their efforts to privatize and revitalize what had been one of the nation's signature industries. Although Mozambique's cashew shelling economy soared to national and international prominence prior to independence in

[23] Jiva Jamal Tharani's name (alternate Jiwa Javal Tharaní) has various spellings in Portuguese sources. I use Jiva Jamal Tharani from Joana Pereira Leite and Nicole Khouri's study, *Os Ismailis de Moçambique; Vida Económica no Tempo Colonial* (Lisbon: Edições Colibri, 2012): 54–66, 235–38.

[24] J. Ismar Parente and Lopes Neto. 'A Agro-Indústria do Cajú em Moçambique', [Instituto de Investigação Agronómica de Moçambique, *Comunicações* 79] (Lourenço Marques: Instituto de Investigação Agronómica de Moçambique, 1973): 56.

Figure 1 Jiva Jamal Tharani,
Founder of Cajú Indústrial de
Moçambique, photo taken
c. 1945
(Credit: Habib V. Keshavjee, compiler.
*The Aga Khan and Africa: His Leadership
and Inspiration. An Illustrated Souvenir
of the Diamond Jubilee Celebrations of
His Imamate and His Visits to Lourenço
Marques and South Africa* (Durban:
Mercantile Printing Works, South
Africa, ca. 1947): 183)

1975, it has not since regained that stature.[25] My focus is on the late
colonial era industry (1945–1975), but the epilogue briefly considers
struggles around the cashew industry and its labour force to 2014.

Chapter 1 includes the full sweep of the production and use of
cashews and cashew products – from home made alcoholic drinks
and hand shelled nuts that circulated within the household, gift and
informal economies to the industrially shelled nuts, paint and lacquer
by-products produced in the formal sector for export. The goal is
to capture the economic and social history of this key late colonial
industry through the experiences and interpretations of its workforce, but also to confirm the full expanse of the cashew economy.
The cashew industry's workforce was very unusual for this period.
It was comprised largely of southern Mozambican women who had

[25] Joana Pereira Leite is the leading economic historian of the Mozambican cashew industry, but
many scholars contributed to debates around the cashew shelling industry after independence:
Joana Pereira Leite, 'A Guerra do Cajú e as Relações Moçambique–Índia na Época Pós-Colonial,'
Lusotopie (2000): 294–332; Pitcher, *Transforming Mozambique*, 225–35; Joseph Hanlon, *Peace
without Profit: How the IMF Blocks Rebuilding in Mozambique* (Oxford: The International African
Institute in association with James Currey, 1996); Hanlon, 'Power without Responsibility: The
World Bank and Mozambican Cashew Nuts,' *Review of African Political Economy [ROAPE]*, 27, 83
(2000): 29–45; Christopher Cramer, 'Can Africa Industrialize by Processing Primary Commodities? The Case of Mozambican Cashew Nuts,' *World Development*, Vol. 27, No. 7 (July 1999):
1247–9; Margaret McMillan, Dani Rodrik, Karen Horn Welch, 'When Economic Reform Goes
Wrong: Cashews in Mozambique,' *Faculty Research Working Paper* (Cambridge: Kennedy School
of Government, Harvard University, 2002).

Figure 2 Cashew Shellers
Rosalina Tembe and Raquelina
Machava, 1993
(© Jeanne Marie Penvenne)

left their rural farms to seek work in the cashew factories. Migrant and local women sometimes worked alongside their mothers, sisters, cousins, aunts, nieces and daughters. Scores of cashew workers, the great majority of them women, generously shared their memories of childhood, family, motherhood, migration, factory labour and the lives they lived in the African neighbourhoods of late colonial era Lourenço Marques.

We necessarily begin with a discussion of the project's rationale and methodology. The following section addresses the following questions: Why was it necessary to anchor an investigation of Mozambique's cashew economy in an oral history project? Who participated in the oral project, how and why? What framed the invitation to participation? How was the project conducted and by whom?

The people & the place

My research has always been driven by curiosity and frustration. In the late 1970s I was curious about colonial era urban workers in the port and railway sector in Lourenço Marques, and about the relationship between volunteer and conscript labour. Given the specific labour sectors I selected, I taped interviews with Mozambican men at the port, railway and municipality. I eventually spoke with scores of men employed in a range of occupations from domestic service to the municipal slaughterhouse.[26] They clearly had women in their lives, but I learned little about them. Many men told me they had 'abandoned' a wife or a partner. I was never really sure what that meant for the man or the partner. The resulting study, *African Workers and Colonial Racism*, did little to ground men in their family lives, and it approached women's experiences much more tentatively than men's.[27] As I wrote up my early research I noted women's very limited presence in the archival and press materials, and confirmed both my distance from Mozambican women, and my ignorance of most of the men's family relationships.

My first transformative experience with Mozambican women completely up-ended the era's clichés about powerful foreign scholars and submissive Mozambican women. I had just begun a public talk in front of a very large audience at Maputo's City Hall auditorium when the scores of women who were standing and sitting at the back of the room started shouting. I was horrified – convinced that I had somehow bungled a translation and managed to insult the whole of Mozambican womanhood. The women were insulted. They wanted to know what I had to say, but I was speaking Portuguese and they did not understand. They brought the meeting to a halt, insisting on being accommodated with an instantaneous translation into Changana or Ronga.

Once I recovered from my fright, and understood what they wanted I was seriously impressed. I could make myself understood among most men by combining Portuguese and very rough Changana. Educated Mozambican women spoke Portuguese, but the great majority of urban African women at that time spoke Ronga, Changana and Chopi, but not Portuguese. With help from the men sitting on the stage with me at that City Hall meeting I closed my talk in Changana saying something like: 'I hope someday my children will know your children.' No matter how mangled my pronunciation, and no matter that I didn't actually have children at the time – the women cheered my effort to address them directly in Changana. That sealed my determination to pursue both a women's oral history project and better Changana. This was more difficult and took exponentially longer than I had imagined.

When I initiated this project my goal was to develop a labour and social history of late colonial Lourenço Marques (1945–1975) based on the experiences of African women working waged labour across a range of sectors. My previous research wrapped up in the 1950s and then the early 1960s, with the legal, political and military changes of the Frelimo insurgency, as their end dates. This research project intentionally shifted the focus from men to women and probed the important changes that took place during the last generation of colonial rule, 1960 to 1975.

[26] I had only three narration sessions with Mozambican women in my earlier research.
[27] Penvenne, *African Workers and Colonial Racism*.

I was immediately struck by the emerging challenges of gendered perspectives regarding both sources and frameworks. Whereas one had to dig to extract Mozambican men as individuals from colonial sources that usually mentioned only so-called natives (*indígenas*), at least those natives were assumed to be men. It was much more difficult to find women in the archives and primary sources. The contemporary models in the enormous literature on southern African urbanization and labour migration supported my earlier work because both basically assumed men as historical actors. Although male actors still dominate much of this literature, we now know that assumptions about urbanization and labour migration work out quite differently for women and men.[28] This fresh material reveals a great deal about those differences.

The initial grant that supported this research was entitled, 'Women in the City – Women of the City.'[29] It interrogated the enduring posture that women could be in the city, but somehow a 'proper' woman could not or should not, be a city woman. The single most important study of the Lourenço Marques African population in the colonial era was undertaken by António Rita-Ferreira, a Portuguese sociologist and civil servant in the 1960s. The study included a section entitled 'the position of women,' but the focus was clearly on men. The questionnaire that anchored the survey asked the assumed male respondent: 'Why do you prefer that your wife remain in the rural areas?' The question also clashed with the survey's data showing that 87 per cent of urban men did not have rural wives.[30] It is one thing to read against the grain and interrogate such sources, but for the most part colonial publications, documents and press coverage simply ignored African women completely. [31]

Any substantive insights would have to hinge on women's recollections. African women were obviously born in and lived their lives in Lourenço Marques, and some rural women accompanied their

[28] Hilary Sapire and Jo Beall, 'Introduction: Urban Change and Urban Studies in Southern Africa,' *JSAS*, 21 (1995): 3–17.

[29] Research for this work was supported by a Fulbright Regional Research Award, Gulbenkian Foundation Fellowship and Tufts Faculty Research Award. It was conducted with an Institutional Review Board protocol through Boston University, African Studies Center.

[30] António Rita-Ferreira, 'Os Africanos de Lourenço Marques,' [separata de] *Memórias do Instituto de Investigação Científica de Moçambique*, Vol. 9 Ser. C [Ciências Humanas] (1967–1968), 'Modelo do Questionário' between pages 100 and 101, 300.

[31] Although their focus is largely Anglophone and Francophone Africa, Helen Bradford, Dorothy L. Hodgson and Sheryl A. McCurdy discuss the tendency for women's history to be warped in any colonial archival paper track, 'Introduction: 'Wicked' Women and the Reconfiguration of Gender in Africa,' in Hodgson and McCurdy, eds, *'Wicked' Women and the Reconfiguration of Gender in Africa* (Portsmouth: Heinemann, 2001); Helen Bradford, 'Women, Gender and Colonialism: Rethinking the History of the British Cape Colony and its Frontier Zones, c. 1806–70', *Journal of African History*, 37 (1996): 351–70; Steven Feierman's classic essay highlights the more general tendency of the colonial era archives to script as invisible whole African populations and practices, but particularly those associated with women, in 'Colonizers, Scholars and the Creation of Invisible Histories,' Victoria E. Bonnell and Lynn Hunt, eds, *Beyond the Cultural Turn: New Directions in the Study of Society and Culture*, (Berkeley: Univ. of California Press, 1999): 182–216.

husbands to the city. However, from the mid-1940s rural women and their children increasingly made their ways to the capital from southern Mozambique, the region called 'Sul do Save.' Despite legislation prohibiting their unauthorized departure from their rural homes and the sustained police action of repatriating them if they were apprehended out of compliance in town, women increasingly came to town, and often with their children.[32] I wanted to know why they came, how they made a life and a livelihood, and what impact their presence had on the city and the city had on them. The first challenge was to decide the people and place for an oral history project centred on women.

The great majority of women in colonial Lourenço Marques worked unpaid in their own households. Many also pursued unlicensed entrepreneurship in petty sales of brewed drinks and agricultural surplus or in services, including prostitution. In both the colonial and independence era, unlicensed sales and services were part of what was called the clandestine, parallel, black market or informal economy and all were technically illegal. Illegal activities were ubiquitous, but could nonetheless be subject to arbitrary and serious penalties. I learned what I could about illegal urban livelihoods through press, archival, photographic, literary and ephemeral sources – including police reports. I was uncomfortable with the ethical implications of placing any women who collaborated with me at risk, so I only considered women in legal waged labour.[33]

For most of the twentieth-century colonial period Mozambicans were administered and controlled by a detailed body of laws and practices that was cumulatively known as the *indigenato*, from the Portuguese word for native, *indígena*.[34] Chapter 3 details how the *indigenato* shaped gender relations, but the point for now is that *indígenas* were required to register with the municipal Native Affairs Office for permission to work legally in the city. Failing that they risked punishment or repatriation. The Portuguese colonial authorities used registration as a tool for urban influx control, and to keep African wages low and upward mobility constrained. Although registration was a great burden for urban African men and women, the registration archive provided a fine trove of information for historians seeking an overview of the

---

[32] Rita-Ferreira identifies and discusses the whole range of influx control legislation for the twentieth century, but note especially that the tightened control in the 1940s was sustained for women, well after it was dropped for men, 'Os Africanos,' 153ff.

[33] Women sometimes raised and discussed these topics in their narrations. I never raised them and if the women raised them I did not follow up. Some suggestive avenues were left hanging because I went as far as women took me on the question of prostitution, but probed no further.

[34] *African Workers and Colonial Racism* details the *indigenato* as a process of engineering inequality by unjustly and fraudulently wringing value from the majority population for the benefit of the state and white minority. The classic works regarding forced labour in Portuguese colonial era Africa are: James Duffy, *A Question of Slavery* (Cambridge: Harvard University Press, 1967) and James Duffy, *Portuguese Africa* (Cambridge: Harvard University Press, 1959). See also, Bridgette O'Laughlin, 'Class and the Customary: The Ambiguous Legacy of the *Indigenato* in Mozambique,' *African Affairs*, 99 (2000): 5–42.

urban African workforce. I took a 5 per cent systematic sample of the capital city's African labour registration records for the period from the late 1940s, when responsibility for labour registration shifted from the police to the municipality, to the early 1960s, when the *indigenato* was legally abolished. The sample provided a quantitative portrait of where African women in Lourenço Marques worked for wages, the wages they earned and their overall rates of attrition and stability. It revealed women as a growing minority in the late colonial era labour force.[35]

I intended to do an oral history project focused on three industries that, according to the sample, historically employed significant numbers of women: the garment industry, tobacco processing, and cashew shelling. I wanted to compare experiences of women who were migrant and local as well as skilled, semi-skilled and unskilled. Garment and tobacco processing workers were semi-skilled and predominantly local. Many more women worked in cashew shelling than any other industry. They possessed a range of skills, but most were unskilled migrants. Unfortunately, most of the industries that employed women in the late colonial era had closed. The garment industry had collapsed, archives were unavailable, and the workforce was dispersed throughout the city.

Although women and girls had comprised an important component of the tobacco labour force in the final processing and packaging stages, I had not noticed in the sample that most of those jobs disappeared with the mechanization of cigarette packaging as early as the 1950s. Despite having adopted mechanized packaging, one firm retained a small female labour force into the 1960s and 1970s. The owner of Sociedade Agrícola de Tabacos [SAT] did not want to turn out women who had worked for him for decades, so accommodated them in custodial and office jobs. The SAT 's colonial archives were lost, but the owner and a small group of retirees participated in this study.[36]

Some oral testimony by women working in a range of urban occupations was also recorded in projects undertaken shortly after independence by Hermínia Manuense, Kathleen Sheldon, Signe Arnfred and a research team working with the Organização da Mulher Moçambicana [OMM].[37] In 1982 the OMM team surveyed the social situation of

[35] The municipal labour registration records were generated by the Administração de Conselho de Lourenço Marques [ACLM]. They were interfiled by the worker's first name in the main file, and also filed by specific firms in the secondary files. The whole collection is now held at the AHM depository. The firm files for Cajú Industrial are unavailable because the file cabinets are packed in storage such that the drawers can not be opened. In principle the information in those files should match the information in the general files of approximately 146,000 records from which I took the 5 per cent systematic sample of the complete employee information. Data from that systematic sample is hereafter referred to as ACLM sample.

[36] Interviews with George Tsilhakis, son of Telemachus Tsilhakis, founder of SAT, Polana bairro, Maputo, Mozambique 1 and 2 July 1993. SAT workers and all other narrators are cited in full in the bibliography.

[37] Hermínia Manuense, 'Contribuição ao Estudo da Mulher Operária no Maputo: o Caso de Cajú,' in Ana Elsa de Santana Afonso, ed., *Eu Mulher em Moçambique* (Maputo: Comissão Nacional UNESCO em Moçambique e Associação dos Escritores Moçambicanos, 1994): 39–59;

women workers in Maputo.[38] Their focus was contemporary, and they interviewed ten workers from each of seven work sites, including the cashew processing plant in Machava – the newer of the city's two large factories.[39] The published and unpublished material from those studies made it clear that the best chance for a substantial oral history project on colonial era labour would be with the city's cashew shelling labour force.

Cajú Industrial de Moçambique was the only colonial era industry based on women's labour that had sustained employment and production. The company's business archives were missing, but some of the personnel records remained. As a practical matter, that confirmed my focus on cashew shellers as a window into late colonial era migration and life on the factory floor and in the city's neighbourhoods. Since many of the cashew shellers had worked in other occupations in the city, their work histories complemented the systematic archival sample and fleshed out the broader situation of women working waged labour in the late colonial era. Workers and administrators in both the Machava and Chamanculo branches of Cajú Industrial de Moçambique participated in the study, but the Chamanculo plant became the focus of this study because it was the oldest factory and retirees returned there to collect their monthly stipends.

More than one hundred women and seven men from the cashew shelling factories and tobacco processing industries contributed to this oral history project. I do not give an exact figure because I did not initially realize that the retirees would appear in large groups at the Chamanculo factory at the beginning of each month to collect their stipends. In the excitement of the first group's arrival I did not get everyone's names in the lively group interview we taped. The audio-tape makes clear that there were many women but it is hard to know exactly how many. The following months I was much better organized, but cannot be sure the groups were the same. The names, date and place of birth information for the participants are included in the appendix. We had follow-up conversations with 20 per cent of the Cajú narrators.

(contd) Signe Arnfred, 'Reflections on Family Forms and Gender Policy in Mozambique,' [unpublished typescript, 1990]; Arnfred, 'Women in Mozambique: Gender Struggle and Gender Politics,' ROAPE, 41 (1988): 5–16; Arnfred, *Sexuality and Gender Politics in Mozambique; Rethinking Gender in Africa* (Woodbridge/Rochester, NY: James Currey, 2011); Sheldon, *Pounders of Grain;* Hermínia Manuense, *Contribution a l'étude de la famille ouvriére à Maputo.* PhD thesis (Paris: EHESS, 1989). The extensive work done since independence by Women and the Law in Southern Africa [WLSA] and the Center for African Studies, UEM on women in Maputo focuses largely on the post independence period. I am grateful to Herminia Manuense for access to her unpublished PhD thesis and her permission to cite it.

[38] Signe Arnfred, 'Estudo da Situação Social das Mulheres Trabalhadoras na Cidade de Maputo,' [Unpublished synopsis of research conducted by the OMM as the basis of their 'Report on the Social Situation of Women Workers in the City of Maputo,' 1982.] Kathleen Sheldon provided a mimeo copy of this report. All of Arnfred's unpublished work is cited here with her permission. I am grateful to Signe Arnfred, Kathleen Sheldon and the OMM for access to this research and permission to incorporate it here.

[39] The other worksites included: Companhia Industrial de Matola, the cleaning staff of Hospital Central de Maputo, Impresa Vestuário Manufátos, Mercado 25 de Junho, Cooperativa de Costura Luis Cabral, and Cooperativa de Zonas Verdes.

According to Chamanculo factory records, approximately 80 per cent of the workers were women, and when the production was at its 1990s peak, it employed 2,500.[40] Given the state of the roads and power and supply disruptions due to the enduring insurgency, production was seldom in full swing. Most of the top administrative and supervisory staff were men, but the vast majority of workers, from the product arrival bay and warehouse to the final sorting, weighing, packaging and shipping stages were women. Some people had worked at Cajú for more than four decades. They included members of the original cohort that founded the Chamanculo factory. Again, some had also worked in other urban industries, in petty sales, domestic service and agriculture. In sum, the oral narratives project recounted a detailed and long-term portrait of the cashew factory's workforce, but also provided comparative perspective from people's experiences in many other sectors.

Although the cashew shellers' narratives provided a complex window into the processes of urbanization and labour migration in the late colonial era, I do not argue that they were typical or representative of urban women or of factory workers, at least in the usual sense of those terms. Following Susan Geiger and James Ferguson, I agree that typical and representative are concepts worth interrogating.[41] Although the cashew workers tended to share certain characteristics with other women in the city, there certainly were no typical cashew workers or typical cashew worker experiences. The diversity of experiences within the labour force was an important finding. Clearly age, ethnicity, fertility, civil status, education and relative prosperity shaped experience and were often revealed in the course of narration, but the project created neither complete sociological profiles nor extensive life histories of the narrators.

Scholars appreciate the ways age and what we call 'civil status' shape one's experiences, perspectives, priorities and memories. Generational tensions and solidarities emerged, particularly when considering change through time among families.[42] In the end, thanks largely to

---

[40] OT, Filipe Guambe, Ministério de Cajú, 10 May 1993, Maputo; Júlio Cuamba, Cajú Industrial de Moçambique in Machava [CIM/M], 26 June 1993; Luis Guila Muhale, 26 June, 29 June and 9 July 1993 CIM/M; OT, Custódio Silva and Paulina Benjamina Hugo, 26 June 1993.

[41] Susan Geiger, 'What's so Feminist about Doing Women's Oral History?' in *Expanding the Boundaries of Women's History; Essays on Women in the Third World*, edited by Cheryl Johnson-Odim and Margaret Strobel (Bloomington: Indiana University Press, 1992): 305–18, esp. 308–9; Geiger, 'Women's Life Histories: Method and Content,' *Signs* 22, No. 2 (1986): 334–351; James Ferguson, 'Mobile Workers, Modernist Narratives: A Critique of the Historiography of Transition on the Zambian Copperbelt,' Part I, *JSAS*, Vol. 16, No 3 (1990): 385–412 and Part II, *JSAS*, Vol. 16, No. 4 (1990): 603–21.

[42] Classic essays capturing changes in family standing and the law under colonial rule are in Margaret Jean Hay and Marcia Wright, eds, *African Women and the Law: Historical Perspectives* (Boston: African Studies Center, 1982.) Lee draws out differences among women in three generational families, and Carton's focus is generational tensions among men: Rebekah Lee, *African Women and Apartheid: Migration and Settlement in Urban South Africa* (London: I. B. Tauris Publishers, 2009) and Benedict Carton, *Blood from Your Children: The Colonial Origins of Generational Conflict in South Africa* (Charlottesville: University of Virginia Press, 2000).

the participation of the retirees, the narrators were fairly evenly divided among three age cohorts: women born between 1910 and 1930, who were middle age to retirement age by 1975 (31 per cent); women born between 1931 and 1940, who were in their mid-thirties to mid-forties (34 per cent); and women born between 1941 and 1954, who were still quite young (35 per cent). The range by region of origin tended to reflect both the population distribution in Southern Mozambique and the overall distribution of migrants among the male population for the same period. Women came from all of the colonial era Districts of Southern Mozambique: Inhambane (35 per cent), Gaza (29 per cent), Lourenço Marques (25 per cent), and Maputo (4 per cent), uncertain (7 per cent).[43]

Information on civil status was both incomplete and complex. Clearly, women at different times during their lives could be variously single, married, separated, divorced, widowed and living in common law relationships. Both women and men used the Portuguese word *abandonar* – to abandon – with respect to leaving a partner or being left by a partner. The ways people discuss their family relationships and forms matter. Later sections more closely interrogate the discourse, tropes and ways of narrating history, but for now, at the time of the study, the eighty two women who clearly stated their present civil status identified themselves as: single (25 per cent), separated from husband (15 per cent), widowed (15 per cent), abandoned by a man (5 per cent), married (4 per cent), married with bridewealth (6 per cent), married without bridewealth (1 per cent), married repaying bridewealth (1 per cent), 'forced' marriage (2 per cent), divorced (17 per cent), woman who abandoned a man (6 per cent).[44] As the fuller narrations make plain, a separated or divorced woman may have also been abandoned by a man or abandoned a man. In sum, the cashew shelling labour force of the oldest and largest factory in the Chamanculo neighbourhood of colonial capital, Lourenço Marques comprised the people and place. We now turn to the process and to issues of interpretation.

The process

The oral history project was conducted with extensive collaboration. First, it was cleared through Institutional Review Board protocols at

---

[43] The percentages are calculated from a base of 107. The place of origin was confirmed for 91 of 98 cashew narrators. As explained in Ana Bénard da Costa and Adriano Bisa's 'Home Space as a Social Construct,' people may identify a range of places as their region of origin, not simply the place they were born, *Home Space Ethnographic Report* [http://homespace.dk/tl_files/uploads/publications/Summaries/HomeSpace_Ethnographic_english_summary_text.pdf]; Abílio Mendes Gil, 'Relatório, Maputo e seus Postos, Administração de Catembe, Catuane, Inhaca e Manhoca,' 1954 & 1960, Inspecção dos Serviços Administrativos e dos Negócios Indígenas [ISANI] caixas 2 and 12 respectively AHM. ISANI reports and the ACLM sample.

[44] Age, marital status and home area statistics calculated from the oral history project. Basic data is not complete for all participants. See the appendix on sources.

Boston University where I was a Research Fellow. I introduced the project in academic and political circles in Maputo through the leadership and staff at Mozambique's national archive, Arquívo Histórico de Moçambique [AHM] and national university, Universidade Eduardo Mondlane [UEM]. I explained my intentions and pursued authorization to record, share and preserve the interviews for this project. I broadly circulated a Portuguese version of my research proposal, invited collaboration and comments from colleagues and students in History, Anthropology, Centre for African Studies, and the Nucleus for Gender Studies. The Chancellor of Mozambique's national university, the Director of Mozambique's national archive and the then Secretary of State for Cashew Nuts all authorized the proposal, the pilot and the final project. When work began at Cajú Industrial, any narrator who wanted a copy of her or his taped testimony was promised that accommodation. At the close of the project all of the oral narrative tapes were deposited in the national archive so that Mozambican and other scholars could hear and interpret them.[45]

All narrators' concerns should be engaged in the research process and their information and assignment of meaning should be honored and treated ethically whether the narrators are men, women, or children. The academy demands different considerations regarding children, but those also devolve from broader concerns for inequality of power and authority. Laura Bohannan famously reminded us that it is not wise to assume or project a specific power landscape, but rather to attend to the developing power dynamics as they emerge while decoding the landscape.[46] Issues of authorship, partnership, appropriation of information and historical methods are important no matter what the topic and no matter who the author.[47]

---

[45] The study was authorized by the late Reitor Fernando Ganhão of UEM, Prof. Dr. Inês Nogueira da Costa, and later Prof. Dr. Joel das Neves Tembe, Directors of AHM, and the then Secretary of State for Cashews, Juliano Saranga. I deposited thirty-nine audiotapes (60 and 90 minute tapes) at AHM in August of 1993.

[46] Bohannan's classic observations are in [Laura Bohannan] Eleanore Smith Bowen. *Return to Laughter; An Anthropological Novel* (Garden City: Doubleday Anchor, 1964): ix. 46, 215: Bohannan, 'Shakespeare in the Bush,' *Natural History*, 75, 7 (August-September 1966): 28–33.

[47] Heidi Gengenbach's introduction explores women's ways of knowing and telling and L. Lloys Frates introduction addresses issues of history and memory; Heidi Gengenbach, 'Where Women Make History: Pots, Tattoos, Stories and Other Gendered Accounts of Community and Change in Magude District, Mozambique, c. 1800 to the Present,' PhD thesis (Minneapolis: University of Minnesota, 1999). This was subsequently published as an ACLS Humanities E-Book, *Binding Memories: Women as Makers and Tellers of History in Magude District, Mozambique,* but references are from the thesis, 1–40; L.Lloys Frates, 'Memory of Place, The Place of Memory: Women's Narrations of Late Colonial Lourenço Marques,' PhD thesis (Los Angeles, University of California at Los Angeles, 2002); Susan Geiger, 'Women and Gender in African Studies,' *African Studies Review*, Vol. 42, No 3 (December 1999) 21–33; Iris Berger and E. Frances White, eds, *Women in Sub-Saharan Africa; Restoring Women to History* (Bloomington: Indiana University Press, 1999); Partha Chatterjee, 'The Nation and Its Women,' and Dipesh Chakrabaraty, 'Postcoloniality and the Artifice of History: Who Speaks for Indian Pasts?' both in Ranajit Guha, ed. *A Subaltern Studies Reader, 1986–1995* (Minneapolis: University of Minnesota Press, 1997): 240–62 and 263–93.

What were my intentions and practices regarding authorship and the reproduction and interpretation of taped narratives in this project and what was my strategy for their incorporation here? The women's narratives taught me many of the broad points I present as arguments in the below chapters. If I understood them correctly, what I present as their truths and insights are clearly theirs, but the narrators are not responsible for what I did with their words. I quote narrators in some length and include their songs. I highlight women's interpretations while distinguishing my voice from theirs. That does not constitute appropriation of their voices. I do not claim to be speaking for the narrators. The women speak for themselves in the recorded narrations that I deposited in Mozambique's national archive. I try to interrogate the lessons and insights I took from our engagement. Like Barbara Cooper in *Marriage in Maradi*, I frankly confirm that the women of Cajú may well contest my interpretations of their narratives.[48] I centre the women's often counter-hegemonic discourses and convey what I understand of their insights.

Efforts toward understanding took place across several languages. Despite having studied Changana and Ronga for years, in the typical dilemma of foreign language acquisition, I could understand much more than I could express orally. Although I am fluent in Portuguese, I absolutely could not quickly formulate questions and respond in either Changana or Ronga. Prof. Dr. Bento Sitoe, whose Ronga and Changana language instruction materials informed my study, introduced me to my language instructors and to Joaquina Boane Machava, who became my research assistant and translator for this project. When I say 'we' below, I mean Joaquina Machava and me. We spent seven months together, preparing for, conducting and tying up loose ends on the oral history project. She took the lead in narrations conducted in Changana and Ronga, and I took the lead in narrations conducted in Portuguese. We were each welcome to interject at any time in any language. Mrs. Machava wrote up free form translations of the narrations from Changana and Ronga into Portuguese, and transcribed some of the Portuguese narrations we worked on jointly. I transcribed the Portuguese interviews I conducted individually. The staff of the National Archive transcribed all thirty tapes in the original languages of narration. Joaquina Machava and I discussed the narrations as we travelled to and from the factory each day, and later as she worked up the transcriptions. Although I am responsible for the way I incorporated the transcribed narratives in this analysis, their richness was without doubt encouraged by Joaquina Machava's sunny spirit, humor, maturity and warmth.

The project was framed by the affiliation I held at UEM's History Department. When my research coincides with Mozambique's academic year,

---

[48] Barbara Cooper, *Marriage in Maradi; Gender and Culture in a Hausa Society in Niger, 1900–1989* (Portsmouth: Heinemann, 1997): 193.

Figure 3
Joaquina Boane Machava,
Research Assistant, 1993
(© Jeanne Marie Penvenne)

I always volunteer to teach a history course. Over the years the number of women in my classes and in positions of authority at the university increased steadily, yet despite the efforts of excellent and creative scholars, the dominant historical narrative of Mozambican history taught at the university at that time was still broadly gendered male. The archival collection of oral history also had many more narratives by men than by women. This was an opportunity to alter the imbalance.

We introduced the project to the administration and workforce of the Chamanculo factory as a component of a broader effort to be sure that young Mozambicans knew as much about women's experiences of the colonial era as men's. The women's testimony would help provide the basis for future works on Mozambican history, including this one. As had been the case with my earlier oral histories among Mozambican men, I anticipated that the narratives would provide material for press coverage, class lectures and future publications. We asked the cashew shellers for help in conveying to a broader audience the meanings women assigned to their experiences as factory workers and urban residents during the closing decades of the colonial era. We emphasized that their taped narratives would be available in the Historical Archive for their children's children to hear. That is how we framed our intentions to the participants. We also invited the women to ask us whatever they liked and to suggest alternative strategies for the project as they saw fit.

The administration at Cajú Industrial de Moçambique authorized
workers to participate in the project individually or in small groups
without compromising their wages. Joaquina Machava and I did not
select women to participate in the oral history project. We presented
the project to the factory administration. As we understood it, they
then put out the word and invited people to participate if they chose.
It was simple luck that we ended up with such a diverse and interesting group of narrators. The retirees who returned monthly for their
retirement checks were not required to spend time with us, but they
did so generously, graciously and to the immense benefit of the overall
project. We usually spoke to women in groups of two, but we spoke to
some women alone and to some groups as large as a dozen. The conversations ranged from about a half hour to several hours. The appendix
reflects the pace of the narrations, but we usually spent four to seven
hours at the factory. Our conversations were spoken and sung, they
ranged from somber to raucous. Although I spoke to several administrators and labour union leaders without Mrs Machava present, she and
I were both present for all the narrations by the rank and file workforce.
During the months at the cashew factory we listened, danced, laughed,
sang and cried. A lot was conveyed through respectful silences. The
goal was to hear what a great range of women wanted to tell us about
the development of the cashew shelling industry, their work and family
lives. That said, however, the women no doubt quickly understood and
discussed among themselves that we were interested in why they came
to work as cashew shellers, and how they recalled their experiences in
the factory and neighbourhoods of Lourenço Marques in the late colonial era. In that respect, they told us what they thought we wanted to
hear, but they also told us a great deal more.

Feminist scholars engaged in oral historical research refer to people
who participate in oral research by a range of terms, including oral
historians.[49] The term locates authority, agency, assignment of
meaning and analytical judgments with the person recounting her or
his history. In that sense it is infinitely preferable to the term I used
in the past, informant. In my early work, I used informant in its most
unimaginative dictionary form – a person who gives information. The
term is obviously unsatisfactory, and I no longer use it. In this study
I have adopted the term narrator. Unlike informant, as a person who
gives information, the term narrator more fully connotes agency,
authority, assignment of meaning and analysis. Many men and
women who took part in this project were indeed oral historians – they
creatively composed and conveyed a sense of the past that included
their personal participation but also went well beyond. They emerge

---

[49] The terms narrator, text, source, informant, respondent, interviewee, interview partner and
oral historian are all present in the literature. Susan Geiger uses the term oral historian and
Lloys Frates follows her lead: Geiger, 'What's so Feminist?' and Frates, 'Memory of Place,' preface
and chapters 1 & 2.

in the following chapters – with their words and song lyrics quoted at length. Some women truly performed their interpretation of the past much to the delight of their audience.

The challenges of women's history and oralcy

Multiple controversies and dilemmas cropped up around African women's oral history. I have addressed some of them elsewhere.[50] Oral narration by African women became something of a lightning rod for ethical concerns regarding power relations in research. Ethical concerns should always be paramount. We need to know about the telling and the listening, and both are complicated. Scholars in South Africa developed ambitious oral history narration collections and archives significantly earlier than scholars in Mozambique, and set the tone of debates.[51]

Judith Lütge Coullie argues that the identification and publication of southern African oral testimony is often motivated, driven and scripted by researchers.[52] Her observation is both obvious and apt. It flags critical methodological dilemmas such as those raised in two classic works of women's oral history: the Personal Narratives Group's collection, *Interpreting Women's Lives* and Susan Geiger's essay, 'What's So Feminist about Doing Women's Oral History?' They critiqued the inherent scripting of any questionnaire, noted the tendency for narrators to tell a researcher what the researcher wanted to hear and urged scholars to provide more open space so that narrators could order and shape what they shared as they judged best. Personal Narratives Group urged a more textured appreciation of what was and was not said in narration, including what provoked nervous laughter or a shifted gaze.[53]

Many scholars have enhanced and critiqued these classic insights, probing the spaces between what is said and what is heard, high-

---

[50] Jeanne Marie Penvenne, 'Elsa Joubert's Poppie Nongena,' in Margaret Jean Hay, ed. *African Novels in the Classroom* (Boulder: Lynne Rienner, 2000): 153–66; Penvenne, 'Rethinking Oralcy: Ways of Knowing and Telling Truths,' Post-graduate module in History and Social Science developed for UEM, July 2006; Penvenne, 'Gender Studies, Area Studies and the New History, with Special Reference to Africa,' in *Curricular Crossings: Women's Studies and Area Studies – a Web Anthology for the College Classroom* (2000). [http://www3.amherst.edu/~mrhunt/women-crossing/penvenne.html].

[51] Ciru Getecha and Jesimen Chipika, et al., *Zimbabwe Women's Voices*, [Photographs by Margaret Waller and David Gombera] (Harare: Zimbabwe Women's Resource Centre and Network, 1995); Suzanne Gordon, *A Talent for Tomorrow: Life Stories of South African Servants* (Johannesburg: Ravan Press, 1985); Hanlie Griesel et al., *Sibambene: The Voices of Women at Mboza* (Johannesburg: Ravan Press, 1987); Belinda Bozzoli with Mmantho Nkotsoe, *Women of Phokeng; Consciousness, Life Strategy and Migrancy in South Africa, 1900–1983* (Portsmouth: Heinemann, 1993); Charles van Onselen, *The Seed is Mine: The Life of Kas Main, a South African Sharecropper, 1894–1985* (New York: Hill and Wang, 1996).

[52] Judith Lütge Coullie, 'The Power to Name the Real: The Politics of Worker Testimony in South Africa,' *Research in African Literatures*, Vol. 28, no. 2, 1997:132–44.

[53] Personal Narrative Group [PNG], eds, *Interpreting Women's Lives; Feminist Theory and Personal Narratives* (Bloomington, Indiana University Press, 1989); Geiger, 'What's So Feminist;' Bender Shetler, 'The Gendered Spaces.'

lighting the power of rumour and gossip, and drawing attention to the textures and contours of women's agency in the ways they slant, submerge and shout history in oral performance.[54] What did women view as an appropriate arena for expression? What forms of expression, discourses and interpretations did they develop? How can scholars begin to understand the meanings and truths in these narrations?

Heidi Gengenbach, working in the rural hinterland of Mozambique's capital city in the 1990s, drew attention to the fact that women considered *matimu*, the Changana word for history, to be none of their business. *Matimu* was men's business. Gengenbach quickly realized women's ideas and ways of recounting knowledge and meaning about the past were important and interesting, but had little to do with men's *matimu*. Women, she argued, mapped history through body scarring, pottery, naming and the stories they told – stories that could be very different from the stories men told.[55] According to Jan Bender Shetler's research in Tanzania's Serengeti region,

> ...women possessed not just another version but wholly different kinds of knowledge about the past...men and women share neither styles of oral narration nor types of knowledge about the past. Men and women occupy separate spheres in their daily routines, sharing the same world but participating in different, though intersecting, sets of discourses about that world... A gendered analysis of oral tradition is necessary for finding its historical meaning.[56]

Elinami Veraeli Swai underscored the importance of women's knowledge systems, cautioning that it is often discounted and misunderstood. Swai highlighted the ways clothing (*khanga* cloth wraps in Tanzania or *capulana* cloth wraps in Mozambique), like body scarring, could be a vehicle to convey meaning.[57] Rebekah Lee explored similar

[54] Luise White, Stephan F. Miescher, and David William Cohen, eds, *African Words, African Voices: Critical Practices in Oral History* (Bloomington: Indiana University Press, 2001); Luise White, *Speaking With Vampires: Rumor and History in Colonial Africa* (Berkeley: Univ. of California Press, 2000); Barbara M. Cooper, 'Oral Sources and the Challenge of African History,' and Kathleen Sheldon, 'Writing about Women: Approaches to a Gendered Perspective in African History,' in John Edward Philips, ed. *Writing African History* (Rochester, NY: University of Rochester Press, 2005):191– 215 and 465–89 respectively.

[55] Heidi Gengenbach, 'Boundaries of Beauty: Tattooed Secrets of Women's History in Magude District, Southern Mozambique,' *Journal of Women's History* 14, 4 (Winter 2003): 106–37; Gengenbach, 'I'll Bury You in the Border!': Women's Land Struggles in Post-War Facazisse (Magude District), Mozambique,' *JSAS* 24, 1 (1998): 7–36; Gengenbach,'Naming the Past in a 'Scattered' Land: Memory and the Powers of Women's Naming Practices in Southern Mozambique.' *IJAHS* 33, 3 (2000): 523–42; Gengenbach, 'Truth-Telling and the Politics of Women's Life History Research in Africa: A Reply to Kirk Hoppe,' *IJAHS* 27, 3 (1994): 619–27; Gengenbach, '"What My Heart Wanted", Gendered Stories of Early Colonial Encounters in Southern Mozambique.' In *Women and African Colonial Histories*, edited by Jean Allman, Susan Geiger and Musisi Nakanyike, 19–47 (Bloomington: Indiana University Press, 2002).

[56] Bender Shetler, *Imagining Serengeti*, 11–12.

[57] As mentioned below, the cashew shellers' insistence on matching capulanas for the members of their work group also signaled identity. Elinami Veraeli Swai, *Beyond Women's Empowerment in Africa: Exploring Dislocation and Agency* (New York: Palgrave Macmillan, 2010): Ch. 3 on *khangas*.

resonances with regard to the living spaces that multi-generations of women built and shared in Cape Town, South Africa.[58]

Working in the 1970s and 1980s in Mozambique and neighbouring Malawi, Leroy Vail and Landeg White explored mapped and gendered versions of history – ways people deemed appropriate and meaningful to convey the remembered past so as to shape the imagined future.[59] Vail and White claimed that Southern Africans 'mapped' their experiences through song and performance.[60] Tumbuka women's *vimbuza* [spirit possession] songs '...constitute a specific reading by women of Tumbuka history...with particular concern for changing relations between men and women within the context of the household.'[61] Furthermore, '...women have insisted on maintaining *vimbuza* because it has been one of the few places where they could express *their* [emphasis in original] view of what the area's history was all about. Rejecting the optimistic views of European missionaries about the value of 'progress,' and finding little comfort in the ethnic boastings of local men, women have used *vimbuza* as their own public voice.'[62] Many scholars have explored the ways southern Africans mocked colonizers and salvaged some dignity from the demeaning circumstances of forced labour through work songs, protected both by language and the nature of the performance space.[63] Both men and women could sing what they would not say, but that was particularly true for women. African men mocked the colonizers, whereas women often performed their contestation with the men who held power over them – whether the colonizers or their families.

History, memory and statist narratives

The historical moment when women paused to share their recollections for this project was 1993.[64] We all view the past through the lens of the present. It is difficult to sort out just how that happens, but the possibili-

---

[58] Lee, *African Women and Apartheid.*
[59] This paraphrases Martin Murray, '...the power of the remembered past to shape the imagined future,' from a paper he presented, 'Crime Talk: Alarmist Fantasies and Youthful Imaginaries in the 'New' South Africa,' African Studies Association Annual Meeting, Boston, November 2003.
[60] Leroy Vail and Landeg White,' Forms of Resistance: Songs and Perceptions of Power in Colonial Africa,' *American Historical Review*, 88 (1983): 883–919; Leroy Vail and Landeg White, *Power and the Praise Poem; Southern African Voices in History* (Charlottesville, Univ. of Virginia, 1991).
[61] Vail and White, *Power and the Praise Poem*, 245–6.
[62] Vail and White, *Power and the Praise Poem*, 248.
[63] Alpheus Manghezi, 'A Mulher e o Trabalho: Entrevistas,' *Estudos Mozambicanos*, 3 (Maputo: Centro de Estudos Africanos, 1981): 45–56; Allen F. Isaacman, *Cotton is the Mother of Poverty: Peasants, Work, and Rural Struggle in Colonial Mozambique, 1938–1961* (Portsmouth, N.H.: Heinemann, 1996); Penvenne and Bento Sitoe, 'Power, Poets and the People – Mozambican Voices Interpreting History,' *Social Dynamics*, Vol. 26, No. 2 (2000): 55–86; Penvenne, *African Workers*; Vail & White, *Power and the Praise Poem.*
[64] Yes, that was a seriously long time ago, so it is just as well that these are historical narratives and not current news.

ties are important and interesting. What factors may have shaped these women's narrations? Secret police activity and heightened political tension shaped activity by men and women in southern Mozambique from the early 1960s. The people of Lourenço Marques did not experience armed conflict in the streets until September and October of 1974, when a failed attempt to challenge the political transition to independence negotiated by Frelimo and Portugal triggered violence. That violence was certainly important for the people who suffered in it, but it was relatively short-lived and contained.[65] By the late 1970s and early 1980s the Renamo insurgency had expanded into Sul do Save and was exponentially enhanced due to the stress of cyclical drought. The result was a famine that took the lives of hundreds of thousands of people. In 1984 the crisis was serious enough to convince Frelimo to sign the humiliating Nkomati Accord – a good neighbour pact – with apartheid South Africa. South Africa spent the political chit it earned at Nkomati with a diplomatic foray in Europe, but continued to support Renamo. As mentioned, the national economy was in ruins and as violence in the South grew, thousands fled to relatively greater safety in Maputo. Increasingly desperate local and displaced people turned to theft and predation.

In the hungry years of the early 1980s scores of cashew shellers were fined, disciplined and fired for eating or stealing cashews.[66] In the early 1990s Mozambique ranked as one of the world's poorest countries.[67] When we initiated the pilot and then the narration project at Cajú Industrial, the city's neighbourhoods were still under curfew and just returning to a modicum of security. The era of Frelimo's socialist food distribution and price controls seemed a very distant past. The extreme shortages of the 1980s had passed, but the plethora of new goods in the city's markets sold at prices most cashew workers could not afford. Despite periodic wage adjustments for workers and stipends for retirees, all of these women struggled with very limited resources. The retirees were particularly hard hit. Their monthly stipend would cover one loaf a day of the city's cheapest bread for 26 days, but for the last 4 or 5 days, the retirees had no money to eat. Nothing was left for tea, sugar, or the women's usual attire of a *capulana* (length of cloth used as a skirt wrap) and a headscarf.[68]

[65] Ndabaningi Sithole's *Frelimo Militant* provides an interesting narrative of this transition period, particularly the violence of September and October 1974, *Frelimo Militant; The Story of Ingwane from Mozambique, an ordinary, yet extraordinary, man, awakened...* (Nairobi: Transafrica, 1977): Chs. 1, 2, 15.

[66] Thefts of cashews were noted on women's personnel records, but for abuses around the transition period in the 1970s see 'O Partido – A Luta dos Trabalhadores na 'Cajú Industrial,' *Tempo*, No. 405 (9 July 1978): 15–20.

[67] Finnegan, *A Complicated War*; Penvenne, 'A Tapestry of Conflict;' Robert Gersony, 'Summary of Mozambican Refugee Accounts of Principally Conflict-Related Experience in Mozambique' (Washington, DC, Department of State, April 1988). Thanks to James McCann for an early copy of this paper.

[68] OT, Julieta Mulungu, 20 May 1993; Laura Nhachunha Tsombe, 20 May 1993; Ofélia Mbebe, 4 June 1993.

The most important characteristics of the historical moment during which the narrators shared their past were poverty and lingering insecurity. The oldest workers felt it most sharply, whereas the youngest women picked up on the promise of peace, economic recovery and potential for upward mobility. Tales of the good old days always reflect age, history and memory, but record inflation put truth to material change. The retirees obviously remembered the past in light of their spent youth and present circumstances. Their long walk from their homes to the factory was increasingly difficult, and even with improving security, the older women were vulnerable to theft and violence from the young thugs they called *maninjas*.[69] The *ninjas* knew retirees collected their pay at the change of the month and that Muslim shopkeepers gave alms to the elderly and poor on Fridays.

These women were all veterans of the threshold passage from colonialism to independence.[70] They lived through the period when Frelimo turned colonial labour policy on its head. Frelimo emphasized that all workers had rights that employers must protect and secure, and that employers and employees were not just white and male.[71] Despite the patriarchal cultural bias against urban women who held jobs, Frelimo President Samora Machel explicitly praised women who worked in the city's factories.[72] In the early independence era Frelimo's public discourse was broadly viewed as pro-woman. Party officials emphasized women's strength, their solidarity and their roles in forging a new Mozambican nation. At this juncture, state media chastized men for polygamy, for demanding subservience from their wives and for discouraging women's political participation in the Organization of Mozambican Women or Frelimo. Scholars have highlighted the disjuncture between Frelimo's and the Organization of Mozambican Women's public discourse, and their practice and policies, but certainly the public narrative regarding women's roles was markedly changed from the colonial era. [73]

---

[69] OT, Group of retirees, 2 and 4 June 1993.

[70] For the many changes in the transition from Lourenço Marques to Maputo, see Brigitte Lachartre, *Enjeux Urbaines au Mozambique: de Lourenço Marques á Maputo* (Paris: Karthala, 2000).

[71] Leroy Vail and Landeg White, *Capitalism and Colonialism in Mozambique: A Study of Quelimane District* (Minneapolis: University of Minnesota, 1980): Ch. 8 and 9; OT, Pedro Timba, 9 July 1993 for specifics at Cajú Industrial.

[72] On the transition see Sheldon, *Pounders of Grain*, Ch. 5–7; Stephanie Urdang, *And Still They Dance: Women, War and the Struggle for Change in Mozambique* (New York: Monthly Review Press, 1989), Ch. 7; 'O Partido – A Luta,' 15–20; Pitcher, *Transforming Mozambique* Ch.1; Sithole, *Frelimo Militant*, Ch. 1, 2, 15.

[73] Isabel Casimiro, 'Paz na Terra, Guerra em Casa: Feminismo e Organizações de Mulheres em Moçambique' (Maputo: Promédia, 2004); Casimiro, 'Situação Legal da Mulher perante o Direito a Alimentos,' in *Eu Mulher em Moçambique*. coord. Ana Elsa de Santana Afonso (Maputo: Comissão Nacional UNESCO em Moçambique e Associação dos Escritores Moçambicanos,1994): 147–72; Kathleen Sheldon, 'Women and Revolution in Mozambique: A Luta Continua,' in Mary Ann Tétreault, ed. *Women and Revolution in Africa, Asia and the New World*, (Columbia: University of South Carolina Press, 1994): 33–61; Urdang, *And Still They Dance*; Arnfred, *Sexuality and Gender*, 5–8.

Frelimo developed the cartoon character *Xiconhoca – O Inimigo* [Chico the Snake – the Enemy] to convey the politics developed by its propaganda department.[74] *Xico*, as he was familiarly known, was the quintessentially irresponsible, corrupt, scheming, domineering male who embodied as many negatives as could be scripted onto his ample being. He was a drinking, smoking, polygamist; he allowed his burdened wife or wives to follow him at an appropriate distance while he strode ahead carrying nothing, and he forbade his wives to have anything to do with the politics of the Organization of Mozambican Women. Although some have read *Xico* as a sinister figure, others found that his very shabbiness and rascality made him an endearing anti-hero.[75] He even inspired twenty-first century progeny in the cartoon figure, *Nhoca Jr. Filho de Xico* – [Snake Jr. *Xico*'s son]. *Xico*'s son took on the new cast of evils that accompanied the country's re-invention as an aspiring darling of the capitalist West. [76]

Xiconhoca was a man, created by men to communicate largely with men, but women noticed how they were scripted in and out of play. *Xico* cartoons opened new spaces for women as tractor drivers, as wives who stood up to their abusive husbands and citizens who put a stop to corruption. Most men and women in the *Xico* cartoons were pro-Frelimo cadres, sketched in dutiful, clean-cut, interchangeable uniformity – undistinguished and un-named, except one. Reminiscent of the mischievous cliché, 'well behaved women rarely make history,' the one woman who appeared in distinctive clothes, was the same size or larger than *Xico*, and had her own name was the infamous *Pita*. *Pita* was neither a factory worker nor a dutiful wife. She was a party girl who sported go-go boots, miniskirt, and what used to be called an 'Afro' hairdo. She looked very much like the late colonial era prostitutes captured by Mozambique's leading photographer Ricardo Rangel in the Rua de Araújo bars and cabarets and the street corners of Mafalala and Lagoas neighbourhoods, the city's notorious red light districts.[77]

Did Frelimo's statements about proud and confident Mozambican women and workers promote those qualities in the narrators for this study? Did Frelimo President Samora Machel recognize pride and confidence among the cashew workers, farmers and market sellers

[74] Frelimo, *Xiconhoca o Inímigo* (Maputo: Frelimo, Edição do Departamento de Trabalho Ideológico, 1979).
[75] Penvenne, 'Tapestry of Conflict,' 250–51; Lars Buur, 'Xiconhoca, Mozambique's Ubiquitous Post-Independence Traitor,' in Sharika Thiranagama and Tobias Kelly, *Traitors: Suspicion, Intimacy and the Ethnics of State-Building* (Philadelphia: Univ. of Pennsylvania Press, 2009): 24–47.
[76] The spirit of Chico lives on in 'Nhoca Jr. – O Filho do Xico,' [Nhoca Junior – The Son of Chico] a cartoon figure featured weekly in *Sacana; suplemento Humorístico do Savana*, No 106, 15 July 2005.
[77] Ricardo Rangel, *Pão nosso de cada noite; our nightly bread*, [Texts by Calane da Silva, José Craveirinha, José Luís Cabaço, Luís Bernando Honwana, Nelson Saúte and Rui Nogar] (Maputo: Marimbique, 2004); Aldino Muianga, *Meledina (ou a história duma prostituta)* (Maputo: Ndjira, 2004).

Figure 4 Xiconhoca and Pita, 1977
(Credit: Frelimo, *Xiconhoca o Inímigo* (Maputo: Frelimo, Edição do Departamento de Trabalho Ideológico, 1979)

and therefore celebrate them?[78] It is difficult to know for certain if Machel's post-independence public talks influenced the testimonies recorded during this era. Machel had been killed in a plane crash six years earlier.[79] Clearly some Mozambican women left their families to join Frelimo, some left their battering or non-supporting husbands to seek waged labour, and some demonstrated a great deal of pride and self-confidence in their workplace before Samora Machel praised factory workers for their labour. Would women have framed their narratives as they did without the potential confidence boost of Frelimo's discourse?[80]

According to Vail and White's research, the late colonial state's authoritarianism, interventionism, and bureaucracy had actually wrung confidence and initiative from Mozambican workers in the Quelimane plantation areas. Despite Frelimo President Samora Machel's call for creative initiatives by workers and farmers, Vail and White argued that Frelimo's inheritance was a pattern of dependency

[78] Richard Roberts, 'History and Memory: The Power of Statist Narratives,' *IJAHS*, Vol. 33, No. 3 (2000): 513–22.
[79] Allen Isaacman highlights oral collection in 'Colonial Mozambique, an Inside View: The Life History of Raúl Honwana,' *Cahiers d'Etudes Africaines*, XXVIII, 1, 109 (1988): 60–2; Centro de Estudos Africanos, Oficina de História, *Não Vamos Esquecer!* Vol. I, Nos. 1 and 2/3, 1983.
[80] Sheldon, *Pounders of Grain* addresses some of these questions.

that would not be easily transformed.[81] The Frelimo government set up worker production councils and appointed political organizers, so-called *grupos dinamizadores*, ostensibly to encourage and fuel worker initiatives. Transitioning from resistance to colonialism to support for independence was not unproblematic.

Many colonial era supervisors left the cashew factory immediately after the 1974 military coup or during the transition to independence. Workers' councils denounced abusive supervisors of all ethnicities and colors. People who taunted African workers during the colonial era, belittling them for their clothing and comportment, were confronted, accused and punished.[82] In some cases Portuguese flight was preceded by sabotage, embezzlement and currency fraud, but in all cases the exodus of management, skilled middle and upper level staff caused disruption and confusion.[83] Frelimo nationalized Cajú Industrial de Moçambique in 1979 in part to head off further capital flight, fraud and sabotage.[84]

Although Frelimo urged worker initiative, not every Mozambican worker initiative was of the sort Frelimo welcomed. Some people took advantage of the confusion to try to defraud the cashew industry, the workers and the state. In a factory where the workforce was over 80 per cent women, it was interesting to note that all of the people apprehended and jailed in 1978 for stealing worker's rent money, embezzling money from the cafeteria, the funeral funds, the cash registers and the main office payroll were men.[85] While most women found it awkward to stand up to men in the factory one on one, the fact that women were the majority and many had gained experience as team leaders facilitated greater leadership.

Whatever the challenges of the historical moment of narration, the women framed the change from colonialism to independence around respect for human dignity, particularly underscoring the colonial era indignities that no longer happened. Carolina Manelele explained:

> In the colonial era there was little respect for people and their lives. Women had to return to work immediately after the birth of a child. *That no longer happens.* Now when there is a death in the family a representative from the factory comes to pay their respects. They give you time. In the past your child or husband could die and they expected you to come to work. *That no longer happens.* Today we have respect; the leaders know to say *xawani vamamana* [respectful greeting for adult women].

Cristina Muzamane recalled: 'When my son died I was called back to work before we had a proper mourning ceremony. The day

---

[81] Vail and White, *Capitalism and Colonialism*, Ch. 9; Pitcher, *Transforming Mozambique*, Ch. 1.
[82] OT, Marta Moiana, 9 July 1993, CIM / M.
[83] Penvenne, 'A Tapestry of Conflict.' 246–59.
[84] For Frelimo's nationalization of the cashew industry see: Pitcher, *Transforming Mozambique*; Pereira Leite, 'A Guerra do Cajú,' 294–332; Hanlon, 'Power without Responsibility,' 29–45; Cramer, 'Can Africa Industrialize?'1247–49.
[85] 'O Partido – A Luta,'15–20.

after my nephew died I had to leave all the people who had come to console us to return to work. In those times the boss would say, "Why did you go to the hospital instead of coming to work?" *That no longer happens.*'[86]

Many retirees were grateful for the benefits, 'Frelimo helped us... thanks to Frelimo we have retirement.'[87] But they also experienced the difficulties keenly, as Saquina Malassahane noted, 'this independence is very difficult for us.'[88] Respect and dignity were critical, but like prestige, you can't eat them. Every person agreed with Amélia Chiconela's baseline, 'What was important was to have enough to eat,' but many others continued: 'In the colonial era we suffered but we could eat. Now we do not suffer, but we can not eat well either.'[89] Julieta Mulungu elaborated: 'I am grateful for the chance to tell you how we worked during colonialism because we suffered to raise our children, but it wasn't like now. I only earned 240 *escudos* [per month] – and often we didn't get all of that – but the money was enough for us to eat. I no longer have little children, but my grandchildren will know from this testimony, as though they could look into our bellies, like looking through a pane of glass, they will see how we lived and what we ate at the time. We did not go hungry like now.' [90]

Colonial era cashew shellers earned the municipality's lowest legal wage, and many did not even manage that. The colonial era *escudo* held its value, in large part because of the state's concern for the welfare of poor whites. When the cost of living index rose, the lowest tier of Portuguese state employees sent up a political howl. Such pressure forced several incremental increases for minimum wage earners between 1945 and 1970. If possible women supplemented their wages by working small food plots at weekends. By developing multiple strategies women with only one or two children could usually cover the cost of food, rent, and water, but women with larger families struggled mightily.[91]

Regarding the changes at independence, the young women with young families prioritized the importance of maternity and sick leaves, while people of all ages valued time off to honor and bury the dead: 'During the colonial era the hardest thing for women was that we had no right to maternity leave, but when we became independent Josina Machel freed women and that changed.'[92] Frelimo President

[86] OT, Carolina Mundao Manelele and Cristina Muzamane – joint testimony, 4 June 1993.
[87] OT, Ester Tafula, 3 June 1993.
[88] OT, Saquina Malassanhane, 13 July and 26 May 1993.
[89] OT, Amélia Chiconela, 17 May 1993; Laura Tsomba, 21 May 1993; and Saquina Malassanhane, 13 July and 26 May 1993; Ofelia Manana Mbebe, 4 June 1993.
[90] *Escudos* were the colonial era currency notes. The contemporary currency is called a *metical*, plural, *meticais*. OT, Julieta Mulungu, 20 May 1993.
[91] Chapters 3 and 4 below and OT, Laura Tsombe, 21 May 1993; Julieta Mulungu, 20 May 1993; Ester Tafula, 3 June 1993; Elina Mulungu, 4 June 1993.
[92] OT, Cristina Duzenta Cuambe, 17 May 1993.

Samora Machel's wife Josina Machel died three years before independence, but with the familiar conflation of person, practice, and place, Josina Machel came to symbolize what many workers felt were Frelimo's pro-woman policies.[93] The cohort of younger workers was somewhat better educated and more apt to be local. In some cases they were second or third generation cashew shellers, working alongside mothers, grandmothers and siblings. Not surprisingly, with their lives still ahead of them the youngest women saw more possibilities for profit and change with independence than did their elders. As more educated, skilled women and men moved into leadership positions at Cajú the reputation of the whole workforce improved.[94]

In sum, I cleared this project for oral research both in the United States and Mozambique. I consulted Mozambicans at the state, archive, university and factory level regarding each stage of my proposed strategy. Mozambican colleagues and people in positions of power provided helpful advice, and ultimately authorized and supported the project. Mozambican Joaquina Boane Machava was the oral project assistant and brought great positive energy to the task. The labour force and retirees at Cajú Industrial in Matola and Chamanculo were clearly at the heart of the project. The women's testimony and their perspectives on the past were shaped by their cumulative experiences up to and including the moment of narration. Their experience, ages, personalities and social positions all factored into the perspectives they brought forth, and again, they were the survivors.

Structure and arguments

Whereas the published and archival record typically ignored, skewed and erased evidence of urban African women's agency and productivity, the narrators for this project forcefully asserted that they made important contributions to the full sweep of the colonial era cashew economy, the vitality of southern Mozambique and the African neighbourhoods of Lourenço Marques. Their narratives and songs provide rich, amusing and deeply astute perspectives on migration, urban labour and social history in the late colonial era. They reveal important themes that linked many women's experiences and also revealed the ways women struggled fundamentally with one another. The women's testimony provides our anchor, but a great range of other sources provide context and support the goal to convey a much broader story.

Chapter 1, 'A Century of Contestation around Cashews,' introduces the region's cashew economy. It explains the many ways cashew plants and by-products were developed in general and by Mozambican

---

[93] Sheldon, *Pounders of Grain*; Vail and White, *Capitalism and Colonialism*.
[94] OT, Luis Guila Muhale, 29 June 1993, CIM/M.

women in particular. Although Portuguese colonial policy eventually promoted some aspects of the cashew economy, it had long proscribed others. This chapter details three arguments that carry through subsequent chapters. First, the cashews women harvested for food security and alcoholic drinks remained important for African producers and consumers in ways standard economic metrics failed to appreciate. The narratives insist on an approach to the cashew economy as whole cloth. Second, Mozambican cashew farmers and cashew factory workers were systematically defrauded of their right to legal minimum compensation for the cashews they produced for, sold to and processed in the formal market economy. Ordinary Mozambican farmers and workers deeply subsidized cashew profits pocketed by others. Third, women's enduring roles in the economic and social place of cashews as a food and drink in the overlapping household, gift, informal and industrial processing economies were essential. Women were not only the main labour force for industrialized cashew shelling, they planted most of the southern cashew orchard, tended trees, harvested nuts, brewed and sold the alcoholic cashew drinks that sustained family support networks much more predictably than the payments and wages of the market economy. Many women regularly participated simultaneously in these overlapping arenas of cashew production and consumption.

Chapter 2, 'Tarana: History from the Factory Floor,' opens with Oselina Marindzi's song of lament: 'Oh, woe is me! Oh, where should I go? Oh, how can I get there?' It posed the questions on the mind of every woman who left her rural home for Tarana: 'what will become of me if I leave?' Chapter 3 more fully explores the broader migration process, but it is necessarily introduced here. Marindzi's song of woe and Filomena Mathaya's song about stoically remaining on 'a flat bare place' capture essential dilemmas that were deeply scripted in the narratives of migration and womanhood.

This chapter closely describes Tharani's experiments that placed the early cashew shelling industry on a permanent footing, and follows the striking changes that took place when Portuguese investors took over in the 1960s. Worker testimony reveals the character of each of the factory's distinct work areas and the labour force's patterns of contestation and solidarity. Despite the narrow parameters of their authority, women took ownership of their spaces through patterns of naming, assignment of meaning and strategies for sharing workloads. They developed counter-hegemonic language that secured their own interpretations of daily life. Women had to make painful compromises to cope with the seasonal work pace and management's efforts to cheat them of their legal wages. They were both proud of their contribution to the industry and incensed by the abuse they faced from supervisors, the industry and the government. Their testimony directly confronts the colonial era's patronizing attitude toward their contributions. It is a story we have not heard to date.

Chapter 3, 'Migration – Pathways from Poverty to Tarana,' confirms that rural impoverishment and extended male outmigration by the 1950s pushed some women and their children beyond their ability to cope. It confirms the historic importance of male migration from Southern Mozambique to employment in South Africa's mines, farms and towns, but also highlights Sean Redding's insight that the movement of women and their children in the making, unmaking and remaking of households everywhere was also a form of labour migration.[95] Considering the movement of labour in a fuller range of possibilities on a single field of analysis enhances connectivity and retains the analysis of women and their labour. It maps women's pathways from rural poverty to the factory floor at Tarana, and identifies patterns that led them to set down the hoe of the field and strike out for the hoe of the city. Who left? Why? Where did they go? How? Who helped and who hindered the process of migration? What meaning did women assign to their moves?

With so many Sul do Save adult men chronically absent, rural women faced an enhanced workload and erosion of economic, social and emotional support. Women recalled that they left when they hit a tipping point. At some point they simply could not see how their situation might change for the better – things were bad and there was little hope that they would improve. Scholarly literature suggests that women who live in patrilineal societies and move at marriage to live with their husband's lineage experience the move as either disadvantageous or ambiguous. Although that was doubtless the case for many it was by no means the whole story. Women developed a great diversity of claims and resources to their advantage in at least three lineages: their father's, their mother's and their husband's.[96] Women learned from other women's experience living among different lineages. Women have more ability and incentive to develop claims in multiple lineages than do men, and that can be a creative advantage rather than a disadvantage.

Chapter 4, 'Lives around Livelihoods – Children are not like Chickens,' probes the central dilemmas most factory women faced trying to manage factory work, housework, and childcare. The title is taken from Rabeca Notiço's observation: 'Children are not like chickens, you can not simply leave them out in the yard for the neighbours to feed.'[97] Men's stories of their work lives seldom mentioned their children. Women's stories of their work lives usually centred around their children. They developed a range of strategies to secure childcare through family networks and factory support. Everyone learned to leverage wages through informal, gift and family sector investments to

[95] Sean Redding, 'South African Women and Migration in Umtata, Transkei, 1880–1935', In Kathleen Sheldon, ed. *Courtyards, Markets, City Streets, Urban Women in Africa* (Boulder: Westview Press, 1996): 31–46.
[96] José Fialho Feliciano, *Antropologia Económica dos Thonga do Sul de Moçambique* (Maputo: AHM,1998): 442ff; Ana Maria Loforte, *Género e Poder entre os Tsonga de Moçambique* (Maputo: Promédia, 2000).
[97] OT, Rabeca Notiço, 24 May 1993.

feed, house, clothe and educate their children – usually in that order. Many narrators insisted that their children had 'no fathers.'[98] Chapter 4 brings the men in single mothers' lives into clearer focus, and probes colonial policy toward African urban families regarding the very different framing of bonuses for family breadwinners on one hand and the penalties women heads of household paid for their fertility and roles as caretakers for the young and sick on the other.

The closing section introduces our third touchstone song by Mindawu Bila and pauses to underscore the richness and challenges of spoken and sung history that have not yet been fully embraced. If we want to understand women's history and experience we have to listen to and work with this material, just as we work with colonial documents and the press. Bila's song bridges migration, childcare concerns and the broader challenges faced by urban African families. It documents continuity, changes and creativity in the clever ways women selected from their remembered past to sing a vision of an imagined future.

Chapter 5, 'African Urban Families in the Late Colonial Era,' extends analysis from the factory into the community. The women of Tarana, like the great majority of the city's African population, lived in zones specifically intended to be impermanent.[99] Lourenço Marques's so-called *bairros de caniço* were neighbourhoods of homes built of *caniço* (cane or reeds), thatch, metal sheets, wooden poles and other impermanent materials. The *bairros de caniço* extended out from the ring road that literally encircled the cement and steel structures of the city's core.[100] This chapter contrasts the colonial and municipal administration's assumptions about socio-economic life in these *bairros* with the quotidian experiences conveyed in the women's narratives and documented by the few social science studies conducted in the era.[101] It concludes that the *bairros* had their own structures, orders and rhythms that the municipality and colonial authorities read as disorder and so failed to see and understand.[102]

---

[98] OT, Elina Chivavale Mulungu, 4 June 1993.

[99] Karen Tranberg Hansen and Mariken Vaa. eds, 'Introduction, *'Reconsidering Informality: Perspectives from Urban Africa* (Uppsala, Nordiska Afrikainstitut, 2002): 7–24.

[100] Except for bakeries and grocery shops (called *cantinas*) that were legally required to be built in masonry, permanent construction was legally restricted to the city core, or cement city.

[101] Rita-Ferreira, 'Os Africanos;' Hilary Flegg [Mitchell] and W. Lutz, 'Report on an African Demographic Survey,' *Journal of Social Research [South Africa]* 10 (1959): 1–24; Norberto Teixeira Santos, 'Avaliação Nutricional da População Infantil Bantu (0–5 Anos) de uma zona suburbana da Cidade de Lourenço Marques,' *Revista Ciências Medicinas [Lourenço Marques]* 17 (Ser. B) (1974) (Lourenço Marques: Tipografia Académica, 1975); 'Inquerito habitacional realizado no bairro da Munhuana,' *Estudos de Ciências Políticas e Sociais*, 72 (Lisbon: Junta do Instituto Superior de Ciências Políticas e Sociais do Ultramar, 1964).

[102] Henri Bergson's observation that 'disorder is merely the order you are not looking for,' and James C. Scott's similar observation about official legibility are both helpful here. Henri Bergson (Quoted by Schuman) in Louise G. White, *Political Analysis: Technique and Practice* (Belmont: Wadsworth Publishing Co. 1994): 211; James C. Scott, *Seeing like a State: How Certain Schemes to Improve the Human Condition have Failed* (New Haven: Yale University Press, 1998).

It also concludes that the municipality's appalling neglect of services and facilities for African neighbourhoods contributed directly to the illnesses and morbidity that meant wives, mothers, sisters and daughters remained at home ill themselves or tending to the ill rather than at work. What employers called absenteeism should be approached from an alternative viewpoint.

Common-law marriages or partnerships, called living *amancebado*, were ubiquitous, complicated and broadly misinterpreted. From the perspective of colonial law, African women's most secure legal and social access to urban residence was through a formally sanctioned marriage to a legally employed man. It is therefore not surprising that common-law marriages were often assumed to be disadvantageous to women, but the women's narratives challenge that framing. Many women had little expectation of male support and had experienced violence and instability with intimate partners. Having secure access to one's home, children and possessions was an important factor in some women's strong preferences for heading their own household and engaging in *amancebado* relationships. It is clearly always difficult to maintain boundaries among intimacy, companionship and control. The narratives reveal that women aspired to control the basics for their and their children's security and safety.[103]

The Conclusion – 'Gendered Perspectives on Work, Households and Authority,' returns to work, households, stakes claims and authority, and recalls what the narratives have taught us. Centring women in an historical narrative necessarily shifts many embedded assumptions regarding colonial labour policy, economic hierarchy and social agency. Women's experiences of migration, urban work and families often begin with households, their making, unmaking and remaking. Women's approaches to staking claims through their parents and partners' lineages and the urban partnerships they pursued and secured were robust, innovative and often successful. Women's multiple and mutually sustaining investments in personal relationships throughout the family, gift, informal, and formal economies were central to their life efforts to build social and material capital.[104] The women with the most robust social networks were the most prosperous and tended to build security buttressed by people, whereas women who, by a turn of circumstances or illness, became isolated and insecure tended to spiral into further misery.

[103] OT, Rabeca Notico, 24 May 1993. Studies from South Africa to Tanzania corroborate this shift. Lee, *African Women and Apartheid, 104;* Margarida Paulo, Carmeliza Rosário, et al., *'Xiculungo'. Social Relations of Urban Poverty in Maputo, Mozambique* (Bergen: Chr. Michelsen Institute, 2007): 4–5; Paulo, Rosário et al., *'Xiculungo' Revisited: Assessing the implications of PARPA II in Maputo, 2007–2010,* (Bergen: Chr. Michelsen Institute 2011), Bender Shetler, 'The Gendered Spaces,' 304.
[104] The Conclusions return to the cashew shellers' narratives as gendered performances in dialogue with points raised by Bender Shetler, Gengenbach, Geiger, Vail and White, and others: Bender Shetler, 'Gendered Spaces'; Gengenbach, 'Women Make History'; Geiger, 'What's so Feminist;' Vail and White, 'Forms of Resistance'; Vail and White, *Power and the Praise Poem.*

The women's narratives provide compelling, gendered and neglected perspectives on urban industrial labour and migrant life in the capital city in the closing decades of the colonial era. By centring women's knowledge, their experiences and interpretations in and about the leading industry, the need to see the cashew economy as whole cloth becomes evident. This analysis confirms connections across the many ways women worked, and pays attention to the multiple strategies they kept in play in their efforts to care for themselves and their families. It highlights the multiple and masked ways the colonial administration and private businesses intentionally squeezed value from their work, while denying them the resources and municipal facilities they needed to be healthy and productive. Ironically and outrageously, the very colonial administration and employers who collaborated to channel health and safety services to white residential areas and grossly neglected them in the *bairros de caniço* then blamed *caniço* residents for the illness and loss of productivity that such conditions inevitably provoked.

Those connections and disconnects are not as obvious if you follow men through their work and daily lives, but they are impossible to miss when you follow women. Men's and women's labour experiences and memories of work may be mutually constituted, but men's memories of labour were more accessible to historians, and were taken as a norm to which women were eventually compared and found to be different. What the colonial government perceived as disorder in the cashew factory, the cashew economy and the Lourenço Marques neighbourhoods where its labour force lived may well have been an important but unacknowledged order – an order they had not anticipated and were ill prepared to see.[105] Resisting the temptation to tidy organically messy and complicated socio-economic and cultural formations, I urge attention to connections through women's perspectives and experiences.

The epilogue sketches the broad lines of Mozambique's cashew economy from 1975 to 2015. It highlights the factors that led to Mozambique's sharp decline as a leading global cashew producer, and argues that continuing failure to see the cashew economy as whole cloth and to appreciate fully both women's roles in all sectors of the economy and the socio-economic context of cashew planting, harvesting and use promotes misleading and incomplete analyses.

Finally, this project leaves many important areas insufficiently explored. I need to mention two. First, in parts of neighbouring Southern Africa women's spiritual and religious associations provided essential kinds of mutual support for urban African women in particular.[106] In

---

[105] Again, drawing from Bergson, quoted by Schuman in White, *Political Analysis*, 211 and Scott, *Seeing Like a State*.
[106] Marc Epprecht, 'Domesticity and Piety in Colonial Lesotho: the Private Politics of Basotho Women's Pious Associations,' *JSAS* 19, 2 (June 1993): 202–225; Deborah Gaitskell, 'Devout Domesticity? A Century of African Women's Christianity in South Africa,' In *Women and Gender in Southern Africa to 1945*, Cherryl Walker, ed. (Cape Town: David Phillip, 1990): 251–72; Gaitskell, 'Wailing for Purity': Prayer Unions, African Mothers and Adolescent

contemporary Maputo such associations are ubiquitous and important.[107] During the late colonial era, however, the Catholic Church was formally associated with the state, and the state was deeply suspicious of Protestant and so-called Separatist or Ethiopian churches, at times subjecting their members to harassment or much worse.[108] During the first generation of independence in Mozambique, Frelimo both formally and informally proscribed religious and spiritual persons and groups and was openly skeptical of healers.[109] Although the oral history project specifically inquired about people or institutions who may have provided support for the workers or their children, it is quite possible that, if women earned extra as healers or if religious groups provided support, women may have chosen not to mention it. When cashew production was in full force, most workers said they spent the precious little time they had reproducing and leveraging their ability to support their households – housework, childcare, petty trade and production filled their time outside the factory. Older women and women without children may have had more time for spiritual healing and church communities, but that aspect is neglected here.

Second, although many women talked about what they thought was ideal, important and of enduring value, this study did not treat symbolic relationships with the same depth and interest as economic and social relationships. Women placed symbolic importance on owning their own home and providing for those in their care. Bento Sitoe underscores the many ways that cultural images, practices and comportment shape the telling, hearing, seeing and understanding of many forms of communication.[110] I was present to absorb the multiple texts of narrators' smiles, laughter, tears, hesitations, movements and silences, but I do not pretend to have understood all by any means. I am sure I missed spiritual and symbolic meanings between the telling and listening. I regret having audio-taped rather than video-taped these encounters for just that reason. The project only contributed the voices of the women who built Mozambique's leading industry in the

(cont) Daughters, 1920–1940,' *Industrialisation and Social Change in South Africa*, Shula Marks and Richard Rathbone, eds, (London: Longman, 1982): 338–57; Gaitskell, compiler, 'Special Issue on Women in Southern Africa,' *JSAS*, 10 (1983).

107 James Pfeiffer, 'African Independent Churches in Mozambique: Healing the Afflictions of Inequality,' *Medical Anthropology Quarterly*, 16, 2 (2002)' 176–99; Pfeiffer, 'Money, Modernity and Morality, Traditional Healing and the Expansion of the Holy Spirit in Mozambique,' in Tracy J. Luedke and Harry G. West, eds, *Borders and Healers: Brokering Therapeutic Resources in Southeast Africa* (Bloomington: Indiana University Press, 2006): 81–100.

108 Teresa Cruz e Silva, *Protestant Churches and the Formation of Political Consciousness in Southern Mozambique (1930–1974)* Introduction by David Hedges, edited by Didier Péclard (Basel: P. Schlettwein Publishing, 2001); Alda Romão Saúte, *O Intercâmbio entre os Moçambicanos e as Missões Cristãs e a Educação em Moçambique* (Maputo: Promédia, 2005).

109 Alf Helgesson, *Church, State and People in Mozambique; An Historical Study with Special Emphasis on Methodist Developments in the Inhambane Region*, PhD thesis (Uppsala: Faculty of Theology, Uppsala University, 1994).

110 Bento Sitoe, 'Translation: Languages and Cultures in Contrast,' Boston University African Studies Center, African Humanities Program; *Discussion Papers in the African Humanities*, No 9 (1990).

late colonial era to the country's history and cultural heritage. Finally, in light of this, I warmly welcome the prospect that Mozambicans, for whom the languages and lilts are mother tongue and the symbolic and spiritual references are most familiar, will listen to the tapes and come away with different points than those that emerged for me.

1 A Century of Contestation around Cashews

'The cashew is a tree of vice and ruin.
Would that the Marquis of Pombal order them all uprooted.'
                    Mozambican High Commissioner António Enes, 1893[1]

'During the three months of cashew season, there is no force
known to mankind that will make the native work ...
they manage to stay constantly drunk.'
                    Mozambican Governor General, A. A. Freire de Andrade, 1907–1910[2]

'Without a doubt cashew nuts will gain a prominent place
in Mozambique's economy, a place that even our
best export products will not be able to surpass.'
                                        Joaquim Viegas, 1952[3]

'In 1974, the income associated with the external trade in cashew products comprised 21.3 per cent to the colony's total exports... At this time the cashew economy out-stripped cotton and sugar, the core commodities shaping the colonial export economy.'
                                        Joana Pereira Leite, 2000[4]

From first fruits to Tarana

Between the turn of the twentieth century and the end of the colonial era the state transformed its image of the importance of Mozambique's cashew orchard and economy. António Enes's late nineteenth-century prescription for the national cashew orchard was explained by Freire de Andrade's early twentieth-century complaint. African drunkenness, he claimed 'deprived European farmers of native labour just when they most need it...Furthermore, just when they should be planting, natives

[1] António Enes quoted in Eduardo Medeiros, *Bebidas Moçambicanas de Fábrico Caseiro* [Estudos, 5] (Maputo: Arquivo Histórico de Moçambique, 1998): 56.
[2] Freire de Andrade quoted in Medeiros, *Bebidas Moçambicanas*, 90.
[3] Joaquim Viegas, 'Problemas Agrícolas em Moçambique: A Castanha de Cajú: Mecanização Indústrial e a sua Influência na Estrutura Economica de Moçambique,' *Império*, (Marco / Abril, 1952): 9, 85–8.
[4] Pereira Leite, 'A Guerra do Cajú,' 295.

do not attend to their own crops.'[5] At that juncture the colonial administration focused on only one aspect of the large and complex cashew
economy. Alcoholic drinks made from cashews, they claimed, not only
competed with the national wine industry, but blighted agricultural
production, public health and safety![6]

Enes called cashews that 'damned fruit', and short of uprooting
the entire national orchard, did whatever he could to discourage
its spread. His early twentieth-century colleagues followed suit. In
Inhambane in 1909, a per-tree tax was levied on anyone owning
more than 300 cashew trees, and the tax was doubled for anyone
owning more than a thousand trees.[7] Cashew-based alcohol production was expressly prohibited in most of the country for most of the
twentieth century. The correlation of cashews, sales of illegal brews,
drunkenness and worker absenteeism remained as more than a
leitmotiv in colonial and missionary correspondence and reports,
especially in the Native Affairs Department, the colonial bureaucracy charged with overseeing the lives and labours of the majority
population. Beginning in the early 1950s, however, the government and local investors increasingly touted cashews as among 'the
great riches of Mozambique,' particularly promising for export.[8] The
business of cashew alcohol consumption remained an important
concern, but mostly for the police and religious communities who
tried to abolish it.

The cashew export economy developed as part of rural commerce
and the export trade linked largely to South Asian traders in Mozambique, like Jiva Jamal Tharani. As a small group of entrepreneurs forged
the development of a cashew shelling industry in the early 1950s, the
government's attention eventually shifted from the suppression of
cashew drinks to the sale of cashew nuts and the industrial processing
of cashew bi-products. Joaquim Viegas urged the state to support
Portuguese entrepreneurs hoping to tap into the cashew export economy.[9] By the time that actually happened in the 1960s, a national
cashew shelling industry was already well underway, spearheaded
largely by South Asians. Eventually Portuguese, South Asian, Italian,
South African and other international investors staked capital in the
cashew 'riches' of Mozambique. Portugal's shifting manufacturing and
industrial profile, its closer economic links with Europe and efforts to

[5] Freire de Andrade quoted in Medeiros, *Bebidas Moçambicanas*, 90.
[6] For example, '... we have all seen how [fermented cashew fruit] has damaged native health.
Natives maintain a permanent state of drunkenness during the season.' Tarquinio Hall,
'Entrevista com Sr. Engr. Gomes e Sousa,' *Império* (4 August 1951):16.
[7] *Notícias* series on cashews, 15, 16, 17,19 and 20 Dec. 1966, quote 16 Dec. 1966.
[8] By the late 1960s Rita-Ferreira opposed 'irrational' police persecution of cashew and other
drinks, and promoted their nutritive value, 'Os Africanos', 440; 'As grandes riquezas de Moçambique; A castanha de cajú e seus derivados', *Lourenço Marques Guardian*, 29 Jan. 1948.
[9] Viegas, 'Problemas Agrícolas', 9, 85–8; José de Oliveira Boleo, 'Conversa inconfidencial sobre
castanha de cajú,' *Notícias*, 1 June 1950; Jose Soares Rebelo Comingos, 'Moçambique pode e
deve marcar uma posição no comércio de castanha de cajú,' *Notícias*, 19 Aug. 1952.

internationalize capital investment in light of the armed insurgencies throughout its African colonies, combined to encourage new policies toward industrialization in Mozambique, and enhanced state support for processing cashews.[10]

Since the 1930s Tharani & Company had purchased unshelled cashew nuts from farmers all over southern Mozambique and exported them as raw material to supply India's large cashew shelling industry. Tharani's firm was part of the extensive network of Indian merchants, small and large-scale retailers, wholesalers and exporters who exchanged manufactured and processed goods for African agricultural products throughout Mozambique.[11] From the late nineteenth century, the largely South Asian networks of small scale rural shops, called *cantinas*, were the front line in efforts to commercialize agriculture in Mozambique. As we shall see, in the 1940s Tharani experimented with shelling cashews through a street-corner cottage industry in Lourenço Marques. In 1950 the firm founded Mozambique's first and largest mechanized cashew shelling factory in the capital city's Chamanculo neighbourhood.[12] By 1951 Tharani & Co. claimed to be '...the only factory in the Province of Mozambique in the business of shelling and processing cashew kernels, cashew oils and cashew shell derivatives.'[13]

Whether cottage style or mechanized, in India or elsewhere, cashew shelling depended extensively on so-called 'nimble fingers' labour to complete the necessary shelling, cleaning and sorting processes. In Mozambique and India women accomplished the great majority of that hand labour.[14] At the close of the colonial era in 1974, from north to south, Mozambique had eleven cashew shelling factories in production and three more under construction. The industry employed more than 17,000 people. The industry developed differently in the south and the

[10] Malyn Newitt compares Portugal's interest in a range of crops and concludes that tea and cashews basically launched and thrived despite the state's disinterest, *A History of Mozambique*, 454ff; Newitt, 'The Late Colonial State,'110–22; Pereira Leite, 'A economia do Cajú,' 640ff; Martin Schaedel, 'The Growth and Consolidation of a Mozambican Proletariat in the Last Phase of Colonial Rule,' [hereafter 'Last Phase of Colonial Rule.'] Excerpt translated by Gottfried Wellmer and edited by David Hedges from *Eingeborenenem Arbeit: Formen der Ausbeutung unter der Portuguisischen Kolonial herrschaft in Mosambique* (Colonia Dahl-Rugenstein Verlag, 1984); David Hedges, 'Protection, Finance and integration in Colonial Mozambique, 1920–1974,' unpublished paper, SIAS Conference, Financial Institutions in the Political Economy, Bergen 11–14, June 1998; David Hedges, 'Transition and Reform, 1957–1966/67: Contradictory Perspectives for Colonial Defense and Development,' unpublished paper, Maputo: UEM, 1993. Thanks to David Hedges for highlighting Schaedel's work and for permission to cite his unpublished work.
[11] Susana Pereira Bastos, 'Indian Transnationalisms in Colonial and Postcolonial Mozambique,' *Stichproben; Wiener Zeitschrift für Kritische Afrikastudien*, 8 (2005): 277–306.
[12] 'Tharani & Companhia Limitada, Principal Associada de Cajú Industrial de Moçambique, Lta, Lourenço Marques: A única fábrica de descasque e extracção de amêndoas, óleos e derivados de castanha de cajú existente na Provincia de Moçambique,' *Império*, 4 (August 1951) ii.
[13] *Império*, 5 & 6 (Oct. 1951); 11 & 12 (March /April 1952) Tharani & Company remains the only cashew processing factory in Mozambique.
[14] Anna Lindberg, *Experience and Identity: A Historical Account of Class, Caste and Gender among the Cashew Workers of Kerala, 1930 –2000* (Lund: Studia Historica Lundensia, 2001); Lindberg, *Modernization and Effeminization in India; Kerala Cashew Workers since 1930* (Copenhagen: Nordic Institute of Asian Studies Press, 2005).

north. Although the overall industrial trajectory is traced below, the focus here is the southern industry, and specifically the largest factory, Cajú Industrial de Moçambique in Chamanculo.

For a brief moment in the twilight of the colonial era, the cashew industry provided Mozambique's the most important source of foreign exchange, but for the entire colonial era cashews provided valued food and highly valued alcoholic drink for the majority population in the household, gift and informal economies.[15] Whereas in the early twentieth century the colonial administration promoted uprooting the national orchard to prevent the majority population from enjoying its fruit, by the end of the colonial era, it promoted the vast expansion of the national orchard for the export of cashew nuts and by-products, with scarcely any mention of cashew drinks. Mozambicans' consumption of cashews and cashew drinks, however, did not diminish over time.

Cashew anatomy: Apples, nuts, kernels and liquid toxins

Cashew shelling never provided easy money for anyone. Whether processing the nuts for home consumption, gifts, local sale or industrial production, cashew shelling is so risk laden, noxious, time consuming and complicated, it is difficult to imagine why people bothered. This chapter introduces the cashew fruit, the cashew orchard, and Mozambique's diverse cashew economy from household and gift appreciation of cashew drinks during the first fruits season, so-called *época de ucanhé*, to industrial shelling and the export economy. It explores the government's schizophrenic attitude, with obsessive attention to cashew alcohol in the early century and obsessive attention to cashew shelling for export at the sunset of the colonial era. Despite the government's split attention, the chapter presents the cashew economy as 'whole cloth'. Mozambicans counted on cashew fruits and nuts for food security, alcoholic drinks to consume at home, share as gifts, and both drinks and nuts to sell for cash. All aspects were important, but transforming the fruit into cashew *aguardente* was probably the most profitable. Those who planted, tended and harvested cashews always had choices about whether to brew, eat, distill, give away or sell their harvest. In Sul do Save the cashew economy was important, complex and fundamentally connected to the interests and labour of women and farming households in general.[16]

Carl Linnaeus attributed the botanical name *Anacardium occidentale* to the cashew nut plant. Cashew anatomy and nomenclature are complicated and counter-intuitive. Nearly every part of the cashew fruit is known by a different name, depending on the literature and the language. Since India and the United States dominate

---

[15] Pereira Leite, 'A Guerra do Cajú,' 295; Parente and Neto, 'A Agro-Indústria de Cajú,' 34.
[16] Parente and Neto, 'A Agro-Indústria de Cajú,' 1–7.

Figure 5 Cashew Apple with Nut [*anacardium occidentale*]
(Credit: url: http://commons.wikimedia.org/wiki/File%3ACashew_apple_with_nut_-_Caju.jpg
FileUrl: http://upload.wikimedia.org/wikipedia/commons/b/b2/Cashew_apple_with_nut_-_
Caju.jpg (Attribution: By Ben Tavener (Flickr: Cashew fruits – Cajú) [CC BY 2.0 (http://creative-
commons.org/licenses/by/2.0)], via Wikimedia Commons, Accessed 11 Feb. 2015))

global cashew production and consumption, the dominant business
language in the cashew trade is English. The cashew tree produces
a cashew apple that is green when young and red when ripe. The
cashew apple is also sometimes called a cashew pear. It is shaped
more like a pear than an apple. Botanists consider the cashew apple
a false fruit. The genuine article is the odd shaped little nut attached
to the base of the apple. The nut has different parts and different
names. Most Mozambicans call the whole nut a *castanha,* but *castanha*
also means chestnut. The hard outer shell of the whole cashew nut
contains a variety of marketable products, but the essential product
is the similarly odd shaped inner nut that most Mozambicans call
an *amêndoa,* but *amêndoa* also means almond. The industry term for
the inner nut is a kernel. The kernel is the edible component that the
reader would probably call a cashew nut. It is an excellent food source,
high in vitamins, protein and healthy fats.[17] Both cashew nuts and
cashew kernels were marketed and exported in the colonial era.
Cashew nuts were exported whole and unshelled – usually to India.

---

[17] Carin Vijfhuizen, Carla Braga, Luis Artur and Nazneen Kanji, 'Liberalisation, Gender
and Livelihoods: the Cashew Nut Case,' *Working Paper* 1 (English) Mozambique Phase 2: The
South, January-December 2003, [hereafter, Kanji et al., 'Liberalisation – South'] International
Institute for Environment and Development [IIED], Eduardo Mondlane University, Faculty of
Agronomy & Forestry (November, 2003): 7.

Cashew kernels were 'shelled' from the cashew nuts, and exported – usually to the United States.[18]

The kernel is separated from the hard outer shell of the cashew nut, by a thin delicate membrane called a testa skin, and a caustic liquid that must be expelled as part of the shelling process. At least the expelled liquid has a sensible name. It is called cashew nut shell liquid [CNSL]. It is 90 per cent anacardic acid and 10 per cent cardol. Cardol, marketed as cardolite, is used to produce resins, varnishes and paints, and is an important commercial by-product. Anacardic acid's commercial value is more limited. The acid chemically burns one's skin on contact and irritates tissues in the respiratory track if inhaled – qualities that obviously complicate the shelling process.[19]

Most shelling strategies entail humidifying and dehumidifying the nuts at different stages. The nuts must be heated enough to cause the shell to break and expel the CNSL, but not enough to scorch the kernel. Cashew kernels are nutritious even if they are scorched or broken in the shelling process, but the most highly prized commercial product – the industry ideal – is the largest white, whole, so-called fancy or dessert type cashew kernel. That industry ideal fetches a significantly higher price than the darker, smaller, misshapen, broken or scorched nuts. After separating the kernel from the shell and expelling the CNSL, removing the testa skin from the kernel is the most labour-intensive step in the cashew shelling process. Removing the skin without breaking the kernel is difficult. Tharani's goal at the Chamanculo cashew shelling factory was to produce and market the ideal large dessert kernels, but also all cashew by-products, from cardolite to the broken cashew kernel crumbs that the industry called 'baby bits'.[20] The hardness and uneven shape of the cashew nut's outer shell, the toxicity of the CNSL, the thinness of the protective skin and the delicacy of the kernel inside render efforts to extract a clean, intact kernel from a whole nut difficult – to say the least. The challenge has kept generations of engineers, inventors, investors and entrepreneurs busy for a long time.

Since the cashew apple gets ripe before the cashew nut, farmers basically have to decide at harvest whether the product they want is the apple or the nut. If the apple is picked while the nut is still unripe, it will not produce a good nut. The majority population's preferred use of cashew apples was distillation or brewing, but cashew apples were also eaten as a fruit, used for juices and, if they spoiled, either when green or over-ripe, they were used for animal fodder.[21] The apple's flesh is an excellent source of vitamin C, although brewing and distillation no doubt compromise that value.

---

[18] Parente and Neto, 'A Agro-Indústria de Cajú,' 47ff.
[19] Viegas, 'Problemas Agricolas,' 9, 85–88.
[20] Parente and Neto, 'A Agro-Indústria de Cajú,' 48.
[21] Parente and Neto, 'A Agro-Indústria de Cajú,' 66.

In light of Portugal's promotion of her national wines, the lively and detailed discussions about the profitability of a range of cashew products that emerged in the business press from the mid-twentieth century seldom suggested the commercial distillation of cashew apples. In the early 1970s the state licensed several Portuguese and Swiss firms to explore industrializing cashew apples for fruit juice or animal fodder.[22] On balance, however, industry owners and innovators around the world have been more interested in cashew kernels than cashew apples. Unfortunately, they have also been more interested in protecting the marketable kernels than the workers who shelled them. Generations of the world's cashew workers have had to remain vigilant on their own behalf in this toxic and dangerous industry.[23] *Anacardium occidentale* can be a seriously nasty plant.

Southern Mozambique's cashew orchard

Cashew trees are among South America's many gifts to Africa; they originated in Brazil's Pernambuco region. From the fifteenth century Portuguese sailors moved South American plants around the world. In the sixteenth century, the Portuguese, who called cashew trees the bread and wine of the people, introduced them to Indian Ocean coastal zones from Malacca to Eastern Africa as far south as Mozambique. In some parts of India cashews are known as *Parangi Andi* or Portuguese nuts.[24]

Cashew trees responded well to local propagation along Mozambique's coastal plain, and by the nineteenth century had spread from north to south. Northern Mozambique has the largest cashew orchard. Despite generally sandy soils and uneven rainfall, the trees grew well in the southern Mozambican Districts of Lourenço Marques, Inhambane and Gaza. Inhambane District became the most important cashew-producing southern region, in part because in the mid-nineteenth century Portuguese military officer João Loforte ignored the government's attitude toward cashews and promoted their propagation for distillation and consumption of the kernels. As Mozambique came out of the 1930s Depression era, sales of raw cashews were particularly robust in Inhambane where Portuguese agricultural entrepreneur Manuel Mendes encouraged marketing. The press picked up on the changing attitudes, wondering what the generations of administrators who advocated destroying the national cashew orchard would say about the promising

---

[22] Parente and Neto, 'A Agro-Indústria de Cajú,' 66; Guilherme de Melo,' A Indústrialização do Cajú,' *Notíciais*, 18 Feb. 1968; 'O cajú na economy de Moçambique,' *Indústria de Moçambique*, Vol. 4, No. 6 (1971): 171–172. In 2005 Maputo supermarkets sold boxed cashew juice, made in Brazil.

[23] Lindberg, *Experience and Identity*; Lindberg, *Modernization and Effeminization*, 42.

[24] Viegas, 'Castanha de Caju,' 9, 85; *Notícias*, Series on Cajú, 15–17, 19 and 20 December 1966.

market in cashews.[25] By the 1960s the region's cashew orchard was touted as 'the gold of Inhambane'.[26]

By the late colonial era the national orchard was estimated at around 45 million trees, most growing in the northern Nampula District.[27] Although a single tree produces fruit over a two to three month period, Mozambique's harvest is extended thanks to the distance and great variation of climate from north to south.[28] With trees producing sequentially, cashew nuts come into the market for as many as six months annually beginning with the northern harvest and ending with the southern.

Portuguese research institutes generated most of the scientific and statistical information about Mozambique's cashew orchards for the period 1945 to 1975. They paid disproportionate attention to production in the small European-dominated commercial agricultural sector at the expense of what they called traditional agriculture, that produced 97 per cent of the south's cashew crop.[29] Government researchers defined traditional agriculture by scale and gender: 'small scale *machambas* [agricultural plots] farmed by women using rudimentary agriculture techniques.'[30] The focus on commercial agriculture and plantations over household production produced a skewed portrait of the cashew orchard and economy.

Between 1955 and 1960 Inhambane alone accounted for about 27 per cent of overall cashew production.[31] In the mid-1960s, the Agricultural Research Project in Sul do Save reckoned the cashew orchard in Mozambique's three southern provinces (Inhambane, Gaza and Lourenço Marques) at more than seventeen million trees; of which less than 3 per cent were owned and managed by commercial farmers, and their distribution was uneven.[32] In contrast with commercial

[25] *Brado Africano*, 30 Jan 1937. Paraphrase translation: 'What would the late Officer Augusto Cardozo say about the brisk market in cashews when he had advocated cutting them all down. We think it was Manual Mendes of Villa João Belo who got this all going in 1933.' Thanks to António Sopa for this reference.

[26] Cajú series, *Notícias*, 16 December 1966.

[27] Parente and Neto, 'A Agro-Indústria do Cajú,' 3, 7.

[28] Parente and Neto, 'A Agro-Indústria do Cajú,' 18; Medeiros, *Bebidas Moçambicanas*, 101.

[29] The most important were the Research Project on Agronomy in the Overseas [Missão de Estudos Agronómicos do Ultramar] and the Agricultural Research Project in Mozambique [Missão de Inquérito Agrícola de Moçambique]. Estimates from *Recenseamento Agrícola de Moçambique* for the southern areas in the mid 1960s, Colin Darch, 'Trabalho Migratório na África Austral; um Apontamento Crítico sobre a Literatura Existente – Análise Bibliográfica,' *Estudos Moçambicanos*, Vol. 3 (1981): 85; Mário de Carvalho, *A Agricultura Tradicional de Moçambique, I. Distribuição Geográfica das Culturas e sua Relação com o Meio* (Lourenço Marques: Missão de Inquérito Agricola em Moçambique, 1969); *Recenseamento Agrícola de Moçambique*, Vol. 9 Inhambane, Vol. 10 Gaza, Vol. 11 Lourenço Marques (Lourenço Marques, 1965–66).

[30] Parente and Neto, 'A Agro-Indústria do Cajú,' 4.

[31] 'Um Comerciante do Chibuto, Mercados de Castanha de Cajú,' *Notíciais*, Series on Cajú, 15–17 Dec, 19, 20 Dec. 1966.

[32] Nearly three quarters of the trees were in Inhambane District with around 2 per cent managed commercially. Gaza had 21 per cent with less than 2 per cent commercial and Lourenço Marques had 4 per cent with 11 per cent commercial, Parente and Neto, 'A Agro-Indústria do Cajú,' Quadro 1, 7.

farmers who planted cashews in stands, Mozambican family farmers regularly inter-planted and managed staple and seasonal crops in the familiar three-tiered mixed agriculture configuration that encourages synergies among plants of many heights and different soil/ sun requirements. Farmers commonly interplant groundnuts, maize, sweet potatoes, manioc, bananas, pineapples, coconuts and cashews.[33] Cashews planted near a working *machamba* were most easily and frequently pruned and cleaned, whereas the bush trees were often left to fend largely for themselves.[34]

Cashew trees can actually produce in their first year, but fruiting more generally begins in the third year with full harvests in the sixth and optimal harvests in the ninth. If regularly pruned and kept disease and pest-free, cashew trees can remain highly productive despite aging. In the colonial era, production of ten to fifteen kilos of cashew nuts per tree was considered optimal, but untreated, older and even compromised trees could still produce two to five kilos per season.[35] Strains introduced in the early twenty-first century promised to produce up to thirty kilos per season, but have yet to prove that boast.[36] Pests and disease can diminish a tree's productivity, but they seldom kill the tree. Fluctuations in temperature, rainfall, wind and humidity affect the trees, and the setting and ripening of their fruit. Wild fires and severe windstorms pose the greatest threats to the trees longevity.[37] By the late colonial era Mozambique's cashew orchard was large and diverse.[38] The Sul do Save orchard that supplied the surging southern industry was overwhelmingly in the care of Mozambican women, who knew its value and attended to its care.[39]

Cashews in the context of family agriculture

Agricultural research in the late colonial period concentrated on three areas: export crops of interest to the state (cotton and rice), export crops of interest to large scale planters (sugar, sisal or citrus), and staple crops

[33] Missão Agrícola, *Recenseamento*; Parente and Neto, 'A Agro-Indústria do Cajú,' 4.
[34] Parente and Neto, 'A Agro-Indústria do Cajú,' 4.
[35] Estimates vary Kanji et al., 'Liberalisation – South,' 6–7; Parente and Neto, 'A Agro-Indústria do Cajú,' 18–20.
[36] 'Disponíveis cinco milhões de Euros para reabilitar o sector do cajú,' *Notícias* (8 July 2005): 6.
[37] The diseases *oidium anacardium* [cashew tree powdery mildew] and *anthracnose* and insects such as helopeltis and cochinilla attack cashew trees, Kanji et al., 'Liberalisation – South,' 6; Parente and Neto, 'A Agro-Indústria do Cajú,' 20–34. In 2005, within three months windstorms killed more than 10,000 cashew trees, 4,700 around the city of Maputo, and 5,193 in the north; 'Vendával destrói mais de 4 mil Cajueiros' *Domingo* (22 May 2005): 1 and 'Vendável desaloja pessoas em Angoche,' *Notícias* (6 June 2005): 1.
[38] In the1970s Parente and Neto calculated the national cashew orchard at 45 million trees. 'A Agro-Indústria do Cajú,'4.
[39] Martha Butler Binford, 'Stalemate: A Study of Cultural Dynamics,' PhD thesis (East Lansing: Michigan State University, 1971): 82.

for the family farming sector (maize, groundnuts, manioc and beans).[40] Although cashews were clearly grown and consumed throughout the twentieth century, they only began to show up in the scientific data when Portuguese interest in export and shelling cashews picked up in the late 1950s.[41] The agricultural census of the mid-1960s focused disproportionately on commercial agriculture, and within that narrow arena on white farmers.[42]

Research on African agricultural production for the market in Sul do Save is uneven, but by the 1940s it seems that families periodically sold some maize and groundnuts surpluses, but usually produced them as staples for household consumption, supplemented by cassava and beans. In 1950, less than 4 per cent of African household agricultural production in Gaza was commoditized, but from the 1960s family participation in the market economy increased sharply, with families marketing up to 27 per cent of their production.[43] The expansion of road and railway networks with the attendant proliferation of *cantinas* and truck marketing probably explained at least some of that increase.[44] Basic transportation networks allowed farmers to take their produce to a market, or to a more promising market than the local *cantina*. Although cashews were abundant in the coastal plains of Sul do Save, colonial era studies did not always clearly distinguish seasonal cashew sales within their estimates of marketed crops.[45] By the late 1960s, corn, peanuts, cashews and mangoes were staple food crops for families around Lourenço Marques, and at least one careful observer noted that cashews had become an important cash crop that people valued.[46]

Colonial era agricultural studies did not detail ownership and management of household cashew trees in Sul do Save. The business and scientific literature focused instead on trade, processing and industry concerns.[47] Early twentieth-century ethnographic studies

---

[40] Fialho Feliciano, *Antropologia Económica*, 126ff., 166.

[41] The *Bibliografia Sobre a Economia Portuguesa* indexed by Amaro D. Guerreiro from the 1940s to 1971 surveyed Portuguese publications for articles of economic interest. A few articles on cashews appeared annually from 1948, but when Portuguese interest in the industry increased in the 1960s, scores of articles appeared (Lisbon: Instituto Nacional de Estatística: 1948/9 to 1971).

[42] Carvalho, *A agricultura tradicional de Moçambique*'; Fialho Feliciano, 'Antropologia Económica,' 291ff; Darch, 'Trabalho Migratório na África Austral.'

[43] Fialho Feliciano, *Antropologia Económica*, 126–7, 167, 291–2.

[44] Arlindo Chilundo makes a parallel argument for commercial expansion with road and transport in Arlindo Chilundo, *Os Camponeses e os Caminhos de Ferro e Estradas em Nampula (1900–1961)* (Maputo: Promédia, 2001): 345ff.

[45] Fialho Feliciano, *Antropologia Económica*, 126–7, 167, 291–2.

[46] Binford, 'Stalemate,' 82.

[47] Joana Pereira Leite is more concerned with trade. The colonial era scientific works on cashew cultivation include: J. do Amparo Baptista, *Moçambique, província portuguêsa de ontem e hoje* (Vila Nova de Famalicão: Centro Gráfico,1962); Baptista, *O cajueiro em Moçambique: série de artigos publicados no 'Diário' de Lourenço Marques* (Lourenço Marques: Tipografia Diário, 1959); A.B. Ramalho Correia, *A Indústrialização da castanha do cajú* (Lourenço Marques: Direcção dos Serviços de Economia e Estatística Geral da Província de Moçambique, 1963); Hélder Lains e Silva, *Parecer sôbre a Industrialização da Castanha de Cajú em Moçambique* (Lisbon: Missão de Estudos Agrónomicos do Ultramar, [1968?]); Lains e Silva, 'O alargamento do

detailed household divisions of labour, crops and food use, but did not detail tree crop ownership.[48] Paulo Soares's historical study of cashew production in northern Mozambique focused on the period 1930 to 1950, and did not address gender differences or tree ownership.[49] José Fialho Feliciano's important economic anthropology of Gaza province in southern Mozambique was conducted in the wake of independence, between 1975 and 1981, and provided rare insight into Gaza families and their agricultural strategies. He considered control over land and the household division of labour, and confirmed that fruit trees were considered part of a household's wealth, but did not explicitly address cashews or tree ownership.[50]

Throughout southern Mozambique men and women claimed access to, use of, and control over land, labour and many resources through their negotiation, mediation and development of social relationships, networks, and practices in both customary and civil law. Such claims staking are now commonly referred to as bundles of rights.[51] José Negrão's classic study of Mozambican farm families underscored multiple strategies for resource claims, management and production. The empirical base of his work was Zambezia where the configuration of cash crops differs and male migrancy had not so badly skewed the region's demography as in Sul do Save, but Negrão's emphasis on multiple strategies and social decisions holds for southern families too. Negrão notes that analysis of rural family economic decisions must take into account things that can not be measured, and may not seem logical or rational in classical economic terms, but are essential because they relate to 'overlapping identities and incentives' for individuals, households, extended families and clans, and are shaped by gender and age.[52]

On a similar note, Fialho Feliciano's observations of Sul do Save households suggested that while men invested socially and econom-

(contd) mercado mundial corresponde a uma ofensiva da União Indiana para eliminar a concorrência da Africa,' *Gazeta do Agricultor*, 14, No. 162 (Nov. 1962):10–12.

[48] Emily Dora Earthy, *Valenge Women: The Social and Economic Life of the Valenge Women of Portuguese East Africa: An Ethnographic Study* (London: Oxford University Press, 1933); Henri A. Junod, *The Life of a South African Tribe*, Vols. 1 and 2 (New York: University Books, Inc. 1962).

[49] Paulo Ribeiro Soares, 'O cajú e o regime de propriadades no Mossuril entre 1930 e 1950,' *Arquivo*, 4 (1988): 91–104.

[50] Fialho Feliciano, *Antropologia Económica*, 189ff.

[51] Bundles of rights mean rights often of diverse, overlapping and complementary origins, like rights to use and inherit (own) and dispose of (lease, lend, sell or give) land and resources. Whether women have any of those rights depends on customary norms and practices as well as intra-household negotiations regarding those rights and practices. See Kanji et al., 'Liberalisation – South,' drawing on Anne Pitcher and Scott Kloeck-Jenson, 'Men, Women, Memory and Rights to Natural Resources in Zambezi Province,' in Rachel Waterhouse and Carin Vijfhuizen, eds, *Strategic Women, Gainful Men: Gender, Land and Natural Resources in Different Rural Contexts in Mozambique*, (Maputo: UEM and Action Aid, 2001):125–52.

[52] José Negrão, *Cem anos de economia da família rural Africana* (Maputo: Texto Editores, 2005): 156–176. The English version is, *One Hundred Years of African Rural Family Economy: The Zambezi Delta in Retrospective Analysis*. PhD Lund: University of Lund, 1995.

ically almost exclusively in their patrilineage lands, women had important roles as stake holders and mediators within and beyond their households and lineages. In particular he noted that women's structural position in at least two lineages – their birth patrilineage and their husband's patrilineage – meant they could develop power, investments and solidarities in each. In that capacity women were both natural mediators and potential scapegoats.[53] As we shall see, the women who shared their experience for this study developed multiple claims strategies in their father's, their mother's and their husband's patrilineages. Women's potential for claims staking within more than one lineage should be appreciated as potentially advantageous.

Sul do Save women and cashew trees

No research turned up regarding tree ownership and management for the colonial era, but a 2003 study, coordinated by the International Institute for Environment and Development [IIED] specifically explored cashew tree ownership and management by men and women in southern Mozambique. Twenty-first century research cannot be simply telescoped back to the mid-twentieth century. The IIEC study was conducted more than three decades after the colonial period; the case study samples were small, and widespread household displacement during Mozambique's post-independence insurgency may well have altered farming and tenure patterns. Nonetheless, the IIED data, approach, questions and premises raise essential issues for this study.

The IIED study alleged that a cashew orchard census conducted at the turn of the century by the World Bank significantly underestimated the number of trees because it failed to count those owned by all family members, and, in particular, those owned and managed by women.[54] Their premise was that rural households are fluid, complex, and embody multiple sets of conflicting interests according to gender, patrilineage and age. Drawing on experience throughout the country, the study highlighted the many different ways women and men assert rights to use, lease, lend, sell, give and inherit resources – their bundles of rights – and further emphasized the importance of women's competence to negotiate those bundled rights.[55] That assertion dovetails with Fialho Feliciano's point about women's structural position in relation to their potential roles as mediators and authorities and Negrão's point about overlapping identities and incentives. Women learned to identify,

---

[53] Fialho Feliciano, *Antropologia Economica*, 436–45.
[54] Ministry of Agriculture and The World Bank, 'Cashew production and marketing among smallholders in Mozambique: a gender-differentiated analysis based on household survey data,' Discussion paper #1, [MAP / Government of Mozambique and World Bank / AFTMA Southern Africa Division] March, 1998.
[55] Kanji et al., 'Liberalisation – South,' 13ff.

navigate and mediate their bundled rights in multiple lineages, and did so by observing other women.[56]

The IIED study found that both men and women planted, inherited and 'owned' trees, but suggested that a term like ownership might usefully be replaced with the term tenure.[57] Ownership and tenure are both apt to be culturally complex and negotiable terms – but tenure at least does not promote an easily misunderstood sense of freehold title, commoditization and marketability. The study documented women planting cashew trees in lands owned by their own patrilineage and also on land assigned to them or to their husband in their husband's patrilineage.

It concluded what one might suspect: that women were most apt to plant and tend trees on lands they held with greater security, and were less apt to plant trees on lands where their claims were less secure. When women planted cashew trees on their husband's or in-laws' lands, they did so more for their children than for themselves. Whereas divorce or widowhood might well separate the women from their rights to trees they planted on those lands, the women's children's rights to those trees would be secure.[58] But widows, divorcees and separated women still controlled trees they planted on lands held by their own patrilineage. Neither a woman's husband nor her father would count the trees she planted as trees belonging to the household they headed. If women were not asked about their own trees, those trees would not have been counted in the orchard census, thus the under-counting.

Finally, the IIED study confirmed what earlier studies suggested, that women were deeply involved with the cashew orchard at virtually all stages: sowing seeds, planting seedlings, pruning, cleaning, weeding, and harvesting. The single activity that was much more strongly linked with men than women was pruning. But even in that case, the authors stressed that in rural Sul do Save, where male labour migration enhanced the ratio of women to men, women who did not have access to male labour accomplished the pruning themselves and with their children. All sources confirmed that women and children harvested the cashew crop, although some indicated that men also regularly participated.[59] In 1960, António Rita-Ferreira, one of the very few Portuguese scholar / civil servants who wrote about Southern Mozambican women, explicitly noted that women and their children

[56] Kanji et al.,'Liberalisation – South,' 13ff.
[57] Kanji et al.,'Liberalisation – South,' 13ff.
[58] Kanji et al.,'Liberalisation – South,' 13ff; Fialho Feliciano, *Antropologia Económica*, 442ff.
[59] W. A. Hance and I.S. van Dongen, 'Lourenço Marques in Delagoa Bay,' *Economic Geography*, 33 (1957):251; 25 and 136. 954 pp. 48,80,121 – Kanji et al., 'Liberalisation – South,' 13ff; Parente and Neto discuss pruning, but with an emphasis on commercial and mechanized plantings. They note that women mostly care for the trees and that women and children usually harvest the crop. Otherwise they make no mention of the division of labour 'A Agro-Indústria do Cajú,' 18.

valued tree crops, including cashews, and harvested and processed their fruits with and without male assistance.[60]

Again, Southern Mozambican adult men were more apt to be away working for wages in South Africa or elsewhere. A farm family's decisions about collecting the cashew harvest for sale or for consumption, whether to focus on the nuts or apples, to prepare them for beverages or for food were always complicated and multifaceted. Such decisions were shaped as much by the ritual and the business of summertime drinking as by the market price for cashew nuts. Although by the 1960s Sul do Save families marketed more than a quarter of their production, most farmers still emphasized social, family and gift exchanges over sales to *cantinas*.[61] They did so for good reasons

The rituals and business of summertime drinking

In Southern Mozambique, late December to late March is summertime. If the weather has cooperated, it is a time when fruits are plentiful: small pineapples, mangoes, avocado pears, papaya, guava, mafurra and passion fruits. These fruits are enjoyed fresh, but are also consumed as juices, beers, wines, or distilled into spirits. The fruit trees not only provide the shade and drinks that are an important part of social renewal and the pleasures of summer, but, since the weather in this region often does not cooperate, they are also valued for the part they play in food security strategies. The sale and consumption of tree crops provide a surplus that boosts household prestige in good times and provides a margin for survival in not-so-good times.[62] Hosting gatherings with plentiful food and drink secured social relations and had important economic implications.[63]

In February, the fruits of both Marula trees, locally known as *nkanyi* [*sclerocarya birrea*] and cashew trees are in season.[64] Depending upon which botanist you believe, cashew trees produce fruit in the south between November and February. The *nkanyi* fruits in the north from December to January and in the south from January through March.[65]

[60] António Rita-Ferreira, 'Labour Emigration among the Moçambique Thonga: Comments on a Study by Marvin Harris,' *Africa: Journal of the International African Institute*, 30, 2 (April 1960): 141–52.

[61] Fialho Feliciano, *Antropologia Economica*, 436–45.

[62] Cashews contribute to food security through market value and as a high quality food, António Sefane 'Devido à irregularidade das chuvas, espectro de fome paira sobre o sul de Inhambane,' *Notícias*, 12 March 2005; Kanji et al., 'Liberalisation – South.'

[63] Negrão, *One Hundred Years*, 202 ff.

[64] The following paragraphs are based on Medeiros, *Bebidas Moçambicanas*. Spelling varies due to orthographic changes and regional language. See also Ministério de Saúde, Direcção Nacional de Medicina Preventiva, *Bebidas Alcoolicas Tradicionais – Algumas Considerações e Resultados Preliminares de um Estudo Bibliográfico e Laboratorial* (Maputo: Ministério de Saúde, 1979).

[65] Parente and Neto, 'A Agro-Indústria do Cajú,' 8; Medeiros, *Bebidas Moçambicanas*, 101–102; Herbert L. Bishop drawing from Henri Junod in 'Recent Works on the Ba-Ronga,' *London Quarterly Review*, Vol. 108, 4th Series, No. 6 (July & October, 1907): 74–86, esp. 81–82.

Although the fruits of both trees are made into alcoholic drinks that are broadly consumed and greatly enjoyed, the drink produced from the fruit of the *nkanyi* tree, *bukanye*, is ritualized.[66] Unlike the other fruit drinks, *bukanye* should not be bought or sold as a commodity.

When the *nkanyi* fruits are ready to be processed into *bukanye*, it is time to begin the *época de ucanhé* – the festival of first fruits.[67] The first *bukanye* are reserved for ritual consumption by the community's political and spiritual leaders – including a ritual libation to the ancestors.[68] Once the leaders have consumed the *bukanye* in the customary gourds, the season has begun and everyone is free to drink whenever they please until the season is brought to a ritual close when supplies run out. The season's songs of social renewal praise the ancestors for another harvest enjoyed among family and friends: 'We drink new *bukanye*! Who would have thought it? That we would again drink from this gourd!'[69]

The brewed and distilled beverages made from cashew trees were not ritualized. Cashew trees were valued as shade trees and the source of alcoholic drinks whose 'effects are stronger than those of any other wild fruit'.[70] Since the mid-nineteenth century, brewed and especially distilled drinks made from the cashew fruit have become the favoured alcoholic drink of the *Ucanhé* season, almost replacing *bukanye*.[71] During the twentieth century, cashew drinks of all sorts became important seasonal commodities, even though their production was illegal and prosecuted. These fermented or distilled drinks are known by dozens of names – every region has a special name for various cashew drinks. For simplicity I call them all *xicaju*.[72]

António Enes blamed *xicaju* for what he called an epidemic of alcoholism during *ucanhé* season: 'When this cursed fruit is in season, and happily it does not produce year round... native labourers put down their hoes, porters abandon their loads, domestic servants leave their employers, soldiers and sailors desert.'[73] Everywhere drums called people to celebrations. A half-century later, observers still noted that

---

[66] Medeiros, Earthy, Bishop and Junod spell the drink alternatively wukanyi, makanye, bukanyi, and bukanye. Junod's bukanye is preferred here. Earthy. *Valenge Women* (1933 ed.), 25ff and 109ff; Junod, *African Tribe*, 1, 397–9.

[67] Henri Junod, *African Tribe*, 1, 397–9.

[68] Medeiros, *Bebidas Moçambicanas*, 46; Junod, *African Tribe*, 1, 397.

[69] Medeiros, *Bebidas Moçambicanas*, 42.

[70] C.F. Spence, *The Portuguese Colony of Mozambique: An Economic Survey* (Cape Town: A.A. Balkema, 1951): 44; Parente and Neto,' A Agro-Indústria do Cajú,' 34.

[71] Medeiros, *Bebidas Moçambicanas*, 55.

[72] Names include *xicaju, bucadju, jukwebee, jujú, chicadju,* or *ucanzu,* Medeiros, *Bebidas Moçambicana,* 55; Armando Jorge Lopes, Salvador Júlio Sitoe, Paulino José Nhamuende, *Moçambicanismos; Para um Léxico de Usos do Portugues Moçambicano* (Maputo: Livraria Universitária, 2002): 148; Pereira Leite, 'A economia do Cajú,' 635 n. 10; Spence, *The Portuguese Colony,* 44; xidanguane means to live by the sale of cashew aguardente, Ana Loforte, 'Migrantes e Sua Relação com o Meio Rural.' *Trabalhos de Arqueologia e Antropologia* 4, (1987): 55–69, 60.

[73] António Enes, *Moçambique; Relatório apresentado ao Governo* [4a edição, facsimilada pela de 1946] (Lisbon: Imprensa Nacional, Agência-Geral do Ultramar, 1971): 50.

during the *ucanhé* season cashew liquor, despite being illegal, was broadly consumed. Administrators complained that 'in the cashew season [workers] like to stay constantly drunk', and 'revelers [are] almost incapable of working or thinking for days afterwards.'[74] Indeed, the party could go on for weeks.[75] Robert Nunez Lyne was perhaps the only European official with anything good to say about *xicaju*. In his early twentieth-century agricultural survey of Mozambique he concurred, that during *ucanhé* season, nearly the whole population got intoxicated, but he went on to say: 'This is a source of inconvenience for the employer, but for the natives themselves it may be as wholesome as taking the waters is with us in Europe, as the fruit is an anti-scorbutic.'[76] Harvest gatherings with feasting and extended 'binge' drinking are very common in agricultural communities worldwide.[77] Recollections of *ucanhé* season reflect both temperance concerns and an appreciation of the rare pleasure of abundance celebrated with family, friends, music, food and drink. Missionaries, colonial officials, and emergent mission-based African elites all took a dim view of drinking that led to drunken partying.[78]

Xicaju and other homemade brews competed for customers with industrially produced wine, rum, whisky, and beer. Portuguese law conflated all indigenously brewed and distilled drinks, calling them simply *bebidas cafreais* [kaffir drinks] and prohibited most of them.[79] Although Mozambicans commonly used the generic term *bebidas* to refer to the beverages they drank, brewed or distilled for gifts or sale, if you asked people about specific drinks, they enthusiastically described dozens, by season, by recipe and utility.[80]

---

[74] Spence, *The Portuguese Colony*, 44; José Firmo de Sousa Monteiro, *Relatório sôbre o Resgate dos Machongos de Sul do Save; Referente á 31 de Dezembro 1951* (Lourenço Marques: Imprensa Nacional [IN], 1953): 28.

[75] Junod and many other observers mention intoxication during this season: 'At the season of *bucadju* there is a enormous amount of drunkenness round the town,' *African Tribe*, Vol. 2, 41–45; Vol. 1, 399.

[76] Robert Nunez Lyne, *Mozambique – Its Agricultural Development* (London: T. Fisher Unwin, 1913): 126.

[77] Charles Ambler, 'Alcohol, Racial Segregation and Popular Politics in Northern Rhodesia,' JAH, 31 (1990): 296.

[78] Alda Romão Saúte and Teresa Cruz e Silva both consider mission strategies regarding alcoholic drinks and society in Southern Mozambique in the twentieth century, Saúte for Anglicans and Cruz e Silva for Swiss Presbyterians. Saúte, *O Intercâmbio entre os Moçambicanos e as Missões Cristãs e a Educação em Moçambique* (Maputo: Promédia, 2005): Ch. 7 esp. 278–89; Cruz e Silva, *Protestant Churches and the Formation of Political Consciousness in Southern Mozambique (1930–1974)* (Basel: P. Schlettwein Publishing, 2001, Ch. 2.

[79] It was legal to produce small batches of low alcohol maize beer, *uputsu* or *pombe* for family consumption. Medeiros probably titled his book *Bebidas Moçambicanas de Fábrico Caseiro*, to avoid the more common phrase 'bebidas cafreais.' The phrase *'de fábrica caseira,'* means 'home brew.' *Bebidas cafreais* translates as kaffir brews / drinks. Kaffir is a derogatory term. It was defined in Portuguese as late as 1980 as 'a perverse person, a barbarian, ignorant or miserly' and *cafrael* (singular of *cafreais*) as savage. *Dicionário do Estudante, Dicionário Português* (Porto: Porto Editora, 1980): 167.

[80] Medeiros, *Bebidas Moçambicanas*, 37ff; Earthy. *Valenge Women* (1933 ed.), 25ff and 109ff; OT, Saul Tembe, Câmara Municipal de Maputo 7 June 1977.

Unlike the missionaries, the colonial authorities were reconciled to the fact that people would drink alcoholic beverages, but they battled about who would be allowed to drink what, where and when. From the turn of the twentieth century, licensing, control, sales and sanctions around alcohol consumption were lucrative, competitive and important in Lourenço Marques and Sul do Save.[81] Portuguese vintners produced high alcohol content wines (24 per cent) specifically for African consumers. The colonial administration wanted the market dominated by Portuguese wines and monopoly licensed industrially brewed beers, so they banned or at least contested local production of sugar, fruit and grain based brews and spirits.[82]

The sense of *ucanhé* as a time for relaxation and indulgence in the pleasures of plenty is gendered.[83] The fruits do not pick, brew or distill themselves. Trees growing in the door yard or bordering women's *machambas* were easily enough harvested, but harvesting trees throughout the distant bush was a chore that often fell to women and children.[84] Production of pots of brewed or distilled drinks from fruits or grains was also a skilled and time-consuming undertaking. Although both men and women distilled, the cashew brewers and sellers were usually women. [85]

Men and women enjoyed drinks and parties, but in Sul do Save men drank first, and more often. The drinking sessions of the *Epocha de Ucanhé* were often portrayed as masculine jostling: who was 'heavy' enough to empty the pots of *ucanhé* brewed by the women.[86] Songs from the *Epocha de Ucanhé* explicitly linked violence with seasonal intoxication: 'This is a new year. Let us not kill each other! Let us eat peacefully! ... May this *bukanyi* [sic] do no harm. May we not slay each other under its influence. May it cause no serious quarrels.'[87] The women who brewed alcoholic drinks were clearly not exempt from domestic or community violence enhanced by drunkenness.[88]

Seasonal brews in rural areas were also gifts for work parties or in anticipation of future agricultural collaboration or services. Women

[81] Penvenne, *African Workers*, 40–43.

[82] José Capela, *A Burguêsia Mercantil do Porto e as Colónias (1834–1909)* (Porto: Afrontamento, 1975); José Capela, *O Vinho para o Preto: Notas e Textos Sôbre a Exportação do Vinho para Africa* (Porto: Afrontamento, 1973); José Capela, *O Álcool na Colonização do Sul do Save, 1860–1920* (Maputo: Edição do Autor, 1995).

[83] 'Taninga em festim de *'ucanhi,'* *Zambeze* (10 February 2005) III, No. 125.

[84] Parente and Neto, 'A Agro-Indústria do Cajú,' 18.

[85] Women do the laborious work of brewing and young men, in particular, move from village to village finishing off the pots until the whole supply is gone. Medeiros, *Bebidas Moçambicanas*, 37ff; Earthy, *Valenge Women*, (1933 ed.), 25ff and 109ff; Junod, *African Tribe*, 1, 398–9.

[86] 'Taninga em festim de 'ucanhi', 125.

[87] Junod, *African Tribe*, 1, 398–9.

[88] *Notícias* 12 Feb. 2005; WLSA, 'Some reflections on the working of the Assistance Centres for Victims of Domestic Violence, 2000–2003,' Outras Vozes, *Suplemento do Boletim*, No. 8 (Maputo, August 2004):1–7; WLSA, 'Research on Violence Against Women,' *Outras Vozes, Suplemento do Boletim*, No. 8 (Maputo, August 2004): 8–11; 'Introduction', Emily S. Burrill, Richard L. Roberts, and Elizabeth Thornberry, eds, *Domestic Violence and the Law in Colonial and Postcolonial Africa* (Athens Ohio: Ohio University Press, New African Histories, 2010):1–29; Lee, *African Women and Apartheid*, 63, 73–4, 186–7.

brewed for other women and men whose labour they might later tap.[89] In contrast with employers whose labour force was diminished by drink, women served drinks to generate an enhanced labour force for their fields. But in both rural and urban areas, women brewed and distilled cashew drinks as a regular business, selling by the cup, mostly to male consumers. Thousands of women depend upon brewing seasonal fruits as part of their larger economic life, leveraging their social and economic capital from the household to the gift and informal economies.[90] Fialho Feliciano and others confirm that Sul do Save families were more apt to invest in household, gift and informal exchanges among neighbours than in capital equipment or market sales. As explained below, Sul do Save farmers had greater confidence in and control over the value and return from personal over market investments.

Brewing and social capital: Household, gift and informal economies

Women all over Southern Africa were extensively involved in rural and urban competition for the cash men spent on alcoholic drinks.[91] Women brewed, distilled, conveyed to market and sold a great range of drinks, and supported their own household and labour interests through alcoholic drinks they offered and bartered in the household and gift economies.[92] Mozambican men of the emerging African middle class, like their counterparts throughout Southern Africa, were conflicted about brewing, distillation and drinking. Many supported household brewing and consumption of low alcohol grain base beers both for their social value and for the often crucial income their sale provided to women of urban elite households, but many also belonged to religious denominations that opposed consumption of alcohol in principle.[93]

[89] Earthy, *Valenge Women*, 25ff; Negrão, *One Hundred*, 202ff.
[90] Medeiros, *Bebidas Moçambicanas*, 56–57; 'Taninga em festim de *'ucanhi'*, 125; Kathleen Sheldon, 'Markets and Gardens: Placing Women in the History of Urban Mozambique,' *Canadian Journal of African Studies* 37, 2/3 (2003): 358–395; Carin Vijfhuizen, Carla Braga, Luis Artur and Nazneen Kanji, 'Cashing in on cashew nuts: women producers and factory workers in Mozambique', in *Chains of Fortune: Linking Women Producers and Workers with Global Markets*, edited by Marilyn Carr (London: Commonwealth Secretariat, 2004): 84, 87.
[91] The literature on women brewers in Southern Africa is vast, but for example, Kathleen Sheldon, *Pounders of Grain*, Charles Ambler and Jonathan Crush, eds, *Liquor and Labour in Southern Africa* (Athens: Ohio University Press, 1992); Teresa A. Barnes, *'We Women Worked so Hard': Gender, Urbanization and Social Reproduction in Colonial Harare, Zimbabwe, 1930–1956* (Portsmouth: Heinemann, 1999); Philip Bonner, 'Desireable or Undesireable Basotho Women?', Liquor, Prostitution and the Migration of Basotho Women to the Rand, 1920–1945', in Cheryl Walker, ed. *Women and Gender in Southern Africa to 1945* (Cape Town, 1990); Ambler, 'Alcohol, Racial Segregation'.
[92] Dora Earthy details women's roles in rural brewing and distilling in Sul do Save in the 1930s, *Valenge Women*, 24ff; Medeiros, *Bebidas Moçambicanas*, 60, raises interesting questions about women's roles and rights in the urban market for cashew drinks; Sheldon, 'Markets and Gardens'.
[93] Ambler, 'Alcohol, Racial Segregation,' 295–313; Saúte, O *Intercambio*, Ch. 7.

The urban African elite's opposition to alcohol sales was also related to their efforts to curb the proliferation of bars in African neighbourhoods and around the compounds where men on contract labour were temporarily housed while in transit to and from the South African mines. In the early twentieth century their newspaper, *Grêmio Africano*, increasingly focused on drunkenness, violence, and prostitution associated with bar culture. They generally supported ritual drinking in *ucanhé* season for spiritual and cultural reasons, but often decried the generally 'scandalous' behavior associated with the seasonal excesses.[94] Not surprisingly the colonial administration, business community and missionaries interfaced a bit differently with the broad array of concerns and opportunities around drinking, and most published perspectives on the topic were men's.[95] In short, women had a hand in virtually all components of the cashew economy, but alcohol production, exchange and sale was the one most closely associated with women's production and income. The colonial era business literature ignored that aspect almost completely. Failure to connect this important use and market for cashews with the larger cashew economy fostered misunderstanding of that economy regionally and nationally.

If farmers decided to sell or barter cashew nuts in the late colonial era, *cantinas* were their essential link to the market that supplied factories like Tarana. In most places, however, even when the market for cashew nuts picked up, farmers continued to harvest the apples as well as the nuts.[96] The cashew economy that focused on *xicaju* was not channeled through *cantinas*. It had its own trajectory, a trajectory controlled largely by women. Well into the sixties, despite growing market participation, farm families still tended to invest what little surplus they had in social relations rather than in capital goods. That suggests that farmers would be more likely to brew or distill cashew apples for investment as social gifts and exchanges than sell them to earn cash for eventual investment in plows and farm implements. They knew that killer famines occurred around once a decade, so they invested and trusted in social support networks in much the same way some people invest and trust in savings accounts, health and life insurance. Social investments were made in various forms, including bridewealth (*lobolo*), *bebidas* and a broad range of gifts.[97] Although *xicaju* was not a ritual drink it nonetheless played a role in these important social investments –

[94] *Brado Africano* reported that in late January some four thousand people from Lourenço Marque took bus and railway transport to the interior 'to enjoy the *época de ucanhé*,' 5 Feb. 1948; Medeiros, *Bebidas Moçambicanas*, 15; Valdemir Zamparoni, 'Copos e Corpos: A Disciplinarização do Prazer em Terras Coloniais,' *Travessias; Revista de Ciências Sociais e Humanas em Língua Portuguesa*, 4/5 (Lisbon, July 2004): 119–37.

[95] See Chapter 5 and Medeiros, *Bebidas Moçambicanas*, 57 ff.

[96] Spence, *The Portuguese Colony*, 44.

[97] Fialho Feliciano, *Antropologia Económica*, 284,288, n.20; Negrão, *One Hundred Years*, 202.

at the interface of the essential household and gift economies.[98]

It is obviously difficult to map and measure the informal and illegal exchange, sale and production of *xicaju* and thus to document its role in the region's markets and social networks. The overall *bebidas* economy remains under-researched. Since I intentionally steered away from discussions of illegal activity of any kind, this study does little to remedy that problem.[99] While evidence for Sul do Save and Lourenço Marques is uneven and circumstantial, it suggests that *xicaju* was fundamental to the household and gift economies and sustained a market in the informal economy beneath the colonial radar screen. Chapter 4 explores the many ways narrators included *bebidas* in their household strategies, but this is an area that needs further research.

The enduring alcoholic beverage economy is revealed in part by reading against the grain, or probing records of sanctions. Employers' complaints about high absenteeism and the impact of *bebidas cafraeis*, particularly during the *época de ucanhé*, provide indirect evidence of the population's continuing production and consumption of *xicaju*. Arrest records and administrative reports corroborate the prosecution of hundreds of women for the production, possession and sale of *bebidas*, and the clandestine collaboration of scores of police and designated chiefs with the women's sales. Finally, municipal arrests for *bebidas* increased during the cashew season. Since the drinks were identified in most of these sources simply as *bebidas*, one cannot be sure the arrests were for *xicaju*, but it's most likely.[100]

Every so often, however, someone lifted the curtain on what was an otherwise obscure trade. In the middle of the 1968 southern cashew season, Lourenço Marques' main newspaper *Notícias* published Guilherme de Melo's question: why was the potential market for cashew apple juice being totally ignored by the cashew industrialists. He noticed that cashew fruit was sold in all the markets in the *bairros de caniço* along the two major roads that ran from the densely populated Infulene and Mahotas peri-urban areas into the neighbourhoods where the majority population lived. People obviously bought them to make *xicaju* for the social party season. 'Control brigades come in and smash up fermentation pots, forbidding people from engaging in these 'abuses'! Ok, but it never does any good! What a shameful waste!'[101]

[98] Alpheus Manghezi, 'Ku Thekela: Estratégias de Sôbrevivência Contra a Fome no Sul de Moçambique', *Estudos Moçambicanos* (1983): 19–21; Kanji et al, 'Cashing in on Cashew Nuts', 84 & 87; Fion de Vletter, *Migration and Development in Mozambique: Poverty, Inequality and Survival* [Migration Policy Series, No. 43] (Cape Town: Southern African Migration Project, 2006): 12.

[99] Medeiros's *Bebidas Moçambicanas* is one of the few published works to detail brewing in Mozambique.

[100] ACLM sample, examples of workers (by registration number) arrested for transgression of regulation 256 of 23 August 1950 (bebidas): 5,361, 6,221, 35,001,45,061, 29,601.

[101] Guilherme de Melo, 'A Indústrialização do Cajú', *Notícias*, 18 Feb. 1968; Rita-Ferreira, 'Os Africanos', 440.

Melo's complaint suggested that, despite police persecution, the trade in cashew brews and *xicaju* enjoyed an excellent seasonal market in urban African residential areas. Many farmers continued to wager that they would earn more selling the apple than the nut. Furthermore the *xicaju* 'value added' accrued to the suburban women who purchased the apples, processed them and sold *xicaju* by the cup in the African neighbourhoods that circled the city. Many cashew shellers counted on *xicaju* income during the season for clothing, school fees and home building materials.[102] *Xicaju* by the cup was an important part of the late colonial era social scene at the Milhulamethini intersection in the Mafalala neighbourhood of Lourenço Marques. The neighbourhood was equally known in this era for its brothels. Ana Loforte observed it was common for widowed, divorced and separated women in the city's *bairros* to live from the sale of cashew alcohol.[103]

Domingos Utuí was one of many regular customers at Milhu-lamethini at least from the early 1970s. He thought that the women could have charged a bit more and still had customers, since this market was known for its good quality and reasonably priced cashew drinks. Utuí concluded, '[xicaju] is a party; and we enjoy it even more intensely because it doesn't last throughout the year – [the fact that it is a transient pleasure] is a penalty for the sins of those who enjoy it'[104] The women who brewed the drinks were subject to arrest and having their investment confiscated or destroyed. Male customers bore no risks except perhaps dropping their cup in a raid. Women who combined prostitution with *bebidas* sales in Mafalala could be arrested for both, whereas their male customers would not. Whereas household and gift exchanges of *xicaju* remained largely outside government control and interference that was not the case in the informal and formal econo-mies.

Cashews in the formal economy:
Export and industrial processing

The market path of Sul do Save cashews began at the small *cantinas* that dotted rural areas throughout the South. The *cantina* locations were more apt to reflect the presence of returning miners with consumer power than farmers with marketable crops. If farmers had convenient access to *cantinas* that offered what farmers considered a reasonable price, farmers sold cashew nuts as a usual part of their management of available agricultural production. Measuring rural commoditization

[102] OT, Christina Jossias Phelembe, 17 May 1993; OT, Celeste Guambe, 17 May 1993; OT, Joana Massacaira, 24 May 1993; OT, Amélia Samuel Muzima, 27 May 1993; *Revista Tempo*, 858, (22 March 1987) in Medeiros, *Bebidas Moçambicanas*, 57.
[103] Loforte, 'Migrantes e Sua Relação,' 60.
[104] Medeiros, *Bebidas Moçambicanas*, 57.

and export of cashews is challenging at many levels. First the state's monitoring capacity was at best inadequate, and second, not all of Mozambique fell under state control until 1941. Statistical profiles of cashew commercialization and exports prior to 1941 include Sul do Save, but exclude important northern regions that always produced more than the south.

Export of unprocessed cashew nuts to India's shelling industry began in the first decades of the twentieth century, but fluctuated considerably until the mid-1920s when they developed a fairly steady increasing pace. Again, like most agricultural products marketed by family farmers, cashew sales typically reflected a great and complex range of factors. Weather and political crises were among the many factors influencing production levels, prices, forms of payment and alternative products. Local conditions were influenced by regional, national and global prices as well as Mozambique's taxes, labour policies, and import / export policies.

From 1920 to 1924, the killer droughts and famines experienced in many parts of the country combined with the state's push to build roads with forced labour to explain the sharp drop in exports. Famines can encourage contradictory responses: some farmers may turn to cashew nuts for food and thus be less willing to sell them; others may push to harvest and sell the maximum number of nuts in order to acquire cash to purchase other foodstuffs. Although the trees are quite hardy, the drought may have rendered the trees too stressed to produce fruit, and labour shortages related to conscription may have severely compromised efforts to harvest and store the nuts. Without detailed inquiries among farmers, the patterns of marketed produce are not easily explained for this period or later.

During the economic crisis of the 1930s, commercial farms in southern Mozambique actually increased agricultural production despite the falling prices for many crops. First, land owners continued to conscript labour for enhanced production, hoping to sustain themselves despite lower prices, and second, they were also able to demand a portion of their tenants' harvests. The value of most agricultural products fell sharply from 1928 to the nadir in 1934, but exports by tonnage increased. Aside from a slight drop between 1931 and 1933, agricultural production actually climbed throughout the period. From 1933 exports increased steadily, and ahead of the price curve until the economy basically recovered in late 1936.[105]

Cashews were one of the very rare crops that did not experience the devastating price drops typical of the depression era – quite the opposite. In one of the worst years of the depression, 1933, the price of cashew nuts increased dramatically from 14.93 *escudos* per ton to

[105] David Hedges, coordinator, *História de Moçambique; Moçambique no Auge do Colonialismo, 1930–1961* (Maputo: Livraria Universitária, 1999–2000): 38–39 Quadro 1 & 2; Newitt, *A History of Mozambique*, 459ff; Soares, 'O Cajú,' passim; Penvenne, *African Workers*, 95ff.

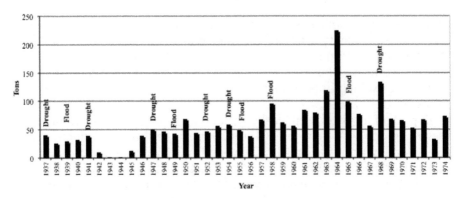

Graph 1 Raw Cashew Nut Exports 1937–1974[106]
(Compiled from Joana Pereira Leite 'A Economia do Cajú em Moçambique e as Relações com a India:dos Anos 20 ao fim da Época Colonial', in Comissião Organizadora, *Ensaios de Homenagem a Francisco Pereira de Moura* (Lisbon: Instituto Superior de Economia e Gestão, Universidade Técnica de Lisboa, 1995): 643 note 29, 651 note 65; Paulo Ribeiro Soares, 'O Cajú e o Regime das Proprie-dades no Mossuril entre 1930 e 1950', *Arquivo* (Maputo, Moçambique) Vol. 4 (Oct. 1988): 91–3)

306.39 *escudos* – a twenty-fold rise.[107] The broader interest in cashew nut exports dates from that price hike. Paulo Soares attributed the price increase to the end of prohibition in the USA in 1932. The USA was the world's largest market for cashews. Soares speculated that the revival of bar culture, enhanced demand for cashew nuts as a favoured bar snack and thus forced up the price.[108] As a post-prohibition condition for serving alcohol, many municipalities required bars to serve food. Bars could evade the expense, space, staff and bother of a commercially regulated kitchen by serving nuts, chips and crackers as convenient alternatives. Cashews were a nutritious food, and like most bar snacks they were salted to fuel a customer's thirst.[109]

The higher exportation figures dating from 1929 also reflected Portugal's resumed administration of the Niassa Company lands. Farmers in those areas had exported cashews right along but those exports had not appeared in state tallies, so the higher figures may not reflect a jump in production, just a widening of reported sales. Mozambican cashew exports to India had increased to 30,000 and even 40,000 tons by the early 1940s, but then plummeted due to shipping and production disruption in India and the Indian Ocean during World War Two.

---

[106] Soares, 'O Cajú,' 93–93; *Estatísticas Industriais*, 1948 to 1955 show up in 'diversas,' but from 1956 fully covered, amendoa, castanha de cajú and personnel.
[107] Mozambique's official currency was the Portuguese *real* (pl. *reis*) until 1910 when Portugal introduced the *escudo*. The *escudo* was tied to and controlled by Portugal until Mozambique's independence in 1975. Independent Mozambique introduced the *metical* (pl. *meticais*) as its currency.
[108] Soares, 'O Cajú,' 101, note 2.
[109] Thanks to Bob Skelnik email 2 April 2008 and postings from contributors to the Alcohol & Drug History Society Listserve, ADHS@LISTSERV.MUOHIO.EDU.

Cashew nut shelling was first undertaken in Mozambique during the 1940s war years to make use of the accumulated nuts that were purchased but could not be shipped to India. At the time Mozambican entrepreneurs did not feel they could achieve the industrial specifications in grading and packing necessary to export directly to the US market, nor could they manage to ship to the US given the war restrictions. Instead they targetted potential local and regional markets for cashew kernels in neighbouring South Africa and Southern Rhodesia. Transport costs were reasonable and southern African industry standards for imported nuts were less onerous than those obtaining in North America. The market experiment was short-lived, however. In 1948, South Africa's Nationalist government tightened import controls and prohibited the importation of nuts altogether, thus putting a quick end to the first attempts to develop industrial cashew shelling. The regional markets re-opened only in the late 1960s.[110] After recovering from wartime disruption in the 1940s, cashew exports became a recognized source of Mozambique's foreign exchange earnings. From 1945 to 1975 exports of cashew nuts for the whole of Mozambique varied from a low of about 12 thousand tons in 1945 to a peak of 133 thousand tons in 1968. During 1974, the last full harvest year of the colonial era, Mozambique exported 73 thousand tons of cashew nuts.[111]

The industrialization of cashew shelling

In 1948 the capital's leading English language newspaper, *Lourenço Marques Guardian*, heralded cashew nuts and their derivatives as one of 'the great riches of Mozambique'.[112] Most of the press in this period promoted a greater role for Mozambique in what they called the 'triangular trade' in which Mozambique exports cashew nuts to India, and India exports the shelled kernels to the United States.[113] By the mid-twentieth century the US imported just under 50 million pounds of various kinds of cashew products with a value of around 15 million USD. India, Goa, Brazil and Haiti were the key producers of shelled nuts at that point.[114] By the early 1970s India supplied 60 per cent of global demand for shelled cashews (Brazil and Eastern Africa, including Mozambique made up the remaining 40 per cent). India depended upon foreign imports for 85 per cent of the raw material that sustained

---

[110] Spence, *The Portuguese Colony*, 46, 74, 75.

[111] Pereira Leite and Khouri, *Os Ismailis*, 239–44.

[112] 'As grandes riquezas de Moçambique – A castanha de cajú e seus derivados,' *Lourenço Marques Guardian* (29 Jan. 1948).

[113] Almeida Figueiredo, 'O Triángulo Económico do Comércio da Castanha de Cajú,' *Notíciais*, (15, 17 Aug and 7 Sept. 1952).

[114] José Soares Rebelo Domingos,'Moçambique pode e deve marcar uma posição no comercio da castanha de cajú,' *Notíciais*, 19 Aug. 1952: 2.

her cashew shelling industry, so clearly had an important stake in sustaining cashew imports.

Chapter 2 details the development of industrial cashew shelling in Lourenço Marques through the workforce's narratives. Joana Pereira Leite's in-depth research on Mozambique's economic history, in particular its cashew economy, fundamentally informs my analysis.[115] She divides the growth of the overall cashew processing industry in two periods. The first, the southern phase, dates from 1945 with postwar experiments with hand shelling on a cottage or satellite basis, and ends in 1962 with the installation of patented shelling machines at the Companhia Colonial de Angoche. During the second or northern phase, Mozambique's installed capacity for the shelling industry began to shift toward the cashew producing areas in the north, and the state became increasingly involved in the cashew economy.

Exports from 1945 to 1962 varied a great deal from year to year. Some observers claimed that harvesting cashews was a 'difficult and onerous' task relegated to women and children, while others argued that Mozambicans found cashew picking 'more profitable and less arduous' than working other crops.[116] No doubt in some cases each observation was true, and again, family decisions about sale of tree crops were complicated. Cashew exporters wanted to be certain that Mozambican households invested their labour in harvesting the cashew crop while it was in season, but their interests conflicted with the settler / planter population who complained that African investment in harvesting cashews 'had the unfortunate result of reducing native labour' available to work on the crops in commercial farmers' fields in the busy summer season.[117]

For much of the colonial period, however, Mozambicans were not free to invest their agricultural labour as they saw fit. Forced production of cotton and rice absorbed a great deal of agricultural labour from the late thirties into the early 1960s. From the late 1930s, cotton was very much at the heart of the colonial state's agricultural project in Mozambique.[118] Some areas of southern Mozambique with particularly

[115] Joana Pereira Leite's essential works on this topic include: 'La formation de l'economie coloniale an mozambique-pacte colonial et industrialisation: du colonialisme portugais aux réseaux informels de sujéction marchande 1930–1974,' Doctorat, Ecole des Hautes Etudes en Sciences Sociales [EHESS], Paris 1989); Pereira Leite, 'A Economia do Cajú em Moçambique e as Relações com a Índia: dos Anos 20 ao Fim da Època Colonial,' in *Ensaios de Homenagem a Francisco Pereira de Moura* (Lisbon: Instituto Superior de Economia e Gestão, Universidade Tecnica de Lisboa, 1995): 631–653; Pereira Leite, 'Colonialismo e industrialização em Moçambique: pacto colonial, dinamização das exportações e 'import-substitution,' *Ler Historia*, No. 24 (1993): 53–70; Pereira Leite, 'A Guerra do Cajú.'
[116] Parente and Neto, 'A Agro-Indústria de Cajú,' 18.
[117] C.F. Spence, *Economic Survey of Colony of Moçambique (Portuguese East Africa)* (Lourenço Marques: Lourenço Marques Guardian, 1943): 15.
[118] Allen F. Isaacman, *Cotton is the Mother of Poverty: Peasants, Work and Rural Struggle in Colonial Mozambique, 1938–1961* (Portsmouth: Heinemann, 1996); Allen F. Isaacman and Richard Roberts, eds, *Cotton, Colonialism and Social History in Sub-Saharan Africa* (Portsmouth: Heinemann, 1995).

inappropriate climate and soil were released from cotton production early, but forced cotton cultivation for many Mozambicans only ended in the early 1960s. Ending compulsion had a direct and marked impact: between 1964 and 1973, cotton production among family farmers dropped by more than half.[119] Overall cotton production dropped 22 per cent between 1960 and 1965, but then resumed a slower pace of growth largely within the commercial farming and cooperative sectors.[120] By 1970 Mozambique still depended upon family farms for most agricultural export production; including an estimated 800,000 cashew producers and 500,000 cotton producers.[121]

Prior to the development of the cashew shelling industry in Mozambique, exportation of cashew nuts competed most directly with local consumption of cashew nuts and drinks. From the 1950s India was Mozambique's main market for the export of raw nuts, and its largest competitor for global sales of shelled kernels. The question of whether it would be more profitable for Mozambique to export unprocessed cashew nuts to India or to shell nuts and export their kernels was famously raised in the mid-1990s controversy between Mozambique's Frelimo party government, Mozambique's newly hatched capitalist entrepreneurs and the World Bank, but the controversy dates back to the 1950s.[122] In an effort to drown out competitors, Indian cashew importers nearly doubled the price per ton they were willing to pay for Mozambican cashew nuts from 3,390 *escudos* in 1963 to 6,128 *escudos* in 1970.[123]

Although the politics of competition changed over time, securing an adequate supply of high quality nuts at harvest time was always the shelling industry's main challenge because it could not otherwise continue full-scale production until the subsequent harvest. That was true for Mozambican and India shellers.[124] Cashew shelling enterprises also aspired to buy the largest, driest, best quality cashew nuts because those qualities correlated directly with the highest quality kernels, the greatest ease of shelling, and thus the most rapid and secure production of the dessert or 'fancy' kernels that earned the industry's top price.

Northern Mozambique produced the most and the best quality nuts, thanks in part to the temperatures and season. In general cashew nuts produced in the south were held to be inferior. The southern harvest coincides with the rainy season, and rain not only complicates efforts to harvest the nuts; it enhances the likelihood that nuts would get satu-

---

[119] Fialho Feliciano, *Antropologia Económica*, 127: 1964 – 98.3 per cent, 1970 – 68.7 per cent, 1971 – 45.8 per cent and 1973 42.8 per cent.
[120] Parcídio Costa, 'A Indústria de Moçambique no Limiar da Década de "70"' *Indústria de Moçambique* [Lourenço Marques] Vol. 4, No. 7 (Julho 1971): 206.
[121] Costa, *A Indústria de Moçambique*, 201–10.
[122] See more details in the Epilogue. Pereira Leite, 'A Economia do Cajú.' Hanlon, 'Power without Responsibility;' Pitcher, *Transforming Mozambique*; Cramer, 'Can Africa Industrialize.'
[123] 'O cajú na economia de Moçambique,' Vol. 4, No. 6, *Indústria de Moçambique* (1971): 171–2.
[124] Pereira Leite, 'A Economia do Cajú.'

rated and moldy in storage. Dampness and mold make the nuts more difficult to prepare for shelling, tend to darken the final kernels, and thus diminish their market value.[125] In short the north produced the most, most easily shelled nuts of the quality that fetched the highest price, and the south produced fewer nuts that were both more difficult to shell and were likely to fetch an inferior price.

Family farmers, whether in the North or South, usually had a single buyer for all their surplus agricultural products – the *cantineiro*. For most of the colonial period in southern Mozambique, *cantineiros* were South Asians who depended upon South Asian wholesalers and exporters for cash, credit and consumer goods. Many *cantinas* worked on a barter basis, directly exchanging food, cloth and manufactured products for agricultural products, rather than buying and selling their products for cash. That, in part, explains why farmers benefited little from the sharply higher prices paid for export cashews in the 1960s. Large wholesalers and cashew exporters benefited from price increases much more than hundreds of thousands of farmers who grew cashews and the hundreds of rural *cantineiros* who handled them. The price increases that did trickle down to growers, however, were sufficient to more than double commercialization of cashews from 61,000 tons in 1960 to 137,000 tons in 1970.[126]

Mozambican rural commerce certainly was not merely a branch of Indian merchant capital, but the links between *cantineiro* credit, goods, export contracts, prices and networks were important. Many of these links connected Mozambique's rural commerce directly to the large scale South Asian import / exporter sector. Rural *cantinas* were almost by definition small-scale enterprises, and, as such, found it difficult to accumulate capital either to buy agricultural produce, or to acquire the stock of goods to barter or sell in exchange for the crops. Cashew exporters contracted with *cantineiros* to advance them credit or goods in exchange for their agreement to supply them with cashew nuts at harvest. [127]

The cashew economy provided an interesting window into the complex tensions among Indian, Portuguese and Portuguese Indian interests in trade in Mozambique. Portuguese colonial administrators, going back to nineteenth-century High Commissioner António Enes, resented the power and presence of South Asian merchants, but frankly acknowledged the critical role they played in rural commerce. Portuguese frequently portrayed South Asians in hostile terms as a de-nationalizing and corrupting influence on Africans. Most South Asian *cantineiros* did not speak Portuguese, practice

---

[125] Parente and Neto, 'A Agro-Indústria do Cajú,' 18.
[126] 'O cajú na economia de Moçambique,' Vol. 4, No. 6, *Indústria de Moçambique* (1971): 171–172.
[127] Pereira Leite, 'A Guerra do Cajú,' 325; Economicus, 'A Castanha de Cajú: Continua `a ser o Melhor negócio dos Indianos,' *Diário* (19 Feb. 1964).

Catholicism or engage with Portuguese merchant capital networks any more than necessary. They were alleged to repatriate as much of their capital as the law allowed, and to share their business opportunities only among themselves. The Portuguese regularly argued that South Asian merchants removed value from the colony; seldom investing value generated from Mozambique back into Mozambique.[128]

Portuguese Indians from Damão, Diu and Goa, however, were imagined to be colonial allies and agents in the colonizing project to the extent that they were Catholic, Portuguese-speaking and connected with Portuguese commercial networks. The Portuguese colonial press decried the supposed domination of *monhés* (South Asian Muslims) in the cashew trade, alleging that it benefited only them and not the colony.[129] However, Goans, such as Domingos José Soares Rebelo, could frame the debate differently, arguing that before India and Goa began to purchase Mozambican cashews, 'Africans completely ignored the cashew harvest to spend time in a more remunerative manner.'[130] Without the strong Indian market for cashew nuts, he argued, commercialization of the nuts would not have achieved high levels, and would not have fed foreign exchange into government coffers.[131]

Joana Pereira Leite located the key shift in Mozambique's cashew economy with the introduction of mechanical shelling at the Companhia Colonial de Angoche in northern Mozambique in 1962, but acknowledged that state interest in the cashew shelling industry began in the mid-1950s and made a difference from the start. Prior to 1955, the state had levied the same export tax by value (9.5 per cent) on both cashew nuts and cashew kernels. Then it issued a new formula that reduced the tax on exported kernels to 7 per cent by value and increased the tax on exported raw cashew nuts to 11 per cent.[132] Kernels had a much higher value per ton than nuts, so the reduced tax on the exportation of cashew kernels curbed colonial customs receipts by as much as 26 per cent, a considerable reduction. However, through this protective policy the colonial administration assured the supply of raw cashew nuts to the shelling factories, supported the continued growth of the shelling industry and also penalized the export of raw cashews to India.

By 1960 growing interest in cashew shelling from Portuguese agronomists, politicians, business leaders, investors and engineers dovetailed to encourage the state to become a more interested partner in the cashew economy. In December 1961 the long-standing tension between Portuguese and Indian merchants in Mozambique was greatly

---

[128] Economicus, 'A Castanha de Cajú.' *Diário* (19 Feb. 1964).
[129] Economicus, 'A Castanha de Cajú,' *Diário* (29 Feb. 1964).
[130] Domingos José Soares Rebelo, 'O Triángulo Económico no Comércio da Castanha de Cajú – Part I, Moçambique – India – EUA.' *Notícias*, 24 April 1952,
[131] Soares Rebelo, 'O Triángulo Económico,' *Notícias*, 24 April 1952
[132] Pereira Leite, 'A Economia do Cajú,' 644–5.

exacerbated when India took over the enclaves of Goa, Damão and Diu that Portugal had long claimed.[133] The Portuguese state responded with draconian measures against Indians in Mozambique, deporting many, stripping them of their property and even tolerating assaults on complete innocents.[134] India's leadership among the non-aligned states and anti-colonial forces in this Cold War period threatened Portugal as much as its position as the world's largest exporter of cashew kernels. Portugal's decision to promote cashew shelling in Mozambique may also have been shaped in part by its deteriorating political relationship with India. Portugal's actions aimed to undermine India's hold on the cashew kernel market.

Pereira Leite argues that the tipping point in Portugal's approach to Mozambican cashew shelling was the development of a mechanical shelling device by a Portuguese inventor, Samuel de Jesus Ferreira de Carvalho. It was subsequently patented by the Sociedade Imperial de Cajú e Óleos. Investment interest was always keenest around the promise of a machine that could somehow simplify the otherwise intractable difficulties of shelling cashews. But that interest only partly explains the Portuguese investment enthusiasm for Ferreira de Carvalho's invention. The machine was a Portuguese invention; built in Italy but bonded by the Portuguese government and Portuguese capital. With the machine's installation in the north at the Companhia Colonial de Angoche, the state confirmed its intention to support Portuguese investment and to enhance processing capacity in cashew producing areas.

One group lobbying for greater investment in cashew shelling included Tharani's business partner Baldini Vissenjou, a Mauritian who worked with the firm Irvington Varnish and Insular Co. as early as 1943 to experiment with cashew by-products. The group emphasized more narrowly technical and mechanical issues, and their lobby did not make much immediate headway. Vissenjou actually successfully patented his idea for mechanized shelling, but then had difficulty funding it.[135] Tharani was one of the few cashew entrepreneurs who remained unconvinced that a shelling machine offered the key to expanded production. Rather he argued that machines typically yielded a much higher percentage of broken nuts than hand shelling, and since whole nuts brought such a premium, Tharani staked his business plan on hand shelling.[136]

---

[133] Pereira Leite, 'A Guerra do Cajú,' and 'A Economia do Cajú;' Parente and Neto, 'A Agro-Indústria de Cajú,'42ff. 56.

[134] Raúl Honwana, *The Life History of Raúl Honwana: An Inside View of Mozambique from Colonialism to Independence, 1905–1975*, edited with an introduction by Allen F. Isaacman, Translated by Tamara L. Bender (Boulder: Lynn Rienner, 1988): 145–46.

[135] Pereira Leite, 'A Economia do Cajú,' 645 n. 37.

[136] Interview with Jiva Jamal Tharani, 'Em Busca da Máquina Perfeita,' *A Tribuna*, [Lourenço Marques] Ano 1 no. 64 (12 Dec. 1962): 4.

Installed capacity increased rapidly: in 1962 five shelling factories were in production, by 1967 seven, by 1972 eleven, and three more were under construction.[137] Government policy addressed the earlier imbalance between installed capacity in the south and agricultural production in the north. The government's involvement with Companhia Colonial de Angoche marked the beginning shift north. In 1969 the south, which produced around 35 per cent of the cashew crop, had 71 per cent of installed capacity. The north, which produced 64 per cent of the crop, had less than a third of the installed capacity (29 per cent). Just three years later, the percentages were quite different; 55 per cent of cashews were processed in northern factories compared to just over 38 per cent in the south.[138] Despite the northern drift in industrial shelling capacity from the 1950s to the 1970s, through the end of the colonial era Cajú Industrial de Moçambique remained the largest factory with the largest labour force.

The cashew industry's labour force exhibited striking differences from south to north. In 1969 Lourenço Marques and Sul do Save still dominated cashew kernel exports and the labour force. Of the more than thirteen thousand tons of cashew kernels produced, the 11 plants in Lourenço Marques produced more than half, and Sul do Save all together produced 82 per cent. Mozambique District, that would later become Nampula, produced only 18 per cent. The next year, the north had increased its share to 24 per cent. Whereas women comprised 84 per cent of the labour force in Lourenço Marques, and just under half the total labour force, they were less than 9 per cent of the Mozambique District labour force. By 1973, the last year of regular statistics for the colonial era, Mozambique District produced 56 per cent of the total tonnage of kernels and employed just under half the total labour force. But whereas women formerly comprised just under half the total labour force in 1969, they had dropped to just over a third, and while they held their share of the labour force at about 85 per cent in Lourenço Marques, they remained at under 10 per cent in Mozambique District. Although between 1970 and 1973, the number of women employed in cashew shelling in the north more than doubled from 390 to 956, by 1973 the northern industry employed under a thousand women. The northern industry not only depended much more on male than female labour, but it also distinguished itself from other regions with more than 10 per cent of the labour force under the age of 18. In short, as the industrialization of cashews moved north it became more dependent on male and youth labour.[139]

[137] Pereira Leite, 'A Economia do Cajú,' 646ff.
[138] Parente and Neto, 'A Agro-Indústria de Cajú,' 79.
[139] *Estatística Industrial* [title and author varies] (Lourenço Marques, 1947–1973).

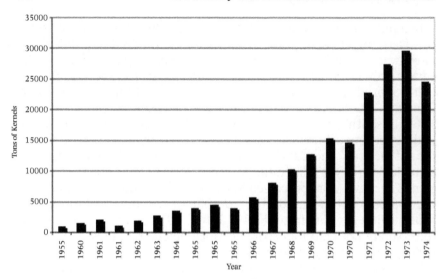

Graph 2 Cashew Kernels Exports, 1955–1974[140]
(Compiled from: Joana Pereira Leite 'A Economia do Caju em Moçambique e as Relações com a India:dos Anos 20 ao fim da Época Colonial', in Comissião Organizadora, *Ensaios de Homenagem a Francisco Pereira de Moura* (Lisbon: Instituto Superior de Economia e Gestão, Universidade Técnica de Lisboa, 1995): 643 note 29, 651 note 65; Paulo Ribeiro Soares, 'O Cajú e o Regime das Proprie-dades no Mossuril entre 1930 e 1950', *Arquivo* (Maputo, Moçambique) Vol. 4 (Oct. 1988): 91–3)

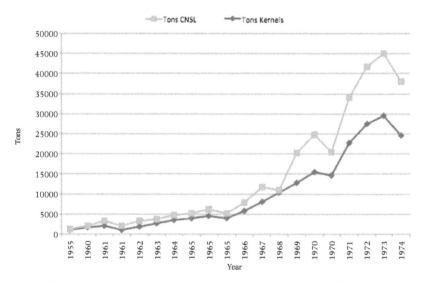

Graph 3 Cashew Kernels and CNSL Exports, 1955–1974
(Compiled from: Joana Pereira Leite, 'A Economia do Caju em Moçambique e as Relações com a India:dos Anos 20 ao fim da Época Colonial', in Comissião Organizadora, *Ensaios de Homenagem a Francisco Pereira de Moura* (Lisbon: Instituto Superior de Economia e Gestão, Universidade Técnica de Lisboa, 1995): 643 note 29, 651 note 65; Paulo Ribeiro Soares, 'O Cajú e o Regime das Proprie-dades no Mossuril entre 1930 e 1950', *Arquivo* (Maputo, Moçambique) Vol. 4 (Oct. 1988): 91–3)

[140] Parente and Neto,' A Agro-Indústria de Cajú,' 50.

To some extent the decline in cashew nut exports to India reflected the increased export of cashew kernels, thanks to growing capacity and production in Mozambique's shelling industry. Marketing CNSL also contributed to the overall commercialization of cashew nut products, but never on the same scale as the nuts and kernels. The Indian and Mozambican shelling industries competed for the same nuts, fueling the demand for cashews that brought more cashews into the market each year throughout Mozambique.

African farmers and cashew sales

Leaving aside the very idea that supply and demand actually shape something called a free market anywhere, farmers in southern Mozambique clearly did not sell their cashews in a free market. From the 1960s farmers experienced stronger demand and higher prices for their cashew. Although that encouraged them to pick and sell more nuts, the colonial state's increasing regulations and the disincentives for competition among rural buyers combined to insure that farmers did not benefit in proportion with price increases.

Joana Pereira Leite shows the inverse relation between the export value of cashew kernels and cashew nuts. She combines the export value of the nuts and kernels to demonstrate the growing profile of the combined cashew economy in relation to the colony's staple exports, such as cotton, sugar and oilseeds. As late as the mid-1960s cashew kernels comprised only 3.6 per cent of exports by value, but then increased more than five fold in less than a decade.[141] Although the combined value of shelled and unshelled cashews peaked in 1972 at more than a quarter of total exports by value, exports of cashew kernels continued to increase significantly until the military coup in Portugal signaled the end of the colonial era and the transformation of Mozambique's economy.[142]

In 1972 the national cashew economy marketed over 200,000 tons of cashew nuts for the first time, but could not sustain it. Economic instability following the 1974 coup reversed the upward trend. Shortly after the Frelimo party came to power in 1975, it imposed a total ban on exports of cashew nuts to India; a move designed to protect and ensure the supply of nuts to the national shelling industry. Despite that drastic step, cashew marketing continued to decline until 1978 when the trend once again rose to an independence era peak of 190 thousand tons in 1981. By 1984 the combination of disruption of commercial networks, drought, transportation problems, contradictory agricultural policies, and growing rural insecurity linked with Renamo's insurgency meant that supplies of cashew nuts and thus exports of cashew kernels plum-

---

[141] Pereira Leite, 'A Economia do Cajú,' 650.
[142] Pitcher, *Transforming Mozambique*, 225–35.

Tons of Nuts

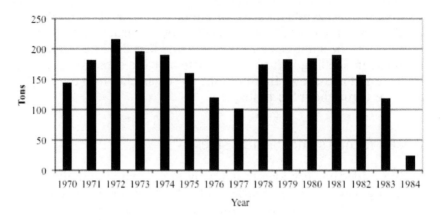

Graph 4 Cashew Nuts Exported, 1970–1984
(Based on Joana Pereira Leite, 'A guerra do cajú e as relaçãoes Moçambique – India na época
pós-colonail', *Lusotopie*, 2000: 295–332, statistics, 325–32)

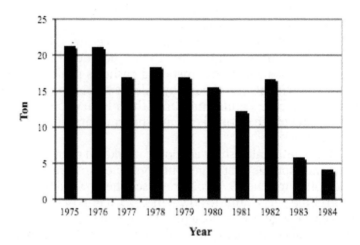

Graph 5 Cashew Kernels Exported, 1975–1984
(Based on Joana Pereira Leite 'A guerra do cajú e as relaçãoes Moçambique – India na época
pós-colonail', *Lusotopie*, 2000: 295–332, statistics, 325–32)

meted: nuts fell by nearly 90 per cent and kernels fell by 80 per cent.[143] The Epilogue continues this story, briefly bringing the situation of Mozambique's cashew shelling industry up to the present.

The Cashew economy: Expertise, policy and practice

The changing profile of Portugal's manufacturing and industrial sector, its increasing links with Europe and the New State's efforts to internationalize capital investment combined to encourage a shift in Portuguese policy toward industrialization in Mozambique. Portugal's enhanced interest in the cashew economy was driven, in part, by those broader shifts.[144] Mozambique's press chronicled the developing inclination to compete with India in the industrial processing of cashew kernels.[145] From mid-century, the champions of local processing raised their voices. Some of those advocates had already invested significantly in cashew shelling and were seeking greater state support for the infant processing industry.[146]

Once Mozambique's kernel exports achieved a certain threshold, the business caught the attention of both India's cashew industrialists and the Portuguese colonial state. In an arena of increased political tension India attempted to crush Mozambique's competition in shelling by raising the price it paid for raw cashew nuts over 200 per cent in less than a decade.[147] That got Portugal's attention. When Portugal finally took a sustained interest in Mozambique's cashew economy, many early advocates undoubtedly reflected on the cliché, 'Be careful what you wish for, because you might actually get it'. Mozambicans, Portuguese and Indians held different, competing and contradictory positions in the chain of cashew production and the overall economic structure. When the state weighed in to support the interests of any one component of the cashew economy, another component was bound to feel aggrieved. By the late 1960s and early 1970s state regulation of cashew prices and licensing of the sale of nuts had alienated nearly everyone with its annually changing and typically complex checkerboard of regions and regulations, suggestive of Port wine demarcations of eighteenth- and nineteenth-century Portugal.

In 1973, the twilight of the colonial era, agronomists Ismar Parente and Lopes Neto published a detailed study of the agro-industry of

---

[143] Pereira Leite, 'A Economia do Cajú,' 650.
[144] Schaedel, 'Last Phase', 7; W. G. Clarence-Smith, *The Third Portuguese Empire, 1825–1975: A Study in Economic Imperialism* (Manchester: Manchester University Press, 1985); Pereira Leite, 'A Economia do Cajú'; Hedges, 'Modernização da cultura de algodão'.
[145] 'A Indústrialização de Castanha de Cajú em Moçambique,' *Jornal de Comércio*, 5 April 1951.
[146] Viegas, 'A Castanha de Cajú', 9, 85, 88; Luis Baldini Vissenjou, 'Apontamentos sobre a Economia de Cajú', *Notícias*, 14, 21 Nov. 14 Dec, 1955; J da Praia, 'A Maior Indústria de Moçambique', *Notícias*, 1,2,3,4 Aug. 1956.
[147] Parente and Neto, 'A Agro-Indústria de Cajú', 42.

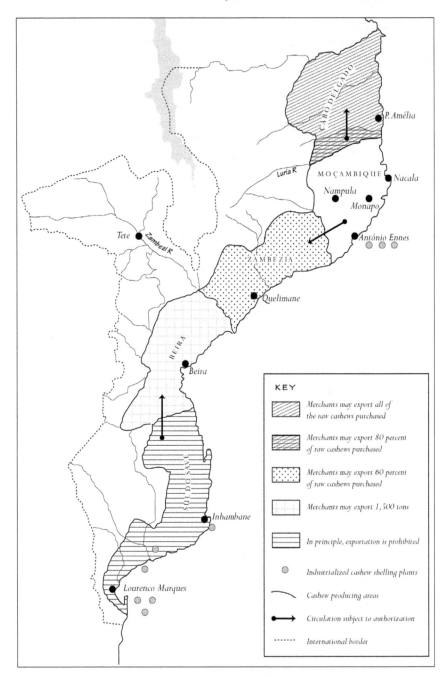

Map 3 Cashew Orchard Conditions for Export, Harvest of 1971–1972
(Based on José Ismar Parente and Alfredo Lopes Neto, 'A Agro-Indústria do Cajú em Moçambique',
Comunicaçao 79 (Lourenço Marques: Instituto de Investigação Agronómica de Moçambique,
1973): 46)

cashews in Mozambique. The map from that study (Map 3 opposite) illustrates just how complex state intervention had rendered cashew exports. Some areas were totally free to export cashews and some areas were in principle prohibited from exporting at all. Other zones had the right to export a certain portion of their harvest, but were only permitted to do so after the national industry had declared that its production needs had been met. Again, like the Port wine demarcations, such formulae simply encouraged people to smuggle their production from one region to another to claim the benefits of the most advantaged zones. Agility, futures and spot markets clearly did not figure in the nightmare of regulations – there was little 'free' about free trade in the late colonial era cashew market.

Prices paid for cashew nuts exported to India increased from between 2.00 to 3.00 *escudos* per kilogram in 1963 to 6.60 and 7.00 by 1971/2, and peaked at 8.00 *escudos* per kilogram during the 1969/70 harvest.[148] Since Mozambique's processing factories could not match India's prices for raw nuts, producers and *cantineiros* all wanted a piece of the higher priced raw nut export market to India. At this point state involvement made a costly difference.

Government involvement proved to be as much a curse as a boon. By the late 1960s the state required all southern farmers to sell their entire harvest to the southern shelling factories. While at first glance that might sound like a good thing, it was also potentially a bad thing, both for the farmers and the factory owners. First, while it was good for the factories to be guaranteed a full supply of nuts, the nuts they were guaranteed were broadly agreed to be the country's worst quality nuts: smaller, more difficult to shell and more apt to be discolored due to the coincidence of the harvest and the rainy season.[149] The southern factories were to some extent saddled with, rather than blessed with southern nuts. Second, southern producers and merchants resented being excluded from the possibility of selling their cashew nuts for the much higher prices offered for export to India. Northern suppliers were not happy either because some of them could not sell their nuts for the higher Indian export prices until the southern factories confirmed that they had acquired their target tonnage from the harvest in the south. Since the southern harvest was later than the northern harvest, northerners further resented having to tie up capital and delay export sales until those they referred to as a 'highly protected minority' of southern factory owners had achieved their quotas.[150]

The broad control system, including price minimums, was even more complicated.[151] It was typically all very tidy, detailed and precise on paper, *'para o Inglês ver'* – for the English to see, as the saying still goes

[148] Parente and Neto, 'A Agro-Indústria de Cajú', 42.
[149] Parente and Neto, 'A Agro-Indústria de Cajú', 18ff.
[150] Parente and Neto, 'A Agro-Indústria de Cajú', 36ff.
[151] Parente and Neto, 'A Agro-Indústria de Cajú', 36ff.

– but it was not put into practice.[152] The pricing and quality evalua-
tion system that was supposed to hold for the factories, *cantineiros*, and
exporters was so absurdly complicated that the interested parties basically agreed simply to ignore it and devise a more efficient, convenient
and mutually acceptable system – mutually acceptable to them.[153] Of
course, no one consulted the farmers, even though they were one of the
groups the price minimums and conditions were ostensibly designed
to protect. Eventually some factories tried to contract directly with
farmers to buy nuts and exclude the *cantineiros*, but in practice most
farmers had few options except to take what the local *cantineiro* offered,
regardless of state regulations. Farmers were generally in debt to their
local *cantineiro* and, even if they were not, the *cantineiro* had the advantage of being their only source of consumer goods and seasonal credit.

State regulations for the purchase of cashew nuts from family
farmers were one of the few clear stipulations. They required *cantineiros*
to do three things: pay the farmer the fixed minimum price set for that
year's cashew harvest, pay promptly and pay in cash.[154] Although few
of the sources go into much detail, it is clear that when the minimum
price was 2.20 *escudos* per kilo, *cantineiros* regularly paid farmers at the
rate of 1.00 *escudos* per kilo, discounting the state's minimum prices,
assuming low quality nuts. *Cantineiros* seldom paid farmers in cash.
Rather they purchased cashews for goods or received them against
accumulated debt.[155]

Parente and Neto's report corroborated information scattered
through the scores of articles published during the fifties and sixties on
the cashew economy:

> Despite the government norms insisting that the pickers be paid
> promptly and in cash; it seems that the latter requirement [payment in cash]
> does not obtain South of the Save River. The nuts there are generally
> purchased with merchandise, and according to our information from
> these [*cantineiros*], quality control is also not possible in practice; rather
> some merchants discount the merchandise exchanged for the nuts in
> anticipation of the fact that the product will weigh less [when delivered to
> the factory] because it will have dried and been cleaned.[156]

The 2003 IIED study also noted the tendency for *cantinas* to barter
rather than pay cash, citing the shortage of cash in rural areas.[157]

Parente and Neto's 1973 report covered the industry's whole sweep
from planting to export. It explicitly corroborated that more than 97
per cent of cashews brought to market from the country's 45 million

---

[152] The phrase remains common, S. Rulane,'Semáforos na capital do país são para 'o inglês ver',
Notíciais (July 2005): 5.
[153] Parente and Neto, 'A Agro-Indústria de Cajú', 36ff.
[154] Parente and Neto, 'A Agro-Indústria de Cajú', 37.
[155] Pereira Leite, 'Economia do Cajú', 648ff.
[156] Parente and Neto, 'A Agro-Indústria de Cajú', 37.
[157] Kanji et al., 'Liberalisation – South'. 18ff, esp. 24.

cajueiros were grown by small scale Mozambican farmers, and that in Southern Mozambique those farmers were women. Furthermore, it underscored that the tree was most valuable to Mozambican farmers for the '...use of the false fruit to make *aguardente*.'[158] The *aguardente* market was in women's hands and they had much more control over the price.

The report only indirectly conceded that the farmers who planted, harvested and brought most of the crop to market did not receive the minimum price that was their legal due. Instead of being paid the minimum price, promptly and in cash, as was their due; farmers receiving goods or debt relief at lower than market or fixed rate prices. It was a long-standing and widespread practice documented by others. Failure to recognize that farmers were often 'paid' at lower rates, in discounted goods or by diminishing their *cantina* debt, reinforced the false notion that prices paid for cashew nuts did not really matter because farmers had, 'minimal subsistence needs' and would not produce beyond those, no matter what the price. On the contrary, prices mattered a good deal to farmers – they regularly made decisions about what to plant, tend, pick, eat, distill or sell based on price.[159] However, the price that mattered to the farmer was not the minimum set by the state, but the price and form of payment he or she actually received.

Finally, Parente and Neto's report only considered the labour force in this labour-intensive industry in its closing section – in connection with what they concluded were factors limiting the industry's potential growth. Their comments about the labour force are introduced at the end of Chapter 2, after the women who claimed that the promising industry grew from their strength, have their say. The contrasts between Parente and Neto's report and the women's narratives are striking.

---

[158] Parente and Neto, 'A Agro-Indústria de Cajú', 34.
[159] Fialho Feliciano, *Antropologia Económica*, 284–92.

2 Tarana
History from the Factory Floor

Layered stories

African women often sing what they are unlikely to say. Oselina Marindzi's work song is the first of our four touchstone songs. Marindzi posed questions that were on the minds of many poor women in Southern Mozambique in the late colonial era: 'Oh, where should I go? Oh, how can I get there? My husband is suffering, Oh woe is me! My husband fled from here a long time ago Oh, woe is me!'[1] Amélia Chiconela, Luis Guila Muhale, and Rosa Joaquim Tembe helped shape answers to some of Oselina's questions. They were among the small group of women and men who joined entrepreneur Jiva Jamal Tharani in the early 1950s and built Mozambique's cashew shelling industry in the capital city; the place the Portuguese called Lourenço Marques, but most people in the region called Xilunguine, the place of the whites or of the strangers.[2]

At an astonishing pace, Tharani and his workforce transformed cashew shelling from a cumbersome street corner enterprise employing scores of women, to a mechanized industry employing thousands in the Chamanculo neighbourhood factory. The official name of Tharani's factory was Cajú Industrial de Moçambique but throughout Southern Mozambique the factory and industry were simply known as Cajú or Tarana. Men and women built the cashew shelling industry, but women comprised the majority labour force in an era when female factory labour was unusual. Tarana quickly gained a reputation as the factory for women.

Amélia Chiconela was one of the thousands of women throughout Southern Mozambique whose suffering drove her to travel to Xilunguine. As she explained: 'I didn't know where Xilunguine was. I got on the train and said I want to go to Xilunguine. I paid 15 *escudos*. I got off at Micoquene, near the slaughterhouse and followed the flow of people to the Ximpamanine market. There I found people from Xinavane.

---

[1] Quote from Oselina Marindzi in Manghezi, 'A Mulher e o Trabalho,' 49.
[2] Xilunguíne, the place of the whites. Alexandre Lobato, *Lourenço Marques, Xilunguíne; Biografia da Cidade, I – A Parte Antiga* (Lisbon,: Agência-Geral do Ultramar, 1970); Lobato, 'Lourenço Marques, Xilunguíne; Pequena Monografia da Cidade,' *Boletim Municipal* 3 (1968): 7–19.

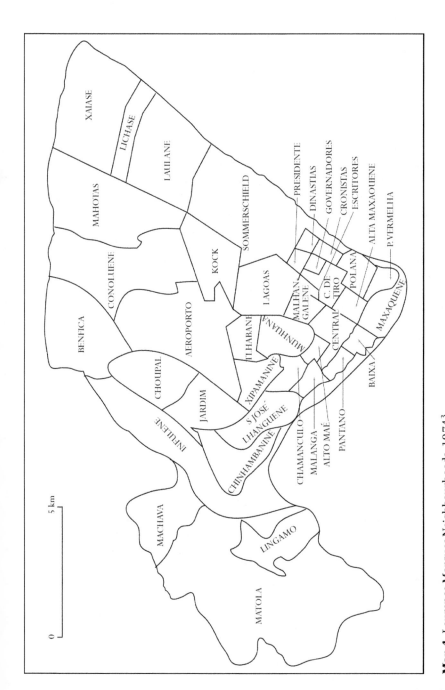

Map 4 Lourenço Marques Neighbourhoods, 1974[3]

(Based on Maria Clara Mendes, 'Maputo Antes da Independencia: Geografia de uma Cidade Colonial', *Memórias do Instituto de Investigação Científica Tropical*, 68, Segunda Série (Lisboa 1985): 76, Fig. 21)

[3] Alternative spellings exist for many *bairros*. Many were added in the colonial era and some have been re-named since independence.

A man let me go live with him. In the house where he lived someone worked at Cajú, so I got a job at Cajú. I did not know what money was. I just got used to this.'[4] Despite having very little idea what might come of it, Chiconela made a way for herself. She learned about money and got used to waged labour in town. Eventually news of experiences like hers spread, and many other women came to view Tarana as a beacon of hope.[5]

Despite its many challenges, the cashew shelling industry was increasingly acknowledged to be one of Mozambique's most promising areas of economic growth. Luis Guila Muhale worked in the industry for decades. He recalled that: 'Until very recently, women who worked in Cajú were despised. People thought they were dirty. People thought they were whores. None, none of our girls from [Lourenço Marques] would work at Cajú.'[6] Muhale may have been right about the way local people viewed the women who toiled in the dust and smoke of Tarana. Much of the work they did was dirty and dangerous, and single migrant woman – employed or otherwise – were culturally suspect in the colonial era. Rosa Joaquim Tembe was one of those women. She was proud to inform anyone who was interested in the colony's leading industry that: 'We worked hard for this factory...it grew from our strength.'[7]

This is a book of layered stories. It is the story of the rise of Mozambique's cashew shelling industry to its apex at the close of the colonial era. Embedded in that narrative are Jiva Jamal Tharani's efforts to build his dream industry despite the power struggles for advantage between Portuguese and South Asian businessmen and financiers.[8] It is also the story of thousands of women who, like Amélia Chiconela and Rosa Joaquim Tembe, made their way to Chamanculo to lend their strength to build the dirty and dangerous cashew shelling industry, and how they interpreted and assigned meaning to life on the factory floor. Embedded in that narrative are the stories of why women set out for Tarana and how they managed to arrive and survive.

The stories among the survivors focused on the lives they lived around their livelihoods. It is a story of men trying to control women, women trying to control or manipulate other women, elders trying to control youth, parents trying to control children and of women, youth and children evading and resisting control. It is most importantly the stories that scores of women told about their work and lives at Tarana. Their stories are rich, painful, funny, generous and truly impressive. Their narratives provide a still too rare window into the day-to-day challenges of women's work on the factory floor and in the neighbour-

[4] OT, Amélia Chiconela, 17 May 1993.
[5] Amélia Chiconela, Marindzi and many others used the term suffering. OT, Chiconela, 17 May 1993 and OT, Virginia C. Massingue, 4 June 1993.
[6] OT, Luis Guila Muhale, 29 June 1993, CIM/M.
[7] OT, Rosa Joaquim Tembe, 2 June 1993.
[8] Pereira Leite and Khouri, Os Ismailis, 54–66, 235–8.

Figure 6 Cashew Sheller
Rosa Joaquim Tembe, 1993
(© Jeanne Marie Penvenne)

hoods of the late colonial era city, and what essentially changed for them in 1975 when Mozambique became independent.

The colonial literature seldom mentioned the cashew industry's majority labour force and badly misrepresented their experiences when it did. Although the following chapters regularly juxtapose women's recollections with impressions from the press, administrative documents and the business literature of the era, the broader challenge is to puzzle out Southern Mozambican women's migration to the capital city, their experiences as the majority labour force at Cajú and the ways they and their families shaped and were shaped by the quickly changing colonial capital. This was a period of rapid urbanization, with migrants outnumbering locals and women becoming a much larger component of the urban African population.

Tarana: The hoe of the city

Life in Southern Mozambique has never been easy for farming families. The region's patrilineal societies located authority over essential resources with senior males, and typically practiced gendered divisions of labour. According to the ideal division of labour, men kept cattle and small stock, hunted, felled trees, built and repaired household structures, protected their families and adjudicated disputes.

Women managed childcare, the daily reproduction of the household and its membership, tilled the light soils with their short-handle hoes and hoped that their sown, gathered and tree crops would be sustained by the region's unpredictable rains. Agriculture near rivers and in the rare pockets of deep moist *machongos* soil was more predictable and productive. Riverine areas, however, were also subject to the periodic ravages of spectacular flooding and to alienation by late colonial-era settlement projects.

Increasingly from the nineteenth century, men and male youth left Sul do Save to seek work in the mines, plantations, farms and factories of what became South Africa and the docks, railways and households of Lourenço Marques. A large literature debates the nature of Sul do Save male outmigration to South Africa and Rhodesia.[9] Men left to earn money to pay taxes, buy consumer goods, and avoid state labour conscription. They were sent out by lineage leaders to earn currency to purchase weapons and ploughs, and eventually were recruited aggressively by South Africa gold and coal mining interests. Some of the nineteenth-century migration was fueled by men's desire to accumulate a bridewealth, or *lobolo*, necessary to legitimate the marriage that confirmed their adult status. Senior men in the husband's family paid *lobolo* to the appropriate male in the wife's family, in part to acknowledge that the wife and her children would live and work with the husband's family (virilocal marriage) managing and enhancing the value of his and his family's property. By the mid-twentieth century long-term male out-migration and a demographic imbalance of widows and rural women became the region's key characteristics.[10]

Cultural expectations regarding marriage and appropriate adult behavior were articulated in law and custom by senior men, but they were also broadly reinforced by older women's discourses and

[9] The classic debate is between Marvin Harris and António Rita-Ferreira in the journal *Africa*: Marvin Harris, 'Labour Emigration Among the Moçambique Thonga: Culture and Political Factors,' *Africa*, 29 (1959): 50–66; Harris, 'Labour Emigration Among the Moçambique Thonga: A Reply to Sr. Rita-Ferreira,' *Africa*, 30 (1960): 243–5; António Rita-Ferreira, 'Labour Emigration among the Moçambique Thonga: Comments on a Study by Marvin Harris,' *Africa*, 30 (1960):141–52; Rita-Ferreira, 'Labour Emigration among the Moçambique Thonga: Comments on Marvin Harris's Reply,' *Africa*, 31 (1961):75–7. Rita-Ferreira wrote a closely detailed challenge to Harris's position in a separate piece: *O Movimento Migratório de Trabalhadores entre Moçambique e a Africa do Sul* (Lisbon: Junta de Investigações do Ultramar, Centro de Estudos Políticos e Sociais, 1963). Core literature also includes, Rita-Ferreira, 'A Oscilação do Trabalhador Africano entre o Meio Rural e o Meio Urbano,' *Indústria de Moçambique*, 2 (March 1969): 96–9; Rita-Ferreira. 'Esboço Sociológico do Grupo de Povoações Meu (Homoíne, Moçambique).' *Boletim da Sociedade de Estudos de Moçambique.*Ano XXVI, No 106, Lourenço Marques (Setembro e Outubro de 1957): 128; Rita-Ferreira, *Evolução de Mão de Obra e das Remunerações no Sector Privado em Moçambique desde 1950 á 1970: Análise da Situação Cambial de Moçambique* (Lourenço Marques: Comissão Coordenadora do Trabalho de Análise de Situação Cambial da Provincia de Moçambique, 1971); Fialho Feliciano, *Antropologia Económica*; Ruth First et al. *Black Gold: The Mozambican Miner, Proletarian and Peasant* (New York: St. Martin's Press, 1983); Patrick Harries, *Work, Culture and Identities: Migrant Laborers in Mozambique and South Africa, 1860–1910* (Portsmouth: Heinemann, 1994).

[10] See Chapter 3.

embedded in work songs that socialized expectations. Women's social location and access to land hinged on their relationships to men, ordinarily their father or husband. Women whose fathers or husbands died or disappeared in South Africa could be greatly disadvantaged and vulnerable to neglect, labour conscription and sexual abuse. Oselina's song centered her suffering, but the chorus in her song and many similar songs emphasized stoicism and the sacrifices expected of a good mother, a good wife, and a good woman. Women were told to remain working their man's land, no matter what the cost.

The second touchstone song is Filomena Mathayi's 'On a Flat Bare Place.' Like Marindzi's lament, it states community expectations of the good woman and wife, but Mathayi revealed the high price women were expected to pay and captured the exact words many women used to explain their predicaments:

> Filomena Mathayi: Oh! On the flat bare place.
> Chorus: Stay there! Remain there!
> Mathayi: Even if they leave me there.
> Chorus: Remain there!
> Mathayi: With the rains falling on me
> Chorus: Remain there!
> Mathayi: Even if they kick me.
> Chorus: Remain there!
> Mathayi: Even if they bewitch me.
> Chorus: Remain there!
> Mathayi: Even if they throw you out!
> Chorus: Remain there!
> Mathayi: Oh! On the flat bare place!
> Chorus: Remain there![11]

Mothers-in-law were advantaged by the labour of their daughters-in-law, so might encourage them to remain on their sons' land – just as they had remained on their husband's lands – even if that land was a flat bare place and they were starving. Song lyrics urged women to stay even if they knew their menfolk would not return, so in effect their 'energy was wasted'.[12] Wasting one's energy on a flat bare place was the phrase many women used to explain community expectations, like standing by one's man even when the man was no longer standing. Thousands of women stayed in difficult circumstances to retain their reputations as good mothers, daughters and wives. They may have stayed out of respect for their husbands and in-laws, but they also may have stayed because they knew that women who left their husband's land sacrificed their social standing, regardless of the circumstances.

[11] 'On a Flat Bare Place' taped by Alpheus Manghezi, was published in First, et al. *Black Gold*, 163.
[12] 'My Energy is Wasted,' taped by Alpheus Manghezi, was published in 'Interviews with Mozambican Peasant Women.' in *Third World Lives of Struggle*. Edited by Hazel Johnson and Henry Bernstein with Raul Hernan Ampuero and Ben Crow (London: Heinemann, 1982): 163ff.

Women also knew, that without a husband's active intervention, her in-laws could also simply send her off. Women who left or filed for divorce might experience support from their birth family, but would likely be taunted in men's songs as whores.[13] Oselina Marindzi's husband had left her long ago, but her song asked where would she go, how she would get there, and what would become of her.[14] Prior to the founding of Cajú Industrial de Moçambique, women like Oselina Marindzi had very limited choices. It is small wonder that many women pounded maize for their family's supper singing the refrain, 'Oh, woe is me!'

From the 1950s, however, the women of Southern Mozambique had somewhere to go. Word got out that poor women, who knew only how to live by their hoe, could feed themselves and their children by going to Xilunguine, to take up a new kind of hoe – a job at Tarana.[15] Women knew that if they left their husband's land to seek work in Lourenço Marques that was tantamount to suing for divorce. If they sued for divorce, they would have to repay *lobolo*, if any had changed hands at their marriage. Tarana became an important destination for Sul do Save women who were suffering. If they worked hard at Tarana, they could repay their bridewealth without starving. When women found themselves in desperate situations, their parents and siblings began to advise them, 'Go to Tarana. You will forget your suffering.'[16]

Luis Guila Muhale had decades of experience with the cashew shellers of Tarana, yet he was of two minds about them. He respected them as hard-working women and mothers who had done nothing to earn reputations as whores. But like most men of his generation, Muhale was uncomfortable with women who were not living under the authority and protection of a culturally appropriate man, a man of the house. The Portuguese term for the man of the house is *dono da casa*. The term for the lady of the house is *dona da casa*. A woman who lived outside the protection of a man was a *mulher sem dono*, a woman without a proper male guardian. Muhale stated a common male perspective: 'Women from Gaza and Inhambane learned they could earn money to repay *lobolo* by working at Tharani's factory. They would threaten their husbands, saying, 'if you annoy me I'll go to Tarana and repay my bridewealth.' Many times families were destroyed by the women them-

---

[13] See also Chapter 5. Classic male perspectives were expressed in the work song, 'Wawuya Celina,' sung by Magomane Pequenino, 15 July 1977, Penvenne, *African Workers*: 214–15; 'My Wife is Suffering' in First, et al. *Black Gold*, 44; Binford, 'Stalemate,' 109.

[14] See also Chapter 5. Alpheus Manghezi recorded extensive Sul do Save oral testimony and song lyrics in the following works: *Trabalho Forçado e Cultura Obrigatória do Algodão: O Colonato do Limpopo e o Reassentamento Pós-Independência c. 1895–1981* [Colecção Documentos, 6] (Maputo: Arquivo Histórico de Moçambique, 2003); Manghezi, *Macassane: Uma Cooperativa de Mulheres Velhas no Sul de Moçambique. Entrevistas e canções recolhidas por Alpheus Manghezi*, [Documentos 5] (Maputo: Arquivo Histórico de Moçambique, 2003); Manghezi, 'O Trabalho forçado por quem o viveu,' *Estudos Moçambicanos*, 2 (1981): 27–36; Manghezi, 'A Mulher e o Trabalho.'

[15] OT, Celeste Mpendane, 26 May 1993.

[16] OT, Amélia Malenguana, 28 May 1993; Felizmeta Namboro, 9 June 1993.

selves – they left their families to come to the factory to be free of their marriage.'[17] Muhale took it for granted that men would migrate and earn money, and conceded that men were much more likely to leave their wives than wives were likely to leave their husbands. He even conceded that women who were in abusive relationships were better off free from their marriages. Nonetheless, he still thought a proper woman should be under the care and control of a *dono da casa*.[18]

By the 1950s, women and youth could increasingly evade the control and authority of senior men through wage labour. If youth and women could earn money by working in town they would be much more difficult to control. As early as the 1960s men and elder women, who depended upon the labour of junior women and youth, expressed that frustration saying, 'What kills us today is money.'[19] By the close of the colonial era, a disgruntled husband complained, 'We, the husbands, are those who know how a woman should work. But at this moment they are employed.'[20]

But, contrary to the tone set by the disgruntled husband and Luis Guila Muhale, women did not leave their families lightly.[21] Rather, women were most likely to go to Tarana because they had no *dono da casa* in their rural household. The *dono da casa* died or contracted himself in South Africa and did not return. Women who actually left their husbands usually did so because they were beaten, starved or just completely fed up. Amélia Chiconela expressed the most common refrain regarding women's tipping point: at some point she could see no way her situation might improve. Her only predictable harvest from tilling her husband's land was a *pancada de graça*, a gratuitous beating.[22] She knew nothing about Xilunguine, had never been to a town, never been on a train or used money. Bravado did not square with most women's testimony. Chiconela was terrified to leave all she had ever known and to plunge into something she knew nothing about and rightly feared.[23] The fact that she 'got used to it' reflected determination, courage and luck, but certainly not bravado.

Tarana may have been the place to which many women who were suffering turned to save themselves, but it was not a place without

---

[17] OT, Luis G. Muhale, 29 June 1993 CIM /M; In the 1950s Rita-Ferreira noted that *lobolo* had lost much of its traditional function, but also confirmed that '... the only woman from the village who was absent working in an urban center left for work because she wanted a divorce and she herself had to earn the money necessary to repay her *lobolo* because it had been spent by her father for his benefit.' 'Esboço Sociológico,' 128.

[18] OT, Luis G. Muhale, 29 June 1993 CIM/M.

[19] Binford 'Stalemate,' 73.

[20] Unidentified man quoted in Sherilynn Young, 'Women in Transition: Southern Mozambique, 1875–1976', unpublished paper, Conference on the History of Women, St. Paul, Minnesota, 1977: 15.

[21] See Chapter 3.

[22] Here as elsewhere in Southern Africa, domestic violence emerged in association with the erosion of patriarchal authority, alcohol abuse and poverty. Burrill et al., *Domestic Violence*; Lee, *African Women and Apartheid*, 63, 73, 186, 198.

[23] OT, Amélia Chiconela, 17 May 1993.

suffering. Local people treated the cashew shellers as sexually suspect. They were marked wherever they went by the scars that cashew acid left on their hands and arms and the acrid smell of cashew ash that clung to their hair. They were stereotyped as *mulheres sem dono*, who had borne 'children of the house,' or children of women; that is to say children whose fathers refused to take responsibility for the pregnancy and child. No corollary derogatory phrases exist for the fathers. Muhale accurately described local people's perceptions that cashew shelling was hard, dirty work for lowly, suspect women; women who might just as easily have ended up in the red light zones in the Lagoas and Mafalala neighbourhoods.[24] One had to have good clothes and make-up to work in the upscale bars of Rua de Araújo, and few migrant women could manage that on their own.

Most clichés contain a nugget of truth. Few cashew factory workers lived in socially sanctioned relationships with men, and they knew that carried a stigma. Again, men who lived in socially unsanctioned relationships with women bore no stigma. The Ronga word for a divorcee, *xungwa*, is also the word for any woman who lives alone. It also connotes sexual promiscuity, and again there is no corollary term for men in precisely the same circumstances.[25] The women of Tarana were more likely to be single, divorced, separated, widowed and to have 'children of the house' than were women who worked in other urban industries.[26] Those very circumstances led many women to Tarana. The women of Tarana also knew that their most likely alternative to day labour at the cashew shelling factory in Chamanculo was night labour as prostitutes in Lagoas and Mafalala bairros. They knew how hard it was to survive and raise children in the chaos and brutality of red light zones, the place they called *Mathlothlomana* – unending chaos. *Mathlothlomana* was another popular conflation. Like Tarana, it denoted a person, a place, and an occupation. In this case *Mathlothlomana* was the name people gave António Nunes, because he was mean and aggressive. Nunes encouraged prostitution in his small shop adjacent to a male labour compound in Mafalala bairro. The compound came to be called *Mathlothlomana*, and 'living in *Mathlothlomana*' meant prostituting oneself. [27] Like thousands of other women, Amélia Chavanguane finally decided she had no choice but to head for Tarana. She was mortified to tears by the implications of that decision for her

[24] OT, Luis G. Muhale, 29 June 1993 CIM/M; Binford, 'Stalemate,' 74.
[25] Binford 'Stalemate,' 74; Laura Longmore's late 1950s study of African women in Johannesburg captured many of the period's embedded prejudices and patronizing attitudes toward urban women, *The Dispossessed; A Study of the Sex-life of Bantu Women in Urban Areas in and around Johannesburg* (London: Jonathan Cape, 1959): 14–15.
[26] See Chapter 4 and Maria da Conceição Tavares Lourenço da Silva, 'As Missões Católicas Femininas,' *Estudos de Ciências Políticas e Sociais*, No. 37 (Lisbon: Junta de Investigações do Ultramar, 1960); Arnfred, 'Estudo da Situação' ; Manuense, 'Contribuição ao Estudo.'
[27] OT, Carlota Samuel Cubay, 20 May 1993; Hilário Matusse. 'Mafalala: Fronteira enter a Cidade e o Subúrbio,' Part 1, *Tempo*, No. 685 (27 Nov. 1983): 18.

reputation: 'I cried when I thought of coming to Lourenço Marques. I am not a loose woman.'[28]

Yet, no matter the cost to their reputations, women who were suffering and could see no way their situation might improve decided Tarana was their place to go. Oselina's next question was how to get there. By the late 1940s the extension of road, railway, and bus service opened avenues out of rural starvation and women and children seized them.[29] The state was so alarmed by the clandestine and legal outflow of women and children from rural areas that it implemented heavy fines on bus, truck or train operators who carried women and children passengers without the explicit authorization of their appropriate male kin. In the late 1940s the state instructed rural authorities to 'take all measures' to prevent further clandestine emigration and instituted a police task force to penetrate and bust illegal migration networks. By 1952 the police had curbed the rapid pace of illegal outmigration, but 'sporadic instances largely involving women' continued for years.[30]

The answer to Oselina's final and most poignant question, 'what would become of me,' depended on each woman's health, her family, her skills, her endurance and her luck. Women who left rural areas on their own were distinct in several ways. Yes, they were often poor, widowed, abandoned and abused but such a journey took courage and determination.[31] People who were familiarly described as the weak, meek and slow probably remained, as the pounding song chorus insisted, suffering on their flat bare place, wasting their energy and crying 'Oh, woe is me'. The women who shared their experiences for this book were more than just determined and courageous. Tembe, Chiconela, Chavanguane, and scores of others were the survivors. Although the city's labour registration records provide some indication of the numbers and rates of turnover at Tarana for the period, absent are the narratives of those who did not survive. The women who shared their stories here were those who managed to hang on year after year

[28] OT, Amélia Chavanguane, 26 May 1993.

[29] Sherilynn Young, 'Fertility and Famine: Women's Agricultural History in Southern Mozambique,' in R. Palmer and N. Parsons, eds. *The Roots of Rural Poverty* (Berkeley: University of California Press, 1977): 67–81; Stephanie Urdang, 'Rural Transformation and Peasant Women in Mozambique,' *Research Working Paper* 40 [World Employment Programme, WEP, 10] (Geneva: International Labour Organization, 1986); Ana Maria Loforte, 'Migrantes e sua Relação com o Meio Rural,' *Trabalhos de Arqueologia e Antropologia*, 4 (1987): 55–69; Circular, 26 August 1946, Nos. 338 & 339/B17/1, Direcção Provincial de Administração Civil [DPAC], Sul do Save; Requerimento, Isabel Mussana to ACLM, 19 October 1948, ACLM archive housed at AHM [ACLM / AHM].

[30] DPAC to ACLM Circular 339/B/ 16/ 1 and 399/ B/17 / 1, 26 Aug 1946, ACLM Caixa [Cx] G; ACLM to Repartição Central de Negócios Indígenas [RCNI], 388/B/ 17/1, 19 Sept. 1952, ACLM Cx NN, ACLM /AHM.

[31] Bilale's study of twenty-first century Maputo argues that women who migrate on their own as a survival strategy often improve their own well-being and self-esteem. This research supports her point that scholarly tendencies to frame single women's migration in negative terms is a residual position, and should be re-framed in a more positive light. Cecilia Castanheira Bilale, *Mulher Migrante na Cidade de Maputo* (Maputo: Centro de Estudos de População [CEP] Faculdade de Letras e Ciências Sociais, UEM, 2007): 11–14.

and raise their children, and even their grandchildren at Tarana.[32]

These women comprised the majority labour force of the most promising industry in the closing decades of Portugal's colonial era. Rosa Joaquim Tembe firmly claimed their due: 'We arrived when Tarana was still poor. This [Chamanculo factory] was a sawmill when Tarana bought it... People suffered breaking open those cashews. Our skin was burned. We worked hard for this factory.'[33] Not every woman who tried to make a life and livelihood at Tarana succeeded, but thousands tried, and thousands more noticed and remembered.[34] Men also noticed that women had new options.

Industrial woman comes to town

The experiences of the women of Tarana shed light on themes that were common throughout mid-twentieth century Southern Africa: erosion of rural resources, changing gender roles, changing household composition, development of industrial labour relations and the impact of women's increasing presence on the character of African urban communities. It was not until the early 1970s that social science and historical literature acknowledged broadly that women's important contribution to African economic development had been overlooked and misinterpreted.[35] Still it is striking that the cashew shellers, who were a critical component in Mozambique's most ascendant industry, could have been so completely invisible in the colonial era archives, press and documents.

Perhaps it is in light of the contemporary shrinking formal economy, that the pervasive informal, gift and household economies of Africa have come to enjoy increasing scholarly attention.[36] Informal production, sales and services clearly play an important role in the daily lives of the majority urban African population. Women, children and youths were as central to these activities in the colonial era as they are today. Most of the cashew shellers of Lourenço Marques, like most

---

[32] See Chapter 3.
[33] OT, Rosa Joaquim Tembe. 2 June 1993.
[34] The growth of the urban industrial labour force is charted in *Estatística Industrial*, 1947–1971, (Lourenço Marques, Imprensa Nacional de Moçambique, 1948–1972).
[35] Ester Boserup, *Women's Role in Economic Development* (New York: St. Martin's Press, 1970); Edna Bay, *Women and Work in Africa* (Boulder: Westview, 1982).
[36] For this growing and dynamic literature see Aili Mari Tripp, *Changing the Rules: The Politics of Liberalization and the Urban Informal Economy in Tanzania* (Berkeley: Univ. of California Press, 1997); Cristina Udelsmann Rodrigues, *O Trabalho Dignifica o Homem; Estratégias de Sobrevivência em Luanda* (Lisbon: Edições Colibri, 2006); Barnes, 'We Women Worked so Hard; Teresa Barnes and Everjoyce Win, *To Live a Better Life; An Oral History of Women in the City of Harare, 1930–1970* (Harare: Baobab Books,1992); Ana Bénard da Costa, *O Preço da Sombra; Sobrevivência e Reprodução Social entre Famílias de Maputo* (Lisbon: Livros Horizonte, 2007); Paulo et al, 'Xiculungo' *Social*, 13; Jane Barrett, Aneene Dawber, Barbara Klugman, Ingrid Obery, Jennifer Shindler, Joanne Yawich, *Vukani Makhosikazi; South African Women Speak* (London: Catholic Institute for International Relations, 1985).

poor people, developed multiple strategies for survival and revenues, including household, gift and informal economic activities, both legal and illegal.[37]

As Frederick Cooper noted, by the 1950s, 'in virtually all' colonial and social science conceptualizations of African labour, the imagined workers were male, thus, 'Industrial man had come to Africa.' But, 'Industrial man had a wife. In fact, women were in colonial debates absolutely central to determining the future of industrial men...African woman would create African industrial man.'[38] Working largely from British and French colonial documents, he noted that late colonial era discourse around 'the stabilization of worker's families' framed African women as 'workers' wives and mothers of future [implicitly male] workers.' According to the same script industrial man would use his family wage or family allowance to support his wife and children. Cooper concludes:

> Colonial regimes did not make African women into workers' wives and nothing more. But the rhetorical construction of African women as workers' wives helped to shape the terms in which women's activities outside of this boundary would be discussed. Defining the workers' wife also defined other roles of women as 'informal' or 'illegal.' Such labels with their implications for law and social and economic policy mark the long-term significance of the colonial construction of industrial man, with his wife and his family.[39]

Colonial policy-makers seemingly had not considered the possibility of industrial woman, but her appearance in the urban formal sector certainly challenged the script; from the proper roles of women as wives and mothers, to the kinds of families that might be supported by family wages and allowances.[40] The recollections of scores of Mozambican women who worked at Tarana open a window into the urban industrial world of the late colonial era and invite a reassessment of the ways African women shaped industrial production and urban social life, and their strategies in light of the demands of industrial production and their own social and economic needs.

Unlike their male colleagues, the women did not receive a family wage, allowance, bonus, or wage enhancement with the birth of a child. In fact, the best they could hope for at childbirth was thirty days of legal unpaid leave. The high rates of child mortality among the cashew shellers suggest that the success of this premier industry

[37] Bénard da Costa and Udelsmann Rodrigues detail such strategies in twenty-first century studies of Maputo and Luanda, *Preço da Sombra* and *O Trabalho Diginfica*, respectively.
[38] Frederick Cooper,' Industrial Man Goes to Africa,' in Lisa A. Lindsay and Stephan F. Miescher, eds. *Men and Masculinities in Modern Africa* (Portsmouth: Heinemann, 2003): 128. Lindsay's work on Nigerian railway workers considers family wages, Lisa A. Lindsay, *Working with Gender; Wage Labour and Social Change in Southwestern Nigeria* (Portsmouth: Heinemann, 2003).
[39] Cooper,' Industrial Man,' 135–136.
[40] Iris Berger, *Threads of Solidarity; Women in South African Industry, 1900–1980* (Bloomington, Indiana University Press, 1992).

came at very high cost to the labour force.[41] The cashew shellers'
contributions were ignored and misrepresented in the print record,
and the urban authorities treated them with hostility and contempt,
but the women grounded themselves in their lived experience on the
factory floor and the lives they honed for themselves and their families in the tight corners they navigated inside and outside the workplace.[42]

Mapping Tarana: From *djamangwana* to *tinumerini*

> 'We counted for something in Tarana's time.'
> Amélia Maciene[43]

> Aiiii, Aiiiii! Roquette Eh! Eh! Eh!'
> Amélia Nhavotso[44]

> '*Malalanyana*, Aiiii! He thought he was "King of the Conselho!"'
> He beat many people...he was bad, truly BAD!'
> Elina Mulungu[45]

The floors of Mozambique's bustling cashew shelling factories were
populated by thousands of women, but key men populated the women's
recollections of life there. Amélia Maciene, Amélia Nhavotso and Elina
Mulungu recalled good men like Tarana, bullies like Roquette and bad,
truly BAD men like *Malalanyana*. This chapter introduces the women
and men of Tarana and conveys the personalities, relationships,
rhythms and discourse of daily life – history from the factory floor
for more than four decades. It maps the flow of cashew nuts through
the Chamanculo neighbourhood factory, before turning to Jiva Jamal
Tharani's early experiments with cashew shelling that led to the foundation of Cajú Industrial de Moçambique – the factory the workforce
called Tarana. It closes with Parente and Neto's 1972 expert report
on the cashew shelling industry and its labour force, allowing us to
contrast the workers' assessments of the industry's development with
Parente and Neto's.

The most cursory tour of Cajú Industrial reveals that cashew shelling
was legally classified and licensed as a toxic and dangerous industry
for good reason. Many of the worst conditions that obtained in the
earliest experiments in cashew shelling were greatly improved when

---

[41] See Chapters 3 and 5.
[42] 'Tight corners,' the title of Chapter 5, is borrowed from John Lonsdale's 'Agency in Tight
Corners: Narrative and Initiative in African History,' *Journal of African Cultural Studies* 13
(2000): 5–16.
[43] OT, Amélia Macaiene, 9 June 1993.
[44] OT, Amélia Nhavotso, 10 June 1993
[45] OT, Elina Mulungo, 4 June 1993.

the industry settled into the factory space in Chamanculo, but it always was and remains today a nasty business. Anyone approaching Cajú Industrial from downwind picks up its signature smell of acrid cashew dust and ash long before the factory comes into view.[46]

In the colonial era the production process began with the arrival of large burlap sacks of raw cashews at the warehouse loading docks. Men and women moved the sacks into the dark windowless warehouse. Even on warm, sunny days the warehouse cement floor was cold enough to drain ones body heat. Processing began with the raw nuts being poured into an enormous oil boiler. The hot oil cracked the outer shell. The cracked nuts then fed out by conveyor belt into the first of the multi-stage hand processing areas. In contrast with work in the damp, bone chilling warehouse, shelling took place in the stiflingly hot shadow of the deafeningly noisy boiler where the air was thick with cashew dust. There the shellers removed the surviving bits of hot, charred outer shell. These women were often 'burned' by the hot nuts, hot oil, and the nuts' caustic anacardic acid. Rosta Muianga worked much of her life in the shelling section under the boiler. Her arms and hands were badly scarred. She recalled that the noise was not only terrifying, but posed as significant a health hazard as the burns: '...we worked until we were deaf under that machine. ...We suffered a lot.'[47]

From the hot and dangerous shelling section the nuts passed to the section where workers conducted the most tedious work, peeling the thin membrane from the kernel. Shelling was done at the exit point of the boiler's conveyor belt, but peeling took place scarcely an arm's length from shelling. Everyone referred to the shelling and peeling sections as *djamangwana*, meaning difficult – difficult conditions and difficult work. By the 1960s *djamangwana* was the popular name for both the Machava Central Prison and the people serving time as political prisoners of the dreaded secret police, Polícia International e de Defesa do Estado, commonly known by the Portuguese acronym PIDE.[48] Difficult in both situations seemed an understated translation.

Double doors separated the dust and heat of *djamangwana* from the cooler, brighter, quieter sorting area where hundreds of women cleaned and separated nuts by size, shape and colour. There the premium fancy dessert nuts parted company with the residual 'baby bits' and other lesser sorts. In the final stages, the sorted nuts were weighed and vacuum-sealed in large metal boxes. This final section was called *Tinumerini*, because people who weighed and packaged the nuts understood

[46] On 10 May 1993, Felipe Guambe guided me through both the Machava and Chamanculo plants with authorization from the Secretary of State for Cashews, Juliano Saranga. See the preface for full acknowledgements.

[47] OT, Rosta Muianga, 9 June 1993.

[48] OT, Amélia Macaiene, 9 June 1993, the Polícia Internacional e de Defesa do Estado [PIDE] was later named the Direcção Geral de Segurança [DGS]. Honwana, *Life History*, Chapter 5; Dalila Cabrita Mateus, *A PIDE / DGS na Guerra Colonial, 1961–1974* (Lisbon: Terramar, 2004): 136–143; 'Desenhos da Prisão de Malangatana,' *Notíciais*, 13 June 2007.

Figure 7 *Djamangwana*, Shelling and Peeling Section, 1993
(© Jeanne Marie Penvenne)

numbers (*ti-numerini*) – they could do the mathematics to weigh and
calculate production. Again Sul do Save discourse conflation obtained:
Tarana and *mathlothlomana* were the person, the place and the job;
djamangwana was the place and the people who did particularly difficult work or had a particularly hard time; *tinumerini* was a place, a
skilled job and the people who did the job.

The least experienced, least educated workers with the fewest
connections did the heavy, dirty and dangerous work in the warehouse
and *djamangwana* sections. Those who had experience, connections,
could speak Portuguese and do mathematics generally enjoyed lighter,
cleaner and less dangerous work. All groups faced their own important
challenges. This study focuses less on the men who worked in the labo-
ratories, carpentry, and metalworking areas, but some of the dangers
they faced became clear the first day of the project. Just as we entered
the building, a metal worker, holding his severed finger, was rushed
out to the hospital.

People in different sections lived with different risks, but no one at
Cajú escaped exposure to the factory's pervasive cashew dust. Everyone
left wearing its acrid badge. The problem was not simply the smell,
though that was bad enough. Within the *Anacardiaceae* or cashew
family, *Anacardium occidentale* is a relative of *Toxicondendron radicans* (or
Rhus radicans), what Americans call poison ivy. Allergy to poison ivy
is relatively common. Anacardic acid is caustic and burns on contact,
and cashew dust, like any other industrial dust is unhealthy, but those

who were allergic to *anacardium occidentale* dust could not endure for long. Sooner or later its noxious effects would catch up with them. [49]

Relations of production:
Names and address on the factory floor

Three generations of Mozambicans who survived those conditions, in some cases for more than four decades, remembered the good and bad times on the factory floor. The oldest generation recounted their work with Tarana before the industry had a factory floor, and when conditions of production made *djamangwana* look like a picnic. The people who lived the rhythms and relationships at Tarana detailed their experience of those years in personal terms. They may have had to assert their agency in 'tight corners', but within those corners workers literally insisted on their own terms.[50] The relationship between hegemony and the power to assign a name and its meaning is broadly recognized.[51] In this colonial arena, as in many others, discourse was separate and unequal. Within their arena naming was an important component of worker ownership. The women transformed Tharani to Tarana, and took that to mean the man, the place and the business. Naming was part of what made Tarana their factory.

At the broadest level, names and forms of address were complex and sharply hierarchical in colonial Mozambique. Most whites were a distant presence from the factory floor. When they interacted with factory workers they presented themselves by surname or position of authority, and expected to be addressed formally. Status hierarchies are embedded in the Portuguese language in ways that underpinned racist colonial assumptions. While whites could address blacks of any age in the intimate/ familiar verb forms that projected authority and required subordination; blacks were expected to use forms that confirmed black deference and social distance – they would certainly never address a white person by his or her given name.[52] To be safe, Mozambicans commonly avoided the familiarity of using even a white person's surname, preferring the social distance achieved by formal titles. Mr Santos (*Senhor* Santos), for example, would be addressed

---

[49] I had not anticipated the occupational hazard of being as allergic to cashew dust as I am to poison ivy. I was only able to get through months of daily work at the factory by using unadvisedly heavy amounts of topical steroid cream to heal exposed skin and subsequent repeated cycles of antibiotics to repair damage to my sinuses, throat and lungs. Those very strong and expensive medications would not have been an option for most Mozambicans, nor were they a long-term solution for anyone.

[50] John Lonsdale, 'Agency in Tight Corners,' See Chapter 5 below.

[51] Bender Shetler, 'The Gendered Spaces.'

[52] Whites could address adult blacks in the intimate verb form [tu] usually reserved for children and family members. Blacks would never presume to use that with whites. Many white memoirs mention this ordering, Nuno Roque da Silveira, *Lourenço Marques; acerto de contas com o passado, 1951–1965* (Lisbon: Edições Calibri, 2011): 174–5.

variously as Mr Boss (*Senhor Patrão*), Mr Supervisor (*Senhor Chefe*), Mr Engineer (*Senhor Engenheiro*).

Relatively few cashew shellers spoke Portuguese and most rarely interacted with whites. In their own arenas, workers assigned names to people in authority. In exceptional cases, women tempered the formal racial hierarchy by asserting fictive kinship. The cast of characters featured in history from the factory floor included: Papa Tarana, *N'wamafasitela, N'wamagange, Ndhondhoza, N'watinhawu, Mamamele, Mudahomu,* and *Cumbula.* The names are often descriptive. *N'wamagange* was the man who wore blue jeans, *N'wamafasitela* was the man who wore eye glasses, *Ndhondhoza* was the man with the booming voice, *N'watinhawu* was the man who smoked a pipe, and *Cumbula* was the man who always mumbled. Surely more than one man fitted these descriptions, but no one confused them.[53] Names in vernacular languages afforded workers modes of control that often escaped those who were formally in charge.

Some men, like António Roquette, were known by several names. Most women recalled him simply as Roquette, but others knew him as *Mamamele,* the man who walked like a cat, such that he was always standing right behind you before you heard or saw him.[54] He was a sneak and a terror. A generation after Roquette left the factory, mere mention of his name still sent women diving for cover, hands thrown over their heads to shield themselves from Roquette's blows: 'Aiiiii, Aiiii, Roquette, Eh, Eh, Eh!'[55] It was a spontaneous performance rooted in years of living in his menacing shadow.

Afonso Ivens Ferraz de Freitas, known as *Malalanyana,* and Roquette come into the story a bit later, but their names evoked the painful, 'Aiiii,' and the sharp warning 'Eh, Eh, Eh!' for good reason. Other names brought smiles, nods, and the soft, long response, 'Ehhhhhh!' Mention of Tarana brought such smiles, 'Ehhhhh!' Most women shared Amélia Macaiene view: 'Ehhhhh! We counted for something in Tarana's time.'[56] Tarana's time spanned from the early cottage industry of the 1950s to the Portuguese takeover of the Chamanculo factory in the mid-1960s. Memories of the early era with Tharani, when women worked hard but 'worked well,' sustained many women through the difficult period after he left.

---

[53] OT, Carlos Maundla, 13 July 1993, confirmed the men's surnames and name assigned by the workers, and Bento Sitoe clarified contemporary orthography. The narrators very likely had similar naming patterns for one another, but I failed to pursue this important line of questioning.

[54] OT, Cristina José Machava, 31 May 1993; Marie Rosa Xavier Sitoe, 28 May 1993; Ofélia Mbebe, 4 June 1993; Amélia Nhavotso, 10 June 1993; Carlos Maundla, 13 July 1993.

[55] When Percina Mungumbe mentioned Roquette, Amélia Nhavotso and four of her colleagues dived for safety, OT, Percina Mungumbe, 10 June 1993.

[56] OT, Amélia Macaiene, 9 June 1993.

Tharani's era: From satellites to Chamanculo

As a cashew shelling entrepreneur, Tharani was well placed. He had knowledge and investments throughout the cashew economy's chain from purchasing agricultural produce at *cantinas* to the import-export trade between Mozambique and India. He experimented in the light of what he had learned from India's dominant role in the global cashew shelling trade.[57] Tharani's experience with and access to largely Indian controlled commercial and export networks was advantageous, but it left him vulnerable to Portuguese allegations that South Asian businesses had no stake in Mozambique. The cliché was that South Asians did business with one another, remitted their profits to the sub-continent, and left little value added in Mozambique. From the colonial administration's perspective Tharani was one of 'them'.

Tharani initiated cashew shelling in Lourenço Marques with a so-called satellite system; delivering nuts to be shelled by groups of women at street-corner clusters and later picking up the shelled and cleaned kernels. Women preferred working in groups on street corners to working at home, not only for the shared charcoal and social solidarity, but because they did not want cashew's caustic oils and fumes polluting their *quintal*, the yard space where most urban African households cooked, cleaned and socialized.[58] Women broke the nuts with hammers they made from tree branches, and all confirmed that it was hard on their hands.[59]

Although the satellite system generated a steady supply of kernels, the dispersed deliveries and pick-ups were cumbersome and time consuming. In March of 1950 Tharani and several other entrepreneurs shifted from this cottage industry to the first small-scale attempt to centralize processing. The trio of Cajú Industrial de Moçambique founders included Tharani, Eduardo da Silva and Bardin da Silva. They were known to the workforce respectively as Tarana or Papa Tarana, N'wamafasitela (the Portuguese man who wore glasses – *fasitela*) and N'wamagange (the Mauritian man who wore blue jeans – *gange*.) They established the city's first cashew shelling enterprise in the Jardim de Gouveia on Avenida de Angola in Lourenço Marques. Tharani's partners N'wamafasitela and N'wamagange were more distant figures for the women. Like Tharani, they both had satellites in the early period, but once the industry moved to Jardim de Gouveia and later Chamanculo, N'wamafasitela and N'wamagange focused on mechanization and technological innovation rather than day-to-day production and labour management.

Tharani began with a small group of workers. Four decades later many of them still worked at Cajú or were active retirees from Cajú.

---

[57] Pereira Leite 'A Guerra do Cajú.'
[58] OT, Group of retirees, 2 June 1993.
[59] OT, Group of retirees, 2 June, especially Joana Chilaule.

Carlos Maundla, Luis Guila Muhale, Joana Chilaule, Rosalina Tembe, Emera Mahochi, Marta Cossa, Carlota Cumbe, Isabel Zandamela, Avelina Bene Manjane and Lina Chivambo were all part of that original cohort and shared their recollections of four decades.[60] When it was clear Tharani would have to hire scores more workers, he brought in David Russell, an Englishman with labour management experience in the Indian cashew shelling industry. The workers named him N'watinhawu because he usually smoked a pipe. Everyone recalled that during N'watinhawu's tenure, if you wanted to work, you worked and were properly paid; if you did not want to 'work well', you were fired. It was as simple as that.

Indeed, the cashew shellers welcomed uniform high standards, fair discipline and positive work attitudes.[61] In an industry where most workers' pay depended upon receiving work from others in the production line, a single laggard could compromise many people's work pace. It was not in workers' or management's interest to retain people who, for whatever reason, didn't want to 'work well.' Tharani, Russell and the factory's two key supervisors, Chefe Lima and Chefe Martins all enjoyed reputations for respect and fairness. Despite the dirt and hard work, respect and fairness were the real hallmarks of Tharani's era. Scores of women echoed Amélia Maciene's assertion they counted for something.

At the original Jardim de Gouveia location, men heated the cashew nuts in barrels of hot oil to force them to crack. The women then completed the shelling and peeling on the spot. The noxious vapor from the nut roasting was recognized as a hazard from the start, so they soon began heating the nuts in cylinders with chimneys to expel the gases.[62] In less than a month Tharani moved from the Jardim de Gouveia to a larger location near the municipal slaughterhouse. The pace of production, however, was such that by September of 1950 they once again relocated, this time to a large sawmill / lumberyard in Chamanculo where they put the business on a permanent footing. The only structures at the outset were long wood and zinc sheds. By December of 1950 about 800 people worked at the Chamanculo location. From that point cashew shelling took place on an industrial footing, complete with a factory floor.

Between March and December of 1950 the business moved three times and the labour force increased from 9 to 800 people. Avelina Manjane remembered those years with calm resignation: 'My hands always hurt, but I had no place to go, so I had no choice but to stay here and suffer.'[63] That was just how it was. Rosa Joaquim Tembe, a tall

---

[60] This section based on: OT, Carlos Maundla,13 July 1993, OT, Luis Guila Muhale, 26 June and 9 July 1993, both in Machava and OT, group of retirees 2 and 4 June 1993.

[61] OT, Carlos Maundla, 13 July 1993.

[62] Viegas, 'A castanha de cajú,' p. 9.

[63] OT, Avelina Bene Manjane, 31 May 1993.

striking woman whose authority within the group remained palpable, knew who bore the cost of innovation and production: 'The cashews were cooked in big pans. People really suffered breaking open those cashews. Our skin was always burned!'[64] She reminded everyone that the cashew shelling industry got its footing when the Chamanculo factory was just a sawmill and Tharani was 'still poor'. She and Manjane were among the hundreds of women who bore the pain and physical scars of the industry's early experiments and expansion.[65]

As the operation increased in scale, the division of labour was clarified and processes streamlined.[66] The nuts were no longer roasted, but treated in hot oil baths. Three 200-litre drums were set on coal-fired stoves that heated the oil to crack the nuts. The nuts, enclosed in a container with a screened bottom, were lowered repeatedly into the hot oil. After the third carefully timed oil bath the nuts predictably cracked and were deposited into a bed of ashes to cool and draw off the excess oil. Men did all of the work with the coal stoves, hot oil, lifting, dipping and timing of the oil baths. The women in this first generation agreed that lifting the large heavy drums and dangerously hot oil baths was men's work.[67]

After the nuts were cracked in the hot oil and drained in the ash beds the men delivered them a short distance away for the women to complete the shelling by hand with small hammers. The men then transferred the shelled nuts to an oven where they were heated to dry out the peel for easier removal. From that point on, women did all the peeling and subsequent sorting by hand. The consensus was that shelling, but especially peeling and sorting was women's work. Although most of the workers corroborated the division of labour that assigned heavy and dangerous work to men and detailed hand work to women, women made it clear that they did not escape heavy lifting in the factory warehouse, in the streets, in their homes and elsewhere.[68] Cajú had a sexual division of labour, but everyone worked long hours and both men and women did heavy, unhealthy and difficult jobs.

Eventually Tharani enlarged the Chamanculo warehouses and further mechanized production. A boiler replaced the coal stoves and oil drums, and the nuts were moved into and out of the boiler on conveyor belts. Some of the men's jobs were displaced through mechanization, but as installed capacity increased ever more women were hired as shellers, peelers and sorters to keep up with the boiler's pace.

---

[64] OT, Rosalina Tembe, 19 May 1993.
[65] OT, Rosa Joaquim Tembe, 2 June 1993.
[66] The below paragraphs on early factory production are based on OT, Carlos Maundla,13 July 1993, OT, Luis Guila Muhale, 26 June and 9 July 1993, both in Machava and OT, Group of retirees 2 and 4 June 1993.
[67] OT, Group of retirees 2 and 4 June 1993.
[68] Carlos Dominguez's photographic tribute to Mozambican women and the elegance of their heavy lifting makes this point nicely, *Com o Mundo na Cabeça: Homenagem as Mulheres de Moçambique* (Figueira da Foz: Impressora Económica, Lda for the Associação do Centro Cultural de Matalana, 1997).

Work in both the shelling and peeling sections remained frustratingly difficult.[69]

'We counted for something': Papa Tarana remembered

Cecilia Chicavo and Rosa Joaquim Tembe knew Tharani before some of the other workers were born. Both women began working with Tharani in his street-corner satellites. They remembered him fondly as a person who worked as hard as they did. They recalled that Tarana cared about the industry and valued the women's place within it. A shared commitment to production at Cajú and the value of working well were striking central features in the worker's narratives. In the collective memory of the workers who knew him in person Tarana emerged as a smart, no-nonsense, fair and compassionate man. He and his founding partners were a good team, because, as Chicavo insisted, and many women echoed, under them the women 'worked well.'[70] The work was hard and expectations were high, but the women agreed they were treated with dignity.

The narratives of Tharani in the early years of production framed relationships as familial and gendered. Some of these *mulheres sem dono* spoke of Tharani as though he were the responsible household head they never had in their own homes. Some referred to Tharani as the *dono da casa,* man of their house, and of themselves as the *donas da casa,* ladies of the house. As the *dono da casa* Tharani oversaw and managed the resources while the *donas* contributed their productive labour within the shared factory household. Obviously one can carry that analogy too far, but the discourse of family clearly marked recollections of the era. These women forged early models of Mozambican industrial women. They drew upon images and relationships they knew and shifted them to fit their unprecedented situation.

Emera Mahochi, a great actress, played this theme beautifully.[71] A tiny woman with seven decades of life behind her, Mahochi entertained the whole cohort of retirees with her lively portrayal of the short stocky Tharani, greeting his workers with '*khissá khissá*' what Portuguese call *beijinhos,* a 'little kiss' on each cheek as a form of greeting. She assumed his stature, and went around the room bestowing *khissá khissá*. She then began a self-praise performance that is more typically done by men. Mahochi performed Tharani's praise for her own fast and produc-

---

[69] Tharani's advertisements in several issues of the periodical *Império* claimed that Cajú Industrial de Moçambique was the only factory in Mozambique to shell cashew almonds and to extract and process cashew oils and derivatives. *Império*, Vol. 4 (August 1951): ii; *Império*, Vol. 11 & 12 (March /April 1952): 14; *Império*, Vols. 5 & 6 Sept. / Oct. 1951): v.

[70] OT, 'we worked well' included Julieta Mulungu, 20 May 1993; Rosalina Tembe, 19 May 1993; Elina Mulungo, 4 June 1993; Cristina Phelembe, 17 May 1993; Elena Machava, 26 May 1993; Emera Mahochi and the group of retirees, 2 June 1993.

[71] This paragraph based on OT, Emera Mahochi, 2 June 1993.

tive work – work that she claimed made her the envy of her colleagues. She boasted that the 'pretty little Indian' Tarana was so delighted by her work that he gave her extra money and bread. That just made her colleagues even more jealous, but she didn't care. Her colleagues may have suspected her of sorcery because of her good fortune, but she considered herself the *dona da casa*, the first lady of the factory, having caught Tarana's eye and pleased the *dono da casa*. Everyone laughed heartily and enjoyed her marvelous performance. Then she sat back and recalled in a more sombre mood, that, like most others, she came to Tarana because of *wusiwana*, poverty. She too was no stranger to hard work, it seems to have been her lot: 'Papa Tarana made us work well. We all worked right along tra, tra, tra, tra.'[72]

If Mahochi was the elder group's sparkling *dona da casa*, Cristina Muzamane was usually the skunk at the group's picnic. She listened to Mahochi rave about herself and laughed with everyone else for a while. Then she took the floor. While Mahochi might have been called *muloyi*, a witch, if she shelled faster than anyone else, there were also consequences at the other end of the spectrum: 'If I didn't clean six cans of nuts a day they would '*tilho dra chitubanana*' [give me the evil eye].'[73] As with factory workers around the world, people were marked for being too fast or too slow. Cristina Muzamane was often taunted for being a laggard.

Mahochi performed Tharani in the role of husband or sugar daddy, but made it clear that it was her successful work pace that caught and sustained his fancy. Many others spoke of Papa Tarana as a caring father, grandfather or uncle. In this era women and children were often merely linked in the common 'women and children' phrase. Women working at both the satellites and the early factory were literally linked – they carried their nurslings on their backs. Despite the dangers, babies were present on the production line. Tharani played with the babies and little children in his 'household,' and was watchful over young girls, but he also disciplined and maintained order in the ranks. Maria Nhantumbo's whole face smiled when she recalled, 'We worked with our children on our backs or tied up in our *capulana* under the table. When Papa Tarana passed he would stop to play with your child.'[74]

Amélia Manena Chavanguane recalled: 'I used to hang around Tarana trying to get work because I had no one to care for me. At first I was too young, but when Papa Tarana saw I had grown he said, "Now you can go to work... and I will feed you."'[75] He and his staff took pity on girls looking for work, particularly if their older family members worked at Tarana. Feeding was the term many people used, but it clearly meant giving people a job so they could earn the money to buy their own food. In the early 1950s, Celeste Marcos Mpende, Matilde Chiduza, and

[72] OT, Emera Mahochi, 2 June 1993.
[73] OT, Cristina Muzamane, 4 June 1993.
[74] OT, Maria Nhantumbo, 3 June 1993.
[75] OT, Amélia Chavanguane, 26 May 1993.

Amélia Chavanguana all hung around Tarana begging for work. All were initially refused because they were underage. Eventually Tarana relented and assigned them to lighter jobs like sweeping or cleaning. He did the same with older people who were good workers, but because of illness or injury could no longer sustain the rigors of their sector.[76]

Tharani's managers enhanced his reputation because they upheld his standards for fairness. Despite the fact that they managed shelling and peeling, the factory's most difficult and dangerous areas, Chefes Lima and Martins enjoyed the workforce's high regard. Maria Rosa Xavier Sitoe's mother began as a hand sheller with Tharani at his first common location in Jardim de Gouveia. When Maria Rosa was only 13, she came seeking work in Chefe Martins' shelling section under the thundering boiler. She was turned away repeatedly, before Martins finally relented. Sitoe and the whole group laughed when she recalled her first attempts: 'It was so hard, I couldn't do it! Everyone made fun of me when I cried about the work. Eventually Chefe Martins let me help one of the other Chefes instead.'[77] Chefe Lima, supervisor in the time-consuming peeling section, was also viewed as one of the few 'good white men'. Lima always carried cookies and crackers for the children and encouraged women to work with their babies. He and Tarana not only liked babies, they knew that keeping babies happy while their mothers shelled nuts was good business.[78]

A strong work ethic, appreciation of fair judgement and full payment for serious work were central themes in the shared memories of Tharani's era of factory labour. Cristina José Machava echoed others: 'if a woman showed up every day and worked, she received her full salary.'[79] Maria Nhantumbo agreed: 'if you came and put in a full day's work you would be paid. If you filled your quota you would get [extra] bread and sugar.'[80] Working well and earning a bonus for more than meeting a reasonable day's quota was fine. Being penalized for not meeting an unreasonable base quota was a different matter.

Carlos Maundla, another of the original cohort, began working for Tharani in 1950 as a metal cutter constructing the boxes used to pack and ship the shelled cashew kernels. He echoed his colleagues' judgment of a golden era under Tarana:

> [Tharani] was a just man, a good man. He set up the factory to succeed. He respected people who worked well, and fired those who were not serious about the work. He was fair. He also always had the end of the year celebration, and gave people meat, soap, rice and sugar and tea as a gift to take home.[81]

---

[76] OT, Celeste Mpendane 13 July 1993; Matilde Chiduza, 28 May 1993; Amélia Chavanguane, 26 May 1993 and Emera Mahochi, 2 June 1993.
[77] OT, Maria Rosa Xavier Sitoe, 28 May 1993.
[78] OT, Maria Rosa Xavier Sitoe, 28 May 1993; Luis Guila Muhale, 26 June and 9 July 1993.
[79] OT, Cristina José Machava, 31 May 1993.
[80] OT, Maria Nhantumbo, 3 June 1993.
[81] OT, Carlos Maundla, 13 July 1993.

The women valued their pay and benefits, but also the dignity with which they and their families were treated. All the workers who knew Tharani valued his fairness, encouragement and the benefits that vanished after Tarana's time. Those benefits might seem small, but for many of the women they made a great difference in their health and sense of wellbeing: a daily provision of a popular corn-flour, water, and sugar mix called *mahéu*, free uniforms, and a new headscarf every six months.[82] Again, Emera Mahochi captured the spirit of her generation's memories:

> 'Tarana fed us, dressed us, and gave us sugar. The clothing we wore came from our work at Tarana. At Christmas we ate beef. We got sugar, soap, rice and cashew nuts. He gave us rice, potatoes, everything we needed to work well. Now we are suffering. We no longer see these good things. Even today we cry over Tarana. He treated us well! When Tarana left we began to suffer.' [83]

The Christmas gifts may have been symbolic recognition of the worker's contribution but were also 'good things' that the workers would not otherwise enjoy.[84]

Cristina Muzamane could always be counted on for healthy skepticism about Mahochi's sense of the 'good old days.' She firmly reminded everyone that people were often burned because of the clumsy handling system, the smoke was suffocating, and the work was bone-breaking hard. Even Muzamane was grateful for Tharani's pattern of rewarding hard work:

> He gave us *mahéu* daily, and when we worked well, he gave us sugar and coca-cola. The money then was not much but it had value. We could afford to buy a *capulana* (a cotton wrap that was most women's standard garment), but now if your daughter-in-law doesn't buy you a *capulana* you simply go without.'[85]

A rare press interview with Tharani corroborated the women's sense that he valued their labour. It is unusual for a historian to have a richer sense of a prosperous colonial era businessman from the oral narratives of his African labour force than from the written record, but that is the case here. The only substantive published information I found about Jiwa Jamal Tharani was an interview with the newspaper *A Tribuna* in late 1962.[86] In it Tharani underscored his firm commitment to expanding cashew shelling based on skilled hand shelling. By 1962

---

[82] OT, Elina Mulungo, 4 June 1993; Leia Papulo Nhavene, 17 May 1993.

[83] OT, Emera Mahochi and group of retirees 2 June 1993.

[84] Most of the retirees commented on the holiday gifts of food, but see also OT, Maria Rosa Xavier Sitoe, 28 May 1993.

[85] OT, Cristina Muzamane, 4 June 1993.

[86] The interview with Tharani is titled 'Em Busca da Máquina Perfeita,' *A Tribuna*, [Lourenço Marques] Ano 1 no. 64 (12 Dec. 1962): 4. Sincere thanks to Dr António Sopa who located and gave me a photocopy of the original article including the photo of Tharani.

he had already sunk a great deal of money and effort into developing his or his colleagues' patents for shelling machines that would boost production and diminish reliance on skilled labour. That frustrating experience made him one of the few industrialists of the era to be skeptical of an otherwise broadly anticipated technological solution to cashew shelling. Instead he was committed to investing in the production of high quality, whole dessert quality cashew nuts hand shelled by skilled Mozambicans. He urged rapid expansion of hand shelling factories, with well-trained and increasingly experienced shellers, working in good conditions. Tharani emphasized the correlation between hand shelling and rendering the premium fancy dessert cashews that fetched the highest price by many fold; something he was certain mechanized shelling could never achieve.[87] The women were right. They counted for something with Tharani; he actually staked his business plan on the value of their hand shelling skills.[88]

Although statistics for the 1950s demonstrated that Mozambican hand shellers were much less productive than their Indian counterparts, by the time of Tharani's interview in the early 1960s he could see important progress. Two generations later Luis Guila Muhale, then manager of Cajú Industrial de Moçambique's Machava plant, maintained that Tharani's faith in the evolution of skilled Mozambican hand shellers had been well placed. Industrial cashew shelling was newly introduced in the early 1950s, but throughout the 1950s Tharani's workforce became increasingly stable, experienced and skilled. Strategies for shelling, peeling and sorting cashews developed differently in India and Mozambique, so exact comparative measurements are difficult, but Muhale maintained that in the 1960s experienced Mozambican shellers actually had become more productive than Indian shellers.[89]

Stability and absenteeism in the Cajú labour force are detailed in subsequent chapters, but the 5 percent systematic sample of the capital's African labour force for much of this period revealed that a high proportion of both men and women were likely to leave their first urban labour contract before the end of the year – no matter what the job.[90] Many first time job seekers were very young. The reasons for

[87] In 2004, António Miranda, working with an NGO called Technoserve made the same argument: 'African Cashews: Stimulating an Entrepreneurial Approach,' *New Agriculturalist*. http://www.new-agri.co.uk/06–5/focuson/focuson6.html Accessed 4 May 2015.
[88] 'Em Busca da Máquina Perfeita,'*A Tribuna*, [Lourenço Marques] Ano 1 no. 64 (12 Dec. 1962): 4.
[89] OT, Luis Guila Muhale, 26 June and 9 July 1993 with corroboration from union leader Elena Machava, 26 May 1993. Fernando Bessa Ribeiro's study argues that hand shelling remains most productive if the goal is to export whole top quality nuts and earn the highest price per kilo: Fernando Bessa Ribeiro, 'Sistema mundial; Manjacaze e fábricas de cajú: uma etnografia das dinâmicas do capitalismo em Moçambique,' PhD thesis (Vila Real, Universidade de Trás-os-Montes e Alto Douro, 2004): 396–7.
[90] ACLM sample overall, and Cajú sample suggest similar patterns for first year attrition.

people leaving their first job before the end of the contract were many.[91] During the 1950s and early 1960s – Tharani's tenure – Cajú's work-force was striking for its polar turnover and retention pattern.[92] The sample revealed the familiar high turnover in the first year of employment, but then showed unusually high retention among workers who survived that first year. Despite being among the toughest, most despised, dangerous and lowest paid jobs in the city, cashew shelling offered steady work. People came to work at the factory because it paid steady wages, and most stayed because they needed those wages to live. The consensus in the workers testimony was that people came to work at the factory because of *wusiwana* and misfortune. They often explained they 'had nowhere else to go.'[93] They also agreed that people left the factory for two reasons. A lucky few found 'somewhere else to go' – that sometimes meant they got married or went to live with a man who earned enough to feed and clothe them and their children, or more exceptionally they found a better job. However, most of those who left did so quickly because they simply '...couldn't take it.'[94] The work pace and hazards of skin and lung irritations from the toxic cashew dust made work at Tarana hard for anyone to take, but people who found they were allergic to cashew dust simply could not survive the daily exposure for long. Allergies clearly accounted for at least some of the short-term attrition.

The BNU Era: Roquette and *Malalanyana*

Ironically it was ambition, drive, and commitment to the industry, the qualities that so many people praised in Tharani and his team, that eventually got them into debt with the Banco Nacional Ultramarino [BNU]. Tharani became overextended in his efforts to expand. Had he been a Portuguese entrepreneur the bank might have worked out a deal, but by the early sixties the Portuguese were increasingly interested in cashew shelling, and India was clearly a major competitor in the industry. Tharani was not among the hundreds of Indians driven out or persecuted by Portugal after the Indian takeover of Portugal's enclaves of Diu, Damão, and Goa in December 1961, but it was not an auspicious era for Indian capital in Mozambique.

[91] Penvenne, *African Workers*, Chapters 7 and 8.
[92] The ACLM sample for men and women working at Cajú revealed just under a third did not make it through the first year contract, and just under a third were steady, long term employees. Women's work lives were often interrupted by childbirth, but in the overall context of instability among women wage workers only seamstresses revealed less turnover than Cajú, and they were a much smaller sample, better paid, local and skilled. ACLM sample
[93] OT, Avelina Manjane, 31 May 1993; Amelia Chiconela, 17 May 1993.
[94] When asked why women left work at Cajú, many women said they only knew about their own experience, and would not speculate about others, but otherwise the most common answer was that people left because '...they couldn't take it.' OT, Group of retirees, 2 June 1993; OT, Ester Tafula, 3 June 1993.

No one claimed that work at Tharani's factory was easy, and if they had, Cristina Muzamane would have begged their pardon, but when the BNU took over operations at Chamanculo everyone agreed the changes were unwelcome and made their work much more difficult. Tharani and his partners left. The BNU fired Russell, and the state became much more involved in the workers day-to-day lives. The smiling 'Ehhhhhh' memories of Tarana and his team gave way to the 'Aiiii' memories of *Malalanyana, Ndhondhoza* and Roquette. Instead of 'working well' as they had under Tarana, *N'wamafasitela, N'wamagange,* and *N'watinhawu,* under the new regime the women were intimidated, coerced, and punished. Carlos Alberto Machado da Silva took over the plant from Tarana. He was known both as *Ndhondhoza* because of his booming voice, and also as *Mudahomu,* a ritual herb necessary to settle disputes.

When *Ndhondhoza* passed by Rosa Joaquim Tembe's child sleeping in the *capulana* hammock she rigged up under her workbench, he did not pause like Tarana to admire the child, rather he demanded: 'Is that a baby goat? Why is he tied up in that bag?'[95] Neither babies nor goats would be tolerated on *Ndhondhoza*'s factory floor. In light of the heightened tensions of the factory floor, he spent much of his time coping with the *zaunzwanas* (gossips and rumour-mongers) who worked their mischief. [96] Jealousy and rivalry erupted, usually ending in punishment that then required dispute resolution – thus the name *Mudahumo.* Suspicion around the growing national insurgency and resistance to what women described as an increasingly hostile work climate fueled the tense atmosphere.[97]

Change on the factory floor was not limited to personalities and style – women also felt it painfully in salaries and production targets. Factories always have their 'witches' like Mahochi, who could work faster than anyone else and earn extra, and plodders like Muzamane, who got the evil eye because she could never work quite fast enough – but most people saw both situations as within the parameters of fairness. It was fair to be paid in full if you put in a full day's labour working your best, and to be paid extra if you produced extra. If you 'didn't want to work' or engaged in '*brincadeiras*' (literally 'little games' but generically foolishness, maliciousness or sexual intrigues) you could be fired – again, most people thought that was fair and appropriate.[98]

The state's footprint was minimal in Tharani's factory. At just the time Tharani moved his enterprise to Chamanculo, however, jurisdiction over African labour registration and the required 'native passbooks' shifted from the municipal police department to the municipal

[95] OT, Rosa Joaquim Tembe, 2 June 1993.
[96] OT, Elina Mulungu, 4 June 1993
[97] OT, Carlos Maundla, 13 July 1993.
[98] This was the consensus of most women, but especially the group of retirees, 2 & 4 June 1993;
OT, Carolina Sigaugue, 24 May 1993.

headquarters of the Curator of Native Affairs at the ACLM. That was also when Afonso Henriques Ivens Ferraz de Freitas, the notorious *Malalanyana*, became Curator of Native Affairs for the city. All workers were required to register at the ACLM within two weeks of arrival in the city and to renew their registration annually thereafter. Women who worked in shelling satellites in the *bairros* did not have to register basically because they were women doing informal labour – men could not do that without registering. But women who worked for wages at the Chamanculo plant had to register.

Ferraz de Freitas was called *Malalanyana*, the skinny one, because no matter how much blood he drank from the city's black labour force he never got fat. He was always hungry and therefore dangerous. *Malalanyana* cultivated his reputation as a fierce disciplinarian, particularly regarding punctuality and work place attendance.[99] Aside from his alleged thirst for Mozambican blood, he was seemingly driven to tidy-up and control. He organized urban African labour throughout the city on a kind of guild basis.[100] When he cast his controlling shadow over BNU's management at Cajú everyone felt the chill.[101] The women particularly resented what they perceived to be a sinister partnership between the BNU and *Malalanyana* to curb tardiness and absenteeism. Carlos Maundla explained: 'When the BNU took over from Tarana things began to change. To deal with absenteeism, *Malalanyana's* police were posted at the gate, and people who missed work for any reason got 6 blows on each hand with a *palmatória*, man or woman.'[102]

A *palmatória* was the Portuguese colonial administration's signature implement for corporal punishment. It is a wooden paddle with a long handle and a head about the size of a ping-pong racket. The head of the paddle has 6 round holes cut into it. The holes suck in flesh with every blow, increasing the pain and swelling. Six blows on each hand

---

[99] Dozens of workers mentioned *Malalanyana*, for example, OT, Julieta Mulungu, 20 May 1993; Celeste Mpende, 26 May 1993; Jalane Machava Elmia, 7 June 1993; Marta Cau, 9 June 1993. For contrasting perspectives on him see Michel Cahen, 'L'État Nouveau et la diversification religieuse au Mozambique, 1930–1974. I. Le résistible essor de la portugalisation catholique (1930–1961),' *Cahiers d'Etudes africaines*, 158 (2000):309–50; L'État Nouveau et la diversification religieuse au Mozambique, 1930–1974, II. La portugalisation désespérée (1959–1974) *Cahiers d'Etudes africaines*, 159 (2000): 551–92; Penvenne, *African Workers*, 141ff; Teresa dos Santos Oliveira, 'Recordações sobre Lourenço Marques, 1930–1950,' *Arquivo* 2 (October 1987): 102 note 18, with alternative spelling *Malalanyani*, meaning *enfezadinho* (stunted). According to Marvin Harris, 'In 1957, it was precisely by the maintenance of artificial urban chiefdoms that the notorious Ferraz de Freitas, administrator of Lourenço Marques, his *chefes do posto*, and puppet urban African chiefs maintained their iron-handed discipline over Lourenço Marques's 100,000 Africans, 'Race, Conflict and Reform in Mozambique,' in Stanley Diamond and Fred G. Burke, eds, *The Transformation of East Africa: Studies in Political Anthropology* (New York: Basic Books, 1966): 166.
[100] Rita-Ferreira, 'Os Africanos', Ch. 10, 323–93.
[101] Ferraz de Freitas's Report underscored that the ten fold increase in prosecuted infractions of the native labour law recorded between 1948 and 1949 was due to the fact that enforcement passed to his office at that time. Relatório, ISANI, ACLM, 1950, R Cx MM/ ACLM/ AHM.
[102] Quote from OT, Carlos Maundla, 13 July 1993; Corroboration of beatings, OT, Amélia Maciene, 9 June 1993; OT Juliete Mulungu beaten at *Malalanyana's* 20 May 1993.

would not only be very painful, it would make it impossible to use one's hands effectively for at least a few days – obviously a counterproductive sanction for absenteeism and tardiness in an industry that depended upon manual dexterity and worker's 'nimble fingers'. Women were also beaten on the breasts, buttocks and the bottoms of their feet. The police similarly disciplined women who worked as seamstresses in the city's textile, garment and other leading 'nimble fingers' factories.[103]

Most women had to get their families and households ready for the day before they embarked on their walk to work. Since rents generally correlated with distance from the city centre, most women lived a great distance from the factory. The few women who could afford transport jostled with men for space on open, overloaded trucks, and fended off groping and harassment.[104] Even when everything went well, it took effort and planning to get to work on time. When it rained torrents in the summer months it was much worse. Amélia Chiconela complained, 'I got up about 4 am every day to arrive here by 7 am. Look, if you arrived after the signal, you went home! They would not let you in to work.'[105] Workers had to pass a guard at the factory gate. In the morning guards like the notorious *Mafumanhane* closed out women who had arrived just after the whistle sending them home or off to be beaten at *Malalanyana*'s. At closing time guards literally shoved women out of the gate if they were not moving fast enough.[106]

The BNU takeover also occurred as the Portuguese increasingly deployed the PIDE as part of their counter-insurgency strategy. The most notorious of the secret police assigned to Cajú was the cat-like *Mamamele*, António Roquette.[107] People remembered him well, because he gave them a lot of trouble: 'When he saw us finish a task, he would tip the scale so you would have to return and do more, and if we dared ask why our full task wasn't marked as complete he would send us off to *xipswahla* the 'jail' or holding cell at the Administrative Post at Munhuana [PAM] – to be beaten [with a palmatória].'[108] Ofélia Mbebe remembered Roquette as, '...the tall balding guy who pushed us around. He was a spy for the PIDE.' Mbebe, distinguished Roquette's behavior from that of ordinary whites who lived well thanks to value extracted unfairly from black labour.[109] Roquette

---

[103] Oliveira Santos' interview with Felizmina in Maputo 1981 confirms that Facobol workers were also beaten with a *palmatório* at the ACLM for absences, 'Recordações,' 89ff.

[104] OT, Julieta Mulungu, 20 May 1993

[105] OT, Amélia Chiconela, 17 May 1993.

[106] OT, Jalane Machava Elmia, 7 June 1993; 'O Partido – A Luta dos Trabalhadores na "Cajú Industrial",' *Tempo*, no. 405 (9 July 1978):15–20.

[107] OT, Carlos Maundla, 13 July 1993; 'O Partido,' 16–17.

[108] OT, Maria Rosa Xavier Sitoe, 28 May 1993; Amélia Macaiene, 9 June 1993; Catarina Tafula, 3 June 1993; Luis Guila Muhale, 9 July 1993; Cristina José Machava, 31 May 1993 and group of retirees, 4 June 1993.

[109] Anyone doubting that Africans understood the nature and extent of wage fraud perpetrated during the colonial era had only to listen to the lyrics of work songs, such as *Loluvaku Lanja!* : 'The Portuguese live by stealing our wages, heave that shovel heave!' Penvenne, *African workers*, 212.

was a sneak, bully and a spy: 'The settlers, they robbed you, but they didn't beat you up.'[110]

Although the difficulty and pace of cashew shelling work was intimidating, particularly for younger or slower workers, no one who worked in the factory under Tarana mentioned brutality on the factory floor. During the BNU era, however, Balbina Tinga and dozens of others recalled being 'beaten and kicked' if they did not make it through the gate on time, if they made a mistake or a poor choice.[111] Many echoed Maria Rosa Xavier Sitoe's sense of Roquette as mean spirited and sadistic: 'Roquette, that crazy little white man, he didn't sleep! I swear he got here at three in the morning. He stood on the first floor to watch and see who ate any cashew kernels. If he saw you eating a kernel, he made you drink a huge bottle of water – the whole thing. Even if you vomited you had to finish the whole water bottle.'[112]

The cashew shellers also freely admitted that they were perfectly capable of bringing trouble down on their own heads. Some *brincadeiras* got you punished but not fired. Everyone laughed when they recalled '*xinvemu*,' the factory discipline meted out to workers who were out drinking, usually around payday, when they were supposed to be at work. The factory police would 'march you right on to the factory floor and put you to work with your [drinking] glass still in your hand.'[113] People distinguished between discipline for one's own foolishness and a beating for tardiness.

Mention of *Malalanyana*, like mention of Roquette, evoked the cry 'Aiiii!' for good reason. Elina Mulungu alleged *Malalanyana* '...thought he was King of the Conselho! He beat many people...he was bad, truly BAD!' [114] Others recalled, 'You had to salute him, stand up when he entered and greet him. He beat many people![115] *Malalanyana's* police disciplined cashew shellers, demanding strict attendance, dismissing 'excuses' for missing work – excuses such as bereavement, childbirth, personal or family illness. Workers practiced conflation of person and practice. *Malalanyana* would not have deigned to administer a beating himself, but police beat people in accordance with his rules and whims, thus in the women's eyes *Malalanyana* beat many people.

The narrators thought his attitude and treatment of the cashew shellers and most other women was demeaning. Women accepted the requirement to register annually at the ACLM, but they resented the indignity of being treated 'like cattle.'[116] Unlike male migrants,

---

[110] OT, Ofélia Mbebe, 4 June 1993.
[111] OT, Balbina Tinga, 27 May 1993.
[112] OT, Maria Rosa Xavier Sitoe, 13 July 1993.
[113] Only one woman in the group drank heavily enough to have it noted on her record as a problem associated with a high rate of absenteeism. Quote from OT, Amelia Samuel Muzima, 27 May 1993.
[114] OT, Elina Mulungo, 4 June 1993.
[115] OT, Juliete Mulungu, 20 May 1993; Carolina Sigaugue, 24 May 1993; Elina Chivavele Mulungo, 4 June 1993; Marta Cau, 9 June 1993.
[116] OT, Jalane Machava Elmia, 7 June 1993.

women had to document permission from the appropriate male family members and administrative officials to authorize their presence in town and at work. Some women fled the very men whose authorization they needed, so their situation could be complicated. *Malalanyana* had no patience for complications, particularly those involving women. He unceremoniously dispatched women to get their papers in order – no matter what. Amélia Chiconela, Lídia Chabana, Elina Mulungu, and Marta Cau all complained that *Malalanyana* 'herded us *kwakwanana*, [rush, rush] as though we were cattle.'[117]

Like the cliché, 'hurry up and wait,' women's business at *Malalanyana*'s tended to be either glacially slow or *kwakwanana*, rush, rush. Like many first time registrants, Amélia Chiconela was intimidated by the journey to register at *Malalanyana*'s ACLM office. The office was in the heart of the cement city, the white residential and business area of Lourenço Marques. The place the women of Tarana called *Xilunguine*. Amélia, who had never seen a sidewalk, had no idea how to navigate in *Xilunguine*. With help from others, she eventually found the ACLM office, went in and took a seat. Paperwork was particularly difficult for women who did not read, write or speak Portuguese. None of the staff took the least notice of her presence, so she just sat there most of the day. Eventually Mozambicans who had come in to register realized she was just sitting there, so they helped her deal with registration. During that long day Amélia saw many women dispatched *kwakwanana*. The experience made her reluctant to get in line for her documents, but also determined that her documents would always be in order.[118]

Although *Malalanyana* was roundly despised for pettiness, arrogance, and the cruel punishments his regime oversaw, Elina Mulungu and others confirmed that he actually pursued some changes that served their interests. First, he took workplace inspections seriously, and although he eventually learned that he had little hope of forcing politically well-connected people to improve working conditions at their businesses, he nonetheless conducted inspections and submitted reports to the Department of Health. He inspected Cajú right after Tharani moved his operation to Chamanculo. He reported to the Department of Health that, whatever the parameters for a toxic / dangerous industry, he agreed with Cristina Muzamane, the smoke and dust at Tarana were just too heavy. He urged that Tharani be required to provide the more than 600 women who worked for him at that time with facemasks, clean drinking water and improved sanitation facilities.[119] The facemasks never materialized – right up to the present, but

[117] OT, Amélia Chiconela, 17 May 1993; Jalane Machava Elmia, 7 June 1993; Lídia Maluzana Chabana, 28 May 1993.

[118] OT, Amélia Chiconela, 17 May 1993.

[119] He also recommended appropriate clothing and protection for men working in caustic and toxic handling at the state-run port and railway facilities and better food and facilities at many urban construction sites, but was not able to enforce his recommendations. Penvenne, *African*

provision of clean drinking water and expansion of latrines in that era were appreciated.

Second, *Malalanyana* believed deeply in what the Portuguese called 'the moral obligation to work,' and he ran a tight ship. By 1950, according to his own reporting, he had almost completely ended what he called vagrancy among day labourers in the Conselho.[120] Whenever he had the opportunity he hauled women out of casual night labour in the street corner sex trade of Lagoas or Mafalala neighbourhoods and sent them to register for day labour at Cajú.[121] *Malalanyana* actually argued that the unreasonably low wages women received were '... one of the principal reasons for widespread prostitution which exists among natives in [Lourenço Marques].'[122] Women no doubt shared his conviction that their wages were unreasonably low and wished that he put as much effort into raising wages for women as he did into keeping women shelling cashews.

Finally, *Malalanyana* disliked having the cashew shellers muddle their ways into the Conselho to register as much as the women disliked doing it. He did not want women wandering around Lourenço Marques looking for the ACLM, arriving in dribs and drabs, standing in long lines, and a wasting the better part of a day's labour for their annual re-registration. In one of the few broadly praised policy changes of the era, he sent the ACLM staff out to Chamanculo for regularly scheduled on-site worker registrations and document renewals. Since the women largely associated the Native Affairs Offices at ACLM (*Malalanyana*), Munhuana (*Xipswahla*), and Benfica (*Nwamupfukwana*) with *palmatória* beatings and routine humiliation, they were grateful for the change.[123] Those small improvements aside, however, the workers argued that under the BNU regime, the work place climate at Cajú shifted from fairness, mutual respect and hard work to unfairness, brutality, petty control and disrespect.

The bonus / quota system: 'Nothing but trouble'[124]

The changes in personalities and tone were bad enough, but other BNU changes had more serious implications for daily life on the factory floor. In an early and callous shift, the BNU revised the workers' pay periods from weekly to monthly. People had to eat daily, and the poorest households found it difficult to hold food money aside for the week, let alone the

(contd) *Workers*, 135–40; Afonso Henriques Ivens Ferraz de Freitas to Delegado de Saude, 'Document of Inspection, 9 Nov. 1950, Cajú Industrial Lda,' ACLM, Red Caixa [RCx] DD, ACLM/ AHM.
[120] Afonso de Freitas to Chefe Gabinete da Repartição do Governo Geral, Lourenço Marques, 11 Dec. 1950, 11971/B/15 R/Cx DD, ACLM/ AHM.
[121] See Chapter 3 and OT, Carolina Sigaugue, 24 May 1993.
[122] Ferraz de Freitas, ACLM to RCNI, 29 Sept. 1949, 50/B/8, AHM.
[123] OT, Marie Celeste Chavane, 2 June 1993; Elina Chiavale Mulungo, 4 June 1993.
[124] OT, Carolina Sigaugue, 24 May 1993.

whole month. The change forced many people, not just the poorest, into the so-called *vale* system. A *vale* is a paper chit or debt note. When people ran out of cash they paid for their necessities with *vales* that stipulated what was to be repaid. When they received their salary at the end of the month they paid off their *vales*. Even if they were not charged interest on their *vales*, they were vulnerable to the merchants who held them.[125] Without cash, people were restricted to buying at a *cantina* rather than purchasing fresher, cheaper food in the so-called 'spontaneous' or 'clandestine' street markets that proliferated along the usual work routes in the city's poorer neighbourhoods from the 1960s.[126] Credit was very difficult for street vendors who, like the cashew shellers, depended upon their daily earnings. Chapter 4 analyses how the change in pay schedule disrupted workers' household strategies to leverage their salaries.

The most important 'factory floor' change workers faced after Tarana's departure was also related to payment, and was much more serious than the shift to monthly payment. The BNU implemented a daily production target tied to payment of one's full salary – the familiar piecework system. Although it was introduced under the guise of a bonus system to reward productive workers, the workers claimed that the production targets were more accurately quotas to penalize workers who did not meet them. The quota system, like the ubiquitous practice of discounts to African cashew producer / sellers, broadly constituted wage fraud. The new management defined the workers' base daily task for full payment at such a difficult level that even experienced women struggled to complete it in a single day.[127] The quota task was different for each section of the factory, but was essentially a minimum number of cans of nuts processed (shelled / peeled / cleaned and sorted) per day.

Women could only punch or mark (*marcar*) their pay card when they had completed the base daily task, confirming that they completed the day's work for full pay. If they couldn't complete the base, they had to clean up (*arrumar*), set the nuts aside and go home without registering the day's work. They would then try the next day or in subsequent days to complete the task so that they could be credited for one full day. When they managed to complete the base task and mark their pay card, they were paid for one day only, not for the extra days it took them to accomplish the basic daily task. Depending upon the worker's skill, the flow of production and the quality of the nuts, it could take three to five full day shifts to complete one base daily task. After the task system went into effect most workers regularly failed to punch their pay card for all work days in the month. The practical effect of the system for the great majority of women was a deduction in the base legal pay, not an increase.

---

[125] OT, Cristina Muzamane, 24 May 1993.

[126] See Chapter 4 for the *vale* system, *cantinas*, and so-called clandestine markets.

[127] Quotas tied to full pay continue to be a point of contention among Mozambican cashew shellers to the present as illustrated by the strike at the Olam plant in Nampula. Joseph Hanlon, 'Cashew Strike 2011,' News Reports and Clippings, *Mozambique*, 182 (11 June 2011) http://www.open.ac.uk/technology/mozambique/ Accessed 4 May 2015.

Thousands of women worked their full shifts every day for the month, but if they did not meet the base daily task each day they did not earn the minimum salary for industrial waged labour that was their legal due.[128]

The full monthly cash wage for cashew shellers – the wage they received if they successfully met the quota every day in the month was the city's legal minimum monthly wage for industrial labour. It was slowly increased from 240.00 *escudos* in 1950 to 245.00 in 1958. As part of general labour reforms in the early 1960s it jumped to 330.00, and finally to accommodate for inflation it was raised to 440.00 in the late 1960s. Strikes at the cusp of independence pushed wages higher, but throughout the late colonial era the best women at Tarana could hope to earn was the legal minimum wage. No one confirmed that her salary was enhanced through the bonus system.

The legal minimum earned by women at Cajú was the same wage paid to male workers conscripted for municipal and state public works. The state could only pay its male conscripts that low a cash wage because the men's pay packet also included room, board, blankets and uniforms at no cost to the worker. Employers also often defrauded the conscript's of their legal minimums by providing very poor quality blankets, soap, and uniforms, rotten food and substandard housing. Nonetheless, the state workers received room, board, clothing and bedding in addition to their minimum cash wage, whereas the cashew shellers had to buy food and clothing and pay rent out of the same minimum wage.[129]

Only domestic servants earned lower legal monthly cash wages than the cashew workers. Like the municipal conscripts, domestic servants received room and board on top of their pay, and those who received the lowest pay were usually boys and girls, too young and inexperienced to be hired in other areas. The cashew shellers did heavy industrial labour in a toxic industry, yet they often did not even receive industrial legal minimum wages, despite having worked full shifts for the full month.

In fact the bonus / quota system disadvantaged workers in multiple and insidious ways. Carolina Sigougau scoffed at the very idea that the quota system was a production incentive or bonus: 'it was nothing but trouble.'[130] First, the workforce paid the price for all kinds of problems that were out of their control. The availability, humidity and quality of the raw nuts influenced the work pace throughout the process. Workers 'ate' the cost of experimentation with mechanization. If the machines broke down, if the nuts were of poor quality or not properly heated, humidified or dried, the hand processing at every subsequent stage was

---

[128] OT, Joana Chilaula, 20 May 1993; Carolina Sigaugue, 24 May 1993; Celeste Mpendane, 13 July 1993; Amélia Samuel Muzima, 24 May 1993; Maria Argentina Mabica, 27 May 1993; Angelica Nequsse Pacute, 31 May 1993; Elena F. Machava, 26 May 1993; Marta Honwana, 31 May 1993; Maria Celeste Chavane, 2 June 1993 all discussed the quota system at length. Sheldon, *Pounders of Grain*, found a similar situation in Beira's cashew factories, 46, 49.
[129] On the poor quality of food, shelter, blankets, soap and uniforms for municipal contract labour see Penvenne, *African Workers*, 135–140.
[130] OT, Carolina Sigaugue, 24 May 1993.

compromised.[131] Even if people worked quickly, they could not control the pace: if people in shelling were slow or sent forward badly shelled nuts to peeling, if the peelers were slow, workers in sorting were compromised, and on and on. The connectivity of the work process is unavoidable, but the high daily quota meant that the basic wage of people throughout was compromised. If women had earned the legal minimum basic wage for each full day worked, with a wage bonus on top if they could manage it, that would have been an entirely different matter.

Second, inexperienced workers, like Celeste Mpendane who began work at age eleven, were the most vulnerable to quota related wage reductions. Despite struggling mightily, she often failed to make her quota. Carolina Rafael Cau typically had 5 or 6 days discounted each month, but Angelica Nequisse had a much harder time, often earning less than half the monthly minimum wage due to task discounts.[132] Women in the selection area had to turn in 12 tins of cleaned sorted nuts a day. Maria Celeste Chavana often managed no more than 6 to 9, so seldom earned her full pay.[133] Even an experienced veteran like Joana Tinga Chilaule who first joined Tarana at the Jardim de Gouveia sometimes took three days to *marcar* under the BNU system if something was wrong with the machines.[134] The ACLM registration records only indicated the minimum wage women were supposed to receive monthly, not what they actually earned. Colonial era archives at Cajú went missing, so what seems to have been a widespread practice of wage fraud is only documented here by the preponderance of oral testimony and corroboration from testimony in Beira.[135]

Third, the quota system gave supervisors increased leverage and excuses to discipline a workforce that needed to claim a full day's wage. When Amélia Samuel Muzima did not manage to *marcar* in the peeling area, she and others were 'punished' with a stint of manual shelling at the boiler's mouth in *djamangwana*.[136] Some women claimed that supervisors only allowed people to *marcar* if workers courted them by giving them headscarves, buying them coca-colas, cakes or breakfast foods to curry their favor.[137] The quota system facilitated abuses by supervisors to exploit vulnerable workers. The women complained they had to find 'a way of paying them [supervisors] to pay you.'[138]

---

[131] OT, Celeste Marcos Mpendane, 13 July 1993.
[132] OT, Angelica Nequisse Pacute, 31 May 1993; Carolina Rafael Cau, 31 May 1993.
[133] OT, Maria Celeste Chavane, 2 June 1993.
[134] OT, Joana Tinga Chilaule, 20 May 1993.
[135] OT, Joana Tinga Chilaule, 20 May 1993; Carolina Sigaugue, 24 May 1993; Amélia Samuel Muzima, 27 May 1993; Maria Argentina Mabika, 27 May 1993; Carolina Rafael Cau, 31 May 1993; Angelica Nequisse Pacute, 31 May 1993; Sheldon, *Pounders of Grain*, 46, 49.
[136] OT, Amélia Samuel Muzima, 27 May 1993.
[137] OT, Maria Argentina Mabica, 27 May 1993; Joana Massacaira, 24 May 1993; Joana Uaichele, 21 May 1993; Raquelina Machava, 21 May 1993; Angelica Nequisse Pacute, 31 May 1993.
[138] OT, Maria Argentina Mabica, 27 May 1993; Joana Massacaira, 24 May 1993; Joana Uaichele, 24 May 1993; Raquelina Machava, 21 May 1993; Angelica Nequisse Pacute, 31 May 1993; Elena Machava, 26 May 1993.

Young women who were newly arrived in town might be particularly desperate to be paid because they had not yet secured shelter. They might also be inexperienced enough to find it difficult to *marcar*, and were therefore vulnerable to demands from their supervisors. Although comparative literature suggests scholars should anticipate sexual abuse of such vulnerable girls and women, I had not anticipated harassment from a lesbian supervisor. Laurinda, a BNU era supervisor in the sorting area was notorious for molesting young girls. Elena Faustina Machava, one of the few *tinumerini*, recalled, 'I worked in Laurinda's section. She was the supervisor who used to feel up the young workers.'[139]

Laurinda also had what people called her 'ways'. Under threat of making women *arrumar* their work day after day, she made people buy her breakfast or a headscarf. Elena recalled, 'On weekends we had to carry water, and wash her clothes or else we couldn't *marcar* on Monday. Not everyone knew about Laurinda's sexual *brincadeiras*, but those who did made little of it. The gist was that the girls she molested were smarter to let Laurinda have her 'way' with them than to spend their weekends doing Laurinda's laundry and hauling her water.[140] Chapter 4 makes it clear that, depending upon their age and the number of children in their households, women had quite enough of their own work to do at the weekend. Laurinda was denounced by the workers' production councils set up after independence. She left the factory in disgrace.[141] In sum, the daily quota system was certainly not an incentive or bonus. Carolina Sigaugue was right – it was nothing but trouble.

Women quickly learned to identify who and what made trouble and to do what they could to avoid it. Sometimes jealousy and intrigue set women against one another within sections. Sometimes one section would posture against other sections for a too fast or too slow work pace. But on the whole, socializing among women within a section was more common. Women recalled sharing out the remaining day's work in their section so that everyone could complete the task, mark their quota and leave at the same time. Women in the sorting and packing areas had the best chance to accomplish that goal. They encouraged one another to keep up a fast pace so that they could finish on time, return home and take care of their families.[142]

---

[139] OT, Elena Machava, 26 May 1993.
[140] OT, Elena Machava, 26 May 1993; Marta Elise Honwana, 31 May 1993; Joana Tinga Chilaule, 20 May 1993; Rosalina Tembe, 19 May 1993.
[141] OT, Elena Machava, 26 May 1993.
[142] OT, Group of retirees, 4 June 1993, OT, Elena Machava, 26 May 1993.

Contrasting perspectives on price, pay, policy and production

Chapter 1 closed with the conclusions drawn from Parente and Neto's 1972 expert report on the cashew industry. The report considered the cashew economy from cashew harvesting and marketing by farmers to commercial shelling and export by the many companies up and running at the peak of colonial Mozambique's cashew exporting era. In 1973 the Sul do Save cashew shelling factories employed some 9,400 of the industry's total labour force of about 17,600 people. Those numbers were clearly a drop in the bucket in comparison with the Indian shelling industry, but they were important in Mozambique. If we look at Mozambique's industrial employment in the decade from 1960 to 1970, taking 1960 figures as the base of 100, overall industrial labour increased to 155 by 1970, whereas labour within the cashew industry increased to 490.[143] Until the report's closing section Parente and Neto scarcely mentioned the labour force in this labour-intensive industry. The report basically ignored 17,600 people.

In the closing section, however, the authors claimed that the factors that cashew industrialists in Mozambique most often cited regarding the industry's limitations were the low productivity, high absenteeism and instability of the industry's workforce. That would seem to be a direct contradiction of Rosa Joaquim Tembe's claim about the efforts of the workforce. It was also at odds with the municipal labour registration statistics that revealed an unusually stable labour force at Cajú. Indeed everything Parente and Neto had to say about workers was strongly contradicted by worker testimony.

Citing a long outdated study of absenteeism and instability among African labourers on the African continent in general, not African workers in the cashew industry in Mozambique in particular, the authors asserted that '...very high levels of absenteeism and turnover among workers [were] common throughout the African continent.' They concluded:

> It is clear that native men and women are not accustomed to any kind of regular and constant labour; the usual pattern being one of work periods alternating with rest periods. Since natives can subsist without recourse to wage labour, given the system of communal living among the tribes, and given the very low level of their ambitions and expectations, one notes that the value of their salaries is actually of secondary importance in this matter; indeed sometimes the highest rates of absenteeism exist among the groups who earn the highest salaries.[144]

The quote reflected the clichés of an earlier era and certainly was a profound misunderstanding of the cashew shellers' ambitions,

---

[143] Anna Lindberg, *Modernization and Effeminization*; Bessa Ribeiro, 'Sistema mundial,' 196–7.
[144] Parente and Neto, 'A Agro-Indústria de Cajú,' 67.

expectations, experiences, wages and reasons for absenteeism. The final assertion that higher wages might actually correlate with higher rates of absenteeism was particularly absurd and troubling. The authors had apparently spoken with cashew industrialists in Mozambique, but not with the industry's labour force. As was typical of other reports of that era, they might blame that on the women's inability to speak Portuguese, rather than their inability to speak Changana.

Parente and Neto followed that broad and wildly off-base generalization with the allegation that, despite management's offer of a 'bonus for good attendance,' sometimes only 1,500 to 2,000 of Cajú's 5,000 registered workers in Chamanculo actually showed up for work.[145] The alleged absenteeism and instability at Cajú Industrial de Moçambique certainly did not correlate with high wages, but rather with the lowest wages and among the worst conditions in the city.[146] By 1973 two decades of experience confirmed that women at Tarana worked shift after shift, year after year, despite the below-minimum wages. The municipal labour force records clearly documented that the cashew workers were among the city's most stable and most poorly paid labourers. Chapter 4 below demonstrates that women at Cajú Industrial did miss work, but certainly not because they received high wages. They missed work because they or their children were ill, a new child was born or a family member died.

Had Parente and Neto checked the Chamanculo or ACLM records or interviewed workers at the Chamanculo or Machava factories they would come away with a markedly different picture. Parente and Neto's report was otherwise very detailed and professional. The fact that they concluded that prices paid to farmers and salary levels paid to workers didn't really matter, suggests they either dismissed or fundamentally misunderstood the interests and experiences of the farmers and workers upon whom the industry depended. Their expert report claimed that worker absenteeism and instability comprised a major barrier to the industry's future. It did so without any contemporary evidence and no substantive exploration of the links between absenteeism and the conditions of life and labour experienced by the industrial workforce.

The law required Mozambican farmers to receive the minimum price for their cashew nuts, to be paid in cash and promptly, yet Parente and Neto confirmed that was not the case for southern farmers. Instead, the buyers enjoyed the privilege to discount the price, simply assuming the inferior quality of the cashew nuts.[147] The low price paid to farmers was

---

[145] Parente and Neto, 'A Agro-Indústria de Cajú,' 67.
[146] Parente and Neto do not name the company, but they say it has 5,000 workers registered, so it had to be Cajú Indústrial.
[147] Bessa Ribeiro noted the tensions around the quality of Sul do Save nuts, but located it between the rural merchants and the factory, rather than the farmers and the rural merchants – the tensions clearly went up the chain, but the farmers took the initial discount, and often with no recourse, Bessa Ribeiro, 'Sistema Mundial,' 197; Parente and Neto, 'A Agro-Indústria de Cajú,' 37–38.

alleged not to matter very much because they had 'minimal subsistence needs,' and would not produce beyond those. That implied that the more you paid farmers the less they would produce. They would just meet their minimal needs more quickly and stop producing. That was simply wrong. The increased marketing of household produce over these decades demonstrates the opposite. If people thought a crop was profitable they invested in that crop.

The same wrong-headed logic was alleged for workers. Since they '...can subsist without recourse to wage labour... and given the very low level of their ambitions and expectations,' it scarcely would matter to raise their wages because '...salary levels are actually of secondary importance.'[148] That implied that the more workers earned the higher their rates of absenteeism and instability – thus higher pay was actually a disincentive for workers to work, and higher payments to farmers were a disincentive for them to produce. How very convenient for those who wished to purchase products and labour at below minimum rates. This discourse reflected assumptions embedded in the press and colonial reports of the era, and had no basis in fact.

What the women of Tarana referred to as a quota system, Parente and Neto framed, reflecting the BNU reports, as a bonus system to encourage production targets. It supposedly allowed conscientious or highly skilled workers like Mahochi to boost their wages. Parente and Neto did not mention or seem to know that, more often than not, the system depressed rather than enhanced wage levels. Wage fraud was pervasive and broadly acknowledged by the colonial inspectors charged with its prevention. The law allowed employers to discount cash wage obligations to workers through the provision of goods, housing and food in lieu of cash, and to discount lost days work or damaged tools.[149] State inspections broadly corroborated worker testimony that employers exaggerated absences, tool damage and grossly skimped on their 'in kind' obligations, providing unhealthy, rotten, and insufficient food, poor quality uniforms, thin blankets, and unsuitable housing. Inspectors' confidential reports repeatedly complained that the food, clothing and housing provided to workers by the state, the municipality and well-connected private contractors were among the worst examples of labour abuse in the city.[150] Quota systems served the same purpose on plantations and commercial farms, providing a loophole for employers to evade paying workers the minimum they were due by law.[151]

---

[148] Parente and Neto, 'A Agro-Indústria de Cajú,' 67.

[149] Parente and Neto, 'A Agro-Indústria de Cajú,' 59.

[150] Schaedel, 'Last Phase,' 25–26, Michel Cahen, 'O fundo ISANI do Arquivo Histórico de Moçambique: uma fonte importante da história contemporânea do colonialismo português,' *Arquivo*, No. 7 (April 1990): 63–82.

[151] Schaedel, 'Last Phase,' 25ff; José Cláudio Mandlate, 'A Companhia do Buzi em transição: uma abordamento de mão de obra e da estrutura de produção agrícola da empresa, 1961–1991' (Maputo: UEM, 2004).

The women explained their steady work history at Cajú saying they '... had nowhere else to go.'[152] Having the wherewithal to care for themselves and their children was fundamental to an adult woman's sense of dignity. Securing that wherewithal was what drove them to wield the hoe of the city: to rise before dawn, carry out their household obligations, walk hours to and from work, struggle to meet their task quotas, and return to feed and care for their families. Luis Guila Muhale confirmed that women usually only missed work when they had important family demands. Workers in rural cashew shelling factories were apt to miss work during the planting season because the food crops they planted were a necessity for their family's survival. In Lourenço Marques, although about 80 per cent of urban women farmed in 1940s, rapid urban development meant that available land was increasingly scarce, increasingly distant and transport was sufficiently expensive that few women of Cajú worked a *machambas* for more than a weekend subsidy.[153]

The women of Tarana missed work because they or their children were sick. Absence was linked to illness and illness was strongly correlated with poverty, inadequate nutrition, poor housing, inadequate clean water and bad sanitation.[154] Absenteeism at Tarana certainly was not linked with higher wages. In short, Parente and Neto concluded that the 'factory for women' and other cashew shelling factories had high rates of absenteeism and labour instability because the labour force was not accustomed to steady labour, did not need wages to subsist, had low ambitions and expectations, and were insensitive to salary levels. Their assumptions were a far cry from the patterns that emerged in oral testimony for this project.

While working under Tarana the women had high ambitions and expectations. Tarana both shared and inspired their ambitions and expectations. His business plan counted on them further developing skilled shelling, and he committed himself to improving their wages and productivity. Under pressure he also enhanced the quality of their working conditions. Under the BNU the women endured, struggling to secure their full pay and assert their personal dignity. They got up each day to go to work, to secure the full value of their wages and aspired to be treated decently.

The workers were not in a position to reshape the factory – as John Lonsdale put it, they asserted agency in tight corners.[155] But their

[152] OT, Cristina Miambu, 26 May 1993.
[153] Women's strategies for food production are discussed in more detail in Chapters 4 and 5. Only 7 per cent of the participants in Rita-Ferreira's survey had worked *machambas*, 'Os Africanos,' 300. OT, Leia Nhavene, 17 May 1993; Julieta Mulungu, 20 May 1993; Maria Celeste Chavane, , 2 June 1993; Marta Honwana, 31 May 1993; Cristina Pelembe, 17 May 1993; Amélia Muzima, 27 May 1993; Rosalina Tembe, 19 May 1993; Cristina Miambu, 26 May 1993; Joana Massacaira, 12 July; Raquelina Machava, 12 July1993. Kathleen Sheldon, 'Machambas in the City; Urban Women and Agricultural Work in Mozambique,' *Lusotopie* (1999) 121–40.
[154] Santos, 'Avaliação Nutricional.' 332.
[155] Lonsdale, 'Agency in Tight Corners.'

collaboration with Tarana and his staff made a difference – to him and to them. They named people as it suited them. They laughed with and appreciated the people they felt valued them and the work they did. In order to feed themselves and their children, however, they hunkered down and patiently endured the hard times under people they feared and despised. Rosa Joaquim Tembe's claim that the national cashew shelling industry grew from their strength was clearly correct, whereas Parente and Neto's claim that the more you paid African workers the less they cared about showing up at work was just as clearly nonsense. Furthermore, Tharani's faith in the efficiency and productivity of skilled hand labour over mechanized labour for the production of whole top quality dessert nuts endured in the period and has proved to be well placed to the present.[156]

---

[156] With reference to the new cashew shelling plant in Sul do Save's Manjacaze area at the turn of the twenty-first century Bessa Ribeiro noted that skilled hand labour brought better results with cashews than any of the technological innovations to date, producing more whole kernels per kilo shelled than mechanical shelling, 'Sistema mundial, '396–7. See also the Epilogue.

3 Migration
Pathways from Poverty to Tarana

> To a small criticism she responds that she can employ herself on the Incomati or Maragra [sugar plantations]. And she will just go. The home is destroyed. Many now live divorced because the women have gone to work to repay the *lobolo*. These women do not know that a woman is meant to be married and to die with her husband. We, the husbands, are those who know how a woman should work. But at this moment they are employed. The Inkomati is filled with workers and they have abandoned their husbands.[1]

Women sang about their dilemmas and the burdens they faced, but they also negotiated with men and children within households for control of labour, access to resources and services. Fathers, husbands and in-laws had customary rights to claim women's labour, but never without boundaries of support and protection. Paid hoe labour in the sugar or rice fields along the Incomati River, referred to by the irate husband above, was also hard work, but the wages women earned there also went into their own hands. Poor women increasingly shifted from seasonal to more full time labour on these plantations. Indeed, women in unsupported or abusive situations concluded that they, not their husbands, were the ones who knew how they should work. Thousands used the money they earned to solve some of their problems, problems that unfortunately might well involve their husbands.

Men's ability as spouses, fathers, siblings and uncles to provide for and protect their families had a great impact on women throughout this period. Women did not 'destroy their homes and abandon their husbands' because of 'a small criticism' or out of sheer bravado. The evidence simply does not support that. Women knew the price they would pay for their decision to leave – nothing about that price was small.[2] It was only when a spouse or parent died, when spouses, parents or others failed to support women or actively abused them, only when women were stretched to breaking point or feared retaliation did they

---

[1] Inkomati is a variant spelling of Incomati, both appear in this quote. Sherilynn Young, quoting an unidentified man interviewed in Chobela Sul do Save 18 July 1975, 'Women in Transition,' 15.

[2] Jean Allman and Victoria Tashjian's book captures the sense of women having limits to what they are willing to suffer or have their children suffer, *I Will Not Eat Stone: A Woman's History of Colonial Asante* (Portsmouth: Heinemann, 2000).

decide to leave.[3] Leaving meant repaying *lobolo* and perhaps having to leave one's children. If women took their children, they also assumed full responsibility to provide for and protect them. Despite having a Catholic mission education, a marriage confirmed with bridewealth, and a healthy son, Avelina Manjane found herself destitute when her husband did not return from work in South Africa: 'When my husband abandoned me and my baby I didn't even have a *nhete* (wrap) to carry my baby on my back.' Like many other women, she made her way to Tarana to support herself and her son and to repay her bridewealth. Women repaid bridewealth out of a sense of fear and pride. If they were going to work on their own, they did not want claims on the product of their efforts from people who failed to support them. None of this was small – it was very big.

All families developed multiple and layered strategies to survive and prosper. The threat of forced labour for tax default shaped the parameters of all strategies right through this period. As explained below, men and women were differentially vulnerable to forced labour.[4] Some women turned from seasonal and occasionally forced labour to permanent day or contract labour on sugar and rice plantations; others tried to navigate advantage against disadvantage in the emerging Limpopo River settlement schemes, and still others heeded the advice when people told them, 'Go to Tarana. You will forget your suffering.'[5] This chapter first considers overall migration from rural Southern Mozambique to the larger region and the colonial state's overarching efforts to control Mozambican mobility and labour. It briefly considers accommodation patterns people developed to remain working the land and herding in the countryside, but then turns to the migration of women to Lourenço Marques. Who left? Why? How did they manage the journey?

The classic scholarly debate about migration from Southern Mozambique to South Africa and the broader region was initiated by American anthropologist Marvin Harris and Portuguese scholar / civil servant António Rita-Ferreira in the late 1950s.[6] Harris wanted to know why hundreds of thousands of Mozambican men from the region migrated clandestinely or with a contract for wage labour in South Africa. He laid out four reasons. First, Sul do Save's sandy soils and irregular rain-

---

[3] Fiction about women's lives in the colonial era portrayed molestation or abuse from shopkeepers, teachers, priests and other people in authority as the trigger for migration, especially among young women. Bento Sitoe, *Zabela: My Wasted Life*, [Translated by Renato Matusse] (Harare: Baobab Books, 1996.); Muianga, *Meledina;* Honwana, *O Algodão e o Ouro*. OT Avelina Manjane.

[4] Bridget O'Laughlin, 'Proletarianisation, Agency and Changing Rural Livelihoods: Forced Labour and Resistance in Colonial Mozambique,'*JSAS*, Vol. 28, No. 3 (Sep. 2002): 511–530; Penvenne, *African Workers*, Chapters 4 and 7.

[5] Many women said this, but for example, OT, Amélia Malanguane, 27 May 1992; Felizmeta Namburo, 9 June 1993; Julieta Mulungu, 20 May 1993.

[6] See Chapter 2 note 9 and the bibliography for full references. Harris, 'Labour Emigration'; Harris, 'Reply to Sr. Rita-Ferreira'; Rita-Ferreira, 'Comments on a Study by Marvin Harris'; Rita-Ferreira, 'Comments on Marvin Harris's Reply'; Rita-Ferreira, 'O Movimento Migratório'; Rita-Ferreira, 'Oscilação do Trabalhador'.

fall limited agro-pastoral growth. The hunger season was an 'annual ordeal' that contributed to family instability and social differentiation.[7] In such conditions, migration was a core famine strategy particularly for disadvantaged families. Second, women were largely tasked with agriculture, although men might supervise production by their wife or wives. Men worked with cattle, built and repaired grain silos, cattle enclosures and homes, but with so much household productive and reproductive labour accomplished by women, men's periodic absence did not directly threaten a household's economic integrity. Third, men who were disadvantaged by birth order placement or the ranking of their polygynous parents aspired to accrue the bridewealth necessary to secure adult status and build a household through waged labour. Finally, the Portuguese administration considered most of what men did to be idleness, and idle males of working age were subject to conscription for state or private contract labour. Faced with the threat of conscription if not employed for wages, men pursued waged labour for the higher wages offered in South Africa or Lourenço Marques.[8]

António Rita-Ferreira contested ethnographic details, but otherwise agreed with much of what Harris wrote. He denied that the threat of conscription drove men to seek employment. Rather he argued that Sul do Save men were attracted by South African and Mozambican urban culture, and women preferred men who had confirmed their masculinity through the rite of passage of a South African mine contract.[9] Harris refuted the latter point, claiming that '...the preference expressed by the young women derives simply from the fact that the man who has worked at the mines has demonstrated his superiority over those suitors too stupid, frightened or lazy to avoid government impressment.'[10] The extensive literature on South African mine migration from Southern Mozambique and the larger area has contributed important textures to many of these core points.[11]

---

[7] Harris, 'Labour Emigration', 53.
[8] Harris, 'Labour Emigration', 60.
[9] Rita-Ferreira, 'Comments on a Study by Marvin Harris'; Rita-Ferreira, 'Comments on Marvin Harris's Reply'; Rita-Ferreira, 'A Oscilação do Trabalhador Africano.'
[10] Harris,'Labour Emigration,' 60.
[11] The key works for the broader region include: Charles van Onselen, *Chibaro: African Mine Labour in Southern Rhodesia, 1900–1930* (London: Pluto Press, 1976); Francis Wilson, *Labour in the South African Gold Mines 1911–1969* (Cambridge: Cambridge Univ. Pr. 1972); Ruth First *et al. Black Gold*; Jonathan Crush, Alan Jeeves and David Yudelman, *South Africa's Labour Empire: A History of Black Migrancy to the Gold Mines* (Boulder: Westview, 1991); Jeeves, *Migrant Labour in South Africa's Mining Economy; The Struggle for the Gold Mines' Labour Supply, 1890–1920* (Kingston: McGill University Press,1985); Jeeves and Jonathan Crush, eds, *White Farms – Black Labour; The State and Agrarian Change in Southern Africa, 1910–1950* (Portsmouth: Heinemann, 1991); Yudelman and Jeeves, 'New Labour Frontiers for Old: Black Migrants to the South African Gold Mines, 1920–1985,' *JSAS*, 13 (1986): 101–24; Patrick Harries, 'Slavery, Social Incorporation and Surplus Extraction: The Nature of Free and Unfree Labour in South-East Africa,' *JAH* 22 (1981): 309–330; Harries, '"A Forgotten Corner of the Transvaal," Reconstructing the History of a Relocated Community through Oral History and Song,' in Belinda Bozzoli, ed. *Class, Community and Conflict: South African Perspectives* (Johannesburg: Ravan, 1987): 93–134; Harries, *Work, Culture and Identities;* T. Dunbar Moodie with Vivienne Ndatshe,

Journalists and short story writers also linked the region's climate and gendered migration patterns. Albino Magaia conveyed his interpretation with the image of the mid-day's hot sun in a deep blue sky amidst puffy white 'fair weather' clouds. He imagined the clouds were laughing at the farmers in the fields below trying to coax corn and sweet potatoes from the region's sandy, stingy soils. Magaia's clouds mocked the farmers, refusing to give up their rain – rain that could stave off their hunger. Hunger, Magaia concluded drove men to work in South Africa's mines and women to prostitute themselves in the country's towns and cities. Neither the miners nor the prostitutes earned easy money. At least when Lourenço Marques prostitutes earned their 'nightly bread' it was secure in their pocket.[12] The threat of drought meant little was certain or secure for the farmers of Southern Mozambique. Scores of women at Cajú also knew that their monthly salary could be discounted and they might have to borrow against it to make it through the month, but it was also secure in their pockets and it was often all that kept them from earning 'nightly' rather than monthly bread.[13]

Gendered rural migration:
Natives and agency in late colonial Mozambique

The men and women of Sul do Save were part of a very large moving tapestry – waves and layers of migration that were often fueled and accompanied by violence; the violence of drought, floods, apartheid, armed insurgencies, forced labour, forced cultivation, domestic violence and the deeply embedded violence of hunger and poverty.

[contd] *Going for Gold: Men, Mines and Migration* (Berkeley: Univ. of California Press, 1994); Corrado Tornimbeni, 'Migrant Workers and State Boundaries: Reflections on the Transnational Debate from the Colonial Past in Mozambique.' *Lusotopie* (Paris: Éditions Karthala, 2004):107–20; Joel Maurício das Neves [Tembe], 'Economy, Society and Labour Migration in Central Mozambique, 1930– ca. 1965: A Case Study of Manica Province,' PhD thesis (London: University of London, School of Oriental and African Studies, 1998); Diana Jeater, 'No Place for a Woman: Gwelo Town, Southern Rhodesia, 1894–1920,' *JSAS* 26, 1 (2000): 29–42; Jeater *Marriage, Perversion, and Power: the Construction of Moral Discourse in Southern Rhodesia, 1894–1930* (New York: Oxford University Press, 1993); Elizabeth Schmidt, *Peasants, Traders, and Wives: Shona women in the history of Zimbabwe, 1870–1939* (Portsmouth: Heinemann, 1992); Penvenne, *African Workers*; Bozzoli, *Women of Phokeng*; Sheldon, *Pounders of Grain*; Sean Redding, *Sorcery and Sovereignty: Taxation, Power and Rebellion in South Africa, 1880–1963* (Athens: Ohio University Press, 2006); Sharon Stichter, *Migrant Labour* (New York: Cambridge University Press, 1985); Fion de Vletter, 'Migration and Development in Mozambique: Poverty, Inequality and Survival' in Jonathan Crush and Bruce Frayne eds., *Surviving on the Move: Migration, Poverty and Development in Southern Africa* (Cape Town: Idasa Publishing House, 2010): 146–163; Stephen C. Lubkemann, 'The Transformation of Transnationality among Mozambican Migrants in South Africa.' *Canadian Journal of African Studies* 34, 1 (2000): 41–64; Luís António Covane, *O Trabalho Migratório e a Agricultura no Sul de Moçambique (1920–1992)* (Maputo: Promédia, 2001).

[12] Albino Magaia with photographs by Ricardo Rangel, 'Prostituição, Tráfico Sexual Mata a Fome,' *Tempo*, No. 211 (13 Outubro 1974): 18–19. See also Raul Honwana. *O Algodão e o Ouro* (Maputo: Associaçião dos Escritores Moçambicanos, 1995.)

[13] OT, Joana Massacaira, Maria Rosa Xavier Sitoe, and Elina Chiavale Mulungu.

Migration was also fueled by the pursuit of many kinds of opportunities. More than elsewhere in Mozambique, migration from the South tied into the regional economy anchored in South Africa.

Although hundreds of thousands of men and women, moved for waged and forced labour and in pursuit of markets and education, the more general population movements in the region were linked with the making, unmaking and remaking of Southern African households.[14] Twentieth-century Southern African conscripts and job seekers were predominantly men and male youth, whereas the historical actors in motion among households were predominantly women, female youth and children. Historians, myself included, were slower to confirm that movement within the household, gift and informal economies was also labour migration. Like so much of women's life experience, their labour and migratory contributions did not quickly or easily attract scholarly attention or shape economic policy and models.[15]

Household formation and endurance was and remains very much about power, labour and resources: who controlled it, by what means, to what ends and against what resistance. Household, gift and informal economies contested and negotiated authority and claims over resources and labour every bit as much as the waged and state-subsidized conscript labour and formal market economies. Although control mechanisms and avenues for redress differed, physical force and pressure to feed oneself and one's children and to secure access to and management of resources shaped outcomes throughout. Family accommodation and alleviation strategies could be ritually masked, and thus difficult to observe and taboo to discuss.[16]

Women in the patrilineal virilocal cultures of southern Mozambique ideally moved from their father's to their husband's home upon

---

[14] Sean Redding's work brought this point home to me most forcefully, 'South African Women and Migration in Umtata, Transkei 1880–1935,' in Kathleen Sheldon, ed. *Courtyards, Markets, City Streets: Urban Women in Africa* (Boulder: Westview Press, 1996): 31–46.

[15] Some of the literature making this point is referenced in Chapters 4 and 5, but Benigna Zimba made this point explicitly in the title of her study of eighteenth and early nineteenth century trade in Southern Mozambique, *Mulheres Invisíveis: O género e as políticas comerciais no Sul do Moçambique, 1720–1830* (Maputo: Promédia, 2003). Aili Mari Tripp's work, *Changing the Rules* is essential with regard to urban areas.

[16] Pioneering work on family and household dynamics, urbanization and gender includes Jane Guyer, 'Household and Community in African Studies,' *ASR*, 24, 2/3 (1981): 87–137; Guyer and Pauline Peters, 'Conceptualizing the Household: Issues of Theory and Policy in Africa,' *Development and Change*, 18, 2 (April 1987):197–213; Meghan Vaughan, 'Which Family? Problems in the Reconstruction of the History of the Family as an Economic and Cultural Unit.' *JAH*, 24 (1983): 275–83; Iris Berger, 'Beasts of Burden' Revisited: Interpretations of Women and Gender in Southern African Societies,' in R.W. Harms, J.C. Miller, D.S. Newbury and M.D.Wagner, eds, *Paths toward the Past: African Historical Essays in Honor of Jan Vansina* (Atlanta: African Studies Association Press, 1994):123–141; Loforte, *Género e Poder*; Lubkemann, 'The Transformation of Transnationality'; Lindsay. *Working with Gender*; Catherine Coquery-Vidrovich, 'The Process of Urbanization in Africa: From the Origins to the Beginning of Independence,' *ASR*, 34,1 (1991): 1– 98; Catherine Coquery-Vidrovitch, 'Urban Cultures: Relevance and Context,' in Toyin Falola and Steven J. Salm, eds, *Urbanization and African Cultures* (Durham: Carolina Academic Press, 2005): 17–22; Tranberg Hansen and Vaa, 'Introduction,' *Reconsidering Informality*, 7–24.

marriage. That was the point at which they created their own *lar* or conjugal household. If a woman decided that her *lar* was unsustainable she left; sometimes returning to her father's lineage, sometimes to the protection of another family member, and sometimes she headed to town. By 1960, the capital's census revealed that divorced, separated and widowed African women living alone in town comprised nearly 15 per cent of the population.[17] Sometimes divorce freed women to migrate and sometimes it forced women to migrate – both avenues were important. Women's place within the layered and contested controls of patriarchy and the colonial legal system was a factor in their mobility. Mobility and labour investment of Mozambicans in the region was heavily controlled by the state in the colonial era, so that is our next consideration.

Raced and gendered labour control concepts

All Africans enjoyed narrow and skewed spaces in the Portuguese colonial state's documented consciousness and imagination. The lynchpin for understanding twentieth-century labour and social history in colonial southern Mozambique was the *indigenato*. The *indigenato* was the cumulative body of legislation and related practices developed by the Portuguese that defined who was to be considered a native, an *indígena*, and then legislated *indígenas* into significant disadvantage in virtually every category one can imagine – civil, commercial, social, political, military, labour.[18]

The *indigenato* was fundamentally gendered. The Portuguese articulated an *indígena* as a man. *Mulhers indígenas,*'native women,' were dependent components of social, cultural, economic and political spheres understood to be the domain of African men. As we heard from Luís Guila Muhale, Portuguese and Mozambican men broadly assumed that, in principle, African women worked within the family sector under the authority of an appropriate male – a *mulher sem dono* was a social threat. That assumption underpinned mobility controls exerted over women. For most of this period, unlike men, women required explicit permission from a man to relocate or travel outside their home district.

The laws, forms, regulations and relationships of the *indigenato* were often articulated and implemented by municipal and state officials in collaboration with employers. It was largely a process accomplished by men for men. The colonial administration understood that Mozambican women were important for any strategy to define and control Mozambican men. The *indigenato* was incrementally developed in early twentieth-century Lourenço Marques, shaped both by maleness and

---

[17] Rita-Ferreira, 'Os Africanos,' 131, 227, 249, 303–05.
[18] Penvenne, *African Workers*, p. 1, Chapter 4 and passim; O'Laughlin, 'Class and the Customary.'

urban conditions. For most of the colonial era the Portuguese broadly scripted African men as either implements for or impediments to the larger goals of the colonial project.[19]

From the first attempt to articulate native status, Africans contested the underpinning assumptions at many levels. By the early second decade of the twentieth century the Portuguese put forth a complementary category for Africans who had culturally assimilated to Portuguese language, education and professions, and would not submit to being *indígenas*. Again the legal, civil, political, commercial and labour scaffolding for this category was gendered male. *Assimilados* were supposed to enjoy full Portuguese citizenship privileges, but the fact that black people had to undergo a tedious and expensive bureaucratic process to certify that they were worthy of Portuguese citizenship, whereas white Portuguese simply had to be born was a complication from the outset.[20]

Assimilado, like *indígena*, was essentially a male form. Although *assimilada* was the term for an assimilated woman, in the great majority of cases, men petitioned for the legal status of *assimilado* on the basis of their educational and social criteria, and women attained the status as the wife of a male petitioner. Women were expected to uphold the social criteria for assimilation in their *assimilado* husband's household.[21] By the early 1960s when both legal categories (*indígena* and *assimilado/assimilada*) were abolished in law only 1,658 *assimilados* were registered in the whole of Mozambique – a telling measure of the hollowness of the concept. At that time more than half the *assimilado* population lived in Sul do Save, with 136 of those registered in the municipality of Lourenço Marques.[22] Whereas the *indigenato* and constraints on *indígenas* were very important throughout the colonial era and were reflected in the narratives; assimilation emerged only as a leitmotif linked with social arrogance. According to Matilde Chiduza, '*Assimiladas* considered themselves different. We were dirty and they were white.' Elena Machava, whose education would have qualified her for assimilation, noted: '*Assimilados* were not equal to whites but they thought the ID card they carried allowed them to devalue their black

[19] Hedges, coord., *História de Moçambique*, esp. 97ff; Rita-Ferreira, 'Esboço Sociológico,' 116–17, 149, 171–2.
[20] Jeanne Marie Penvenne, '"We are all Portuguese!" Challenging the Political Economy of Assimilation, Lourenço Marques, 1870 to 1933,' in Leroy Vail, ed. *The Creation of Tribalism in Southern Africa* (Berkeley: University of California, 1989): 255–88.
[21] Thanks to Kathleen Sheldon for underscoring women's contributions to the maintenance of assimilated households. The gendered nature of assimilation was detailed in a *Voz de Zambezia* open letter written by José Roldão and reproduced in Direcção de Secretaria de Negócios Indígenas [DSNI] Informação 59/M/3 PF/ AC, 8 July 1959, signed by Pinto de Fonseca: 'O Estatuto dos Indígenas Portugueses e a Carta Aberta dirigida por José Roldão, a Sua Excia o Min. do Ultramar, publicada em *O Brado Africano*, 29 Junho de 1959.' The DSNI Informação inaccurately cited *O Brado Africano*.
[22] Confidencial Proc. M/3, 'Resultado do inquérito promovido pela circular no. 4461/ M/ 3 de 31 /10/1953 sôbre o número de casos de obtenção de assimilação ou cidadania, nos últimos 10 anos (1950–1960), DSNI, 10 Março 1962, signature illegible, ACLM.

brothers.' Elina Mulungu claimed they even disdained the common practice of bargaining with street sellers, saying simply, '... give it here and I'll pay you!'[23]

The *indigenato* targeted African men between mid-adolescence and late maturity; men who were essentially fit to work for or to contribute tax revenues to colonial or settler projects within Mozambique and to contribute foreign exchange to the colonial state through bureaucratic interventions regarding their work abroad. Able-bodied male labour was regularly referred to as though it were a commodity, like sisal and sorghum, or a factor of production, like fertilizer and hoes.[24] In many periods and places young and old, able and fragile men and women were conscripted and worked beyond their capacity – to the point of breaking their health and even to death.[25] They were forced to clear and maintain roads, railways and canals, work on settler plantations, plant the crops mandated by the state, and do any and every description of task that did not draw volunteer labour.

Mozambican men were not only commoditized and de-humanized, colonial sources framed them as a problem, *o problema de mão-de-obra indígena*, or as a 'question,' *a questão de mão-de-obra indígena*. The phrases, 'the problem of native labour,' and 'the question of native labour' were ubiquitous to the point that the words seemed indivisible.[26] The problem from the colonial perspective, of course, was that there were simply never enough Mozambicans willing to labour for the wages and under the conditions that the state and many settlers were willing to provide. The question was how to solve that problem, and into the 1960s the answer was conscripted contract labour backed up by prison labour or violent punishment.

In 1957 Native Affairs Officer and sociologist António Rita-Ferreira put it diplomatically: 'The term 'preference' [for jobs] is used here in a relative sense... the native who works, whether within his home locality or elsewhere within Mozambique, very often does so at the suggestion of the Administration.'[27] Two years later, L.M. Pinto da Fonseca, Rita-Ferreira's superior officer was less diplomatic in his confidential report on conditions for native labour. He confirmed that the conscript labour system still supplied on average over eighteen thousand workers annually to colonial agriculture and almost twenty thousand to industry. He

---

[23] OT, Matilde Chiduza, 27 May 1993; Elena Machava, 26 May 1993; Elina Chivavele Mulungu, 4 June 1993.

[24] José Rodrigues Júnior, *A Voz dos Colonos de Moçambique' (Inquérito)* (Lourenço Marques: Tip. 'Notícias,' 1945): 222–3, 230.

[25] Although gross over-working of conscripts was most pervasive in the early twentieth century, it persisted throughout the era of the *indigenato*, Penvenne, *African Workers*; Eric Allina, *Slavery by any other name; African Life under Company Rule in Mozambique* (Charlottesville, VA: University of Virginia Press, 2012); Hedges, *História de Moçambique*.

[26] Ismaal Alves da Costa referred to the 'age old' question of native labour: 'A Velhissima Questão de Mão de Obra Indígena,' *Lourenço Marques Guardian*, 15 and 21 January 1948; Rodrigues Júnior, *A Voz dos Colonos*, 222–3,231.

[27] António Rita-Ferreira, 'Esboço Sociológico,'153.

described the system as unjust, inefficient, obnoxious and intolerable. It prevented market conditions from bidding up wages, and penalized employers willing to pay above the minimum wage, while supporting '...the worst employers [who] pay the absolute minimum, requisition the most labour and make the most trouble when the workers resist the poor conditions.'[28]

From the late nineteenth century to the 1960s, families could be conscripted for labour for nonpayment of taxes, failure to comply with their 'moral obligation to work,' or simply being in the wrong place at the wrong time when the government or Portuguese settlers needed workers.[29] Most men premised their labour strategies on escaping low wage forced contract labour – what everyone called *xibalu*, or *trabalho de graça*, unpaid labour.[30] From the 1940s adult men and women were responsible for payment of a head tax, and both could be sentenced to terms of *xibalu* for tax default. Men and women in poor families were regularly harassed for forced labour due to tax default. The head tax rate for women was set at half that for men because it was assumed that adult women were married. Perversely, the lower level of women's taxes and the assumption of marriage were marshalled by the state and employers as a reason to legislate and hold women's legal wages below those for men.[31]

By the early 1960s local, regional and international pressure was building for Portugal to institute labour reform. Armed insurgencies in all three of her African mainland colonies were the most compelling drivers for change. The *indigenato* remained economically useful for employers in Mozambique, but it had become a political liability.[32] Unfortunately, the reforms of the early 1960s were more about masking continuing control over the majority population than about genuine labour reform. Portugal replaced the despised *indigenato* with the so-called Code of Rural Labour. The new categories barely masked the prior system of white advantage and black disadvantage.[33] White workers kept their privileges through union membership and educa-

---

[28] Luciano Maia Pinto da Fonseca. Inspector Administrativo, 'Relatório da Direcção dos Serviços de Negócios Indígenas e da Curadoria Geral da Provincia de Moçaambique. Periodo de 7 Junho de 1958 á 31 Dezembro, 1959,' Fundo do Governor Geral, [FGG] 721, AHM.

[29] Penvenne, *African Workers*.

[30] Preferred orthography now is *xibalu*, variants include *shibalo*, *chibaru* and *xibalo*, Lopes, et al. *Moçambicanismos*, 148; Bento Sitoe, Narciso Mahumana, Pércida Langa, *Dicionário Ronga – Português* (Maputo: NELIMO – Centro de Estudos de Linguas Moçambicanas, (2008): 348.

[31] Ferraz de Freitas, alleged that '...hundreds of women working in Lourenço Marques industry do not have husbands.' He argued that the unreasonably low wages women received were '...one of the principal reasons for widespread prostitution which exists among natives in the *concelho.*' ACLM to RCNI, 29 Sept. 1949, 50/B/8, AHM.

[32] Hedges, *História de Moçambique*, Ch. 4 and 5; Penvenne, 'A Tapestry of Conflict': O'Laughlin, 'Class and the Customary'; Amélia Neves de Souto,'As Reformas Coloniais Portuguesas na Década de 1960s e o Seu Impacto em Moçambique,' unpublished paper, UEM, May 1993. Thanks to the author for access and permission to cite.

[33] Schaedel, 'Last Phase of Colonial Rule.'

tional or technical qualifications that were essentially inaccessible to the majority black population.[34] The words shifted more than the experience; a former native (*indígena*) was briefly renamed an uncivilized labourer (*mão-de-obra nãocivilizada*). That choice was quickly recognized as a blunder, but was replaced by another negative placement – uncivilized became unqualified (*mão-de-obra não-qualificado*) or non-unionized (*mão-de-obra não-sindicato*). Again, these were essentially male categories that defined the majority population by what they were not, rather than what they were.

Rural or urban workers who did not qualify for membership in labour unions or staff positions, looked and were treated very much like their *indígena* predecessors. Within the growing urban and peri-urban industries, unqualified, non-unionized workers ate in separate canteens, not in the factory dining hall, and had no right to the privileges whites enjoyed: company transportation, childcare, vacation, international travel and bonus packages.[35] Non-unionized workers in the processing industries in the late 1960s comprised 92 per cent of the labour force, and were paid about one-seventh the salary received by unionized workers.[36] The fact that the Code of Rural Labour was implemented and managed by the former Native Affairs bureaucracy suggests the essential continuity.[37] In sum, the agency, migrancy and labour investments of Mozambican men and women were shaped by the *indigenato* and the follow up Code for Rural Labour. Both sustained privileges for white urban workers. Although the *indigenato* and Code mostly targeted men, women were also conscripted and, all women's lives were made more difficult if the men in their households were conscripted.

---

[34] Although white, East and South Asian women also entered waged labour in Lourenço Marques in the colonial era they were a small minority. The focus in this section is white males as the great majority of privileged workers.

[35] A tiny group of *assimilados* who worked in the printing industry were union members, but most remained trapped as apprentices, thus unable to take advantage of the full range of union privileges.

[36] Figures for 1968, for example show that of the 71,653 person labour force in the processing industry, 66,047 were not unionized. They earned 23 *escudos* per day in comparison with 174 *escudos* per day earned by organized labourers. The administrative and technical staff earned 260 *escudos* per day. Parcídio Costa, 'A Indústria de Moçambique,' 201, 203; Nuno Castel-Branco, 'An investigation into the Political Economy of Industrial Policy: The Case of Mozambique,' PhD thesis, University of London, 2001.

[37] Amélia Neves de Souto, 'A Administração Colonial Portuguesa em Moçambique no Período de Marcello Caetano (1968–1974): Mecanismos e Relações de Poder,' PhD thesis (Lisbon: Universidade Nova de Lisboa, 2003): Chapter 3. This was later published as *Caetano e o Ocaso do 'Império'; Administração e Guerra Colonial em Moçambique Durante o Marcelismo (1968–1974)* (Porto: Afrontamento, 2007), but references here are to the thesis. See also, Harris, 'Race, Conflict and Reform'; Lorenzo Macango, 'Um Antropólogo Norte-Americano no 'Mundo que o Português Criou' : Relações de Raça no Brazil e Moçambique segundo Marvin Harris,' *Lusotopie* (1999):143–61.

The women in men's migration: *Magaiça, n'wamacholo* and *n'wasalela*[38]

> 'It is not for nothing that fathers wish their daughters to marry *magaiça*
> [South African mine migrants]. It is because of hunger.'[39]

As early as the mid-eighteenth century, men from Sul do Save and Lourenço Marques left their farms to participate in raids, trade and eventually wage labour in the hinterland of what became South Africa.[40] From the mid-nineteenth century, southern Mozambican men worked in increasingly large numbers in neighbouring South Africa, first in sugar fields and eventually in diamond, coal and gold mines.[41] Men who returned to Mozambique having worked in South African mines were called *magaiça*. The word has multiple meanings, both the positive image of a man returning with wealth and goods to assume adult status through marriage, as suggested by the above quote, and the negative image of a man robbed or swindled in his travels.[42] The negative experience was common enough to have generated another name *mamparra magaiça* or *mambarha gayisa*. A *mamparra magaiça* was a miner who spent, squandered, or lost all of his wages before returning home or who did not return home at all.[43] By the mid-twentieth century *magaiça* were very common in Sul do Save, and no longer referred just to mine migrants. It came to embrace men returning from all kinds of jobs in South Africa, including farming and manufacturing jobs.

By the 1920s, and increasingly from the 1930s, farmers also had to contend with state run forced cultivation of cotton and rice. By the late 1940s and throughout the 1950s growing white settlement brought the additional burden of land alienation.[44] Large tracks of the region's best agricultural lands along the Limpopo River were taken from area

---

[38] The male terms *magaiça, n'wamacholo* and *n'wasalela* are defined and discussed below. No precisely parallel terms emerged for women, but I also failed to probe explicitly for gendered corolaries. As noted throughout, women who migrated, lived alone or left the authority of a socially significant male were commonly denoted in negative terms, like *xungwa* linked to prostitution or promiscuity, Binford, 'Stalemate,' 75.

[39] Unidentified man quoted from 1983 OT research project by Urdang during a famine period in Sul do Save. *Magaiça* has many various spellings. Urdang, 'Rural Transformation,' 109.

[40] Allen Smith, 'The Peoples of Southern Mozambique: An Historical Survey,' *JAH*, Vol. 14 (1973): 565–80; Harries, *Work, Culture*; Zimba, *Mulheres Invisíveis*.

[41] Harries, *Work, Culture*; Patrick Harries 'Kinship, Ideology and the Nature of Pre-colonial Labour Migration: Labour Migration from the Delagoa Bay Hinterland to South Africa up to 1895,' in Shula Marks and Richard Rathbone, eds, *Industrialisation and Social Change in South Africa. African Class Formation, Culture and Consciousness, 1870–1930* (London, Longman, 1982): 142–66.

[42] Lopes, et al, *Moçambicanismos*, 90; Sitoe et al. *Dicionário Ronga – Português*, 46.

[43] It is from the Afrikaans term *baar* meaning raw, inexperienced, or spendthrift. Luís Covane, 'The Impact of Migrant Labour on Agriculture in Southern Mozambique, 1920–1964,' unpublished paper, 9; Lopes, et al., *Moçambicanismos*, 94–5.

[44] Manghezi, *Trabalho Forçado*; Otto Roesch, 'Migrant Labour and Forced Rice Production in Southern Mozambique: The Colonial Peasantry of the Lower Limpopo Valley,' *JSAS*, 17, 2 (June, 1991): 252ff; Kenneth Hermele, *Land Struggles and Social Differentiation in Southern Mozambique: A Case Study of Chokwé, Limpopo, 1950–1987* (Uppsala: Scandinavian Institute of African Studies, 1988) [Research Report, No. 82].

families to be developed into irrigated farm complexes designed largely to benefit Portuguese settlers and planters. The remaining lands were less fertile and further from reliable water sources. As we shall see, environmental, economic, and state-driven challenges combined to fuel male outmigration in the south. Eventually patterns of male labour migration resulted in a higher ratio of women to men, a greater number of widows, divorcees and separated women in Sul do Save's population than elsewhere in Mozambique, and a heavier work burden on women in households with absent males.[45]

Men resorted to migrant labour for many reasons, but two of the most important related directly to women.[46] First, men had to acquire bridewealth to secure marriage and adult status in their community. Without repatriated wages from employment in South Africa many young men, particularly younger brothers, might not have been able to acquire a marriage size bridewealth from their elders until middle age. Second, assuming support from their lineage and good luck, migrants were able to rely on women's labour in hoe agriculture and farm management to accommodate their periodic absences without seriously threatening household food production and resources. Although the women's narratives suggest that this reliance had important limits, many analyses of Sul do Save labour migration argue that it was an important factor.[47] That suggests that women were at the heart of men's migration – men left to acquire the money necessary to access women in formal marriage and, in their absence, men relied upon their women's capabilities to manage their household assets.

Although all areas of the colony experienced drought, flood and famine, Southern Mozambique's climate, the topography of its rivers and characteristically sandy soils contributed to its enhanced vulnerability. During the twentieth century, Mozambican farmers who worked rich riverine soils in the Limpopo and Incomati valleys were displaced to drier, more marginal areas to accommodate white settlement schemes. The region experienced seasonal drought or flooding in dozens of years throughout the twentieth century. Drought or floods, with the potential to trigger a killer famine, struck least once in each decade.[48]

[45] The disproportionate population of widows in Sul do Save is broadly referenced in census and commentary, Roesch, 'Migrant Labour and Forced Rice,' 249; Eulália Tembe, 'The Significance of Widowhood for Women,' *Outras Vozes Suplemento do Boletim* 8 (August, 2004): 36–8; Salim Crimpton Valá, *A Problemática da Posse da Terra na Região Agrária de Chókwé (1954–1955)* (Maputo: Promédia, 2003).

[46] Chapter 2 note 9 has full references for the Harris / Rita-Ferreira debate and associated works. See also Ruth First et al. *Black Gold*; Manghezi, 'Mulher e Trabalho'; Covane, *Trabalho Migratório*; Fialho Feliciano, *Antropologia Económico*.

[47] Marvin Harris, 'Labour Emigration Among the Moçambique Thonga'; Harries, *Work, Culture*.

[48] Covane, *O Trabalho Migratório* for strategies to cope with drought. The following weather events were culled from the *Brado Africano* newspaper: severe drought and famine in 1941, drought and famine in 1947–1948, seasonal drought and hunger again from 1950 to 1954, followed by record flooding on the Limpopo in 1955, flooding again in 1958, 1964–1965, Cyclone Claude 1966, drought 1968–1969, and record flooding of the Limpopo in 1977.

When residents were asked in the late colonial era about region-wide killer famines, the so-called *amapaka* famine of 1922 was the last they recalled.[49] For the rest of the colonial era in Southern Mozambique, the extension of roadways, increased prevalence of rural *cantinas* and commercial agriculture meant that people who had access to cash no longer starved to death.[50]

In the nineteenth century people relied on chiefly authority and rain prayers to manage the threat of famine. The early penetration of state administration, sustained demand for conscript labour and the eventual alienation of riverine, roadside and rail line lands combined to diminish the power and authority of many area chiefs. People eventually altered their famine strategies; they courted broad social networks of reciprocity, counted on worker remittances and purchased food at *cantinas*.[51] Mine labour remittances became a core element of the South's famine strategy, underscoring that: 'It is not for nothing that fathers wish for their daughters to marry *magaiça*. It is because of hunger.'[52]

A great economic range characterized the households who send out migrants for waged labour. Most poverty measures hinge on Amélia Chiconela's mantra: 'What was important was having enough to eat.' Families count as extremely poor when 80 to 100 per cent of their income is spent on food. Many migrant families, including those of some narrators for this project, were extremely poor. However, families who sent out multiple migrants, whose migrants were skilled, experienced and better paid could be quite well off. Of that group, some invested in tools, plows, tractors and transportation to facilitate rural businesses and potentially leverage investments in the informal economy and truck gardening. In many cases male migrants relied on siblings and wives to manage those investments.[53]

But men were also at the heart of women's household strategies. Loss of a man's labour and protection was always a burden to the household's women and children, but some labour loss was more burdensome. *Magaiça* were absent for a long time – twelve to eighteen months. Accidents and venereal or lung diseases were always a threat, but these factors were increasingly counterbalanced by the stability and improved safety record of migration through the South African mine

---

[49] Sherilynn Young, 'What have they done with the rain? 20th Century Transformation in Ceremonial Practice and Belief in Southern Mozambique with Particular Reference to Rain Prayers,' unpublished paper, 1978, 20.
[50] Tragically, thousands starved to death in Sul do Save in the 1980s when the Renamo / Frelimo / South African Defense Forces fighting closed roads, shut down commerce and forced people into internal displacement or international refuge, Penvenne, 'Tapestry of Conflict,' 256; Phyllis Johnson and David Martin, eds, *Frontline Southern Africa: Destructive Engagement* (New York: Four Walls Eight Windows, 1988): Introduction.
[51] Young, 'What have they done with the rain?' 20.
[52] Urdang, 'Rural Transformation,'109.
[53] First, et al., *Black Gold*; Covane, *O Trabalho Migratório*; Fion de Vletter, 'Migration and Development,'146–63, esp. 159–63.

labour recruitment agency, the Witwatersrand Native Labour Association [WNLA], known by the vernacular rendering of its acronym,
Wenela. Living and working conditions at mines varied greatly, but
by the late colonial era the food, medical care and working conditions
men experienced on a Wenela mine contract had improved such that
most men returned home safely and with their health. [54]

Before leaving and upon return from South Africa, magaiça generally
bestowed gifts on their village's senior males and local authorities to be
sure that their wives and families would not be harassed for tax default
or conscripted in their absence. Public visiting and feasting, both prac-
tically and symbolically, thanked families and chiefs for the protection
and support they lent the miner's family in his absence. Although men
were expected to do the travelling in this process, women clearly were
at the heart of feasting and provision of the required supplies of beer.
Wenela provided an advance bonus, and, except for mamparra magaiça,
most men returned with a lump sum payment of deferred wages. Even
if families were unable to pay taxes in the magaiça's absence, they might
be spared xibalu conscription because local authorities could count on
taxes being paid up quickly upon the men's return. In short, while
magaiça were absent in distant places for a long time in objectively
dangerous conditions, they could plan to protect the family before they
left, and, barring accidents, most returned with their health and a sum
of money sufficient to cover debts the family accrued in their absence.

If miners and their families had spent their savings at a time when
famine struck, the men would have to join others begging for food
throughout the region in a ritual process that called in social debt to
secure family food – a process called ku thekela. Unlike forced labourers,
magaiça could leverage their ku thekela efforts with their history of
generous gifts, visits and parties.[55] They used goods and cash earned
in the formal economy to built social capital through the family and
gift economies that would tide them through lean times.[56]

Workers contracted or conscripted for local road and farm work could
not leverage pleas for support. Unlike Wenela recruits, xibalu conscripts
seldom received their legal minimum of food, clothing, soap and blankets. Their payment for a three-month contract seldom amounted to
more than the sum of their tax burden. They did not return with a
significant packet of deferred pay, but rather a paid tax receipt. Most
importantly, food supplied to xibalu labour was often of such poor
quality and so badly prepared it could compromise the workers' health.

[54] This assessment clearly does not take into account the impending HIV / AIDS epidemic.
First, et al. Black Gold; Covane, O Trabalho Migratório; Fion de Vletter, Sons of Mozambique:
Mozambican Miners and Post-Apartheid South Africa, [Migration Policy Series No. 8] (Cape Town:
Southern African Migration Project, 1998); Fion de Vletter, 'Labour Migration to South Africa:
The Lifeblood for Southern Mozambique' in David A. McDonald, ed. On Borders: Perspectives on
International Migration in Southern Africa (New York, St. Martin's Press, 2000): 46–70.
[55] Manghezi, 'Ku Thekela,'19–29.
[56] Rita-Ferreira, 'Os Africanos,' 282–3.

If family members were taken for conscript roadwork or settler field-work in the area, women and children continued to provide food to them if at all possible. That could require sending a youth to deliver food to the conscript's workplace daily or periodically. Conscripts working far from home, might be accompanied by a youth to be sure he had proper food and water to survive without sacrificing his health. In short, families not only suffered the loss of a conscript's labour and protection, but also had to invest additional household labour and food to sustain conscripts during their contracts.[57]

One stint of *xibalu* was costly enough, but multiple members of the poorest families could end up being chronically targeted for conscription – almost invariably leading to ill health, exacerbated vulnerability and deeper poverty. Men who were repeatedly seized for forced labour were called *n'wamacholo*, or 'old boys' – the police and forced labour overseers grew familiar with them during the repeat contracts.[58] With so little to show for their repeated absences, and such burdens on their households, *n'wamacholo*, like *mamparra magaiça*, sometimes didn't return at all. Fathers wanted their daughters to marry a *magaiça* who could provide increasingly necessary cash for her and her children; hoping, of course, the *magaiça* would not turn out to be a *mamparra magaiça*. Clearly no one set out to be or to marry *n'wamacholo*.

Social capital was and continues to be strongly linked with reciprocity, generosity and the successful navigation and accumulation of staked claims – for men and women. Material and social capital are clearly linked, but the specific linkages are important. Margarida Paulo and Carmeliza Rosário explored twenty-first century urban social networks and relations in Maputo and titled one of their studies *Xiculungo*. The term refers to the city's poorest, most isolated and vulnerable people. *Xiculungo* 'are not only defined with reference to material poverty and lack of assets but also on the basis of the nature of their social relationships outside their household...'[59]

People distinguished between migrants who used their migration to build status and wealth and ne'er-do-wells who either could not make headway or actually went from bad to worse. People also distinguished among the fortunate.[60] A *magaiça* held promise, but the wealthiest men in the most enviable positions were called *n'waselela*. *N'wasalela*, from the verb *salela* to remain, was the man who stayed behind. This kind of

---

[57] This paragraph, OT, group of retirees, 2 June 1993; Young, 'Women in Transition,' 5–8; Penvenne, *African Workers*, 49–50; Roesch, 'Migrant Labour and Forced Rice,' 247–53ff; José Cláudio Mandlate, 'Moçambique, decadas de 1960–1970: reforma da legislação laborale e sua implementação: um estudo de caso – recrutamento de mão de obra Africana pela Companhia do Buzi,' unpublished paper, Maputo, 2004.

[58] Also spelled *mwamu cholo*, Penvenne, *African Workers*, 50–52.

[59] Paulo, et al., 'Xiculungo,' *Social* 3.

[60] This social discourse ranking of promising and less promising people and distinguishing between deserving and undeserving poor is similar to that discussed in Paulo et al. 'Xiculungo,' *Social*, and the social spectrum highlighted in Gareth Stedman-Jones's classic *Outcast London: a Study in the Relationship between Classes in Victorian Society* (New York: Pantheon, 1971).

'stay behind' did not carry a 'stick in the mud' connotation. Rather, men stayed behind if they had enough good land, livestock and resources to marry, to pay taxes and comply with the colonial 'moral obligation to work' without having to sell their labour at home or abroad. They did not have to migrate to accumulate and retain capital. Some men accumulated wealth to marry through the years as *magaiça* and were eventually successful enough to become *n'wasalela*. *N'wasalela* did not have to risk leaving wives, children and elders to manage and secure their land, fields and livestock. They were few, and theirs was the most enviable status. Every father wished their daughters the security of being in a *n'wasalela* family.

Not surprisingly, none of the women who shared their narratives left *n'wasalela* familes to travel to Tarana – but many left *magaiça, mamparra magaiça* and *n'wamacholo* spouses or parents. We will follow the women who heeded the advice to 'Go to Tarana,' but first we consider the range of options for Sul do Save women who were suffering. If access to land and social protection was tied to males, but one's husband or father died or did not return from South Africa, what could women do? If one's husband or father could never generate enough to cover the family's tax burden how long could people survive cycles of *xibalu* as *n'wamacholo*?

Rural women without men:
Layered ironies of the Limpopo scheme

Although men migrated to secure their household and counted upon their wives to manage their holdings while they were away, Otto Roesch's research in rural Sul do Save led him to conclude: 'The absence of large numbers of men from their home communities for long periods of time ...made a number of traditional subsistence arrangements impracticable...The prolonged absence of one or more male members of a household, of course, also entailed a significant increase in the work load for women.'[61] *N'wasalela* households were likely to have been secured with a substantial *lobolo* and to have multiple adult males resident. Stable households where men, women and youth were healthy and productive could be prosperous if they had access to good land.

Men and women acknowledged their quite different places in the production and power landscapes, but appreciated and counted on the complementarity of each other's strength, productivity and contributions.[62] *Magaiça* wives had a fighting chance to sustain their families if absent husbands regularly repatriated wages and returned healthy

[61] Roesch, 'Migrant Labour,' 249.
[62] Arlindo Chilundo, Joel Neves Tembe, Ana Loforte and Luís Covane all make this point: Chilundo, *Os Camponeses*, 345ff; Neves [Tembe], 'Economy, Society and Labour Migration,' 30–40; Covane, *O Trabalho Migratório*, Ch. 7; Loforte, *Género e Poder*, 16–18.

and on time. They were much more likely to remain on the land than were the wives or daughters of *mamparra magaiça* or *n'wamacholo*. The latter rightly feared they might end up working *xibalu* right alongside their husbands – then who would care for the children and elderly.

Widows and women who were divorced, separated or abandoned by their spouses sought ways to support themselves and their dependents, earning wages on plantations and seeking alternative access to land. Throughout this period many women and children worked so-called *mugwaza* labour. *Mugwaza* was supposed to be volunteer labour paid on a daily quota basis. The hitch was that planters could conscript workers if insufficient volunteers materialized – thus *mugwaza* could easily elide into *xibalu*.[63] The irate husband who opened this chapter referred to women working *mugwaza* labour at Xinavane sugar planations on the Incomati river.

Rural and urban women, who had a mostly absent husband or who did not and probably would never have a resident husband, learned to partner with siblings and women within their mother's family, their matricentric family or matrikin, to secure land, opportunities and household labour.[64] Women ordinarily cultivated allies in their husband's patrilineage, their father's patrilineage and their mother's patrilineage. Women's strategies to shape the impact of migrancy and marriage on their lives were often miss-framed when viewed primarily through a lens focused on their husbands and fathers. The important colonial era Limpopo river valley settlement / irrigation project spectacularly miss-framed women's experiences in the service of hyped patriarchy. Thousands of women made a way for themselves in the Limpopo scheme – although you would not know that if you did not read colonial reports very carefully.

In the 1950s, building on earlier initiatives, the Portuguese greatly expanded a high profile irrigation, development and settlement project on the Limpopo river valley. It combined swamp drainage, settlement of Portuguese and Mozambican families, and large-scale crop irrigation systems. The project was called the Resgate dos Machongos, or the recovery of the fertile, water-retentive so-called *machongos* soils by draining riverine lands. It was the most ambitious such southern project in the colonial era.

Between 1951 and 1959, the project's lead engineer, José Firmino de Sousa Monteiro, produced a series of detailed reports.[65] They revealed that the Resgate dos Machongos had both stated and intentionally

---

[63] Roesch, 'Migrant Labour.'

[64] Fialho Feliciano, *Antropologia Economico*, 437–43. For an urban corollary in Laulane suburb of Maputo in the late twentieth century see Ana Loforte, *Género e Poder*, 16–18.

[65] Sousa Monteiro, *Relatório sobre o Resgate*. See also the same author and title for reports referring to 31 Dec. 1953, 31 Dec. 1957 and 31 Dec. 1959 and *Resgate dos Machongos do Sul do Save, Um Caso Típico; Primeiras Jornadas de Engenharia de Moçambique* (Lourenço Marques, Empresa Moderna, 1965); Junta Autónomo do Povoamento de Baixo Limpopo, *Relatório 1967*; Luís Covane, 'Migrant Labour,' 266.

masked objectives. The stated objectives were: settling Portuguese immigrant families, enhancing opportunities for the existing settlers, alleviating the south's labour shortage by discouraging the migration of men to South Africa, securing the residence of African families, adding value to the province, and 'looking after the well-being and socio-economic uplift of the native.'[66]

According to the preface: 'The goal of the [Lower Limpopo] project is to promote a ...new [Mozambican] man...a good Christian, a less ignorant man, and a capable artisan.'[67] The words industrious, moral and prosperous pepper the rationale.[68] The idea was to develop an *agricultor*, a black so-called European type farmer, akin to the British progressive farmer model, who was presumed to learn better agricultural techniques and habits from working in proximity with white farmers. Despite the fact that the vast majority of farmers in Sul do Save were women, the term *agricultor* was firmly raced and gendered as a black male, and the project explicitly promoted 'a new man.'[69]

To the extent African women figured at all in the rationale, it was as wives of *agricultors*. Agricultural support for the region's majority farming population was basically absent from the project's rationale. Portugal had long ignored the south's increasing crises – shortage of male labour, land alienation, and diminished access to reliable water. They failed to anticipate the impressive exodus of women and children in the late 1940s and early 1950s – when they overtook men as the majority of so-called clandestine migrants from the south. Rather than support rural women, the state legislated and enforced sanctions on travel by women and children, levying fines on bus drivers, truck drivers and train conductors who transported women and children without authorization from the men whose very neglect may have fuelled their departure.[70]

The Limpopo scheme was layered with dissonance, ironies and deception. The assumption that whites would embody the best agrarian practices, and promote the '...evolution of the native' merely by their presence was particularly galling to the mission-educated, well-off *n'wasalela* who eventually became *agricultores*.[71] Many of the Portuguese settlers, *colonos*, were poor, illiterate and plainly inexperienced in farming tricky tropical soils. *Colonos* enjoyed such low standing among *n'waselela* that, if a *n'waselela* was asked to do something he considered to be beneath his dignity, he would protest that, after all,

[66] Sousa Monteiro, *Relatório sobre o Resgate*, 10; Roesch, 'Migrant Labour and Rice'; Hermele, *Land Struggles*.

[67] Quote from the Preface, Sousa Monteiro, *Relatório sobre o Resgate... 31 de Dec. 1953* (Lourenço Marques, 1955): 3; José Rodrigues Júnior, *Transportes de Moçambique* (Lisbon: Editorial Ultramar, 1956): 219–54. 241.

[68] Rodrigues Júnior, *Transportes de Moçambique*, 241.

[69] Frelimo adopted the idea of a new man, *homen novo*, with many of these characteristics as part of its Socialist project immediately after independence, Buur, 'Xiconhoca,' 26 ff.

[70] Penvenne, *African Workers*, 141–53.

[71] Manghezi, *Trabalho Forçado*, 81ff; Covane, 'Migrant Labour,' 271ff.

'he was not a *colono*!'[72] Despite projections of settling hundreds of thousands of Portuguese families in the Limpopo showplace, by 1954 only a dozen 'European-type' farmers worked less than a thousand hectares of land in the scheme. A decade later fewer than 70 Portuguese farmers cultivated less than 9.000 hectares.[73]

Instead of promoting prosperity, the Limpopo project directly undercut the region's most prosperous rural men on many levels. First, in each of the project's five locations families were evicted from scarce riverine lands. 'Title' in traditional land resided with men, so men who controlled these desirable lands were effectively dispossessed. Second, the very heavy and unhealthy job of digging out the drainage ditches, clearing and maintaining the infrastructural canals was initially accomplished by hundreds men working *xibalu* gang labour.[74] Hundreds more men made sure they had a mine labour or urban wage contract so they could not be conscripted to do the hard and dangerous work digging out the swamp. Rather than admit that the project's land was alienated and its footprint was inscribed by *xibalu*, the reports emphasized the numbers of Africans who came forward to sign on for a plot of good land once the dangerous foundational work was completed and the evictions seemed confirmed.[75] However, even some of those people faced forced cultivation quotas and obligatory annual labour maintaining the irrigation ditches.[76]

The preface made little of one of the basic criteria for male participation. Participants had to forswear seeking future labour contracts in South Africa. Yet, migration to South Africa was the most familiar, widespread, multi-generational famine and risk management strategy practiced by Sul do Save men.[77] Residents knew they could expect droughts and floods of killer magnitude at least once a decade. The only men who were likely to forsake mine contracts were *n'wasalela* – and many of them were aggrieved and dispossessed by the Limpopo scheme.

Despite the propaganda value that *agricultores* and the Limpopo settlements held for Portugal's pluralism campaigns of the 1950s and anti-insurgency campaigns the 1960s and 1970s, their practical impact was less auspicious for Mozambican males. First, the few Portuguese who took up residence in these projects clearly received a greater portion of resources, and more government support than did the Mozambicans, and Mozambicans noticed.[78] If even *n'wasalela* had

---

[72] Manghezi, *Trabalho Forçado*, 81ff; Covane, 'Migrant Labour,' 261 and 273ff.

[73] Covane, 'Migrant Labour,' 271ff.

[74] Covane, 'Migrant Labour,' 261ff; Rita-Ferreira, 'Esboço Sociológico,' 116, 150, 172.

[75] Rita-Ferreira, 'Esboço Sociológico,' 116, 150, 172; Hermele, *Land Struggles*.

[76] Roesch, Covane and Hermele all discuss these aspects.

[77] Sousa Monteiro, *Relatório sobre o Resgate*; Rodrigues Júnior, *Transportes de Moçambique*, 219–54.

[78] *Agricultores* are considered for this period in Neves [Tembe], 'Economy, Society and Labour Migration'; Covane, 'Migrant Labour'; Faria Dutra, '9,500 famílias de agricultores Europeus no Vale do Limpopo?' *Notícias*, 9 Oct. 1952; Bowen, *State against the Peasantry*, 27–44, 65–92.

to fight for their stake amid the settlers, few *magaiça* judged they had much of a chance – let alone the *n'wamacholo*.

But the key dissonance in the Limpopo settlement was gender. Reading the narrative of Sousa Monteiro's many reports from 1951 to the 1960s, one scarcely would have known there were women and children living within the project. Even the photographs appended to the reports mainly featured buildings, vistas and formal portraits of Portuguese men in positions of authority. One slightly blurred distance shot revealed the half naked male gang labourers digging the original infrastructural ditches while others clearly revealed the hard work men accomplished standing in knee to waist deep water shoveling mud.[79] Several photos showed women and children waiting their turn to collect water from new communal taps or to use the sparkling new bathroom and health posts.[80] By 1967 the project had only attracted twenty-seven 'European type' farmers, four of whom were Africans. Photos featured these four African *agricultores*, including their wives and other women in their families. They appeared like indispensable props, particularly when greeting visiting dignitaries.[81]

It is then fairly astonishing to read plot census figures included as an appendix. In 1959 the census revealed that Mozambican women occupied all of the plots, while Mozambican men lived on less than a third. The majority of plots were occupied by single, divorced or widowed women, or by married women whose 'new man' husband was off working the same 'old' jobs in Lourenço Marques or South Africa.[82] A decade later the situation was even more dramatic: 87 per cent of the total occupants were women and only 13 per cent were men.[83] The indisputable evidence of African women's absolutely critical role in the project was buried without comment in the project's plot census appendix while the preface, text and photography strongly emphasized men.

Once the Limpopo project was up and running, its day to day industry and prosperity depended on the Mozambican women who lived and farmed there. Except for the handful of *agricultores*, the 'new' Mozambican men were largely imagined as props in the print material. The ironies did not stop there. One of the *agricultores* was Alberto Chissano. By the time Alberto Chissano had become an *agricultore* in this politically showcased colonial development scheme, his son, Joaquim Alberto Chissano, was in exile in Paris working as a diplomat for Frelimo.[84]

[79] Sousa Monteiro, *Relatório sobre o Resgate*, 1957, figures 9 through 12 between pages 64 and 65.
[80] Sousa Monteiro, *Relatório sobre o Resgate*, *1957*, figures 19– 22 between pages 88 and 89.
[81] Sousa Monteiro, *Relatório sobre o Resgate*, *1957*, figure 25 between pages 120 and 129.
[82] Luís Covane and Rodrigues Júnior both made use of Sousa Monteiro's set of reports: Covane, 'Migrant Labour,' concluded, 'Settlement schemes aimed also to attract and stabilize African male labour in the rural areas...but men continued selling their labour to the mine industry,' 344; Rodrigues Júnior, *Transportes de Moçambique*, 219–254.
[83] Covane, 'Migrant Labour,' Chapter 8.
[84] Covane, 'Migrant Labour,' 266ff, 273–83.

Joaquim Alberto later headed Frelimo's transitional government (1974–1975), while Samora Machel prepared the political leadership. After independence in 1975, Machel became President and Chissano served as Foreign Minister. After Machel's death in a suspicious plane crash, Chissano became independent Mozambique's second president. Obviously Joaquim Alberto Chissano was not the sort of 'new man' the Portuguese hoped to promote through the Limpopo scheme.

Mátchiuassane Boa takes matters into her own hands

The *Machongos* narrative provided names for the four symbolic male *agricultores*, but their wives, who appeared in the photographs and reports that promoted the project, remained un-named. The thousands of African women who farmed the project were submerged in the report appendix, un-named and broadly unacknowledged. Also buried and ignored in the narrative of Monteiro's report, was the annexed documentation for the project's first transfer to a Mozambican of a private house and land plot in the Inhamissa sector of the larger project. The inaugural deed was important enough to be retained in the appendix, but not important enough to merit comment in the narrative.

The new owner, like the majority of others living on the Limpopo, was an African woman, Mátchiuassane Boa, also known as Rosalina Boa. Like thousands of women, and the majority of Limpopo project women, Mátchiuassane Boa had no man in her life. The project's framework completely ignored women like her, but she initiated the process to consolidate her claim to land without a 'new man,' imagined or otherwise. She lived with her 59-year-old mother, her 78-year-old maternal grandmother, and her eleven-year-old cousin, a boy. The deed does not reveal if the cousin was related through the maternal or paternal line, but the three adult women of this household comprised a classic matrikin.[85] The officials who conceived, rationalized and oversaw these projects clearly knew that the overwhelming majority of people living on and farming the Limpopo plots were women and children. In a region of Mozambique supposed to be firmly patrilineal, Mátchiuassane Boa lived in a matricentric household, and secured the symbolic first deed. Even assuming someone had a sense of humour or irony, it would be a stretch to portray Mátchiuassane Boa or her little cousin as a 'new man.'

Despite the scheme's androcentric framework and the region's patrilineal society, Mátchiuassane Boa took matters into her own hands. She secured title to good land, moved her family and farmed. Like many others, she made no pretence of holding a space for some imagined man in her household. She realized her situation would 'not change,' so she

[85] Monteiro, *Relatório sobre o Resgate dos 'Machongos' do Sul do Save Referente a 31 de Dezembro de 1957* [Anexo II, pp. 157–161] documentation of sale to Mátchiuassane Boa.

claimed her dignity and her stake in land to support her household. The state conveyed the deed – without comment.

Boa's situation stood in sharp contrast with the project's rationale and the extensive press coverage. The absent men were imagined present and the scheme's reports rendered the present women largely absent. The document did not reveal whether Mátchiuassane Boa once had a husband, who, like the disgruntled husband quoted above, might complain that only he knew how she should work. But she and thousands of other women took matters into their own hands, many because they had few other options. It is also unclear if Mátchiuassane Boa's deed implicitly committed her to planting and producing certain quotas of rice and working to keep the irrigation channels clear. In any case, she secured good land in freehold, and four generations of her family farmed it.

The Limpopo agricultural project, like the cashew shelling industry, was a high profile success story in the late colonial era. African women's productive labour was absolutely central to the viability and prosperity of each. Their roles were not simply neglected; they were actively eclipsed from the era's touted success stories. At best their contributions were noted in passing, as an aside, at worst, competent, hardworking Limpopo farmers and Tarana cashew shellers were patronized as being in need of 'uplift' or devalued as impediments to a promising industry's expansion. In both cases women laboured in difficult circumstances, often having to accommodate a larger labour load in light of male migration.

Men in women's migration:
'Go to Tarana! You will forget your suffering!'[86]

> 'Married life was over for me. There was nothing to be done about it. The best thing for me was to go to Cajú to find work'
>
> Felizarda Bila[87]

Mátchiuassane Boa had secured enough land and labour to sustain herself and her household. She was a *n'wasalela* in that she could stay, work her land, pay her taxes and neither she nor her household members would be harassed for conscript labour. I know of no female equivalents for the terms *n'waselela*, *magaiça* and *n'wamacholo*. All are gendered male. Women from very poor families were definitely vulnerable to repeated conscription for *xibalu*, and thus could become *n'wamacholo*. Many of the women who ended up working *mugwaza* or for wages on contract at Xinavane sugar plantations first worked there

---

[86] OT, Felizmenta Namboro, 9 June 1993; Julieta Mulungu, 20 May 1993; Amélia Malanguane, 27 May 1993.
[87] OT, Felizarda Bila, 21 May 1993.

as conscripts to cover their tax obligation. They were simply finding their way like Amélia Chiconela found her way out of desperate poverty by following a flow.

The outraged husband seemingly dismissed the experiences of women who were beaten, abandoned, poor and suffering – women who left because 'married life was over,' and they could not see any way their situation would change for the better if they stayed. The thresholds and details were different for every woman, but, again, leaving one's household to seek wage labour carried such a heavy social penalty no woman would do so lightly, certainly not for any small criticism. We first met Amélia Chiconela, telling us that she knew nothing of Lourenço Marques, busses, trains, money or anything else urban. In some ways she simply inserted herself in a path and process and went with the flow until she could once again find her feet. Violence set her on that path. Her husband beat her no matter what she did. It went on over a long period and finally she could no longer endure what she knew would invariably recur. Furthermore, she could not imagine any way the situation with her husband might change. In her case there was no single trigger, no small thing, just a breaking point when the combination convinced Amélia to leave.[88]

Some women recalled an actual event or events that sent them on their way. Some triggers might actually seem trivial to an outsider, but many women's disaffection was cumulative and the trigger was best understood as the tipping point when they could no longer face their situation and maintain their self-esteem. Carolina Manelele's situation might have seemed enviable. She was the wife of a *magaiça*. During her husband's long absences, she struggled, harvesting groundnuts and maize to feed her family. She was a hard working farmer, and year in and year out she brought in a good crop. Men were supposed to build, maintain and repair their wives' houses and storage silos, but Carolina was chronically frustrated because neither her husband nor his family complied. The day her maize storage silos finally collapsed under the weight of the harvest she worked so hard to produce, Carolina reached her tipping point. She had done her job well, but no one met her efforts even half way. Without a proper silo, her harvest was vulnerable to rain, rot and rodents – her energy would be 'wasted.' The silo's collapse focused her cumulative anger and she left with the familiar refrain, 'I could not see how my situation would change.'[89]

Like so many others, if Carolina stayed, she could look forward to more of the same, and she was too proud and too disgusted for that. She set down the hoe that she had wielded so successfully, left and joined hundreds of other women and children in Lourenço Marques. It was just as well that Carolina never balked at hard work, because her first jobs in town were hauling dirt, timber and building materials at

---

[88] OT, Amélia Chiconela, 17 May 1993.
[89] OT, Carolina Manelele and group of retirees, 4 June 1993.

the port lighterage yards, the lumberyards and various construction sites. She laboured in the winter's cold and rain and summer's hot sun and dry wind. The dirty heavy material she carried on her head wore an unsightly and uncomfortable bald spot in her scalp. When Cajú opened, Carolina applied right away. Whatever the health hazards and difficulties of working at Cajú, at least she would work with a roof overhead and not wear a hole through her hair![90]

Felizmenta Namboro's path was different, but no less difficult. She ended up at Tarana thanks to the support and betrayal of family members. When one of her three children died, her husband kept their son but sent her and her youngest daughter back to her parents. Her parents took her in and Felizmenta eventually married again, but she had not been married long when the whole family was shocked to discover that her second husband and her young niece were having an affair. Despite the disgrace of child abuse and a technically incestuous relationship the husband and niece ignored family pressure to end their relationship, and when the niece became pregnant the two began to live openly together. Once again Felizmenta returned to her parents, but this time the family suggested she go to Tarana to put some distance between herself and the scandal. Felizmenta asked herself how she could sustain her dignity in the circumstances. She could not imagine anything getting better so she left – no small thing.[91]

Unlike Chiconela, who had to figure out everything from train fare and money to where she would live and work, Felizmenta went to town knowing she had support. Another cousin lived in Lourenço Marques and worked at the Central Hospital. She gave Felizmenta a room and some advice. Although a range of processing industries were hiring when she arrived, her cousin advised Felizmenta to go to Tarana. She told Felizmenta that work there might be dirty and hard, but it would be steady and she was unlikely to be laid off. Carolina was happy to have a roof, Amélia felt lucky to have made her way by muddling onward, and Felizmenta was grateful for the promise of a steady job – it was all so little, but all so much.

Mapping migration: death and misfortune
Protestations from outraged husbands aside, men were central to most women's migration. Women's lives, their strategies to make a livelihood and their capacity to secure themselves in difficult times were socially intertwined with men and families. When the idealized social relationships failed to materialize or were upended, women had to innovate. Although some men walked away from women and the children they conceived with them, some women raised their children at Cajú because their husbands or fathers died. Men died in South Africa

---

[90] OT, Carolina Manelele and group of retirees, 4 June 1993.
[91] OT, Felizmenta Namboro, 19 July 1993.

or went missing with no subsequent explanation.[92] More than a score of women who shared their stories embarked on their journey to Cajú due to the death or disappearance of a parent or a husband.[93]

Certainly the death of either parent deprived their child of emotional, material, and social support and protection.[94] If a father died, his children and their mothers were often also vulnerable to abuse from the father's family, from older male siblings or sons. If a mother died, her children were potentially subject to abuse by relatives who were unenthusiastic about assuming the mother's burden of services and support. Women exploited, neglected and resented other women. With death and divorce came disadvantage and loss of protection. Stepmothers have difficult reputations in many societies. Difficulties with stepparents or co-wives could be as important as difficulties with a parent or spouse. Amélia Malanguane, Cristina Duzenta Cuambe, Joana Alberto Chivangue, Carlota Samuel Cumbay and Celeste Marcos Mpende were all touched by death, but each shaped her subsequent experience depending upon her energy and her luck.[95]

Amélia Malanguane's path to Cajú began when her mother was widowed. She couldn't support Amélia, so she sent Amélia to live with her own mother. Patrilineal dominance did not prevent women from seeking support in their mothers' families. It was common for women to approach people within their own and their mother's patrilineage for support. Amélia lived with her maternal grandmother until she was around 16. Amélia's mother then sent her money and told her to, 'go to Tarana.' In 1962 Amélia rented a room with a cousin and began working twelve-hour days in Cajú's peeling section. As we shall see, she eventually forged an energetic and largely successful path at Cajú but her mother's widowhood initiated her journey. [96]

Widowhood also marked Cristina Duzenta Cuambe's path. Her husband died when she was a very young nursing mother. It soon became clear that her husband's family would not support her, so she returned to her father. Her father could barely support those who already lived in his household, but he gave Cristina money and advised

[92] Rita-Ferreira,'Os Africanos,'131; de Vletter, *Migration and Development*, 9.
[93] All of the following women began their migration due to death: Rabeca Notiço, Amélia Muzima, Albertina Utane, Helena Chemane, Ofélia Manana Mbebe, Rita Novela, Matilde Chiduza, Maria Celeste Chavane, Amélia Nhavotso, Rosa Cau, Carlota Ncutana, Matilde Chilengue, Catarina Tafula, Serafina Langa, Lídia Chabana, Joana Chilaule, Virginia Massingue, Ester Tafula, Percina Mungumbe, Caferina Nhatsane, Helena Adelino, and several in the groups of retirees, 2 and 3 June 1993.
[94] In a photographic study of Mozambican and Finnish women, the authors asked all of the women they photographed: 'What changed your life?' The single life-changing event most mentioned by Mozambicans was the death of a parent, usually a father. Almost a third of the Mozambicans, but only one Finnish woman gave that answer. Magi Viljanen and Rui Assubuji, *Photos: Women from Finland and Mozambique – Fotos: Mulheres de Moçambique e da Finlândia* (Maputo: Embassy of Finland, 2005): unpaginated.
[95] Following paragraphs based on OT, Amélia Malanguane, 28 May 1993; Cristina Cuambe, 17 May 1993; Joana Alberto Chivangue, 19 May 1993.
[96] OT, Amélia Malanguane, 28 May 1993.

her to 'go to Tarana.' She got a job at Tarana and lived with her older
brother for several years until she could rent a home of her own. Amélia
counted on maternal kin, but Cristina depended upon her paternal kin.
Her father and brother helped her establish herself in town. Although
she seldom managed to earn a full salary without discounts for failure
to achieve the daily quota, what she earned covered the basics for
herself and her son – rent, rice, sugar and groundnut staples. She
lived alone in part so she would have no more children and would not
become trapped in chronic debt.[97] Cristina, like Amélia, took matters
into her own hands, and did well for herself.

Joana Alberto Chivangue's burdens in life also accrued from death,
abandonment and neglect – by men and women. Her mother died
before Joana married. When Joana's husband went missing in South
Africa, she returned to her father's home. Her father had remarried and
his new wife felt burdened by Joana's presence. She had enough people
under her roof without this unwelcome woman. Since Joana couldn't
imagine how the situation with her stepmother would improve, she
decided, 'The best thing for me was to go to Cajú to work.'[98] Like Cristina Cuambe, Joana headed to the city to live with family. In Joana's
case, her sister paid for her transport to Lourenço Marques and let her
move in while she got settled, and her sister's son helped her get a job
at Cajú.

Joana never married again, but she raised three sons and two daughters at Cajú – each with a different father – that was not an unusual
situation in the capital's *bairros de caniço*.[99] Tragically, two of her sons
were killed in the post-independence war, and in the wake of her sons'
deaths the mothers of her son's children 'abandoned' the children
with Joana. In a turnaround from the usual practice of men going off
to South Africa, Joana's widowed daughters-in-law went off to South
Africa, never to be heard from again. Unlike her stepmother, however,
Joana did not shun the children as burdens. She embraced them, and
at age 54 she was the breadwinner for six people. Joana made sure her
household did not fall into debt.[100]

Carlota Samuel Cumbay and Celeste Marcos Mpendane also lost
their mothers as infants or young children. Both were neglected or
mistreated by stepmothers, and could easily have ended up in prostitution.[101] Celeste arrived in the city very young. She quickly learned that
prostitution was the obvious entry opportunity, but she aspired to a
job. *Malalanyana* first tried to place her in domestic service, but without
Portuguese language and counting skills, Celeste was hard to place.
She was among the many who hung around Cajú teasing administra-

---

[97] OT, Cristina Duzenta Cuambe, 17 May 1993.
[98] OT, Joana Alberto Chivangue, 19 May 1993.
[99] See Chapter 4 and Rita-Ferreira, 'Os Africanos,' 301–08.
[100] OT, Joana Alberto Chivangue, 19 May 1993.
[101] The following paragraphs are based on OT, Carlota Samuel Cumbay, 20 May 1993 and
Celeste Marcos Mpendane, 26 May 1993.

tors for a job, and when she was only eleven she finally was hired to do cleaning. Celeste was grateful for the opportunity because it kept her from having to 'live in Lagoas' – the euphemism for prostituting oneself in the Lagoas red light district.[102]

Celeste's older sister took her in when she arrived in Lourenço Marques. She shared with Celeste what many considered to be the working women's mantra:

> ...behave and work hard in the city. Take care of yourself, your father and your family...If you have a job, you don't have to chase down men. If you are working you can support yourself and buy what you need... when you are sick, ok be sick, but you better get well quickly and get back to work.... Hide money away so you will be able to save yourself when you are sick.[103]

Celeste's sister underscored to her: the only person who will ever take care of you is you, so do it! Like many of her colleagues, Celeste's life was largely restricted to work and home. She had all she could do to hold tight, feed and care for her children. Two of her seven children did not survive, but she raised five at Cajú. Death put her on the path to Tarana, but her older sister helped her secure herself and her children. Most people in Lourenço Marques, migrants included, looked first to family, but as narratives by Carlota Cumbay, Matilde Chiduza and Helena Lissenga revealed, it did not always work out well.

Carlota Cumbay's mother died when Carlota was a nursling. She was encouraged by her stepmother to marry very young, and had three children with her husband before he left her to go to South Africa. She stayed with her in-laws for a long time but felt she was 'wasting her energy' on 'a dry bare place'. Without her husband's protection she was shuttled among her father-in-law's five wives; each woman had work for Carlota to do but none was particularly interested in feeding her and her three children. Perhaps it was all her father-in-law's wives could do to feed themselves and their own children, but they failed to exhibit any solidarity with Carlota's struggle. Finally Carlota fled to Lourenço Marques. If she was going to work hard, she wanted to work to feed herself and her children.

Carlota's cousin was a prostitute in *Mathlothlomana*. She paid Carlota's bus fare and tried to convince her to enter prostitution. Carlota did not want to live that way with three children, so applied for work at Cajú right away. Angelina, a colleague at Cajú, knew how difficult it would be for Carlota and her children to live with her cousin in *Mathlothlomana*, so invited them to live with her. Many women at Cajú were never in the position to offer shelter or much else – they were simply too poor to reciprocate let alone be generous. Angelina could squeeze in other areas to make a place for Carlota – at least for the short term.

---

[102] OT, Celeste Marcos Mpendane, 26 May 1993.
[103] OT, Celeste Marcos Mpendane, 26 May 1993.

Initially Carlota struggled to complete her daily quota to earn full pay. But little by little she managed to save enough to buy pots and pans, and eventually accumulated materials to build a home for her children. She was grateful for Angelina's generosity, but wanted to be on her own. For Carlota, life at Tarana was hard, but as was the case for so many of her colleagues, it was better than prostitution: 'Those who didn't want to suffer left Cajú a long time ago, but those of us who want to live by our own sweat have worked here right up to the present. Even though we are now old we don't have to depend on anyone but ourselves.'[104] That sense of not having to depend on anyone but oneself was the steel girder, rather than the silken thread, that bound together so many of the cashew shellers. They shared Celeste's sister's advice on self-reliance.

Carlota managed to escape *Mathlothlomana*, and eventually saved enough to build her own home. Despite her self-reliance, courage and stamina, she was one of the saddest people we met during the whole project. Her experience underscored the importance of dignity, family and matters of the heart: 'My poverty is not so heavy. It is more a poverty weighing on my spirit because my three children died and the only child I have left doesn't even remember he has a mother. I came to *Xilunguíne* to raise this child – not to prostitute myself.'[105] Dread, joy and bitter experiences at the hands of one's family and children are obviously part of the human condition. Family members were both key supporters, and instigators of the worst pain.

That was the case for Matilde Chiduza and Helena Lissenga too. They ended up at Cajú thanks to the treachery of their brothers. Matilde and her siblings lived in the Ximpamanine neighbourhood of Lourenço Marques in a house the family had built from the money her father earned in South Africa and her mother earned selling firewood. When Matilde was young her father died in an accident. Her eldest brother seized house and then beat his mother until she and the children fled from the neighbourhood. Perhaps her mother could have pled her case to the municipal authorities, but she did not. Matilde's brother's greed and her mother's vulnerability left an impression on Matilde. She built herself a small house with the money she earned at Cajú.[106] She eventually had a child, but she never had a man in her house. Her child eventually had a child, who also did not '...have a father.' They lived in a three-generation family – two generations 'children of women.' No man would have a claim on her, her daughter, her granddaughter or her home.[107] Chapter 4 considers household arrangements in more detail, but some women preferred to live alone or to live *amancebado* – in a

[104] OT, Carlota Samuel Cumbay, 20 May 1993.
[105] OT, Carlota Samuel Cumbay, 20 May 1993.
[106] OT, Matilde Chiduza, 28 May 1993. She saved for her house using the rotating savings system, the *chitiki* system discussed in Chapter 4.
[107] OT, Matilde Chiduza, 28 May 1993.

common-law marriage relationship – they were particularly concerned about violence from men and the security of their family's shelter.[108]

Helena Lissenga's move to Cajú also began with her brother's abuse of authority. When Helena's parents separated, her oldest brother asserted authority over her as the acting head of household. He insisted Helena live *amancebado* with a local man. The man did not want to marry Helena, he just wanted her as an *amancebado* partner, and was willing to pay her brother if Helena moved in with him. When Helena refused, her brother beat her, trying to force her to acquiesce. She fled to escape her brother's violence and the threat of sexual exploitation.[109]

Helena made her way to Cajú, and eventually had nine children in an *amancebado* relationship with a man who also worked at Cajú. They never married but they had an enduring relationship and he contributed regularly to support her and the children. He eventually left to work in South Africa and did not return. Helen appreciated both the vulnerability of single women to male authority and the potential of having a protective and contributing male in one's household. She knew that her long *amancebado* relationship was unusual, and when it ended she did not risk another.

Mapping migration: The solidarity of siblings and hahánis[110]
Women who managed to get to Lourenço Marques and land a job at Cajú, formed a diverse array of households, and looked mostly to each other for support. Someone may have urged them to 'Go to Tarana,' but they had to somehow get there, and find support until they could support themselves. Family members from a woman's father's, mother's and husband's lineages could be essential supports along the journey.

In mapping migration, support and solidarity, a *haháni* emerged as special. The position of *haháni* among the patrilineal people of Southern Mozambique was anchored in the practice of *lobolo*.[111] The sister who brought in a *lobolo* that was used by her brother so he could marry was a *haháni* to him, his bride and his family. A *haháni* enjoyed status and authority within her own patrilineage for having brought in a *lobolo* and within her brother's family because her *lobolo* was used for his marriage.

In principle, all parties who shared a *lobolo* enjoyed special relationships. Some sisters, who had not brought in a bridewealth, because they did not marry or married without *lobolo*, nonetheless contributed

---

[108] Chapter 4 and Rita-Ferreira, 'Os Africanos,' 301–305.

[109] OT, Helena Malemo Lissenga, 31 May 1993.

[110] E. Dora Earthy uses a alternate spelling of *haháni (hahane)* and discusses the relationship in *Valenge Women*, 12–15ff.

[111] Earthy notes that the *haháne* 'ranks as the female counterpart of the father.' Earthy, *Valenge Women*, 12–15ff; Carin Vijfhuizen suggests that paternal aunts have special relationships in southern African patrilineal social relations with or without bridewealth, Vijfhuizen, 'The People you Live with': Gender Identities and Social Practices, Beliefs and Power in the Livelihoods of Ndau Women and Men in a Village with an Irrigation Scheme in Zimbabwe (Wageningen: Grafisch Service Centrum van Gils B.V., 1998): Chapter 2; Loforte, *Genero e Poder*, 18ff.

to a brother's *lobolo* through personal savings. In that case they too were considered *haháni*. The importance and authority of a *haháni* in relation to siblings and spouses shaped women's complex approaches to *lobolo*. In scholarly literature, *lobolo* is often demeaned as a bride's ball and chain, but the potential status and authority that the *lobolo* conveyed within the bride's and groom's patrilineages should not be underestimated. *Lobolo* merits textured consideration for its advantages and disadvantages. The narrators for this project held a great range of views on the subject, and their views could be contradictory. Women who resented paying off their own *lobolo* after their marriage ended through no fault of their own, might be quite happy to contribute to their brother's *lobolo*.[112]

In 1949–50, Mechtild von Bosse Casquiero walked from village to village, taking particular note of women's social conditions throughout Mozambique. Her firmly Western and Christian perspective led her to broadly condemn *lobolo*, polygamy, and witchcraft, arguing that they were more prevalent in the South than the rest of the country, but she tempered her judgment with regard to *lobolo*: 'What do those who call *lobolo* servitude make of it when a woman who is not *loboloed* turns to her husband and says, "Am I so insignificant that you will not even *lobolo* me?"' She then confirmed that *lobolo* could be understood as advantageous; noting that whether paid in gold backed pounds or in cattle, *lobolo* for women of status and education was a substantial accumulation and sacrifice for the husband and his family. It confirmed the bride's status and capacity to stake claims in both her own and her husband's lineage – as a wife, a sister, a sister-in-law, a mother, an aunt, a grandmother, a *haháni* and a widow.[113]

Women were well aware of opportunities to stake claims and authority in their own, their mother's and their husband's lineages. Scholars have paid more attention to the ambivalences and disadvantages women experience in their husbands' lineages than to the advantages they experience in their own. Furthermore, in most authority and obedience relationships in life, people eventually experience both sides of the coin: a child / daughter-in-law owes obedience to a mother / mother-in-law, a mother / mother-in-law demands obedience from a child / daughter-in-law. In the ordinary scheme of things, children and daughters-in-law became mothers and mothers-in-law. Aging and life cycle passages move women from disadvantage to advantage and possibly back to disadvantage.[114]

[112] Loforte, *Género e Poder*, 18ff; OT, Rita Famisse Novela, 27 May 1993; Cacilda Gulene Fumo, 21 May 1993.
[113] Mechtild von Bosse Casquiero, 'A Mulher Indígena,' *Boletim da Sociedade de Estudos de Moçambique*, Vol. 21, No. 68 (Jan. Março, 1951): 5–25, quote 14; Manghezi very similar quote, 'Interviews,' 164–72.
[114] Contemporary and historical research suggests that elderly women with or without resources can be targets of witchcraft accusations. Terezinha da Silva, 'A Journey of an Old

Contributing a *lobolo* potentially enhances advantage in staking claims.

However, claims to authority have structural, informal and personal aspects. Speaking about Valenge women earlier in the twentieth century, for example, Dora Earthy confirmed that, 'Women have hardly any authority in legal or political matters, though they accomplish a good deal by the power of the tongue.'[115] *Haháni* relationships potentially place women in positions to make claims and assert authority, but individual women have to pursue those claims and assert that authority. Not everyone will assert the power of the tongue or the power of specific relationships, and some will do so more successfully than others. A woman's luck and force of personality made a difference in every case.

A *haháni* shaped Rita Novela's and Ester Tafula's paths to Cajú and their experiences as urban women. Rita's husband died, leaving her with two children. Seeing Rita struggling, her *haháni* asked her oldest daughter to bring Rita to town to seek work at Cajú. Hers was the helping hand Rita needed to embark on a new life. She began in *djamangwana*, crushing nuts by hand. It was the most difficult work she had done in her life, but she too managed to hold on. Rita took credit for her own hard work, but acknowledged the important bridge provided by the *haháni* mother and daughter team.

Ester Tafula's father died shortly before she was born. His parents had not approved of his marriage to her mother, so, without his protection, their situation quickly became precarious. Ester's mother returned to her birth family, but her *haháni* stepped in to protect and raise Ester as her own child. In Ester's case that meant she had a significantly more prosperous upbringing. Ester was eventually married with *lobolo*, and left her *haháni*'s protection to live in her husband's lineage. Unfortunately, when Ester's husband left to work in South Africa her mother-in-law worked her very hard and Ester felt she disliked her. Ester soon gave birth to a son, thus consolidating her position within the family, so despite continuing trouble with her mother-in-law, she and her son remained.

Like many others, Ester aspired to live out the morality play of a faithful wife working her 'flat dry place' though hopefully not 'wasting her energy' until her husband finally returned. He had not been home long when he died. Widowed and facing a hostile mother-in-law, Ester worried she would be accused of witchcraft and blamed for his death. Hers was precisely the situation that would trigger witchcraft accusations. She could not see how her situation would improve, and feared it would deteriorate.

(contd) Woman,' in Viljanen and Assubuji, *Photos: Women from Finland and Mozambique;* WLSA, 'WLSA Mozambique – Research on Violence against Women,' *Outras Vozes: Suplemento do Boletim,* 8 (August 2004): 8–11; WLSA, 'Some Reflections on the Working of the Assistance Centres for Victims of Domestic Violence, 2000–2003,' *Outras Vozes: Suplemento do Boletim* 8 (August 2004): 1–7; Redding, 'South African Women and Migration.'
[115] Earthy, *Valenge Women,* 11.

Once again, her *haháni* stepped in. She helped Ester make her way to Cajú to get a job and raise her son. Like Cristina Cuambe, Ester decided not to have more men or children in her life. It was somewhat easier to make ends meet on her salary with just one child. Despite her *haháni's* help and her own fine efforts, misfortune seemed to stalk Ester. Like most women Ester aspired to build a home for herself and her son. She returned from a family visit in Inhambane to find that her son, her only child, had sold all her accumulated building materials and absconded with the money. At age 68 she was once again starting to accrue corrugated iron sheets and concrete blocks to build a house. All she could say regarding this bitter betrayal was '...and this was the child I came here to raise.'[116]

Virginia Massingue's experience highlights the diversity and complexity of migration, authority and support networks. Virginia's father died just after she was *loboloed* as a very young bride. Her husband beat her, and the one child she had with him died. With her brother's help, Virginia left the marriage and made her way to Lourenço Marques. Virginia's brother had used her *lobolo* to marry, so she was *haháni* to him and his family.[117] He helped her get a job at Cajú and committed to repay the 2,500.00 *estudos lobolo* to her husband's family so they would not harass her further. The fact that repayment of Virginia's substantial *lobolo* would come out of her brother's household assets obviously caused tension, and soon his wives, including the one with whom Virginia enjoyed a *haháni* relationship, began to drive her out.

Using familiar witchcraft discourse, they accused her of having poisoned her own marriage so she could order them around in their marriages. They challenged both Virginia's presence and their husband's intention to repay her *lobolo*. They may have picked up on Virginia's vulnerability due to the divorce, or simply judged she did not have the spirit to resist. They were right. Virginia, a gentle soul, left her brother's family to live with a cousin, his wife and their seven children. She repaid her *lobolo* out of her wages at Tarana. In her brother's home, aggressive sisters-in-law challenged Virginia's status as *haháni*, but in her cousin's home she simply became another mother to the household's many children. She explained that, although her only child died, her cousins were now 'her children'. Personality clearly figures in family dynamics, but gender, age and location shaped the parameters within which to stake claims.[118]

Finally, Balbina Tinga's experience revealed links among family members and between household formation, taxation, forced labour, *lobolo* and savings.[119] Her father was a very poor and ill man. His situation echoed the familiar plight of trouble paying taxes and conscription

---

[116] Above paragraphs from OT, Rita Novela, 27 May 1993 and OT, Ester Tafula, 3 June 1993.
[117] OT, Virginia Massingue, 4 June 1993.
[118] OT, Virginia Massingue, 4 June 1993.
[119] The following paragraphs based on OT, Balbina Tinga, 27 May 1993.

for plantation labour. The work was hard and he was weak. He feared the work would kill him, and then his wife would be conscripted, leaving no one at home with the youngest children?

In order to spare himself and to pay the family's taxes, he accepted a *lobolo* payment from a man who wanted to marry his oldest daughter Balbina, even through she was still a child. Balbina had no say in the choice. Soon, however, her father saw how badly she was being abused in the marriage, and negotiated for another man to marry her for twice the amount of *lobolo*. Again, Balbina had no say. Her father used half of the second *lobolo* to repay the first marriage *lobolo* and the balance to pay his taxes. Balbina was barely more than a child and yet her bride-wealth had twice paid the family's taxes.

Unfortunately Balbina had no better luck in her second marriage. She did not want to disrespect her father or to continue as a pawn in his tax strategies. Her father died shortly after the second marriage, and Balbina decided it was time to save herself, and if possible, her mother and siblings. She heard about Tarana and struck out for it. However, she was not done with bridewealth payments. She saved her first wages to repay the *lobolo* from her second marriage so that no one could harass her family on that account. Then, fearing that her mother and siblings would all suffer from conscription for tax default, she saved her wages and eventually brought the remaining family to the city.

Balbina eventually gave birth to four children, but only one daughter survived. When we spoke seven people shared her household. She lived without bridewealth payment with a local man. Their household included Balbina's daughter, her sister, two nieces and one nephew. Balbina's daughter and sister had both separated from their husbands. Balbina continued to save her wages to help repay both her sister's and daughter's *lobolos*. She made the payments formally through the appropriate elders and recognized authorities. There would be no question that the marriage had ended.

Some people argued that women whose husbands mistreated them were not obliged to repay *lobolo*, but many people in those circumstances did repay it – including Balbina's father. Women often explained that decision as part of their quest to be 'done with it'. They wanted to be on their own without social claims on them or their children. Indeed, attention to the positive and negative potential of all kinds of social claims was an important current in the narratives.

In sum, the paths from rural poverty to the hoe of the city were many. Women confronted quite different configurations of possibilities and constraints, and each women's strength and ability to pursue her claims to make a life for herself differed. Death and the relationships enjoyed with family members were two key factors in the larger trajectories of women's migration both among rural households and between rural and urban households. Chapter 4 begins by opening the lens on the many ways women expressed themselves, taught each other about new possibilities and framed their claims on men, women and each other. It highlights emerging and culturally steeped self-images and aspirations, but then turns to the most important concern in most women's lives – how to care for the members of their families. In most cases it was their children. The chapter underscores the point that Mozambican children can become backdrop or statistics if you follow formal sector and androcentric data and narratives. If you follow the women you cannot miss the children.

4 Lives around Livelihoods
'Children Are Not Like Chickens'

Childcare dilemmas

The women of Sul do Save and the women of Tarana were dispro-portionately widowed, divorced and separated. Dozens of narrators became single mothers when their husbands died leaving them to support the children alone.[1] Many women simply said their children 'had no fathers.'[2] They had always looked after their children alone. Some women said they had 'problems' with the fathers of their chil-dren, so had to support their children alone. Everyone echoed Amélia Chiconela and Rabeca Notiço's mantra: to have enough to eat you had to go to work, but while you were at work someone had to care for your children.

Perhaps nothing was more difficult for the women of Tarana than the fact that staying at home to care for their children was undercut by their need to leave their children and go to work so they could earn the money to feed their children. Despite Parente and Neto's correla-tion between higher wages and higher absenteeism at Cajú, women and supervisors with decades of experience were perfectly clear about why women missed work: they or their children were ill, or a family member had a serious crisis. The long work day, poverty, seasonal malaria in areas with a lot of standing water, inadequate supplies of clean water and inappropriate handling of sewerage in their neigh-bourhoods made it much more likely that people would fall ill, espe-cially young children. Women remembered nothing worse about the colonial era than that supervisors pressured women to return to work immediately after childbirth, and dismissed illness and bereavement as appropriate reasons for missing work. Many women, fearing loss of their jobs or simply loss of wages, returned to work ill or left a sick child at home.

Clearly bearing, nursing and rearing children comprised a very large component of most women's daily work during their child-bearing years. As women aged, many continued to sustain household reproductive labour, providing for grown children, nieces, nephews,

[1] OT, Carlota Cumbe and group of retirees, 2 June 1993.
[2] OT, Elina Chivavale Mulungo, 4 June 1993.

155

siblings and grandchildren. Most women stoically accepted that their fertility was largely out of their hands. Older women had few options for birth control: 'We had many children. It was not for us to say. We had the number of children God destined for us.'[3] Some women expressed gratitude that God reconsidered their destiny. Matilde Chilengue, who struggled to raise her three children with no support from their fathers, was relieved: 'God helped me that I didn't have any more children.'[4]

In 1960, God gave Cristina Miambu the first of eleven children who included two sets of twins. Sul do Save cultures generally viewed the birth of twins as inauspicious, and initially that seemed to be the case for Cristina.[5] Her husband couldn't cope and left her after her sixth child. She confirmed the obvious: 'He did not want all those children.'[6] Cristina headed for Cajú with her first six children. While working at Cajú she lived *amancebado*, in a common-law marriage and had five more children with her new partner. She explained, 'It is God who gives us our children, I did not decide this.'[7] Her second partner did not necessarily support his five children, but they remained in a stable relationship, and Cristina found that helpful.

Nine of Cristina's eleven children survived. When she had school age and pre-school children, Cristina staggered their school shifts so that an older child would always be home with the younger children. When we spoke Cristina was an energetic woman aged 54. Her oldest daughter was 33 and had her own young family. Cristina had survived the particularly trying period with a long sequence of infants and toddlers, and finally enjoyed support from her children. She and her children worked together on weekends producing extra food in a *machamba* she had secured outside of the city. Cristina's patience, hard work, health and good luck combined to her advantage. She had a large social and support circle of family members who counted upon and supported one another – but getting to that point had not been the least bit easy.

In Tarana's time women brought their infants to the factory floor, but care of toddlers and young children posed a major dilemma.[8] The cost and availability of housing in Xilunguine meant that many women left their children in homes that were long distances from Tarana. Many women walked more than two hours a day.[9] The workday and time it took to get to and from work left little time to gather and process fuel, water and food. Families who went to bed hungry eventually got sick.

[3] OT, Joana Tinga Chilaule, 20 May 1993; Rosalina Tembe, 19 May 1993.
[4] OT, Matilde Chilengue, 27 May 1993.
[5] Paulo, 'Xiculungo' Social, 60.
[6] OT, Cristina Miambu, 26 May 1993.
[7] OT, Cristina Miambu, 26 May 1993.
[8] Kathleen Sheldon, 'Crêches, Titias and mothers: Working Women and Child Care in Mozambique,' in Tranberg Hansen, ed. African Encounters, 292–5; Urdang, And Still They Dance.
[9] OT, Amélia Chiconela, 17 May 1993; Leia Nhavene, 17 May 1993.

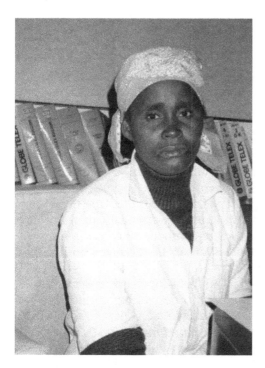

Figure 8 Cashew Sheller
Cristina Miambu
(© Jeanne Marie Penvenne)

More than half of the women who shared their stories had lost a child
to illness and accidents, and many had lost more than one. Amélia
Chiconela told us, 'Many children died because women left newborns
at home alone so they could go back to work. Children died from their
mothers' neglect'. Then, with a combination of sadness and resignation, she told us that seven of her eleven children died – more than any
of the other women.[10]

Amélia Maniquete cried whenever she had to leave her four-year-old
alone at home. She left milk for her daughter to drink, but she knew
that if she couldn't work, she couldn't even give her child milk.[11] Eventually Amélia brought a niece to live with them so her daughter was
no longer left alone. Perhaps no one felt the cost of having to choose
between caring for and working to feed her children more than Marta
António Nhamave. The cost for her was simply unbearable. In her soft
voice, with her eyes downcast, she told the group how her older child
had accidentally killed her younger child when they were home alone
playing with a hoe. Those listening felt her agony as though it were
yesterday. Many stories left the circle of listeners silent in empathy and
pain. The most painful stories always concerned children.[12]

[10] OT, Amélia Chiconela, 17 May 1993.
[11] OT, Amélia Manhiquete, 26 May 1993.
[12] OT, Amélia Chiconela, 17 May 1993; Amélia Manhiquete, 26 May 1993; Marta António
Nhamave, 27 May 1993.

The Chamanculo factory eventually transitioned from allowing women to carry their infants on their backs or rest them in sling hammocks on the factory floor to the establishment of a factory child-care centre. Nursing mothers took time during their shifts to feed their babies. In principle their children were better off in the childcare centre than at home alone or vulnerable to many dangers of the factory floor. It was clearly in the factory's interest to keep women and their children safe and healthy. After the formation of Frelimo in the early 1960s, factory childcare centres also played into the late colonial era's 'hearts and minds' campaign. Colonial social services, called Acção Social, supplemented the babies' diets in response to the acknowledged crisis in nutrition among the city's poor black families that threatened a generation suffering from stunting and its attendant mental retardation. Accão Social was an important component of Portugal's social welfare counter-insurgency strategy, implementing several housing, health and nutrition initiatives.[13]

The childcare centre at Tarana had a starkly checkered reputation. Elina Mulungo was enthusiastic about it, despite having no personal experience with it. Her children were grown before it was established. She was impressed that it was clean and children were all provided with smocks.[14] Most women who actually left their children at the centre were less enthusiastic. Marta Else Honwana and others said they kept their children and grandchildren in the childcare centre in the late 1960s because they had no other option and it was a lesser evil, particularly for infants. Several women found their children unattended, naked and soiled on the childcare centre's wooden berths. One woman found her child eating another child's faeces. That particular story spread quickly and many women responded by removing their children. Honwana immediately sent for a niece to care for her children in exchange for room and board. Not all women had a trusted relative they could call on, or if they did, they did not have enough space or food to support her.[15]

Women who had no alternative except the childcare centre eventually got up the courage to raise their voices with their supervisors and Accão Social, insisting on greater vigilance and better conditions. At the close of the colonial era, conditions in the centre had improved a

[13] Detailed in Chapter 5. Teixeira Santos, 'Avaliação Nutricional'; Comissão Provincial de Nutrição de Moçambique, *Inquérito nutritional e alimental a 262 operários indígenas da Fabrica de Cimentos da Matola e suas famílias* (Lourenço Marques, typescript, 1960); Junta de Investigação d'Ultramar, 'Inquérito habitacional realizado no bairro da Munhuana,' *Estudos de Ciências Políticas e Sociais*, 72 (Lisbon: Junta de Instituto Superior de Ciências Sociais e Política Ultramarina, 1964); Lília Maria Clara Carriére Momplê, Junta dos Bairros e Casas Populares. 'Relatório Sintese de Sector Social – Ano 1966,' December 1966, unpublished report from the archive of the Ministério de Coordinação da Acção Ambiental in Maputo. This 55 page unpublished report covers September 1965 to December 1966 and includes the survey observations of the 1966 inquiry at the Bairro de Munhuana. My sincere thanks to David Morton for copying and sharing this document.

[14] OT, Elina Chivavale Mulungo, 4 June 1993.

[15] OT, Marta E. Honwana and Carolina Cau, 31 May 1993; Rosalina Tembe, 19 May 1993; retiree group 2 June 1993.

great deal. In light of the factory administration's consensus that illness and childcare were the key factors in worker absenteeism, a well-run childcare centre would seem to have been an obvious investment in productive capacity.[16]

Leveraging discounted wages: *Vales*, *chitikis* and *biscates*

In light of their low monthly salaries and discounts due to the quota system, women at Tarana had to save where and how they could and leverage all their assets to make ends meet. Women walked to work, carried their lunch, and found ways to make more money and make the best of their income. Stretching a paycheck 'to have enough to eat' was particularly tough for large, young households. Poverty meant malnutrition, which meant ill health, which meant absenteeism, lower wages and rolling crises. It easily became a vicious circle. Women resisted that possibility by buying food with *vales*, saving money through *chitikis* and making more money where possible from *biscates*. We'll take them in order.

With eleven children to feed, Cristina Muianga often had to borrow against the promise of her monthly paycheck. As mentioned in Chapter 2, merchants in the *bairros de caniço* did business with clients on the *vale* credit system. When Cristina's paycheck ran out she paid for food by signing a *vale* or chit. When she was paid, she paid off the chits she had accumulated, but was soon back to borrowing. Portugal's currency in this period was quite stable. For much of the period the cost of living rose only gradually, but Cristina had a lot of people to feed, shelter and clothe. On the positive side, merchants trusted most cashew shellers with the *vale* system because they knew the work and the women were both steady. On the negative side, however, the *vale* system tied women to a specific merchant and the quality of his food. If women were ill or something went seriously wrong they could end up in significant debt, basically eclipsing any access to cash. Whatever the disadvantages, the *vale* system tided many women through their most difficult years. As Cristina's family grew and she could count on the labour of the older children, weekend work in their shared *machamba* provided them with fresh, high quality food and diminished the family's need to buy food.

If *vales* were the credit system for the city's poor, *chitikis* were their savings strategy. *Chitiki* is the southern Mozambican name for a rotating savings circle, of the sort practiced in many parts of the world, but extensively in Eastern and Southern Africa. This ubiquitous practice was engaged in by friends, colleagues and family members to accumulate cash. Each payday every member of a *chitiki* paid in a fixed amount of money. One by one, each member of the *chitiki* circle in turn

---

[16] Sheldon, 'Creches, *Titias* and Mothers', 295–306.

received all the money contributed by all the members. For example, if you were in a *chitiki* of ten women who each put in 10 *escudos* a week, you would pay your 10 *escudos* every week for nine weeks and on the tenth week you would receive 100 *escudos* – your ten plus ten from everyone else in the circle. The payments continued until all members of the group had received the payday lump sum of cash, and the group then decided whether or not to begin anew. No one took out more than they put in, but the point was that, without the *chitiki*, no one would ever be able to accumulate the sum of 100 *escudos*. The money would simply have to be spent for one thing or another. Poor households globally spend all or virtually all of their income on food, fuel, shelter, and clothing.

Many women could never manage to commit any money to a saving strategy – they could barely borrow enough to live.[17] The amount of money put into *chitikis* varied greatly, and only people who could achieve a certain threshold could participate in even the smallest *chitiki*. To some extent life cycle factors shaped women's participation in both *vales* and *chitikis*. Women who had no children, few children, or grown children found it easier to accumulate some savings through *chitikis*. When most women's families were young they depended on *vales* as a lifeline, but when children became more productive, women could engage in *chitikis*, either with women who also sold surplus from their *machambas* or with women at Cajú. Market sellers, particularly women who sold fish and other popular and relatively high price products with daily turn around and a steady cash flow, were much better placed to participate in and benefit from *chitikis*.[18]

Cristina Cuambe had a small family, so was well placed to participate in *chitikis*, both to make her salary last and to buy clothing for herself and her son. When she began work at Cajú in 1962 her salary was 240 *escudos* a month. Eventually she and her colleagues earned 330 and then 450 a month. When she first moved into a very simple *caniço* home, her rent and most of the staples she needed were within her reach. Charcoal for cooking, for example, cost 7.50 for two bags. Her basic diet was rice, groundnuts, tea and sugar. As a 'good Changana woman,' she would have liked to pound maize for porridge, but she didn't have time, so she and her son ate rice instead.[19] Shortage of time shaped women's choices as much as shortage of money. Like many women, Cuambe also put her

---

[17] Rita-Ferreira, corroborates the prevalence of indebtedness and rent default, 'Os Africanos', 311.

[18] OT, Joana Chivangue, 19 May 1993; Carlota Cubay, 20 May 1993; Joana Nhacumbi, 21 May 1993; Joana Massacaira, 24 May 1993; Saquina Malassanhane, 26 May 1993; Cristina Miambu, 26 May 1993; Maria Argentina Nhasinde, 27 May 1993; Balbina Tinga, 27 May 1993; Rosa Joaquim Tembe, 2 June 1993; Melita Msague Tete, 2 June 1993; Rita-Ferreira, 'Os Africanos,' 367ff. Their testimony dovetails with a late twentieth-century study by Adriana Cândida Biosse de Caifaz, 'O Xitique, a Mulher e a Economia Familiar nas Zonas Urbanas: O Caso da Cidade de Maputo, 1992–2002' (Maputo: Têse de Licenciatura, UEM, 5 July 2005). Thanks to the author for permission to cite.

[19] OT, Cristina Duzenta Cuambe, 17 May 1993.

savings toward building materials. Although her son absconded with her first significant stock of building materials, she had begun again, and still planned to build her own home.[20] No matter how simple, a home of one's own was an important goal for many women at Tarana, and their path to that home was invariably through *chitikis*.

Ofélia Mbebe agreed that a home was important: 'When the *chitiki* money came to me I bought poles and zink sheets to build a little shanty just to hide my head.' [21] Again, many women linked the capacity to own their own home with the ability to protect their children. Rabeca Notiço told her lover: 'if you like me I will raise my children in my own course, later we can live together.'[22]

Young women who did not yet have children, women who for many reasons had few or no children and older women whose children were grown were likely to have a bit more time to leverage their income in a variety of ways – many of which were illegal in the late colonial era. Petty sales and service opportunities, basically all odd jobs, were called *biscates*. They were typically unlicensed, unregistered, and illegal. Men and women commonly worked *biscates* if possible, but men had many more *biscate* opportunities that carried lower risk than those available to most women.

In the late colonial era, as it is today, women planted any and all odd plots of land in and around the city with groundnuts, cassava, beans and greens. Although the great majority of African women in Lourenço Marques lived from or supplemented their livelihoods through agriculture in peri-urban or in-town *machambas* in the 1940s, as early as December 1945, the city's leading black newspaper claimed that urban agriculture was in crisis due to the uncertainty of land tenure. It was increasingly difficult for the women who grew produce for African consumers to secure claims to land.[23] From the mid 1950s the white residential and industrial footprint of the capital city pushed into the *bairros*. The further outside town women had to travel to find available and appropriate land to plant, the more costly the investment in time spent walking to and from the land, or in transport fees.

It was easier for local women like Rosalina Tembe and Raquelina Machava to arrange access to land for a *machamba*. Migrant women, Cristina Miambu, Cristina Phelembe, Joana Massacaira, Amélia Muzima and Leia Nhavene all worked weekends in *machambas* in and around the city to feed the many people in their households. Families with grown daughters, like Raquelina Machava, had a sufficiently large and energetic labour force to make the bus or truck ride to a weekend garden productive. The women worked in matrikin groups

[20] OT, Cristina Duzenta Cuambe, 17 May 1993.
[21] OT, Ofélia Mbebe, 4 June 1993.
[22] OT, Rebeca Notiço, 24 May 1993.
[23] *Brado Africano*, 24 Dec. 1945; *Censo da População em 1940*, Vol. 2, *População Indígena*; Barry Pinsky, *The Urban Problematic in Mozambique; Initial Post-Independence Responses, 1975–1980* (Toronto: Centre for Urban and Community Studies, 1982): 8; Loforte, *Genero e Poder*, 26ff.

and shared out the produce as well as the work.[24] As the price of transport increased some women had to give up their distant *machambas*.
Some then turned to brewing alcoholic drinks or to petty trade, buying
small quantities of produce at the large markets and selling them for a
tiny profit in their neighbourhoods.

Celeste Guambe and many of her colleagues regularly stretched
their low pay by producing and selling *bebidas* on the weekends: *uputsu*
(a low alcohol maize beer), *khalhavadlaha* (melon wine), *usura* (palm
wine), and *xicaju* (cashew brandy). Celeste explained: 'It was easy
to make or buy *bebidas*. When people finished their drinks they just
dispersed. There were no problems.'[25] Cristina Phelembe and others
valued their *machambas* because they produced the basic ingredients
for drinks like *uputsu*. Many women made *uputsu* at home and sold
it in the dooryard just outside their homes. Brewing is exacting and
time consuming, so best accomplished by women with grown children or without children.

At least as told by the narrators, *bebida* sales were not generally associated with casual prostitution. Women insisted that they worked at
Tarana and managed multiple *biscates* because they did not want to
end up in prostitution. Fear of getting to the point where the only way
they could feed their family was 'living in' Lagoas, Mafalala or *Mathlothlomana* kept women at Tarana. Most narrators sympathized with
colleagues who had resorted to prostitution – knowing they did not
do that lightly. A few women spoke of prostitution with disdain rather
than empathy. They alleged that women who were either lazy or too
proud to do Cajú's dirty work turned to prostitution – preferring to earn
'nightly bread,' but such opinions were a minority.[26]

As mentioned in Chapter 1, researching illegal activity is tricky, but
by most accounts brewing was pervasive. Although women down-
played social problems regarding brewing, they all knew it was illegal.
It was also lucrative, and the press and archival evidence make it clear
that police, soldiers, *régulos* and hundreds of women were deeply imbricated in alcohol sales. The women did the work and the authorities
took their cut as protection money. When an in-depth investigation in
the late 1940s revealed that the police, soldiers, and *régulos* who were
supposed to control the trade were instead living nicely off their cut,
the administration proposed deporting three *régulos* to Quelimane to
make an example of them.[27]

Malalanyana's police periodically went on a rampage to shut down
any and all brewers.[28] When that happened the sentences could be
stiff. Flora Inhatunguene and many other women were arrested in

[24] OT, Raquelina Machava, 21 May and 12 July 1993.
[25] OT, Celeste Guambe, 17 May 1993.
[26] OT, Maria Celeste Chavane, 2 June 1993.
[27] ACLM to Secretaria Geral,1808/A/42, 15 Nov. 1947.
[28] Marta Mahumana, ACLM sample registration card 35001 in 1955 and 1956 arrests and
forced labor for *bebidas*, ACLM / AHM.

December of 1951 for *bebidas* and sentenced to a full year of forced labour. In the mid 1950s Angelina Nhaca of the Mafalala neighbourhood and scores of other women were imprisoned multiple times for *bebidas*. [29] If women brewed and sold in their door yards rather than in the popular brisk seasonal markets they were less apt to be arrested.

Cashew nuts and drinks were seasonally important economic activities for thousands of producers, sellers and consumers. Women initiated and sustained production, and men's earnings moved to women's hands through sales of *bebidas*. That income was important to women, and in the aggregate, the *bebidas* sector of the informal economy in the *bairros de caniço* was very strong. Economists in the colonial era ignored the social and cash value of informal cashew nut and drink sales in the urban African economy. Instead the police and Native Affairs Officers focused on such production and sales as aspects of urban crime. Many cashew shellers, like many other women in Lourenço Marques, counted on extra income from informal seasonal sales of cashews and cashew drinks. Women who did not work full time for wages were better placed to make extra income from brewing because it was so time consuming. Comparatively well off African families also defended brewing and home sales of maize beer because such earnings contributed toward the family's rent, clothing and school fees.[30]

Resilient and collaborative households

Women came to Tarana because of *wusiwana*, poverty and *xaniseká*, the kind of poverty that caused deep suffering. Although most were poor by the urban standards of the era, some were very, very poor. The poorest people, then and now, were invariably the most socially isolated. They could not even minimally reciprocate within the gift and household economy, and experienced the humiliation and trauma of important debt that could not be paid. The women's testimony illustrated the multiple ways that bad luck and illness increased poverty, fuelled fear and enhanced isolation.[31] Although no clear polar spectrum emerged from isolated desperation to corporate prosperity, it was clear that women considered the optimal strategy to be collaboration among all members of an extended household in layered efforts to tap revenue and resources and diminish stress.

---

[29] ACLM sample registration cards reveal *bebidas* arrests and forced labor for cashew workers registration numbers 29601, 6221, 5361 and 45061.
[30] Amélia Alfredo Muiane and Lídia Tembe, educated women who were among the best off of the African urban population in the late colonial era confirmed maize beer sales were important for many elite women to contribute to the household needs. OT, Muiane, 13 Sept. 1977, Câmara Municipal de Maputo; OT, Tembe, 12 Nov. 1977, Maternidade de Matola. See also *Brado Africano*, 23 Feb. 1946, 10 Jan. 1948, 5 Feb. 1949.
[31] Distinct understandings of social correlations of poverty and wealth were revealed in a recent study of poverty in Maputo by Paulo et al, *'Xiculungo' Social*, 52–71.

Two women came to Cajú from quite different circumstances, but each illustrated the personal capacities women used to secure their households. They distinguished themselves as among the strongest, most prosperous of the women at Cajú – assuming leadership on the factory floor, among their colleagues and across the various work sectors. Joana Tinga Chilaule and Raquelina Machava each struggled with poverty and crises, but these women were resilient, strong and persistent.[32] Other women at Cajú also managed to build and sustain resilient households, but Joana and Raquelina's experiences combined important elements of patterns that emerged more broadly. Their key lesson was that social investment both trumped and was a necessary component of material investment. Both women invested in and depended upon people, and both built homes where their families felt safe, valued and invested.

Raquelina was a 'very married' woman, and her seven children were the focus of her household. Her path to Cajú began with a shock in midlife. In contrast, Joana was barely married, and her household revolved largely around her siblings, nieces and nephews. She was very young when she headed to Cajú and began to assume responsibility for a large household. Parents, partners, children, siblings, nieces or nephews served up beatings, betrayal and heartache as well as support and solidarity – nothing was magical about shared heritage. Courage, health and strength often combined with good luck when things actually turned out well. Indeed, the sense of 'there but for the grace of God (or the luck of the draw) go I' was palpable in people's empathy for their colleagues in general and for those who experienced crises in particular.

Joana Tinga Chilaule: '...Someone had to look after those children.'[33]

Joana was born and raised in Morrumbene, Sul do Save, the oldest of her parents ten children. She married young and was pregnant with her first child when both her father and husband died. Despite her own vulnerability as a pregnant young widow, Joana was more concerned about how her mother would be able to support herself and cope with her nine siblings. Even in distant Morrumbene Joana had heard of Tarana. As a widow, she did not have to repay her *lobolo*, but she looked to Tarana to secure her whole family's survival. In 1964, Joana secured her young son across her back in her *capulana* and headed off to pick up the hoe of the city.

Once she got her feet on the ground at Cajú, Joana returned to Morrumbene to get travel documents for all nine of her siblings. Her

---

[32] OT, Joana Tinga Chilaule, 20 May 1993; Raquelina Machava, 21 May and 12 July 1993; Eugenia Salamandze, 24 May 1993..
[33] The following paragraphs based on OT, Joana Tinga Chilaule, 10 Mary 1993.

mother stayed in Morrumbene to work their land. Joana sent her mother money and developed a strategy for the family to invest in both Lourenço Marques and Morrumbene. She made sure that everyone who could work and contribute did so. Like her colleagues, Joana managed childcare, cooking and reproduction of the household by staggering school hours and having older children look after the younger ones while she worked. Women's management of children's labour and household participation was essential. If women could afford to have their children in school, having older children attend school in shifts meant someone would always be home with the younger kids – it accomplished two goals.[34]

Many narratives confirmed that girls were less likely to be sent to school than boys, in part because their households counted on their labour, and in part because their families could not manage the cost of education.[35] The women of Tarana knew that their lack of education limited their options, and aspired to educate both boy and girl children, but many were not able to keep their children in school for long because their household's income barely covered food, water and shelter. School fees, clothing and supplies were often beyond their reach.[36] Helena Muzimba did not have schools in her area as a child, and in principle wished to educate her daughters and sons: 'Even though there were schools in Lourenço Marques my children did not study. How could they? They had to have clothes and school fees. I also had to have clothes and I have no husband'[37]

Joana consistently leveraged her wages through *chitikis* and invested her savings to spread the risks. Some household members worked peri-urban *machambas,* some went to school, some worked in the household, some conveyed money and goods to Morrumbene, some sold garden produce brought back from both the local *machambas* and Morrumbene. Joana first built a masonry house for the family in Lourenço Marques *caniço.*

Despite the low wages, it was not uncommon to find women saving to repay their own *lobolo* or to contribute to a brother's bridewealth. In Joana's case it was also not a successful strategy. With her *chitiki* savings Joana invested in her brother's *lobolo* and eventually paid for him and his family to return to farming in Morrumbene where she also built them a masonry house. Despite the *lobolo*, her brother's wife left him and their two-month-old child. He remained in Morrumbene and the child survived. The wife was never heard of again, and the *lobolo*

[34] Although most women talked about their experiences as girls, and we talked with several mother and daughter families, I paid insufficient attention to children's perspectives. OT, Marta Elisa J. Honwana, 31 May 1993.
[35] Beverly Grier 'Child Labor and Africanist Scholarship: A Critical Overview,'*ASR*, 47, 2 (Sep., 2004): 1–25; Grier, *Invisible Hands: Child Labor and the State in Colonial Zimbabwe* (Portsmouth: Heinemann, 2006).
[36] OT, Serafina Langa, 3 June 1993; Maria Rosa Xavier Sitoe, 28 May and 13 June 1993.
[37] OT, Helena Muzimba, 19 May 1993.

was never returned, however thanks to the brief marriage Joana had one more member in her household.[38]

When I met Joana, she supported at least a dozen people, and had built two masonry homes – all on the strength of her wages from Cajú. Joana had not achieved her managerial and material success without cost. Her story was not at all onward and upward. Two of her children died and one son spent time in jail. She worked a lot of overtime, and when she was in a pinch, needed food or the last bricks to finish one of her family's houses, she engaged in casual prostitution, and made nothing of it. She simply said she needed quick money, and prostitution paid daily and on the spot. She was just as unassuming and unromantic about her farm income, it was simply another component of her multi-stream income generating strategies. Her household, like many others, revealed how the waged, household, gift and informal economies combined in people's lives. She seemed neither impressed nor intimidated by what she had accomplished. She fed her household 'at Tarana,' and leveraged and enhanced that income as she judged possible and necessary. It was straightforward, she concluded, '...someone had to look after those children.'[39] Joana never assumed that anyone had to look after her.

Raquelina Machava:
'Our mothers suffered to hold together their marriage.'[40]

Raquelina Machava was born in Pande, a distant rural area of Sul do Save where, Raquelina recalled, 'people wore bark cloth and knew nothing about the value of money or vaccines.'[41] Raquelina's family moved to Boane, just outside Lourenço Marques, but she retained her respect for traditional marriage ritual and male authority. For her, dignity and value hinged upon a good marriage, and the birth of healthy children. Women, she argued, should make their marriage work: 'Our mothers suffered to hold together their marriage. Today women do not know the value of having children and a home. Who will take care of us when we are old if we do not have children?'[42]

Unlike many women at Cajú, Raquelina Machava married with *lobolo* and had all seven of her children with one husband. She and Salvador Cossa had prospered, and built a masonry home for their large house-

[38] OT, Joana Tinga Chilaule, 20 May 1993; Allison Butler Herrick et al. noted some women in Sul do Save in the mid-1950s paid *lobolo* to secure a 'wife' of their own. 'These were lent to their husbands or brothers for procreation and their children were claimed by female 'husbands' as their own.' *Area Handbook for Mozambique* (Washington: US Government Printing Office, 1969): 78.
[39] OT, Joana Tinga Chilaule. 20 May 1993.
[40] OT, Raquelina Machava, 21 May 1993.
[41] Quotes in the following paragraph from OT, Raquelina Machava, 21 May and 12 July 1993.
[42] OT, Raquelina Machava, 21 May and 12 July 1993.

hold. That was before Raquelina learned that Salvador had seduced her sister's young daughter. Relations between mature husbands and young nieces were something of a leitmotif in the narratives. In Raquelina's and Salmina Cuma's cases the husband seduced the niece, but in Felizmenta Namboro's case the niece seduced the husband.[43] In every case the relationship between an older married man and young niece provoked the dissolution of a household.

Raquelina was horrified and humiliated by the seduction. For all that she believed women should work hard to make a marriage work and soldier on in the face of adversity, she basically viewed her husband's act as incest, and in cultural terms it was incest. Incest was simply beyond the pale. In light of the assault on her dignity and the potential threat to her own daughters, Raquelina felt she had no choice. She divorced Salvador Cossa saying: 'One day you will make a woman out of your own daughter!'[44]

Not only was loyalty to a marriage important to Raquelina, divorce was difficult even if women could prove a serious grievance like incest. If a husband sent his wife off, Raquelina explained, he could not reclaim the *lobolo*. If the wife was at fault or if she was the one who left, she had to repay the *lobolo*. If she went off with another man, that man repaid her *lobolo* to the husband. If the husband or wife died no one had to repay the *lobolo*. She and her colleagues agreed that women often repaid *lobolo* even if they could make a case for not paying, because most women wanted to keep their former husband out of their lives. As many said, they wanted the matter finished.

Negotiations over the payment, non-payment or repayment of *lobolo* could go on interminably. Bridewealth and divorce comprised the core of the colonial administration files labeled '*Milandos*,' meaning complicated problems, disputes or imbroglios.[45] Men even tried to claim *lobolo* for daughters raised by women they never married and never supported, or women who had divorced them and repaid *lobolo* years earlier. Everyone nodded and many women fairly roared when Elina Chinavale Mulungo performed a very familiar situation. She shouted:

'*Loku uku inhimba yakule? Aku heee! Ahi Nhimba hanga.*' You would challenge the man like that: 'Is this your pregnancy then?' 'No! Not my pregnancy!' These children do not have fathers, but we feed, clothe and educate these children. But when the child grows up, then the father says, 'Yes this is my child.' Why did you deny that this was your child when the child was small?' The men were like that – they were useless for anything except what you do between the sheets.[46]

[43] OT, Raquelina Machava, 21 May and 12 July 1993; Salmina Cuma and Felizmenta Namboro, 19 July 1993.
[44] OT, Raquelina Machava, 21 May 1993.
[45] Milando defined in Lopes et al, *Moçambicanismos*, 105; Tenente Simões Alberto, 'Ethnografia Moçambicana,' *Império*, 5 / 6 (Sept. Oct. 1951): 30; ACLM R Cx II, run of B/11 files from the late 1940s include complaints about relationships and damage to property.
[46] OT, Elina Chivavale Mulungo, 4 June 1993.

Despite the possibility of some future contest regarding bridewealth for their daughters, Raquelina decided not to return Salvador Cossa's *lobolo*. The *lobolo* was probably not enough for anyone to contest. Besides, his behaviour clearly caused the break-up of a mature marriage. She judged that he would have very little standing in any potential dispute. Raquelina was determined to rebuild the security and prosperity her children had enjoyed until the divorce. She invested anything she managed to set aside into better circumstances for herself and her family. She had originally followed one daughter to work at Cajú. Eventually several other daughters entered the factory, some of them in good jobs. Raquelina eventually worked her way up to the level of supervisor, so the whole family earned better than average. She then encouraged all family members to leverage their earnings in a variety of strategies.

Raquelina and her daughters worked weekends on four *machambas* in Boane, just outside Lourenço Marques. Like Joana's family, they kept several income generating schemes going at once, and pooled individual resources. Savings from wages were the base, but market gardening and food savings leveraged wages. They first managed to build a house of *caniço*, and eventually improved it with corrugated metal sheets. Finally they completed a masonry home with running water. Like all the others who built homes of masonry or corrugated metal sheets, construction was accomplished one sheet or one block at a time over a long time.[47]

While some women never seemed to make any headway and wondered why they had worked at all, other women sustained themselves and many other people with the fruit of their labour at Tarana. Despite their great difficulties Joana and Raquelina were resilient, formidable women. In both cases, family members, mostly women, cooperated to complete the necessary tasks across the board. They shared childcare, gathered and processed fuel, food and water, they risk-managed *chitikis* based on Cajú wages, and they a kept a range of *biscates* going. Leveraging, cooperating, and being resilient in the face of blow after blow were all hallmarks of successful lives lived around livelihoods at Cajú. Despite lifetimes of hard work, not every worker got the balance of family relations, *biscates* and much else right. Sometimes it just came down to bad luck.

Poverty, humiliation and isolation

The anxiety of poverty is often lost on people who have not lived with its weight and experienced its wages. Elina Chiavale Mulungu was one

---

[47] David Morton writes about incremental construction in Maputo. Morton, 'Chamanculo in Reeds, Wood, Zinc & Concrete,' *Slum Lab – Made in Africa, Sustainable Living Urban Model*, 9 (2014): 43–46.

of the poorest women at Tarana: 'Poverty is so worrisome. Sometimes I am sick at heart for fear that my brother might come to see me. I will not even have tea to offer him. I always am tormented by the thought of visitors arriving when I have nothing to offer them.'[48] She could barely feed herself, but the humiliation of lacking the wherewithal to greet a visitor with appropriate dignity was more painful than her own hunger. Leia Papulo Nhavene agreed: 'It is important to receive family members in the proper way.'[49] A proper reception at a minimum required tea, and for the poorest families, even tea was a luxury.

Isolation was both a characteristic and a strategy of the most distressed women. Some women pursued isolation and some felt isolated when they were actually not alone. Given the paths many women took to Tarana, they were wary of relationships with people who might throw them out, leave them, beat them or rob them of what little they had gained to date. Most women confirmed and protected their autonomy, but many of the poorest women were fearful of depending on anyone. All relationships, including among the generally safer matrikin, were potentially complicated. Family members could assert claims as well as offer support.[50] As we have seen, women experienced some of their most devastating betrayals at the hands of their children or siblings.

Cacilda Fumo, Celeste Guambe, Ofélia Manana Mbebe, and Amélia Chiconela were among the poorest women in any of the cohorts. All felt isolated, even desperate. Cacilda Fumo and Celeste Guambe actually pursued isolation. Cacilda was one of the few women at Cajú who never had children. She used to live with her nephew but preferred to live alone, explaining: 'I did not want to have his problems.'[51] Celeste Fumo had one child, but when that child died she fought with her husband and left. She repaid her bridewealth because she wanted to be 'finished' with that marriage and back on her own. Celeste claimed, 'I have no friends, men or women. I don't want friends because I don't want problems.' For years she had made her living in the shelling section, and leveraged her discounted wages with brewing. She could call on the nephew for whom she was a *hahâni* if she needed, but in Cacilda's and Celeste's experience relationships just brought problems – problems they feared. Both were limping along, but barely.[52]

In contrast to the actual isolation lived by Cacilda and Celeste, Ofélia Manana Mbebe felt utterly alone despite being the pillar of a family of more than a dozen people. She clearly experienced relationships as a burden. Ofélia began working at Cajú before any of her children were born, but in the end she lamented: 'I have worked so much, but I can't say I know why I worked. I suppose I worked to feed

---

[48] OT, Elina Chivavale Mulungu, 4 June 1993.
[49] OT, Leia Nhavene, 17 May 1993.
[50] Loforte, *Poder e Género*, passim.
[51] OT, Cacilda Fumo, 21 May 1993.
[52] OT, Celeste Guambe, 17 May 1993.

my children, but my children still have no homes and now they are having their own children, and I am still working to support them. I can barely feed all these children, so I am always sad. I worry all the time and bear all of this alone. I work, but I don't know why I am working.'[53] Ofélia's was not the conjunctural stress experienced by young mothers exhausted by their efforts to juggle the particular challenges of nurslings and toddlers. Unlike Joana and Raquelina, Ofélia had not been able to leverage her contribution with broader efforts from other members of the household. She remained the only breadwinner in a growing family. Hers was chronic grinding poverty and it was taking its toll.

Reflecting on her decades at Cajú, Amélia Chiconela also worried that all her efforts were for naught – everything had been so hard for her, and her losses were so painful. This book opened with Amélia muddling her way to Lourenço Marques. She did not know what money was and 'just got used to this'. She spent most of the day at *Malalanyana's* office because she didn't know how to register and was afraid to ask. She told us that seven of her eleven children died. The cumulative impact was very difficult: 'I think I will never have peace in this life. I am very poor. I just want to rest!'[54] Cacilda, Celeste, Ofélia and Amélia experienced their children and families as burdens and disappointments.

Most women took pride in their endurance, and viewed their work and family as anchors of meaning and concern. Some women considered their colleagues at Tarana as their family, and knew they could count on them. Given what it took for women to get to Tarana in the first place, self-reliance seemed like a core characteristic. Catarina Tafula put it well: 'In some ways the factory helped me. I raised my children on Cajú money, but I earned that money with my own two hands.'[55] The women in that workforce also accomplished work outside the factory to support their families and raise their children in the hours they had before and after work. They had to live their lives around their livelihood at Cajú. In so doing they shaped the city and the city shaped them.

Seeking gendered perspectives through song

The book opened with the observation that Southern Mozambican women often sing what they will not say. Whether in song or speech, women framed what they did in terms of their womanhood and responsibility for their children. Songs provide a lens into what women valued and how they assigned meaning to their experiences. All the touchstone songs in this work were recorded by Alpheus Manghezi. More than

---

[53] OT, Ofélia Manana Mbebe, 4 June 1993.
[54] OT, Amélia Chiconela, 17 May 1993.
[55] OT, Catarina Tafula, 9 June 1993.

any other scholar, Manghezi has focused on songs of southern Mozambique.[56] A South African whose mother tongue is Changana, Manghezi was among the cadres of researchers who recorded testimony and songs in the wake of Mozambican independence. After months of taping among men and women in the late 1970s and early 1980s, he realized that his own patriarchal assumptions blinded him to some aspects of women's agency and empowerment, and began to listen more critically.

Oselina Marindzi sang the questions on every woman's mind when she considered heading to Tarana: 'Oh, where will I go? Oh, how can I get there? What will become of me?'[57] Filomena Mathayi sang many women's experience of pressure to remain working stoically on a flat bare place, waiting for a man who would not return. Stoicism was a standard theme in laments, pounding songs and group work songs. There was not much in either woman's song to suggest they would defy their elders.[58]

Our third song is '*Magostinho nuna wa mina, mamani!*' or 'Agostinho, my husband, Oh mother!' The lament was originally sung by Agostinho's wife. It tells us that he left to work on contract in South Africa but didn't come home to her and their children. Agostinho returned to Mozambique, but became involved with a Ronga woman in Lourenço Marques, and remained in town living with her. Agostinho's wife eventually heard that the Ronga woman was fine, 'with hips round like a pumpkin.' Everywhere beauty is a form of power, and women were well aware of their own and other people's powers. The power of this Ronga woman convinced her that Agostinho would never return. She considered herself abandonned and knew that her children would suffer. Her lament's refrain, 'Oh mother,' was the equivalent of Oselina Marindzi's 'Oh woe is me!'

Manghezi heard the song several times. He then heard what he initially thought was a different song with a similar theme. He then realized that it was the same song, but that the singer, Mindawu Bila, had transformed the lament into something of a lesson. Bila's version of '*Magostinho nuna wa mina mamani*' was significantly less woeful than the original. Bila, who was born around 1910, sang the song in Changana with a group of unidentified women supporting her as the chorus. Unlike the original, Bila's version was neither true nor autobiographical. Bila changed the original lyrics, and imagined an alternative to a lament.[59]

What follows is my free-form English translation of Mindawu Bila's version of '*Magostinho nuna wa mina, mamani!*'[60]

[56] The following paragraphs are based on Manghezi, *Trabalho Forçado* and my conversation with him on 28 Nov. 2004, *Bairro Residencial Universitária*, Maputo. I am grateful to Alpheus Manghezi for permission to include the unpublished backstory for this song.

[57] Oselina Marindzi in Manghezi, 'A Mulher e o Trabalho,' 49.

[58] 'On a Flat Bare Place' taped by Alpheus Manghezi, was published in First, et al. *Black Gold*, 163.

[59] Manghezi, *Trabalho Forçado*, 56–60.

[60] The original Changana with a Portuguese translation is included in Manghezi's *Trabalho Forçado*, 56–60.

'Agostinho, My Husband – Oh Mother!'

Lead singer [S] & Chorus [C]

S: Ahhh, Agostinho my husband, oh mother!
C: Yes, let's go home
S: The children are crying for their father, oh mother!
C: Yes, my husband
S: [Children], I can't find your father, oh mother!
C: Yes, let's go home
S: They weren't delayed in South Africa, they were delayed in Lourenço Marques where there is a Ronga woman!
C: Yes, my husband
S: Her hips are round like a pumpkin, oh mother!
C: Yes, my husband
S: She's squandering my husband's money.
C: Yes, let's go home
S: I make the bed, but only the lizard sleeps in it, oh mother!
C: Yes, my husband
S: I roast groundnuts, but it is just food for the rats, oh mother!
C: Yes, my husband
S. I spread the straw on the floor, but it is just food for the termites, oh mother!
C: Yes, my husband
S: What can I do my husband? oh mother!
C: Yes, let's go home
S: Oliveira [rural bus company] help me please.
C: Yes, my husband
S: I'll take a bus to Lourenço Marques, oh mother!
C: Yes, let's go home
S: And when the woman arrives in Lourenço Marques, oh mother!
C: Yes, my husband
S: He says: 'Where did you come from?'
C: 'What do you want?'
S: Yes, let's go home
C: Yes, my husband
S: She says: 'The children are sick my husband'
C: Yes, my husband
S: I have no money, my husband.
C: Yes, let's go home
S: He says: 'Now you start this again [with your problems!]'
C: Yes, my husband
S: 'You start this again'
C: Yes, let's go home
S: She says: 'Father, are you refusing to come with me?'
C Yes, let's go home
S: 'I will file a complaint [with the Native Affairs Office]'
C: Yes, my husband
S: 'Why don't you want to come home?'
C: Yes, let's go home.
S: They [the neighbours] say: 'Aiiii! She will file a complaint!'

C: Yes, my husband
S: He says: 'Please, be patient; now I understand, my dear wife.'
C: Yes, let's go home
S. He says: 'We will go tomorrow.'
C: Yes, my husband
S. He says, 'Let's leave tomorrow.'
C: Yes, let's go home
S: But I have to return [to the city].
C: Yes, my husband
S: When they arrive at home
C: Yes, my husband
S: They find a desperately poor situation
C: Yes, let us go home
S: He says to his wife: 'Let's leave'
C: Yes, my husband
S. They return to the land of the whites [*Xilunguine* –Lourenço Marques]
C: Yes, let's go home
S: He decides that he no longer likes the one whose hips are round like a pumpkin.
C: Yes, my husband
S: He says: 'Get out: you made me suffer!'
C: Yes, let's go home.
S: 'You squandered my money and made me abandon my wife.'
C: Yes, my husband.

Mindawu Bila's version underscored familiar tensions among town and migrant women, and created spaces among old and new expectations and practices for women to secure their goals. Typically, she first addressed the wellbeing of children and the importance of a father and his resources in their protection. She then documented her adherence to a community's expectations for adult women's behavior as a dutiful wife and proper housekeeper: waiting patiently for her husband; staying with the children even though they were ill and she was poor; making a proper bed for her husband; roasting groundnuts to feed their family properly, and spreading fresh straw on a clean swept floor.[61] The parallel dutiful husband narrative required Agostinho to support and protect his family, yet he had left his wife without money and their children were ill, suffering without food. Agostinho spent the money due to his wife and children on another woman. The narrative thus deepened claims on the cultural expectations of how a dutiful wife might challenge an errant husband.

Bila juxtaposed some stock images of Mozambican women with new images. Bila's wife takes advantage of the expanding rural transportation network, the Oliveira bus system that used to just carry men to towns and the mines, but now carried many women to towns and to Tarana. She left her village by bus and arrived in the unfamiliar colo-

[61] Many parallels exist here with Deborah James's anthropological analysis of Kiba dance lyrics among Sotho women in the late twentieth century, *Songs of the Women Migrants: Performance and Identity in South Africa* (Edinburgh: Edinburgh University Press, 1999). See also Deborah Gaitskell's review of James in *Journal of Religion in Africa*, 32, 2 (May 2002): 256–61.

nial capital city, much like many of the women of Tarana. In Bila's narrative Lourenço Marques was not only *Xilunguine*, the place of the whites, it was also the place of Ronga women who were powerful because they were native to the city and more powerful still if they were beautiful. Her song opens to the black city.

Bila's dutiful wife image was immediately challenged by Agostinho's retort that she was a nag or a scold, thus the kind of wife a husband might properly ignore. Bila pivoted with the image of a smart wife, one that a man ignored at his peril. Bila's smart wife would pursue all means necessary to make her husband comply with his obligations to their conjugal partnership. She afforded him fair warning that he was dealing with determination: 'Father, are you refusing to come with me?' When he ignored that, she stepped squarely into the crocodile's mouth and threatened to file a complaint of abandonment with the municipal Native Affairs Office. She confronted an old problem with a new resource. From the 1940s women increasingly directed complaints of spousal non-support, abandonment and inequitable treatment to the Native Affairs Office, in some ways playing off one patriarchy against another.[62] In Bila's version that threat did the trick. Agostinho's Ronga neighbours were so astonished by her audacity that Agostinho decided to rethink his posture toward this courageous woman.

While it is tempting to assume that Bila's version picked up on Frelimo's pro-woman legal reforms, and telescoped that attitude back to the colonial era, that was probably not the case. The Portuguese administration in Lourenço Marques developed a reputation in the late colonial era for supporting married women in family disagreements, including non-support, custody of minor children, and widow disinheritance. *Malalanyana*'s strategy was to keep married women supported at home and unmarried or divorced women out of town. Senior men complained that 'disgruntled' wives could seek recourse both in the Native Affairs Office and the cashew factories – undermining senior male authority in either situation.[63] Regardless of women's rights in law and custom, men frequently retained control over women in their households through the threat or execution of violence.[64] Even a successful claim

[62] The ACLM files contain hundreds of complaints from men trying to fetch back wives and wives claiming child support from husbands. My broad sampling of these files revealed that women and men were most likely to be successful if their claims were against a spouse by civil or customary law, whereas people seeking claims in *amancebado* relationships seldom prevailed except in cases of domestic violence or theft. PAM to ACLM, 12 Sept 1947, 93/B/5, ACLM R Cx GG, ACLM / AHM; Ana Daili against Agostinho Dias, RCNI to ACLM 29 Jan. 1947, 273/M/1, ACLM R Cx X, ACLM / AHM.

[63] Binford, 'Stalemate,' 108–109.

[64] Corroboration for women's testimony regarding domestic violence is extensive: Ungulani ba ka Khosa's memories of women being beaten in colonial Mafalala, Chamanculo and Ximpamanine in Nelson Saúte, *Moçambique: A Oitava Côr do Arco-íris* (Madrid: Agência Española de Cooperación Internacional (1998): 242–3; WLSA collaborative, Mozambique, 'Research on Violence against Women' *Outras Vozes*: Suplemento do Boletim. No. 8 (August 2004): 8–11; WLSA 'Some Reflections on the Working of the Assistance Centres for Victims of Domestic Violence, 2000–2003,' *Outras Vozes*: Suplemento do Boletim. No. 8 (August 2004): 1–7; Ribeiro, *África no Feminino*, 81ff.

through the colonial administration carried the risk of a *pancada da graça,* a gratuitous beating, from an angry husband or an unsympathetic policeman. Challenging male authority was never without risk.

In Bila's version the legal / abandoned rural wife triumphed, but the song also revealed the dilemmas of what were effectively polygamous extended households. In Bila's song, both husband and wife blame the entire situation on the Ronga woman. Agostinho was not responsible for his profligate behavior and non-support: 'You [Ronga woman] squandered my money and made me abandon my wife.' The song ends having resolved a conjugal disruption by creating an *amancebado* disruption. Agostinho tells the Ronga woman to 'Get out!' Unlike Agostinho's legal wife, the Ronga woman living *amancebado* would have little standing at the Native Affairs Department. However, if the house were actually hers, the Native Affairs Office would take her side. This Changana song does not pursue the fate of the Ronga woman, but it seems that one woman's claim costs another woman her home. That would be in keeping with many of the narratives, and was a major driver for women's aspirations for home ownership.

Percina Mungumbe spoke directly to the Ronga woman's situation when she said, 'a man could send you away any night – then what would you do? If a woman doesn't work for wages she depends on a man.'[65] Mungumbe was twice widowed. She built her own home and lived with her daughter. She and others preferred to control their incomes and the roofs over their heads so that men could not exert claims on them, their children or their homes.[66]

The song explored the ways women navigated the stakes claiming opportunities available to them in familiar and emerging arenas. The colonial and lineage laws and those who enforced them favored the legal (usually rural) wife over the *amancebado* partner. Yet despite a legal wife's advantages in law, Sul do Save rural women were more apt to live without men in their households than were women in Lourenço Marques. Although both men and women played the powers and images of multiple arenas off against one another, by the late colonial era, public transportation, the colonial legal system, and, most importantly, increasing opportunities for women to earn wages and to work in both rural and urban informal trade opportunities, combined to shift the power landscape somewhat to women's advantage. Following Ali Mari Tripp's insight, relationships and rules were both changing.[67] Some women no longer settled for a lament – they made their own way.

---

[65] OT, Percina Mungumbe, 10 June 1993.
[66] OT, Amélia Manhiquete, 26 May and 13 July; Matilde Mussongue Chiduza, Ofélia Manana Mbebe, 4 June 1993; Elina Chivavale Mulungu, 4 June 1993; Percina Mungumbe, 10 June 1993.
[67] Tripp, 'Changing the Rules.'

The women who came to make a life and livelihood in the Chamanculo factory arrived with their individual spirits, identities, personalities and understandings. They made choices within what they understood to be possible, even if difficult. People do not make impossibly difficult choices lightly. Women often found the people and the new practices of mission posts, urban markets, factories, transport systems, Native Affairs Offices, and *cantinas* intimidating, and all could interfere in their lives in bothersome ways. Many women learned to navigate the era's changing possibilities and resolve some of the problems they faced in their day-to-day lives. They developed a capacity to forget their suffering, solve their problems, alleviate their poverty and raise their children. In the manner highlighted by Frederick Cooper:

> ...ordinary people were trying to live their lives: to use resources that were new and others that were old, to struggle against the oppressiveness of the new by using the old and against the oppressiveness of the old by using the new. What they were producing did not fit a pre-packaged modernity, nor did it constitute 'tradition' or 'community.' People were fashioning and refashioning forms of connections and associations.[68]

In that sense, the cashew factory in Lourenço Marques opened a new pathway for Southern Mozambican women. They heard about Tarana whether they lived in Catembe, just across the bay from the city, or in Pande, deep in the southern Mozambican hinterland – word spread. Women knew that their key qualifications, being strong, patient and smart, were inadequate for the many urban jobs that required knowledge of the Portuguese language, counting and reading skills. The calculation and communication skills that served them well in their rural lives were not necessarily equivalent to what they would need in town.

The colonial state and senior men and women resisted the movement of young women and children to urban areas. Helen Bradford reminds us that that '...many male lives were premised on exclusion of women from most property and political rights, [and] on access to unpaid female productive and reproductive labour.'[69] The interests of both men and senior women, who counted on unpaid labour by younger women, were potentially threatened if they made their way to work at Tarana. Ronga men's songs in the 1960s complained of 'the disrespect of women for their male superiors and their wanton recourse...to jobs in the cashew factories.'[70] Sul do Save men complained that, 'to any small criticism,' women responded by going off to get a job and divorcing their husbands.[71] As lineage authority

---

[68] Frederick Cooper, *Africa since 1940: The Past of the Present* (New York: Cambridge University Press, 2002): 118.
[69] Bradford, 'Women, Gender,' 351–2, 356, 369.
[70] Binford,' Stalemate,'109, 117–18; Sheldon, *Pounders of Beans*, Ch. 2, esp. 57.
[71] July 1975, un-named man in Chobela, southern Mozambique, quoted by Young, 'Women in Transition,' 14.

and control over resources diminished, some women were actually driven away from lineage households. Women, who in prior eras would have been 'fetched back' to their homes by their menfolk, were left to fend for themselves in the city.[72] As we have heard, few women upped and left before they were pushed far enough to convince them to jump.

The space between expressing a lament and an action to address its root cause can be great, and not everyone has the spirit, health or luck to bridge it. Some women found the courage to leave for Tarana whereas many others did not. We heard from those who had the courage to leave an untenable situation and survived Tarana. The threshold of suffering that propelled women along the unfamiliar and frightening pathway toward Tarana shaped them, as did their experience of work when they arrived at Tarana.

Women who formed the original cohort at Tarana, and worked in subsequent generations, individually and cumulatively created narratives of factory work, life on the factory floor and their developing identities as cashew shellers. 'Industrial woman' was not anticipated in the colonial labour script, but neither did she emerge as an essential figure with a uniform narrative.[73] Important differences existed between women who worked as *tinumerini,* weighing, counting and sending out packaged cashew nuts and women who worked in *djamangwana,* peeling the hot cracked shells in the heat, dust and thunder of the factory boiler. Little at the factory was like women's rural home experience, but they nonetheless drew on rural and familial language and images when fashioning new narratives to claim ownership of the spaces, relationships and work they did in town.

Wealth, status, maturity, ability, personality and other factors shaped choices and possibilities among women. The more we know of women's history and where we might seek it, the more we appreciate the textures and fault lines of women's strategies, solidarities and competition. Heidi Gengenbach suggested we find women's past in their body scars, potshards, story telling and names.[74] Elinami Veraeli Swai suggested women spoke through clothing, explicitly their Khangas (*capulanas*).[75] Mindawu Bila's song is particularly instructive regarding the making, unmaking and remaking of households and also underscores Cooper's point about ordinary people's eclectic strategies to pursue their interests by asserting the old and picking up on the new.

Southern Africans express their experiences and aspirations in complex and culturally coded ways. Efforts to read southern African

[72] Shula Marks, 'Patriotism, Patriarchy,' 227.
[73] Frederick Cooper, 'Back to Work: Categories, Boundaries and Connections in the Study of Labour,' in Peter Alexander and Rick Halpern, Eds. *Racializing Class, Classifying Race; Labour and Difference in Britain, the USA and Africa* (New York: St. Martin's Press, 2000): 217.
[74] Gengenbach, 'Where Women Make History.'
[75] Swai, *Beyond Women's Empowerment,* Ch. 3.

voices in praise poetry and song are challenging and promising.[76] Songs embody contending gendered perspectives.[77] Men and women working conscript labour under colonialism contested the brutality and indignity of their labour through song. Women's pounding, spirit possession and field songs often contested the tensions around their labour and standing in their households. Men sang about their cheating wives and their sense of the untrustworthiness of women in general.[78]

Mine workers worried in song that their wives, who secured their property and status at home, might take up with other men during their long absences. Men's songs often conflated women's resistance with disrespect and laced praise for women who dutifully held the family's investments with insults and threats of divorce for women who did not. Women's songs were more apt to lament than to threaten, and men's songs more apt to sanction and intimidate. Women's songs featured the refrain 'woe is me!' or 'oh mother!' The refrain for the popular men's song about the bride named Celina was, 'But in the end she is a whore....Ho Celina!' According to the song, 'Wawuya Celina,' Celina was wed at great expense by her husband, but ultimately she was sent packing back to her family in disgrace because she had seen other men in her husband's absence.[79] Catembe men similarly sang about the 'whores' who left their marriage for a job in the cashew factories? [80] Popular men's songs in Mozambique's second largest city, Beira, carried familiar male images of African urban women. The songs claimed women schemed and cruelly played men for their money and yet revealed that men treated women as mere objects of pleasure or lineage property. Men's songs also idealized women as wives, mothers and guardians of a peaceful hearth and prosperous household.[81]

[76] Vail and White, Capitalism and Colonialism; Vail and White, Power and the Praise Poem; Manghezi, 'Entrevistas,' 45–56.
[77] Patrick Harries, Alpheus Manghezi, Allen F. Isaacman and I have developed song texts in our work on Mozambique: Manghezi, Macassane, Trabalho Forçado and 'Entrevista;' Isaacman, Cotton is the Mother; Harries, 'A Forgotten Corner of the Transvaal,' 93–134; Penvenne and Sitoe, 'Power, Poets and the People;' David Coplan, Elizabeth Gunner, Isabel Hofmeyr and Deborah James have done extensive work with gender, song and performance in Southern Africa: David Coplan, In Township Tonight!: South Africa's Black City Music and Theatre (London: Longman, 1985); Coplan, Songs of the Adventurers [Videorecording produced and directed by Gei Zantzinger] (Devault, PA: Constant Springs Productions, 1987); James, Songs of Women Migrants; Elizabeth Gunner, 'Songs of Innocence and Experience: Women as Composers and Performers of Izibongo, Zulu Praise Poetry,' Research in African Literatures, X (1979):239–67; Isabel Hofmeyr, 'We Spend Our Years as a Tale that is Told': Oral Historical Narrative in a South African Chiefdom (Portsmouth: Heinemann, 1993).
[78] Estévão J. Filimão, 'Imagem da Mulher nas Canções da Música Urbana na Beira (1975–1989): Contribuição ao Estudo das Literaturas Marginais,' in Santana Afonso, coord. Eu, Mulher em Moçambique,125–45.
[79] This quote and paragraph based on 'Wawuya Celina,' sung by Magomane Pequenino, Maputo, 15 July 1977.
[80] Binford,' Stalemate,' 109, 117–18.
[81] Filimão identifies eight images of women: gold digger, two faced, cruel, ideal domestic guardian, invisible, mother, object of pleasure, and property: Filimão, 'Imagem da Mulher nas Canções.'

Women's spirit possession chants could be confrontational because the spirit spoke, not the woman. When possessed, women took the men of their households and villages to task for their infertility, betrayals, harassment, incest and adultery. Given the limited alternatives for women to protect themselves and their children, they had a lot of incentive to endure in their households: to care for their children, be respectful to authority, work hard and well, and keep their *machambas* productive while their husbands worked for wages.

We draw gendered and generational perspectives on the making, unmaking and remaking of Mozambican households from a final song in Manghezi's archive. Emereciana Alfredo Mazivi's song 'Keep Quiet,' speaks to men as husbands and men as fathers of married daughters. The song cautioned a daughter and her migrant husband about malicious gossip that could sow distrust and jealousy between them and undermine their marriage. When the husband returned from South Africa, his kinsmen might tell him 'look here, that wife of yours is lazy, stupid and always on the footpath.' In the song, the wife's father cautioned his daughter, and, implicitly her husband, to keep quiet, ignore the gossip and be confident that her husband and father both trust her. The father's trust was explicit: '...keep quiet my daughter, I know you are not like that!'[82] The husband's trust was essential, but could not be assumed.

---

[82] Song included in First, et al., *Black Gold*, 165.

5 African Urban Families in the Late Colonial Era[1]
Agency

Africans [in Lourenço Marques] live in total promiscuity... numerous families together with no thought of hygiene. These poor people not only live miserably in shacks built of all kinds of junk but also pay rents for the space they occupy on lands, that in other times perhaps belonged to their grandparents, but are now held in legitimate title by Europeans.[2]

Adelino José Macedo, Municipal Administrator, 1947

Why do you prefer to have your wife and children live in the rural areas?[3]

António Rita-Ferreira – 1967 Survey 'Africans of Lourenço Marques'

The social history of everyday life in late colonial Lourenço Marques supports John Lonsdale's assertion that Africans navigated in quite tight corners.[4] Lourenço Marques municipal authorities created, perpetuated and exacerbated those tight corners, and the city's willful neglect cost African urban businesses and families a great deal. This chapter reveals that families formed by cashew shellers were broadly similar to those of the overall urban African population. The daily lives of people living in the *bairros de caniço* revolved around work, wages, housing, rents, strategies to leverage wages and struggles to keep families intact, fed and healthy.

Many urban women, not just cashew shellers, formed *amancebado* families, not because it was their last option, but because such arrangements allowed them a measure of autonomy that they valued and pursued. Poor women in particular had limited expectations of service and support in relation to employment, child bearing, formal marriage, common-law marriage and polygamy. Although the status as head of household was unusually common among women of Tarana, their family forms and lives were otherwise broadly similar to those of their neighbours. Women throughout the suburbs of Lourenço Marques

---

[1] A portion of an earlier version of this chapter was published as Penvenne, 'Two Tales of a City – Lourenço Marques, 1945–1975,' *Portuguese Studies Review*; Special Issue in Honor of Jill R. Dias. 19, 1–2 (2011): 249–69.
[2] ACLM to Secretaria Geral da Colonia de Moçambique, 12 Nov. 1947, 'Relatório Annual Referente ao Ano 1946 Respeitante ao Administrador Adelino José Macedo, ACLM/ AHM.
[3] Rita-Ferreira, 'Os Africanos,' 'Modelo do Questionário' between pages 100 and 101.
[4] Andreas Eckert and Adam Jones, 'Historical Writing about Everyday Life,'*Journal of African Cultural Studies*, 5, 1 (2002): 5–16; Lonsdale, 'Agency in Tight Corners,' 6.

experienced the essential economic and social connectivity of productive and reproductive labour in the working lives of their families.

Lourenço Marques was a settler city, and increasingly through this period a sophisticated cosmopolitan destination for white tourists. The white city was completely supported by black workers whose neighbourhoods and urban social history is as diverse and interesting as the settler city, but much more difficult to extricate. To retrieve the daily challenges the great majority of African families faced living in what everyone called *caniço*, the diverse and sprawling *bairros de caniço*, we have to extricate *caniço* from the projection of a white city.

Drawing out the black city from projections of the white city

Lourenço Marques – the Lourenço Marques that captivated me, was a white city, served entirely by blacks, of course, but a white city.

Rodrigues da Silva[5]

Every city and small town in Mozambique is surrounded by *caniços*. They are the out-buildings of the towns – the places where the servants and labourers live.

Amâncio d'Alpoim Guedes[6]

[In colonial times] there was a border area, it was called the *Estrada da Circunvalação*. There were those who lived on this side, and those who lived on that side.

José Craveirinha[7]

As was the case across the settler areas in Southern Africa, the population and geographic footprint of Lourenço Marques expanded rapidly in the postwar era.[8] The scholarly lens for the colonial era focused on and projected images of Rodrigues da Silva's beloved white city.[9] Despite the fact that the white city was completely served by blacks and dwarfed by what the famous Portuguese architect Amâncio d'Alpoim Guedes, commonly known as Pancho Guedes, called its out-buildings; the documentary record featured the highly resourced cement city of Lourenço Marques as *the* showplace city. José Craveirinha, Mozambique's leading poet, had one parent in the *bairros de caniço* and one

---

[5] Curado da Gama, *Era uma vez...Moçambique* (Lisbon: Quimera, 2004): 9.
[6] Amâncio d'Alpoim Guedes, The '*Caniços* of Mozambique,' in Paul Oliver, *Shelter in Africa* (London: Barrie & Jenkins, Ltd. 1971, paperback 1976): 200.
[7] Craveirinha in Nelson Saúte, *Habitantes da Memória: Entrevistas com Escritores Moçambicanos* (Praia-Mindelo: Embaixada de Portugal, 1998):113.
[8] David Anderson and Richard Rathbone, *Africa's Urban Past* (Portsmouth: Heinemann, 2000); Bill Freund, *The African City: A History* (New York: Cambridge University Press, 2007); Catherine Coquery-Vidrovitch, 'The Process of Urbanization in Africa: From the Origins to the Beginning of Independence,' *ASR*, 34, no. 1 (1991); Paul Maylam, 'Explaining the Apartheid City: 20 Years of South African Urban Historiography,' *JSAS*, 21, 1 (1995): 19–38; Maylam and Iain Edwards, eds. *The People's City: African Life in Twentieth-Century Durban* (Portsmouth: Heinemann, 1996).
[9] Michel Cahen, ed. '*Vilas*' et '*Cidades*' *Borges et Villes en Afrique Lusophone* (Paris: Editions L'Harmattan, 1989).

in the cement city. Thanks to his white Portuguese family, he enjoyed the privileges of the cement city, and thanks to his black Mozambican mother and her family he knew that people in Lourenço Marques lived on different sides of privilege.

Key changes in the capital city from 1945 to 1975 included the rapidly growing white population and migrant African population, the gendered profile of new employment opportunities for Africans, enhanced social and political incentives and sanctions linked with the initiation of Frelimo's political and military challenge, and the checkered implications for urban workers of the end of the *indigenato* (1961). Just as the print record ignored or obscured the fact that the cashew economy's meteoric rise fundamentally depended upon the strength of thousands of African industrial women; the municipal press, photographs, statistics, and eventually dozens of published memoirs and blogs detailed the growth and changes in Rodrigues da Silva's white city, while the much larger *caniço* city remained ignored, blurred and misunderstood. [10] The *bairros de caniço* housed the people who were the force behind daily production, reproduction and growth. It was home to the thousands of Africans working in domestic service, industry, civil construction, markets, warehouses, public works, ports, railways and the informal economy. They did not live in 'total promiscuity,' and they gave a lot of thought and attention to the few aspects of sanitation that they could control.[11]

Before New State censorship was imposed in the 1930s, Lourenço Marques' diverse and lively press provided a reasonable window into the city's majority neighbourhoods, their societies, politics and problems.[12] *O Brado Africano*, published by the city's black and *mestiço* elite, featured aspects of daily life in these *bairros*, albeit from the perspective of local writers who were often hostile to migrants. Local people fought hard to squeeze even limited infrastructure from the municipality, and

[10] For greater detail about the white city and the impact of late colonial era settlement see the essays in *Os Outros da Colonização: Ensaios sobre Tardo-colonialismo em Moçambique*, Cláudia Castelo, Omar Ribeiro Tomaz, Sebastião Nasimento, Teresa Cruz e Silva, eds. (Lisbon: Imprensa de Ciências Sociais, 2012), including Penvenne, 'Fotografando Lourenço Marques: A Cidade e os seus Habitantes de 1960 á 1975,' 173–191; Penvenne, 'Two Tales of a City;' Penvenne, 'Settling against the Tide.'
[11] Scores of nostalgic websites, blogs and Youtube videos exist of Lourenço Marques in the high colonial era. João Loureiro's collection of photographs very much captures what people of the era wanted to remember. João Loureiro, *Memórias de Lourenço Marques: Uma Visão do Passado da cidade de Maputo* (Lisbon: Maisimagem-Comunicação Global, 2003). See among others: www.youtube.com/watch?v=kiheHNbUpmA; www.youtube.com/watch?v= M_fyD8EM3bEmaputophotoblog.wordpress.com/category/old-pictures-lourenco-marques-new-pictures-maputo/ Accessed 1 March 2015.
[12] Valdemir Zamparoni's fine published work on Lourenço Marques urban social history focuses largely on the period prior to the New State: 'Copos e Corpos;' Zamparoni, 'Lourenço Marques: Espaço Urbano, Espaço Branco?' *Actas do Colóquio Construção e Ensino da História de África* (Lisbon: Comissão Nacional para as Comemorações dos Descobrimentos Portugueses, 1995): 89–109; Zamparoni, *De Escravo a Cozinheiro; Colonialismo e Racismo em Moçambique* (Salvador: Universidade Federal da Bahia, 2007).

increasing numbers of urban migrants severely taxed those gains.[13] Taken together some memoirs, biographies and *Brado Africano*'s social news shed light on the lives of the city's small *mestiço* and black elites. The focus was largely on men, but a small group of women emerged in association with the two urban African social associations, Instituto Negrófilo and Associação Africana or with the Protestant church communities.[14]

Between direct censorship and press ownership by New State political allies only good news appeared in print for most of this period. That made it difficult to probe urban challenges through the press.[15] When complaints about low wages, unemployment or housing shortages appeared, they usually focused on poor whites. Articles scarcely mentioned the much greater difficulties faced by urban Africans.[16] Only in the early 1970s did journalists publish substantive pieces about the majority population, a trend that expanded rapidly after independence. Journalists who founded the newspaper *A Tribuna* and the weekly magazine *Tempo* led that opening.[17]

The few contemporary social surveys organized by the colonial state or municipality provided some information, but African women were the least likely to participate or to be the focus of attention.[18] António

[13] Penvenne, *African Workers*, Ch. 2, 9, 10.

[14] Raúl Bernardo Honwana, *Life History;* Lina Magaia, *Recordações da Vovó Marta* (Maputo: JV Editores, 2010); Santos Oliveira, 'Recordações sobre Lourenço Marques,' 85–108; Olga Iglésias Neves, 'Em Defesa da Causa Africana: Intervenção do Grêmio Africano na Sociedade de Lourenço Marques, 1908–1938,' MA thesis (Lisbon: Universidade Nova de Lisboa, 1989), Aurélio Rocha, *Associativismo e Nativismo em Moçambique: Contribuição para o Estudo das Origens do Nacionalismo Moçambicano (1900–1940)* (Maputo, Promédia, 2002).

[15] Malyn Newitt viewed Salazar's use of censorship and propaganda as one of his most important strengths. Newitt, *History of Mozambique*, Ch 17; Newitt,' The Late Colonial State,' 110–22; Fatima Mendonça, 'Dos confrontos ideológicos na Imprensa em Moçambique,' *Os Outros*, 193–220; Fatima Ribeiro and António Sopa, Coordinators, *140 anos de Imprensa em Moçambique: Estudos e Relatos* (Maputo: Associação Moçambicana da Língua Portuguesa, 1996).

[16] Ernesto Casimiro Neves Santos Barbosa, *A radiofusão em Moçambique: o caso do Rádio Clube de Moçambique, 1932–1974* (Maputo: Promédia, 2000); Cláudio Jone, 'Press and Democratic Transition in Mozambique, 1990–2000,' *Les Nouveaux Cahiers de l'IFAS / IFAS Working Paper Series* (Johannesburg, Institut français d'Afrique du Sud, 2005); 'O problema dos bairros clandestinos urge solução,' *Notícias*, 5 Abril 1971; 'Suburbios, O problema maior da cidade,' *Notícias*, 22 June 1971.

[17] Calane de Silva,'Alguns Aspectos da Cidade de Caniço,' *Notícias*, 24 July 1971; Albino Magaia, 'Os Senhores dos Subúrbios de Lourenço Marques,' *Diário*, 26 March 1971; Emídio Machiana, *A Revista Tempo e a Revolução Moçambicana: Da Mobilização Popular áo Problema da Critica na Informação, 1974–1977* (Maputo: Promédia 2002); Magaia with photographs by Ricardo Rangel, 'Prostituição; Hilário Matusse,' 'Bairros de Maputo: Chamanculo: Memórias de um Bairro,' *Tempo*, No. 682, 6 Nov. 1983; Matusse, 'Mafalala: Fronteira.'

[18] Junta de Investigação do Ultramar [JIU], 'Inquerito habitacional realizado no Bairro da Munhuana,' *Estudos de Ciências Políticas e Sociais*, No. 72 (Lisbon: Junta de ISCSPU, 1964):16–23, 42–87; 'Direcção Provincial dos Servicos de Estatística, 'Inquérito as rendas e a outras caracteristicas das habitações arrendas na cidade de Lourenço Marques em 1961–1962,' Estudo No. 1, *Supplemento ao Boletim Mensal de Estatistica* (Lourenço Marques, Direcção Provincial dos Servicos de Estatística, 3 Março 1962; Momplê, 'Relatório Sintese de Sector Social;' Hilary Flegg Mitchell, 'Aspects of Urbanization and Age Structure in Lourenço Marques, 1957,' *University of Zambia, Institute for African Studies, Communication*, No. 11 (1975); Hilary Flegg and W. Lutz. 'Report on an African Demographic Survey.' *Journal of Social Research* [South Africa] Vol. 10 (1959): 1–24; Teixeira Santos, 'Avaliação Nutricional.'

Rita-Ferreira's 1967 survey was by far the most important exploration of African life in Lourenço Marques in the colonial period. Although he included a section titled 'The Position of Women,' his framework was firmly androcentric. As the above quote makes clear, he addressed the survey to men, although one can learn a good bit about women between the lines.[19]

Colonial era Portuguese historians and photographers were so much more interested in the built environment and white population than in the African majority, their work portrayed a white city – often eerily empty.[20] Maria Clara Mendes and João Sousa Morais extensively documented aspects of the late colonial city's demography, economic geography, and architectural history. They captured what they could of all parts of the city, but both were frustrated by the imbalance of sources.[21] Some scholars focused explicitly on the city's white Portuguese population, including only peripherally their views on the African majority.[22] Explorations of the way the city's African women remembered specific spaces in the colonial city, confirmed the tendency of the majority of women to stay within their own neighbourhoods, but acknowledged that *mestiça* and assimilated women were more mobile and comfortable in areas understood by the majority to be white.[23] Recent research on contemporary Maputo includes innovative and important work on women that is often suggestive for the colonial period, but clearly it must be used critically regarding analysis of the colonial past.[24]

Hilary Flegg Mitchell and Norberto Teixeira Santos conducted research in the *bairros de caniço* in the late 1950s and the early 1970s

[19] Rita-Ferreira, 'Os Africanos,' 247–253.
[20] Lobato, 'Lourenço Marques, Xilunguíne'; Lobato, 'Conhecimento da Baia a Criação do Município,' *Boletim Municipal* [Lourenço Marques], 2 (1968):9–20; Lobato, 'Lourenço Marques, Xilunguíne; Pequena Monografia; Alfredo Pereira de Lima, *Edifícios Históricos de Lourenço Marques* (Lourenço Marques: Livraria Académica,1966); Pereira de Lima, *História dos Caminhos de Ferro de Moçambique* (Lourenço Marques: Admin. do Porto e dos Caminhos de Ferro de Moçambique, 1971); Pereira de Lima, *O Palácio Municipal de Lourenço Marques* (Lourenço Marques: Livraria Académica, 1967); Pereira de Lima, 'Para um Estudo da Evolução Urbana de Lourenço Marques,' *Boletim Municipal*, 7 (1967); Pereira de Lima, *Pedras que já não falam* (Lourenço Marques: Tipografia Notícias,1972); Carlos Alberto Vieira, *The City of Lourenço Marques Guide* (Johannesburg: Cape Times, 1956); Carlos Alberto Vieira, *Recordações de Lourenço Marques* [Fotografia de Carlos Alberto Vieira, Texto Ana Paula Lemos, Coordenação Joaquim Carlos Vieira] (Lisbon: Alétheia Editores, 2005).
[21] Mendes, 'Maputo;' Castelo, *Passagens para África*; João Sousa Morais, *Maputo: Património da Estrutura e Forma Urbana; Topologia do Lugar* (Lisbon: Livros Horizonte, 2001).
[22] Castelo, *Passagens para a África*; Margarida Calafate Ribeiro, *África no Feminino: As Mulheres Portuguesas e a Guerra Colonial* (Porto: Afrontamento, 2007).
[23] In Frates, 'Place of Memory,' women identified the following as specifically white places in the city: the beach, the central hospital, museums, government buildings, and the central business district or *baixa*, 118, 194, 197, 203–4; OT, Amélia Alfredo Muiane, 13 Sept. 1977, Câmara Municipal de Maputo, Maputo; OT, Lídia Felizmina Tembe, 12 Nov. 1977, Maternidade de Matola, Matola, Mozambique; OT, Joaquim Costa, 11 Nov. 1977 and Roberto Tembe, 12 Nov. 1977, Port and Railway, Maputo; Magaia, *Vovó Marta*; Honwana, *The Life*.
[24] Bénard de Costa, *Preço de Sombra*; Udelsmann Rodrigues, *O Trabalho Dignifica*; Paulo et al. *Xiculungo* and contemporary work on gender and sexuality by Teresa Cruz e Silva, Conceição Osório, Terezinha da Silva and Maria José Artur and other scholars in the Women and the Law in Southern Africa [WLSA] collaborative, http://www.wlsa.org.mz Accessed March 2015.

respectively. Both struggled to delineate the population where streets and households were more fluid than fixed. Both also had an appreciation of the fact that conceptions and definitions of what a household is could be shifting and dynamic.[25] In Flegg Mitchell's 1957 study, the difficulty went beyond trying to get a fix on the fluid; she had to walk the fine political line set by the colonial government. Inquiries by foreigners about '...occupations, income, use of amenities and involvement in town life,' were out of bounds.[26] Marvin Harris did not heed such warnings. In 1956 he was deported, but the consequences for his Portuguese collabourator António Figueiredo were much worse. Figueiredo was arrested, deported to Lisbon and committed to a mental hospital until he managed to flee to London in 1959.[27] Colonial civil servants could pursue sensitive questions, but they too knew to tread carefully with critiques or policy implications.[28]

Flegg Mitchell and Rita-Ferreira, for example, posed critiques differently. Flegg Mitchell sharply contrasted '...the attractive [white] city with tree-lined streets...and every amenity' with the basically random and un-serviced population in the surrounding *bairros*. She asserted that '...[The municipality] either ignored the presence of over 60,000 people living within 5 kilometers of the Town Hall or found it an embarrassment...[its] lack of provision for the needs of people drifting into towns was astonishing.'[29] Rita-Ferreira corroborated the stark differences between the black and white cities, but spun them differently:

> The contrasts in our capital city jump out at you when you compare the center, laid out in cement, steel and asphalt and the [*bairros*] chaotic expanses of *caniço*, zinc and sand. One could interpret these differences as rooted in racial privilege, were it not for the fact that so many assimilated well-paid Africans would not trade the advantage of the conviviality and prestige they enjoy living in the suburbs for the impersonal relations and anonymity associated with the large modern apartment buildings in the city center.[30]

Some individuals and families no doubt preferred the *caniço* neighbourhoods to living in high-rise buildings where they could be mistaken for servants, beaten by suspicious whites and deprived of back yard spaces for children, laundry, gardening and cooking.[31] However, Rita-Ferreira knew perfectly well that the differences he noted were indeed deeply

---

[25] Guyer, 'Household and Community;' Guyer and Peters, 'Conceptualizing the Household;' Flegg and Lutz. 'Report.'

[26] Flegg Mitchell, 'Aspects of Urbanization,' xi.

[27] Obituary of Marvin Harris in *The Guardian* (London, 13 December 2001).

[28] António Rita-Ferreira and Lília Momplê dodged or carefully framed the critiques raised in their research. Rita-Ferreira, 'Esboço Social,' 171; Momplê, 'Munhuana,'50–55.

[29] Flegg Mitchell, 'Aspects of Urbanization,' xii.

[30] Rita-Ferreira,'Os Africanos,'180.

[31] Writer José Craveirinha was famously wedded to his home in Mafalala. He simply explained, 'I feel good here.' Saúte, *Habitantes da Memória*, 117–19.

rooted in racial privilege – from access to municipal funding for water, sewers, roads, parks and trees to the ability to join a union, graduate from an apprenticeship or earn a living wage.[32]

Finally, a handful of photographic collections from the colonial era's professional black portrait and news photographers and photos appended to reports or studies provide insight into the urban social life of the era, including some glimpses into ordinary life in the *bairros de caniço*. Although most professional photographs highlight the lifecycle events of elite families, some photos of individual or small groups of women, barefoot and dressed in *capulanas* and headscarves, cooking on wood fires or pounding maize within small *caniço* enclaves captured the quotidian many women described. However, connecting anonymous images to individuals is challenging.[33] In sum, scholars know a great deal more about the colonial era white city than about the black city, and the lens into the black city is more likely to highlight elite men's activities than the daily lives of women, children, ordinary people and the poor.

Interface of cement and *caniço*

Rita-Ferreira's narrative that Africans preferred the conviviality in *caniço* paired with the equally misleading white narrative of the relationship between the two cities. Whites imagined that the populous *bairros de caniço* threatened to swamp the central city. In fact the opposite was true. From 1945 to 1974, the cement city's new buildings, neighbourhoods, roads, and businesses pushed into surrounding areas. The white city consistently gained ground at the expense of *caniço*. In peak years of white immigration and high unemployment from the mid 1950s, poor whites competed with Africans for housing, water, jobs and business opportunities in *caniço*.[34] The black population was forced to look further afield for agricultural and residential land. Whole neighbourhoods were uprooted and relocated further afield by municipal development schemes designed to house whites, encourage tourism and accommodate the service needs of the growing white city – that pattern went back to the turn of the twentieth century.[35]

---

[32] Just after the abolition of the *indigenato*, a Mozambican man described to Marvin Harris the changes he observed: 'It used to be that the faucet was completely shut. Now it has been opened and the water is coming out: Ping.., ping.., ping...' Harris, 'Race, Conflict,'180.

[33] *Sebastião Langa*; *Retratos de uma vida* [Photograph selection and research by António Sopa, Maria das Neves and Maria Deolinda Chamango] (Maputo: Arquivo Histórico de Moçambique, 2001): 50; Rangel, *Pão nosso de cada noite*; *Inquérito nutritional...Fabrica de Cimentos*; Teixeira Santos, 'Avaliação Nutricional.'

[34] Penvenne, 'Two Tales of a City.'

[35] Penvenne, *African Workers*, 28–43; Eviction from Sommerschield Concession, 1070 A/11/ ACLM to Direcção Provincial de Administração Civil [DPAC], Sul do Save, 21 Nov.1946, R / Cx R, ACLM / AHM; Ingemar Saevfors, *Maxaquene: a Comprehensive Account of the First Urban Upgrading Experience in the New Mozambique*, (New York: UNESCO, 1986): 9.

The rhythms and scope of the city's growth emerged dramatically in many forms. People generally described the rapid transformation with a big sweep of their arm saying: 'And then the city grew all of this was just bush!'[36] Mozambique's colonial era municipal and national census statistics are infuriatingly inconsistent and unhelpful, but whatever the statistical shortfalls, it is clear that between 1940 and 1970 the city grew from about 68,000 to almost 400,000 people. Africans accounted for at least 46,000 to over 300,000 of the totals. The growth was driven by African migration and Portuguese immigration. By the late 1960s only 21 per cent of the city's African population was born in the city. Even if one counted the people born in the neighbouring areas of Namaacha, Matola, and Marracuene as local people, locals still would have comprised under a third of the African population. Around 70 per cent of the city's African population originated well outside the local neighbourhood.[37]

While the number of African men increased by 153 per cent between 1940 and 1960, the number of African women increased by 194 per cent.[38] As we saw in Mindawu Bila's song Agostinho, tensions between locals and migrants were important and mixed. Migrants did not necessarily feel themselves subject to the authority of local 'native' or 'ethnic' authorities, and municipal Native Affairs Officers confirmed that the great majority of complaints and problems in poorer neighbourhoods were between locals and newcomers and people of different ethnic and linguistic heritages.[39] The migrant women of Tarana knew those tensions. Some, like Ester Tafula wanted nothing to do with local men, explaining: 'I did not want *Xilunguine* women to think we were after their men. I thought about looking for a man here, but saw it was not worth it. Their women would beat me saying I was trying to take their husbands, while they were unable to feed their children because of women like me. So I just stayed by myself, living from Tarana until today.'[40]

From the 1950s Portuguese whites arrived in the city in unprecedented numbers.[41] Rodrigues da Silva's captivating white city was whiter in the late colonial era. Between 1940 and 1970 the white population of the District of Lourenço Marques increased from 5.44 per cent of the total population to 10.44 per cent. With the formation of Frelimo and the initiation of armed insurgency Portuguese troops further swelled the white population. Although the troops were stationed all over the

---

[36] OT, Joaquim da Costa and Roberto Tembe, both born in the late nineteenth century and lifelong residents of Lourenço Marques, 15 and 16 June 1977, interviewed at Port and Railway, Maputo; Lloys Frates, 'Memory of Place,' 181 and 191.
[37] *Censo da População em 1940; Recenseamento Geral,* 1950; *Recenseamento Geral,* 1960; *Recenseamento Geral,* 1970.
[38] Rita-Ferreira, 'Os Africanos,' 229.
[39] Momplé, 'Relatório Sintese,'10–11.
[40] OT, Ester Tafula, 3 June 1993.
[41] Castelo, *Passagens para África.*

country, they and their families were processed through the capital and most took their leave there. Despite the fact that Portugal increasingly Africanized its military, the presence of white troops remained strong in Lourenço Marques.[42] Despite some instability due to the fear of insurgency, white tourism from Southern Africa and Europe climbed into the 1960s, such that during the high tourist season the city was whiter still, particularly around Polana Beach, Costa do Sol and the central business district.[43] In these closing decades, the white city grew ever whiter, ever more luxurious and highly resourced.

In 1963 Pancho Guedes, an internationally known Portuguese Architect who had designed signature homes in Lourenço Marques, spent a lot of his substantial political capital when he published a sharp, satirical and ironic 'Manifesto' in the city's newspaper, *A Tribuna*. Guedes was incensed by the expansion of luxury residences in the Chronistas and Sommerschield neighbourhoods at the expense of *bairro de caniço* residents. Guedes challenged the city's residents, black and white, to get together to fundamentally restructure the city to be 'home to everyone.' His grand plan was to '...repair houses, construct roads through to heart of *caniço*, bring in sewers, water, electricity... Create 300,000 hopes for 300,000 improved lives.' His 'Manifesto' made reference to apartheid in neighbouring countries and the frustrating Portuguese bureaucracy:

> Will we continue with a divided, sick, schizophrenic city?
> Will we continue with a city betrayed by men's laziness, stupidity, and greed, or will we start tomorrow to build a city that will be home to everyone?
> Get outraged voters![44]

The courageous and passionate challenge failed. Guedes probably anticipated insufficient support from white voters, but he should not have been surprised when black residents also failed to back the plan. Black residents would have to temporarily relocate to accommodate reconstruction in large areas. Based on decades of displacement and eviction, they had plenty of reason to fear their removal would be permanent even if their original neighbourhoods were improved.[45]

Although blacks comprised over 86 per cent of the city population, colonial and municipal documentation during this era portrayed

---

[42] Cann, *Counterinsurgency in Africa*; Thomas Henriksen, *Revolution and Counterrevolution; Mozambique's War of Independence 1964–1974* (Westport, CT: Greenwood, 1983); Califate Ribeiro, *África no Feminino*.

[43] 'Tourismo,' *Lourenço Marques Guardian*, 5 May 1950; José Rodrigues Júnior, 'Turismo – Series,' *Diário*, 26 Feb. 13, 18, 26 March 1957; 'Turismo em Lourenço Marques há 56 Anos,' *Notíciais*, 8 March 1962; Florentino Serrano, 'Centro de Attracção Turística,' *Diário*, 24 July 1971; 'Nem só a praia vive de turismo,' *Capital*, 13 Outubro 1970.

[44] Amâncio d'Alpoim Guedes, 'Manual de Alfabetização do Vogal sem Mestre.' *A Tribuna* 228 (Lourenço Marques, July 1963) [Quoted in full in Sousa Morais *Maputo: Património*, note 38, 239–41, esp. quote 240.

[45] Guedes, 'Manual de Alfabetização,' in Sousa Morais *Maputo: Património*, note 38, 239–41.

Lourenço Marques as a white city.[46] All aspects of the white city's growth (population, formal economy, cement and asphalt footprint and skyline) were dramatically portrayed in photographs, graphs, statistics, charts and maps.[47] The visualization of those changes was facilitated by measurements embedded in the surveying, licensing and registration of civil construction, new and expanded companies and roadways. Maria Clara Mendes graphed, charted and mapped Lourenço Marques in almost all imaginable manners, many with striking visual impacts. Her graph of municipal construction from 1913 to 1973 seemed to mimic the city's transformed skyline with its peaks and plunges. It showed the dramatic boom in residential construction fueled by white settlement, and the dramatic downturns caused by the initial insurgency of the early 1960s and the balance of payments crisis of the early 1970s.[48]

The equally dramatic growth and changes in the *bairros de caniço* were notoriously difficult to map because almost all construction, markets and roads were not surveyed, licensed, taxed and registered.[49] While the rapidly growing footprint and skyline of the white city was understood to be orderly, growth in the environs was framed as clandestine, illegal, spontaneous, chaotic and therefore a crisis. The municipal authorities also viewed their limited access to and knowledge about these neighbourhoods as a problem, particularly once the insurgency took form in the early 1960s.[50] The city's leading colonial historian Alexandre Lobato viewed these neighbourhoods as: 'the zone that is not yet the city but is also no longer the *mato* [bush]... where people make their houses according to their means, a mix of huts, shacks and houses, circled with *caniço* fences and within a maze of sand footpaths.'[51]

João Sousa Morais captured the 'othering' discourse regarding *caniço* residents: 'No one knows how many live in the immense belt of *caniço* that surrounds the city, from 150,000 to 1 million. They live without sewers, water and electric lights. Their houses are precarious shacks made of old zinc, tin cans, cardboard boxes and *caniço*. At night it is dangerous to travel through the corridors and labyrinths.'[52] To the extent that *caniço* was mapped, it was mapped from above. Much of what social scientists of the era thought they knew

---

[46] *Recenseamento Geral da População, 1970* [Vol. I, Distrito de Lourenço Marques], xxxi–xxxiv; *Boletim Municipal*, Vol. 1 (10 Nov. 1967): 46; Alexandre Lobato and Parcídio Costa, *Moçambique na Actualidade, 1973* (Lourenço Marques: Imprensa Nacional de Moçambique, 1974): 39; Frates, 'Memory of Place,' 193–4.

[47] Mendes, 'Maputo;' Loureiro, *Memórias de Lourenço Marques*; Penvenne, 'Fotografando Lourenço Marques.'

[48] Mendes, 'Maputo,' 91 fig. 27; Lobato and Costa, *Moçambique na Actualidade*, 119.

[49] Mendes, 'Maputo.'

[50] Harris, 'Race, Conflict and Reform,' 165–70.

[51] Lobato quoted in Sousa Morais, *Maputo Património*, 182. See also his 'Os Subúrbios,' 149–51, 'O 'Caniço,' 182–7.

[52] Sousa Morais, *Maputo Património*, 38.

about the *bairros* came from enhanced aerial photographs. From the sky view path patterns could be puzzled out and dwellings could be counted by their rooftops. Formulas for the number of inhabitants per dwelling then comprised the basis for estimating area's population growth. [53]

Mendes argued that, although it was possible to discuss the cement and *caniço* cities as separate, in her judgement, 'despite its particular characteristics, [the *bairros de caniço*] comprise[d] an integral part of the city.'[54] Although her study was much less detailed for the *bairros de caniço* than for the cement city, it produced statistical evidence where any was to be found. She demonstrated, for example, that the populous neighbourhoods of Ximpamanine, Munhuana, S. J. de Lhenguene, and Tlhabane had the most *cantinas*, and those sold groceries, water, alcoholic drinks and building materials. That clearly reflected the limited disposable household income and priorities of the residents. Over this period the population grew and employment opportunities and wages that shaped household priorities and spending also changed rapidly.

Changing employment profiles: Housework and domestic service

Between 1945 and 1975 daily reproduction in most urban households required a lot of work. When women and children did that work within the household and gift economy it was called housework. When African men, boys and women did it as paid labour it was called domestic service. Particularly between 1945 and 1970, domestic service was a very large component of the urban African labour force. Housework consumed a very large proportion of women's time throughout the whole period. Most women who worked for wages did not stop work when their shift ended. They went home after work and on weekends to accomplish the necessary household labour to reproduce themselves and the people in their households so they could produce another day. They secured food, hauled fuel and water, cooked, washed clothing, cleaned the household, bathed and tended children, the aged and infirm.

Conditions in *caniço* made this reproductive work much more important for a family's health and wellbeing. If the water was not clean, and the food not properly cooked people became seriously ill, medical care and the time to seek it were beyond peoples' means. *Caniço*'s sand streets made it difficult to keep homes, people, shoes and clothing clean in the dusty dry season, and almost impossible in the rainy season

---

[53] Flegg and Lutz. 'Report,' 1–24; Rita-Ferreira, 'Os Africanos,' 168; Mendes, 'Maputo,' has several photos and maps of *caniço*.
[54] Mendes, 'Maputo', 157.

when poorly drained streets turned into rivers of mud, rubbish and sewerage. Cashew workers had to accomplish essential reproductive tasks before and after work. They may have been the breadwinners, but if they did not have older children or relatives to help at home they did that work themselves. The immediate need to feed and care for families drove most women to work long hours every day in the formal, informal, gift and household economies.

Residents of the cement city hired domestic servants to do cooking, cleaning, washing, ironing, yard and garden work, to run errands, deliver meals, haul water, and tend children, elders and small stock.[55] Servants in the city were invariably undercounted. Employers avoided municipal registration of servants to evade the fee or because the employee was too young or paid too little to comply with the law. Domestic service was a particularly important entry occupation for young African males. Thirty-five per cent of all Africans employed for a wage in Lourenço Marques in 1940 worked in domestic service, almost 9,500 people. At that time, more than three quarters of all domestic servants were male youths under the age of twenty, with ten to fifteen year olds comprising nearly half. Domestic service employed more urban males than the next three largest employment categories combined.[56] It was obviously an important category in the urban formal labour economy, and with the influx of Portuguese immigrants it became even more important. [57]

In 1950 more than 21,000 men worked for wages in Lourenço Marques, over 60 per cent of those in domestic service. Most were employed as *criados*, basic domestic workers who did most household reproductive chores. From the early 1940s the colonial government and municipality encouraged employing women as domestics, arguing it was more 'natural', and that youths and men should be doing more strenuous work in agriculture, construction and industry.[58] Only about 1,700 women worked for wages in the city in 1950, but 53 per cent of those worked in domestic service. Within the domestic service sector, women were also mostly unskilled *criadas*, the feminine version of *criados*.

All domestic servants struggled with the long hours, lack of privacy, tedious work and the threat of living intimately with white families, but for most males it was a bridging opportunity to better jobs, whereas for

---

[55] I have not paid sufficient attention to children's labour here. Karen Tranberg Hansen 'Body Politics: Sexuality, Gender and Domestic Service in Zambia,' *Journal of Women's History*, Vol. 2, No. 1 (Spring 1990): 120–42;Tranberg Hansen, ed. *African Encounters with Domesticity* (New Brunswick: Rutgers, 2002); Tranberg Hansen, *Distant Companions: Servants and Employers in Zambia, 1900–1985* (Ithaca: Cornell University Press, 1989); Beverly Grier, *Invisible Hands*.

[56] 8,832 males in domestic service in 1940, 5,001 in state port and railway work, 1,277 in public works and construction and 1,639 in industry. Moçambique, Repartição Técnica de Estatística, *Censo da População em 1940* (Lourenço Marques, 1944): 10–11.

[57] On Portuguese immigration to Africa from 1920–1974 see Castelo, *Passagens*.

[58] José Tristão de Bettencourt, *Relatório do Governador Geral de Moçambique; Respeitante ao Período de 20 Março de 1940 á 31 de Dezembro, 1942* (Lisbon: Imprensa Nacional, 1945): 47–48.

most females it was not.[59] Most adult male domestics who worked as cooks, gardeners or other specialized jobs had mothers and wives who accomplished domestic labour in their homes and took care of their children.[60] By 1960, Portugal's decade-long efforts to feminize domestic service combined with other labour trends to make a difference. Men moved increasingly to alternative employment in industry, transportation and especially civil construction that fueled the city's changing skyline.[61] Also by 1960, land for peri-urban *machambas* was increasingly scarce. Scarcer peri-urban land and the burden of long term male outmigration in rural areas forced many more women into waged labour.[62] As we have seen, *Malalanyana*'s office tried to place such women in domestic service, but it was difficult to place women with no Portuguese language skills in domestic service.

In 1960 service occupations, including domestic service, comprised around 35 per cent of total waged opportunities for men – a major shift from the pattern that existed in 1950. At the same time women moved rapidly into service industries, comprising around a quarter of all urban domestic servants, up from around 7 per cent in the 1940s and 1950s. Indeed, 60 per cent of women who worked for wages in Lourenço Marques in 1960 were domestic servants.[63] Domestic service was becoming increasingly important for women and less so for men, but even so, three quarters of the urban domestic service labour force in 1960 remained male.

In the last generation of colonial rule, 1960–1975, the rapidly expanding urban economy provided many more attractive jobs for both men and women. Policy changes in Lisbon provided an opening for the expansion of Portuguese and some international companies into Mozambique. The great majority established themselves in and around the capital. The result was a construction boom, rapidly increasing investment in processing industries and expansion of the colonial staple businesses like cement, beer and tobacco.[64]

Given the opportunity, women moved strongly into the processing industries. By 1970 these industries employed almost twice as many women as domestic service. Between 1960 and 1970 the number of women working as domestics in Lourenço Marques actually dropped

---

[59] Moçambique, Repartição Técnica de Estatística, *Recenseamento Geral da População em 1950, III: População Não Civilizada* (Lourenço Marques, 1955).

[60] OT, Amélia Samuel Muzima, 27 May 1993; Penvenne, *African Workers*, 142–53.

[61] Rita-Ferreira, 'Os Africanos,' 124

[62] Documented for Sul do Save by: Roesch, 'Migrant Labour and Forced Rice;' Fialho Feliciano, *Antropologia Economico*; Rita-Ferreira, 'Esboço Sociológico;' Hermele, *Land Struggles*; Bowen, *State against the Peasantry*; Covane, *O Trabalho Migratório*.

[63] Moçambique, Repartição Técnica de Estatística, *Recenseamento Geral da Populaçãona Província de Moçambique, 1960*, I, Distrito de Lourenço Marques (Lourenço Marques, Imprensa Nacional, 1960) reveals around 5,200 women.

[64] Martin Schaedel's thesis provides important analysis of this period and Mendes's economic geography closely charts the city's changes. Schaedel, 'Last Phase of Colonial Rule' and Mendes, 'Maputo.'

by nearly 700.[65] That shift was linked to many factors, including the white population's shift to multi-storey housing, and the increased availability of household appliances, piped water and electricity in middle and upper class neighbourhoods.[66] People who lived in high-rise flats did not require gardeners, and could not keep small stock. The availability of piped water, electricity, prepared foods, refrigerators, freezers and kitchen electronics made cooking and shopping less time consuming, so households employed fewer domestic workers. Most of those changes did not extend to families in the *bairros de caniço*.

Mozambique's industrial statistical records for the colonial era covered 1947 to 1973 unevenly. From the early 1960s the statistics no longer disaggregated by race, but they continued to differentiate the labour force by sex, and so provided some basis to compare developing employment opportunities for African women in Lourenço Marques.[67] To some extent one can project patterns from the years when statistics recorded race or 'civilized / uncivilized' into the subsequent period when they did not, although clearly not without risk.[68] European women who worked in industry, largely staffed the office, administrative and technical jobs, although some worked sewing machines in the garment industry, an industry which developed significant and rapidly growing employment opportunities for African women especially in the 1960s. In 1956 only 11 black women worked in the garment industry, but by 1964 that had increased to 280 and between 1969 and the end of 1973, jobs for women in the garment industry held steady at around eleven hundred.

Between 1956 and 1973 job opportunities for men and women in rubber plants that made sneakers and all kinds of rubber goods increased rapidly. Men outnumbered women, but women's employment jumped from under 30 in 1956 to 174 in 1970 and 273 in 1973. Within a decade of independence, a woman named Felizmina recorded her recollections of working in the rubber industry during the colonial era.[69] Like so many at Cajú, her father never returned from South Africa, so she came to the capital to look for work. She scavenged for wild fruit and firewood to exchange with the soldiers at the urban military barracks for maize flour and beans. It was a very insecure living,

---

[65] *Recenseamento Geral, 1960*, included 2,242 women employed in the processing industries and 5,193 women domestic service, and Instituto Nacional de Estatística, Direcção Provincial dos Serviços de Estatística, República Portuguesa, Estado de Moçambique, *IV Recenseamento Geral da População, 1970*, Vol. I, Distrito de Lourenço Marques (Lourenço Marques: Imprensa Nacional, 1973) included 8,074 women in the processing industries and 4,522 in domestic service, so almost reverse proportions.

[66] Ribeiro, *África no Feminino*; Penvenne, 'Fotografando Lourenço Marques.'

[67] The following paragraphs based on *Estatística Industria*l [title and author varies] (Lourenço Marques, 1947–1973)

[68] Whenever possible, evidence from oral narratives and the ACLM sample is cited to support statements about race when the statistics no longer rolled it into their equations.

[69] The following based on an interview with Felizmina in Santos Oliveira, 'Recordações sobre Lourenço Marques,' 89–108.

and in 1949 she got casual labour at the rubber plant. Every day the boss would choose among people waiting at the gate and paid them but not the legal minimum.

Like the members of the original cohort at Tarana, Felizmina began working in rubber when the operation was just a small garage in Malhangalene. By the time the business expanded and moved to a factory on Avenida de Angola in Ximpamanine, she was an experienced worker. The employer paid overtime and the conditions were better than in the garage. She worked crack of dawn, and when necessary straight through to ten in the evening. The work was relentless: 'We didn't get a lunch hour. We ate while we stitched. How could we buy food in the bazaar and cook it? We ate sardines with bread. We ate the same thing at night if you had to work through to finish the order.' Unlike the women of Tarana, Felizmina got 15 days of vacation, and some benefits: 'The boss gave us some kilos of rice and sugar as a way to say happy holidays. We would eat those happy holidays and stay home for 15 days...We used to say, 'Iaa! the boss likes me a lot, he gave me rice. Forgetting that you worked hard, how long you worked, how hard you worked. I didn't know because I never studied.' Even without an education Felizmina knew her wages were low, but she took pride in being a 'vulcanizadora'. She took pride in the fact that the work of her own hands had contributed to a major urban industry, and that her own house was built 'with sneakers and rubber'.[70]

Everywhere poverty is expensive, time consuming and inconvenient. Water purchased by the can, cigarettes by the cigarette, and firewood by the small bundle are all more expensive than water piped into the house, cigarettes bought by the carton and firewood purchased by the cord. The Ximpamanine market, the first and only municipally built and subsidized market in the bairros de caniço, did more business than the other broadly scattered cantinas because it was located on the main roads serviced by municipal transportation that specifically targeted African workers, and also attracted white customers and tourists.[71]

Ximpamanine's prices were lower than those prevailing at Vasco da Gama, the major municipal market in the heart of the cement city, but higher than those of informal street corner sellers throughout caniço where most families both bought and sold food. Most of the women of Tarana could not afford the time or transport to shop at Ximpamanine regularly. When they had cash, they could buy fresh produce closer to home from unlicenced vendors. For people without cash, cantinas with vale credit were the only option. The thousands of caniço residents who did not live near municipal taps, purchased water from the nearest cantina. Most African women who lived in caniço bought food and water close to home because they had little disposable time and money, lived by vale credit and appropriately feared being in the wrong place

[70] Santos Oliveira, 'Recordações sobre Lourenço Marques,' 89–108
[71] Mendes, 'Maputo,' 160.

at the wrong time. All women knew enough to stay in after dark if at all possible and to stay away from areas where they might encounter drunken or predatory men.[72]

The informal economy in the *bairros de caniço* was extensive and growing, particularly in the closing decade of the colonial era. Although *cantinas* were almost all owned and run by South Asians and Portuguese, Africans handled the trade in *caniço* and poles – the very items the women of Tarana saved to buy – and also competed in the market for cement blocks and corrugated metal roofing sheets.[73] African women dominated the *caniço* trade in firewood, charcoal, *bebidas*, cooked food and informally sold fresh produce.[74] The *cantinas* and informal economy served the majority of residents, and they would have been hard pressed to get what their families needed daily without it.

Cashew shellers in context

Local people may well have viewed the cashew shellers as dirty and suspect and avoided work at Tarana unless they had no other choice – the place was dirty, stinking and dangerous. [75] But scores of local women also worked and raised their children at Tarana. Local women like Marta Moiana and Raquelina Machava worked at Tarana right alongside their mothers and daughters – three generations of local women supporting one another and taking care of children, without counting on the children's fathers.[76] Just how different were these industrial women and their families from their neighbours in the *bairros de caniço* in this era? As reflected in Felizmina's narrative, life among factory women was not so different, but how about the rest of the population.

Rita-Ferreira's 1968 study found that around 40 per cent of all urban African children's birth and paternity was not registered. They did not

---

[72] In 1947, 1949 and 1950 significant violence broke out between residents of *caniço* and soldiers, particularly those of the *Esquadrão de Dragões* (special forces), housed in the Malanga military barracks. Luis Augusto Pereira de Azambuja, the administrator at the time reported: 'All of these disorders without a doubt were motivated by struggles over women. The soldiers look to satisfy their sexual needs by molesting any woman who passes them, a mother accompanied by husband, parents, and siblings – always resulting in disorder.' The same report confirmed that some women lived in houses around the military barracks in *amancebado* relationships with soldiers, and that the soldiers protect these women. PAM to ACLM, 242 B/11, 20 Nov. 1950, ACLM / AHM; OT, Group of Retirees, 4 June 1993.

[73] OT, Joana Tinga Chilaule, 20 May 1993, Carlota Samuel Ncutlana, 6 March 1993, Julieta Mulungu, 20 May 1994, Ester Tafula, 6 March 1993, Rosa Nau, 10 June 1993; Langa, *Retratos*, 50.

[74] *Brado Africano*'s coverage of African sporting teams suggests sport is another important and neglected economic area for African business, but it was clearly a male arena. Rita-Ferreira, 'Os Africanos,' 280, 367; Nuno Miguel Rodrigues Domingos, 'Football in Colonial Lourenço Marques: Bodily Practices and Social Rituals,' PhD thesis (London: University of London, 2009).

[75] OT, Luis Guila Muhale, 29 June 1993.

[76] OT, Marta Moiane, 9 July 1993, Marta, her mother Alice Massinga and daughter Antoineta Moiana all worked at Tarana; OT, Raquelina Machava, 21 May 1993, 12 July 1993.

have the documents they needed to attend school. Although women asserted, 'These children do not have fathers,' they of course did, and most mothers and fathers knew whose child was whose. Registering a child's birth at the municipal office was another matter. It meant money, time off work to stand in line, and likely as not, a problem that would require a return visit and more money.

As early as the mid-1950s when Rita-Ferreira began research in rural Sul do Save, he found that stigmatization for having children of the house and living *amancebado* was greatly diminished, even in what were presumably more conservative rural areas. Having a child prior to a *lobolo* sanctioned marriage sharply limited a woman's chances of becoming a first wife in a *lobolo* sanctioned marriage. By the 1950s young people were less convinced than their parents of the benefits of marriage with *lobolo*. Rita-Ferreira found that formal polygamy had sharply declined whereas living *amancebado*, or what he called living in concubinage, was increasingly common.[77]

By 1960 more than 8,500 women who lived in Lourenço Marques, were registered as heads of household providing for their own children. Thousands of urban women avoided registration if possible, so it is difficult to document how many women lived as single heads of households with dependent children.[78] Women who did or did not work for wages developed multiple income streams and strategies: collecting fruits, nuts and edible plants in public areas, collecting shellfish at low tide, and harvesting the pruned branches from municipal streets to use or sell as firewood for cooking. Charcoal and firewood were the usual fuels in much of the city not serviced by electricity, and women were the usual purveyors.

Although all families leveraged wages if possible, the fact that only 7 per cent of *caniço* residents in Rita-Ferreira's 1967 survey worked *machambas* underscored the enormous shift from 1940 when over 80 per cent of urban women worked *machambas*. Although aerial photos revealed that virtually every small patch of land that could be planted was, these small bits could not produce like a proper *machambas*.[79] Instead, women bought staples at area markets and either resold them or processed them to sell as food and drink, again providing convenience and staples for people who lived in poorly served neighbourhoods and did not have time in their day to walk to the main markets.[80]

The narratives deeply document that women from all kinds of household configurations participated in the firewood, charcoal, *bebidas*, cooked food and fresh produce trades in *caniço*. They worked in hairdressing and sewing enterprises for themselves, their families and as

[77] Rita-Ferreira, 'Esboço Social,' 121, 128–9.
[78] Rita-Ferreira, 'Os Africanos,' 304–27.
[79] Rita-Ferreira, 'Os Africanos,' 315.
[80] Rita-Ferreira, 'Os Africanos,' 300; Mendes, 'Maputo.'

small businesses. Unless they belonged to churches that prohibited any consumption of alcohol, even women from elite households brewed *uputsu* or *pombe*, millet based low alcohol beer, both for home consumption and neighbourhood sale. Brewing remained an important method for all families to leverage income.[81] In short, most African families in *caniço* pursued the same multiple stream strategies as the women of Tarana: borrowing on *vales*, saving with *chitikis*, enhancing income any way they could. Most families also counted on the active contributions of as many urban and rural family members and friends as possible to keep their households together.

A 1959 / 1960 study of 262 workers and their families at the Matola cement factory was one of the rare studies of workers and their families in this era. It found a good deal of diversity among the workers and their families, but made many observations that rang true with the cashew shellers, and provided a basis for comparison. It confirmed that the standard fuels for cooking were charcoal or firewood. They were essential to cook the maize, rice and groundnut staples most people counted on for all their meals. Most families used a mortar and pestle to grind the maize and groundnuts. That and the use of charcoal and firewood suited the usual pattern of preparing and cooking food either in the open or in a structure with an open roof to vent smoke. The study estimated the 1956 to 1959 minimal weekly cost for these staple foods and the fuel to cook it at 70 *escudos*.[82] If the cashew shellers were paid in full, 13 per day, for each day in a six day week, their maximum earning was 78 *escudos*.

Even though the men at Matola's cement factory earned higher wages, their families still planted *machambas* near the factory housing to enhance access to food.[83] More than half those families depended upon a man who earned the factory's lowest wage, 18 *escudos* per day. Around 8 per cent of the men earned the top wage, 40 *escudos* a day. Of those people who ate regular meals: breakfast was tea with sugar and bread, both the midday and evening meals were maize porridge or rice with groundnuts or some vegetables. People had fish or meat when possible, but the study revealed that all the women in the study consumed around a third too few calories, 82 to 100 per cent of the children and adolescents consumed between a third to more than half too few calories, and all the women and children were either somewhat

---

[81] OT, Christina Josias Pelembe, 17 May 1993; Celeste Guambe, 17 May 1993; Joana Massacaira, 24 May 1993; Amélia Samuel Muzima, 25 May 1993.

[82] The *Anuário Estatístico* for 1956 listed prices for key staples: charcoal 60 *escudos* per kilo x 8 kilos per week total 4.70, maize flour 1/5 kilos per day at 2.28 week total 23.23, groundnuts at 1 kilo per day at 5.2 week total 36.40 and 1.5 kilos of chicken for the week at 18 total 27.00, Moçambique, Repartição Técnica de Estatística, *Anuário Estatístico*, Lourenço Marques, Imprênsa Nacional,1956. This study confirms 70 to cook and eat per week, leaving most workers with 29 *escudos* per week for tax, rent, clothing and everything else. See also *Inquérito nutritional...Fabrica de Cimentos*, un-paginated.

[83] *Inquérito nutritional...Fabrica de Cimentos*, un-paginated.

or very protein deprived.[84] Women were consistently the most calorie and protein deficient, despite the fact that they carried pregnancies, nursed and produced food for everyone else. The only people in the cement factory study who consumed more calories and protein than they needed were the small number of men who earned 40 *escudos* per day. Their wives and children did not benefit to the same extent.

Although the cement factory workers' accommodations were rudimentary, they did not have to pay rent. Most of the women of Tarana prioritized food. A secure roof over their heads came next. Several surveys found that residents of *caniço* in general prioritized food, and that took so much of their income, it was not uncommon for people to be late with or to default on their rent payments.[85] Food, fuel and rent were basic. The women of Tarana and many others in *caniço* struggled to meet the basics.

Norberto Teixeira Santos's 1970 study surveyed diet and nutrition for the general population of 200 African households in the *caniço* neighbourhood of Josefa, with specific emphasis on children under age five. It revealed that almost half (48 per cent) of the children examined were malnourished in basic caloric and protein intake. Although nurslings suffered less from malnutrition, 5 per cent of children between ages one and five were gravely malnourished, to the point of suffering from kwashiorkor or marasmus, and 6 per cent suffered from rickets.[86] The study concluded that infant and childhood illness and mortality in *caniço* was due to 'poverty, ignorance, poor housing and sanitation conditions as well as high rates of diarrhea, respiratory-illness, parasitism and malaria.'[87] Poverty and poor municipal services contributed to flimsy housing, inadequate clean water, and unreliable bucket sanitation that could have lethal consequences.

Prejudices faced by the women of Tarana were familiar to the rest of the population. Despite the fact that urban African families clearly depended upon women to feed and reproduce their households, men were apt to frame the presence of African women in urban areas as a problem, and the colonial administration repatriated women to rural areas if their migration and employment papers were not in order. The archives revealed cases of locally born women and long term residents facing relocation to rural areas in the 1960s when pressure for housing was stiff.[88] The state and senior males conceptualized African women's proper place as working a *machamba* in a rural area. In the late 1950s, Flegg Mitchell, speaking about the *caniço* population in general, concluded that women's presence was a positive factor: 'in spite of their

---

[84] Sources of protein were one third from groundnuts, one quarter from maize flour and only about 16 per cent from some combination of meat or fish. *Inquérito nutritional...Fabrica de Cimentos*, un-paginated.

[85] Rita-Ferreira, 'Os Africanos,' 311; JIU, Inquérito habitacional,' 42–87.

[86] Santos, 'Avaliação Nutricional,' 325–32.

[87] Santos, 'Avaliação Nutricional,' 325 –32.

[88] ACLM, petitions file 134 / B 1950s to 1962.

illiteracy and lack of remunerative employment, and even without formal marriage, the women of Lourenço Marques appear to represent a stabilizing force in the urban area. This may have been because the men and women lived in family units with their children and [unlike South Africa] not in separate labour units.'[89] Rita-Ferreira's analysis a decade later concurred with Flegg Mitchell's judgement almost word for word: 'women can be an eminently stabilizing force in urban society in spite of the numerous illegal and precarious [family] unions.'[90]

Flegg Mitchell also questioned the lopsided sex ratios the municipality reported. She argued that the municipality promoted a skewed understanding of the urban population because it included several all-male populations in the count of the urban African population. Those men and boys did not live in *caniço*, they were employed as live-in domestic servants in the cement city and as contract workers and soldiers living in compounds at the port and the military barracks in Malanga. In practice, she argued, the population who actually lived in the *bairros de caniço* had a much more balanced sex ratio.[91] In sum, scholars who focused on life in *caniço*, argued that African women's presence benefitted, rather than blighted, the city.

Families, fertility and poverty

Clearly many women looked to Lourenço Marques for the possibility of a better situation for themselves and their children, but the diversity among women migrants was significant. Rita-Ferreira argued that infertility was a major cause for divorce and separation in Sul do Save, but that argument did not emerge as true among the narrators, despite the fact that many of them were divorced and separated.[92] Although several of the women with the highest fertility were in long stable relationships, many more husbands left women for high fertility than divorced them for infertility. Only 10 per cent of the narrators never had children, and some of those had never married, were widowed before they had a child or never lived with a man. Another 15 per cent of the narrators had only one or two children, but three quarters of the narrators had three or more children. Of that group, more than a third had between three and six children and 40 per cent had between seven and eleven children. Again, sometimes large families correlated with enhanced security and prosperity and sometimes not.

Within the broader African urban community in the 1960s, the fertility profile was the opposite: 73 per cent of families had less than three children, whereas 75 per cent of Tarana narrators had three or

[89] Flegg Mitchell, 'Aspects of Urbanization,' 14–29, 35.
[90] Rita-Ferreira, 'Os Africanos,' 247–53, quote, 253.
[91] Flegg Mitchell, 'Aspects of Urbanization,' 14–29.
[92] Rita-Ferreira, 'Os Africanos,' 291–3.

more children. In the broader community, 44 per cent of households had no children living with them, about 29 per cent had two or fewer children and 27 per cent had three or more children.[93] Women came to the city to be sure they and their children or their siblings would be able to eat and have shelter. The great majority of women working at Tarana were not infertile. They had children and brought those children to town with them, in part because they did not have family in rural areas to take care of their children.

Although three quarters of the narrators had three or more children, about half of those mothers experienced the death of a child. Amélia Chiconela's tragic loss of seven of her eleven children was exceptional, but several women buried more than four children. Poverty contributed to high levels of child mortality among the urban African population as a whole. Cashew workers were a majority of wage earners among urban women, but by the late 1960s at least 18,700 urban women worked for wages, many in order to support themselves and their families.

In the late 1960s many African families were in some level of debt: owing back rent on their residences, taking out loans against the payment of their salaries, and spending 60 to 75 per cent of their overall income just on food.[94] Inquiries in 1963 and 1966 in the significantly more prosperous Munhuana housing project, where heads of household had to be men, residents reported that their entire incomes were consumed by the cost of basics: food, fuel to cook, rent for housing and electricity, batteries or kerosene for light. Their food rarely included luxuries like meat and fish.[95]

Although many women recalled that food and fuel prices in these years were accessible in comparison with inflation after independence, women with larger families always had to combine income generating, leveraging and borrowing to make ends meet. Rita Ferreira's survey revealed that 68 per cent of men did not tell their wives or the women they lived with what they earned and how they spent their money. Women who responded in the 1960s to similar surveys in the Munhuana *bairro* also said they did not know their family's income. [96] I suspect that even if they did, they would not want to share that with a stranger, through a translator.

The Social Agency professionals who conducted both inquiries in Munhuana worked with and focused mostly on men. The Bairro de Munhuana – originally the *Bairro Indígena de Munhuana* – was one of

[93] Rita-Ferreira, 'Os Africanos,' 178–97.
[94] Rita-Ferreira, 'Os Africanos,' 309 –22.
[95] JIU, 'Inquérito habitacional.'
[96] It is worth noting that 41.5 per cent of women and 49.3 per cent of men invited to participate in the 1963–64 Munhuana survey did not show up to participate. In the end the survey results for 500 families rested on information from 35 men and 25 women – sixty people. 'Inquerito Habitaçional', 24, 31; The numbers who actually engaged in the 1966 pilot seem to have been a bit more balanced, Momplê, 'Relatório Sintese,' 12.

the very few places the municipality invested in housing for the majority population. Many of the male heads of household held what would be considered good jobs, and most spoke at least rudimentary Portuguese. Both surveys, however, noted that virtually none of the women and children spoke Portuguese. The languages of the Bairro were Ronga or Changana. In this way the women of Cajú were not unusual.[97]

The professionals also noted that while men were generally in favor of the Municipality building blocks of apartment buildings rather than single-family dwellings, the women overwhelmingly disliked apartment buildings. Women valued a space where their children could play, and they could hang out a wash and sit in the open air with family when the house was hot. In an apartment they could not use their accustomed firewood or charcoal for cooking, but had to purchase more expensive fuels, and they could not pound maize with a large mortar and pestle, even if they found time to do that. Apartment living, they said, seemed to them like being hung out on a line without a backyard.[98]

Very few homes in *caniço* had piped water, electricity or chimneys for indoor cooking. None had municipal sewerage. Ninety four per cent of cooking was done in the back yard with firewood or charcoal. Women did meal preparation on top of the food, fuel and water gathering that entailed. Malarial mosquito populations bred in standing water from summer floods. Diapers and bedding did not dry. Charcoal prices soared, and wet fuels were difficult to light. Commutes on foot or by public transport were slowed. It took more time to do everything, and people got sicker from malaria and water borne diseases. The last weeks of each rainy month were particularly miserable, since people accumulated so much debt they couldn't get more credit and simply had to eat less. Hunger and illness combined with damp and mud to tax everyone's spirit.[99]

Despite the fundamental importance of food, the nutritional survey's attention to malaria, diarrhea and parasitism as contributing factors highlighted the importance of other aspects of health and wellbeing. In neighbourhoods with inadequate clean water, lack of sanitation, and poor drainage, women's ability to keep their children, their food and homes free of parasites and mosquitoes often hinged on their ability to manage their time and housework: hauling water from distant public fountains or purchasing it at the nearest *cantina*, cleaning surfaces, dishes, clothes and bodies. Absenteeism at Cajú was strongly linked to family illness, usually children's illness, so in effect, women missed work because the municipality did not invest in providing the basic services to their neighbourhoods that would have greatly enhanced their ability to live healthy lives.

[97] JIU, 'Inquerito Habitaçional,' 31; Momplê, 'Relatório Sintese,' 12, 23; Saevfors, *Maxaquene*, 69–71.
[98] JIU, 'Inquerito Habitaçional,' 31; Momplê, 'Relatório Sintese,' details 37–38, quote 38.
[99] OT, Carlota Cumbe and group of retirees, 2 June 1993.

Urban family forms

Like the women of Tarana, thousands of urban women lived *amance-bado* and the children of those relationships were considered children of women. Rita-Ferreira's query, 'Why do you prefer to have your wife and children live in the rural areas?' comes from the questionnaire at the core of his 1967 social survey – the one that he argued was factual and objective.[100] The survey posed no questions explicitly to African women and the quoted question clearly pre-judged men's answers. Not surprisingly, the survey concluded that urban men did not consider urban women suitable for marriage.[101] That may well have been true, but given the way Rita-Ferreira posed the question, it's not clear how he could have reached any other conclusion.

By rights, men who paid *lobolo* for their wives were supposed to support them and their children. Throughout this period both men and women asserted claims for support and service from their spouses and partners through the Native Affairs Department. Although the treatment of such petitions was hardly uniform, in general, men and women living *amancebado* had a much smaller chance of having their claims addressed than those in licensed civil marriages or *lobolo* sanctioned marriages.[102] Many women lived *amancebado* and raised children with men they knew were married to other women. Men lived *amancebado* and had children with women who were not their wives. Many people had longer or shorter term relationships with people who were their lovers, but not their wives or husbands.[103] Some women had long and satisfying relationships with their *amancebado* partners, with little expectation of anything but emotional support.[104] Some women had a series of men in their lives, and simply commented, 'We didn't necessarily live together we just had children.'[105] Matilde Chiduza went back to the same man who had repeatedly disappointed her, but smiled when she said, 'What can you do? A woman is a woman!'[106]

In short, many women and men lived in common-law relationships and the tensions and expectations in their households varied greatly. It is difficult to tell from the census figures how many of the households in the vast African residential areas were comprised of a man, his legal wife and their children. The mathematics in Rita-Ferreira's survey are also challenging. He estimated that around 26 per cent of

---

[100] Rita-Ferreira, 'Os Africanos,' 'Modelo do Questionário' between pages 100 and 101.

[101] Rita-Ferreira, 'Os Africanos,' 247 ff and 291ff.

[102] ACLM correspondence files documenting so-called *milandos* (disagreements / litigation) are a promising source for more details on social history. For example, PAM to ACLM, 29 Jan. 1949, 13 / B / 8; PAM to ACLM, 28 Nov. 1949, 222/ B/ 11; RCNI to ACLM, 19 Jan. 1947, 273/M/1/1; Circunscrição de Guija, 16 June 1950, 829/B/ 8. ACLM / AHM.

[103] Paulina Chiziane brings playful insightful into such urban relationships in her novel, *Niketche: Uma Historia de Poligamia [Romance]* (Lisbon: Caminho, 2002).

[104] OT, Amélia Manhiquete, 13 July 1993; Cristina Miambu, 26 May 1993.

[105] OT, Maria Argentina Nhasinde, 27 May 1993.

[106] OT, Matilde Chiduza, 27 May 1993.

men lived with their legal wives and children, and about 15 per cent of married men were living *amancebado* with a woman in town.[107] The figures were much higher in both categories for women. About 45 per cent of women lived with their husbands, and more than 28 per cent lived *amancebado*. Rita-Ferreira confirmed that the proliferation of *amancebado* relationships was strongly linked to poverty and the fact that once a woman with children from an earlier relationship struck out on her own in the city she would probably not marry again, but rather enter into *amancebado* relations. He raised these issues under the sub-heading concubinage.[108]

The experiences of women at Cajú mirrored those described by Rita-Ferreira, but most women did not adopt a sense of shame or second rate standing. Often the unmaking of their marriage was the trigger that sent women to Cajú, but the trigger of unmaking usually was not of their making, so they were not to blame. If simply being an urban woman was a strike against a woman's marriageability, being divorced or separated cast a woman as used goods – not suitable as a first wife. Of course, no one described men of any civil status as 'used goods' – that too is a gendered female concept.

However, Maria Argentina Mabica and Marta Elisa Jorge Honwana revealed that *amancebado* relationships could be satisfying and of long standing. They arrived at Cajú in 1964 in quite different circumstances, but both enjoyed sustained *amancebado* relationships. Maria Argentina was single and arrived in town with her mother.[109] They had fled Zavala district for the capital to escape the beatings they both experienced regularly from Mabica's father. Shortly after she started work at Cajú Mabica began an *amancebado* relationship with José Braço. After their second child was born Braço wanted to marry her, but his family viewed her as used goods and they insisted on what they and Maria Argentina called a 'fresh wife' from Gaza.[110] Braço eventually went through with the marriage to the Gaza woman to appease his family, but he continued to live and raise a family with Maria Argentina. They eventually had a family of six children and were still together nearly thirty years later. All parties to these relationships compromised. Maria Argentina Mabica basically lived with Braço while Braço's fresh wife lived mostly alone in Gaza. The sanctioned relationship between two families with bridewealth rested in the Gaza household.

Marta Elisa Jorge Honwana was barely 18 when she first married, but less than three years later she was widowed.[111] Although she was

---

[107] Rita-Ferreira, 'Os Africanos,' 299–300.
[108] Rita-Ferreira, 'Os Africanos,' 301ff under heading 'Concubinagem.'
[109] This paragraph based on OT, Maria Argentina Mabica, 27 May 1993.
[110] Maria Argentina used the words 'used goods' and 'fresh wife' when narrating her experience, OT, Mabica, 27 May 1993. By the twenty-first century the term *Xicalamidade*, meaning used clothing, 'used goods' was also applied to women who were separated, widowed or divorced, Lopes et al. *Moçambicanismos*, 39.
[111] This paragraph based on OT, Marta Elisa Jorge Honwana, 31 May 1993.

just 21 and had no children, she knew she would be considered used goods, not suitable as a first wife. She moved to live in the city with her father and began a long career at Cajú. The following year she had a daughter, a child of the house, and that confirmed Marta's status as used goods. Marta then began an *amancebado* relationship with Américo Cossa. Cossa was already married to a woman in Gaza, so Marta had no particular expectations of support in their relationship. However, thanks in part to Américo's support for her household, Marta managed to finish a second grade education and learn to sew. Her skills provided opportunities beyond farming and brewing to earn a bit extra on her own. She also leveraged Américo's wages with her skills.

Between 1967 and 1980 Marta and Américo had four sons and two daughters. Marta continued at Cajú. Her stepmother helped her when the children were young. On weekends Marta, her stepmother and several other women worked on a *machamba* just outside of the city. The combination of a stable relationship, education, technical training, consistent help with her children and the opportunity to enhance the family's income with produce from their gardens made Marta one of the most secure women among the narrators. Marta was not Américo's wife, but they made a good life together. Marta benefitted from Américo's protection, as well as her own skills and collaboration with a group of women drawn from her family and beyond. They had a deeply satisfying personal relationship despite the Gaza wife and the stress of many children and step-families. Perhaps it was simply that the narrators for this project were the city wives, not the country wives, but they seemed to enjoy a lot of satisfaction. Had they been living with an Agostinho things may have been different.

Rita-Ferreira's survey question was loaded with regard to rural wives, but his research findings were parallel to those in nearby Catembe: men married rural women and did not want to bring their wives into an urban area, because the city had a licentious and ostentatious reputation.[112] The women of Cajú came in for special disdain: 'Women who work in those factories ... all bear the stigma of being prostitutes ... A woman who is unwilling to live with [her husband or father] is a wanton woman whose only interest can be to sell her favors to as many men as she can.'[113]

The practice of men (Portuguese and African) hinging the status of community morality on the control and subordination of women, and projecting women as innately in need of domination was both regional and of long standing. Unsurprisingly, the narrative of cultural propriety and women's experiences of insecurity did not always square. Women's desire for independence and the right to hold property in their own right were due, in part, to the erosion of the familial protections and rights they formerly enjoyed. Focusing on women in Tanzania,

[112] Binford, 'Stalemate,' 109; Rita-Ferreira, 'Os Africanos,' 299–300.
[113] Binford, 'Stalemate,' 109.

Liv Haram's work suggests some single urban women with children fashioned reputations as so-called modern women, and spun it to their advantage. She also confirmed that poor women were the least likely to develop such a strategy.[114]

Rita-Ferreira concluded that women's final option after living *amancebado* was prostitution.[115] Certainly the single women migrants, widows and divorcees who worked at Cajú knew that their used goods reputation left them suitable only as *amancebado* partners, or second (small) wives, but many forged living arrangements with other women, with nephews or with their own children – without turning to prostitution. Migrant and local cashew shellers knew their reputations, but they did not have to live up to them. Many had sacrificed their perfectly fine reputations because men divorced them, left them, beat them, or in some other important way failed the women's culturally appropriate expectations for support and protection from a husband or father. The correlations between single motherhood and poverty remain strong. In his history of Africa's poor, John Iliffe cited a mid-twentieth century Burundi proverb: 'The poverty of the solitary is exceeded by that of the woman with a child on her back.' Half of Iliffe's four categories of Africa's very poor people were exclusive to women: unfit elderly widows and women with dependent children.[116]

Elina Chivavale Mulungu's statement that men in general and husbands in particular were useless for anything except what you do between the sheets was exceptionally frank but the idea of a husband as a nuisance was not at all beyond the pale. A study of South African women living and working in town in the late 1970s found similar sentiments among both single and formerly married women. A separated woman frankly stated: 'A husband is just a nuisance – he wouldn't let you work or, if he does, he doesn't work but takes your money. He is jealous and beats you. No, I'm better off without a husband.' A single woman had a similar attitude: 'What do I want a husband for? I can earn money and I can have a baby: I can bring my baby up myself and with no trouble from a man.'[117] Urban women could enjoy companionship in a relationship with a man without counting on him for support. Many women considered their jobs or

[114] Liv Haram specifically warns that single women's leveraging strategies to have children with multiple men who they can play off against one another, 'is not a real option for the poorest [women],' Haram, '"Prostitutes" or Modern Women: Negotiating Respectability in Northern Tanzania,' in Arnfred, ed. *Re-Thinking,* 225.

[115] Rita-Ferreira, 'Os Africanos,' 299.

[116] John Iliffe, *The African Poor: A History* (New York: Cambridge University Press, 1987): 63, 275.. More recent studies support this observation: Rosemary Galli, 'Household Surveys of Women in Urban Mozambique: A Statistical Overview,' *Africa Update,* 1, 3 (Summer 1994): unpaginated; International Labour Organization [ILO], *Women and Poverty in Mozambique: A Synthesis of an ILO study on Feminization of Poverty in Mozambique* (Geneva: ILO Office, 2001).

[117] Eleanor Preston-Whyte, 'Women Migrants and Marriage,' in Eileen Jensen Krige and John L. Comaroff, eds. *Essays on African Marriage in Southern Africa* (Cape Town: Juta & Company Ltd 1981): 166–7.

cash crops to be a more secure source of uncontested income than support from a husband.[118]

Analytical biases suggesting that male headed households were preferred and that conjugal rather than the kin bonds were core in household formation may be particularly unhelpful among poor populations or farming families in which women share field and household work.[119] Evelyn Blackwood, working on a case study in Sumatra suggests that: 'The assumption that at base most households are nuclear and headed by men ...be replaced by the assumption that households are groups of kin operating in a variety of cross-cutting relations, one of which may be the conjugal relation. '[120] Ofélia Manana Mbebe plainly stated the situation many women experienced: 'The men gave us children but never took any responsibility for them.'[121] She and others counted on family members to raise their children. Certainly a variety of cross-cutting relations among kin emerged as more usual and sustained in the cashew workers households than a conjugal relationship, and that was not unusual among other families in the *bairros*.

Poor women knew they could expect little in the way of support if they gave birth to a poor man's child. *Mestiço* and white populations living in the city's poorer neighbourhoods like Xavane and Chamanculo in the early 1960s also had significant populations of common-law partnerships and children born of women: in Xavane more than a quarter of couples lived in common-law households and more than 27 per cent of children were considered illegitimate in civil law.[122] In Chamanculo more than half the population lived *amancebado* (54 per cent), and 43 per cent of single women had children. Rita-Ferreira linked common-law unions to widows, infertile women and women cast out of their households, but made no mention of whether the men who entered *amancebado* relationships were widowers, infertile or also from unmade households.[123] His statistics just show that around 13 per cent of the city's African men lived in *amancebado* relationships, whereas more than 29 per cent of urban women lived *amancebado*. Only thirteen per cent of the men in Rita-Ferreira's sample were married with wives in rural areas – and they did not want them living in the city.[124]

Rita-Ferreira highlighted a range of factors that suggested the parallel between urbanization and the proliferation of *amancebado* households.

---

[118] OT, Elina Chivavale Mulungu, 4 June 1993; Preston-Whyte, 'Women Migrants,' 166–7.

[119] Gracia Clark, *Onions are my Husband: Survival and Accumulation by West African Market Women* (Chicago: University of Chicago Press, 1994); Gracia Clark ed., *Gender at Work in Economic Life* (New York: Rowman & Little Field, 2003) especially Evelyn Blackwood 'Women Headed Households in Agrarian Societes – Not Just a Passing Phase,' in Clark, ed. *Gender at Work*, 41–59.

[120] Blackwood, 'Women Headed Households,' 56.

[121] OT, Ofélia Manana Mbebe, 4 June 1993.

[122] 'Inquérito as rendas' and 'Inquérito Assistência Pública' details in Rita-Ferreira, 'Os Africanos,' 300 ff.

[123] Rita-Ferreira, 'Os Africanos,' 310.

[124] Rita-Ferreira, 'Os Africanos,' 300.

He emphasized the rationale and basic practices of patrilineal marriage with an exchange of *lobolo*, some of which held regardless of the form of household.[125] The idealization of generous hospitality and reciprocity among family members was general, as was the assumption of family support, and the authority of senior males. Those ideals could also be burdensome. People turned to extended family for life cycle thresholds (birth, death, marriage) and in times of crisis / distress (illness, unemployment, conjugal disputes). The importance of maintaining one's place within the family given the inevitability of these events and crises fueled people's commitment to sustain family links. Absenteeism to attend family rituals around birth, death, and marriage were an investment and form of insurance for many.[126] Poverty and misfortune greatly strained these ideal relationships, and the poorest and least fortunate were the most likely to be wrung into isolation, while the lucky and those who had maintained health could build resources and be generous with family.

The narrators of Tarana experienced much trauma in their family lives: death, domestic violence, adultery, abandonment, incest, and gross neglect. Most were poor and some were wrung into isolation, but others scrapped their way into something more prosperous. Whatever their circumstances, most had not given up on stable, enduring conjugal units as an ideal, or as a path through which they might exert influence to secure their interests as they aged. Women claimed space for themselves within socio-cultural notions that were usually articulated in law by senior men but also broadly present in women's songs and narratives: a man should provide *lobolo* to marry a respected woman and together they should create and sustain their family in dignity, with the man earning wages and the woman feeding the family through hoe labour in her *machamba*.[127]

Although Emera Mahochi dramatically joked about being Tarana's *dona da casa*, most women's ideal was indeed to be the senior woman in a *lar* – the conjugal unit.[128] What the Portuguese called the woman of the house, *dona da casa*, implied that the house had a *dono da casa*, a man of the house. While men absolutely disapproved of a woman living as a *mulher sem dono*, outside the authority of a man, women also

---

[125] Rita-Ferreira, 'Os Africanos,' 282–332.

[126] Rita-Ferreira, 'Os Africanos,' 282–89.

[127] The themes raised here were deeply embedded in the narratives. The most extensive quotes are from the following narrators: Cristina Jossias Pelembe, 17 May 1993; Salmina Cuma, 7 June and 19 July 1993; Raquelina Machava, 21 May and 12 June 1993; Cacilda Fumo, 21 May 1993; Celeste Marcos Mpendane, 26 May 1993; Marta Nhamave, 27 May 1993; Joana Tinga Chilaule, 20 May 1993; Rosalina Alberto Tembe, 19 May and 12 July 1993; Joana Massacaira, 25 May and 12 July 1993; Angelica Guamba, 4 June 1993; Caferina Malunguane Maletsuane, 9 June 1993.

[128] The Portuguese term is *lar*. There is some controversy over the Ronga and Changana terms for house and household. The Ronga terms used here follow Binford: *yindlu* or *kaya* for house / hearth and *muti* for household with a man and wife or wives, married sons and their families, unmarried children and widowed or divorced sisters or children and their children. Binford, 'Stalemate,' 71.

ideally preferred being the wife in a conjugal unit to being a women head of household – but as underscored throughout, every woman had her limits.

Regina Nhantumbo recalled, 'In the past our mothers were very good. They stayed suffering in their *lar* to take care of the children.' [129] Speaking in a group of retirees, with colleagues nodding their heads, Joana Massacaira claimed, 'A good home, with a single marriage for a lifetime – that is dignity and value. It is not good to have many husbands. It isn't good, but it happens. Our mothers suffered, but held together one *lar*. Today's women do not know the value of having children. Who will help you in your old age if you don't have children? Having one's own house is good. At one time you could do that, but now it is much harder.'[130]

Women distinguished between house and household – woman of the house and homeowner, but both were important. If your *lar* became undone, you did not want to lose your house in the bargain. Recall Rabeca Notiço's position: 'A woman of value has a home. When a man wants to live with me OK, but when he no longer wants me – he goes. I have my home, and that is my value.'[131] Like so many others, Rabeca rented a room and then a small house, and eventually she build her own home through *vales* – one cement block, one metal sheet at a time. She never moved in with a man.

Scores of women agreed with Leia Papulo Nhavene's judgment: 'The best and most important thing is to provide well for your children; get along well with them and with the head of your family. Save and plan so that you can receive family members in the proper way.'[132] Clearly cultural definitions of proper comportment and reception of family differed somewhat, but the retirees peppered their descriptions of ideal households and homes with the words respect, discipline, and harmony.

Those values anchored people's aspirations even when everything had gone wrong for them personally. Caferina Nhatsene, like so many others, followed her description of a harmonious household, capable of receiving family in the proper manner, with the fact that, 'We are at Cajú because our parents died, our husbands left us and we are poor.'[133] Poverty, death and irresponsibility undercut aspirations for respect, discipline, and harmony in people's lives. Some things one could not change or escape, but since 'somebody had to take care of those children', many women carried on in pursuit of the most dignified harmonious accommodation they could manage. It was never easy.

The narratives were not all tales of suffering and stoicism. Young women especially made time to play when they could manage it. As

[129] OT, Regina Nhantumbo, 26 May 1993.
[130] OT, Joana Massacaira, 24 May and 12 July 1993.
[131] OT, Rabeca Notiço, 24 May 1993.
[132] OT, Leia Papulo Nhavene, 17 May 1993.
[133] OT, Caferina Malunguane Maletsuane, 9 June 1993.

happens in most places, factory friends in Chamanculo gathered on payday to dance and drink: 'When we left work we went to the *cantina* and had a good time. On pay day, when the Indian saw us coming, he said to himself "today I'll make money".' When women were past struggling with infants and toddlers, many remembered enjoying one another's company over a beer or tea after work.[134]

Cashew workers sooner or later learned to navigate the usual workplace tensions of personality, competition and jealousy. Migrants and local women might frequent different *cantinas*, gathering with colleagues who shared their mother tongue, and neither group was above taunting the other. Local women belittled migrants because they spoke Changana or Chopi rather than Ronga. Many migrant women had no money for nice clothes and no time for socializing because they were working every minute to pay off their *lobolo*. Migrants could be intimidated by more experienced local women. Migrants complained that locals were haughty, entitled, and jealous of competition for their menfolk, while others built enduring workplace friendships.[135] Social capital accumulated at the workplace was an important part of many workers' gift and informal economy investments. Beyond workplace *chitikis* co-workers might trade or barter the products of their shared *machamba* labour.[136] In sum, the women of Tarana, like most people in the city navigated the potential and tensions of relations among families, work colleagues, neighbours and friends. Their wages were important, but so was their social capital.

---

[134] OT, Leia Papilo Nhavene, 17 May 1993; Joana Massacaira, 25 May 1993; Joana Uaichele, 21 May 1993; Raquelina Machava, 21 May, 12 July 1993.

[135] OT, Marta Moiana, 9 July 1993; Serafina Langa, 3 June 1993 and song *'Magosino nuna wa mina mamani!'* Manghezi, *Trabalho Forçado*, 56–60.

[136] OT, Christina Jossias Phelembe, 17 May 1993; Celeste Guambe, 17 May 1993, Amélia Samuel Muzima, 27 May 1993; Christina Miambu, 26 May 1993; Leia Nhavene, 17 May 1993; Marta Elise Honwana, 31 May 1993; Rosalina Tembe, 19 May 1993.

Conclusions
Gendered Perspectives on Work, Households and Authority

The value and visibility of women's work

Basic concepts like work, history, household, migration and authority can look quite different through the lens of gender. Women's daily productive and reproductive work regularly cuts across analytical categories, and they experience work in the household, gift, informal, and formal economies on much the same footing. Furthermore, since women birth, nurse and raise children, even if they work in the formal sector many hours a day, the household and its related gift and informal economies are often an essential part of women's lived workdays. It is true that in the field of labour history, '...because of the differing perceptions of what constitutes work, women's active participation in the economy tends to remain undercounted.'[1] Although, particularly since the 1970s, the naming and measuring of previously ignored arenas of productive and reproductive labour has proceeded apace, scholars still struggle to understand and value work, but gender has emerged as one of the more productive and challenging lenses into such inquiry.[2] Gender is no longer simply a residual category.

Although scholars still debate what to call it and how exactly to define it, the informal sector is now broadly recognized as important, ubiquitous, gendered and deeply connected across space and within authority hierarchies and networks.[3] Social and labour historians realize that 'the boundaries between formal and informal subsistence strategies are especially blurred for women, even those employed, at one point or another, in the formal sector,'[4] and moreover, 'the

---

[1] R. Jhabvala, 'Labor Markets, Labor Movements and Gender in Developing Nations,' *International Encyclopedia of the Social and Behavioral Sciences* (Elsevier Science Ltd, 2001) 8185–8191, quote 8186.
[2] Jan Lucassen, ed. *Global Labour History: A State of the Art* (New York: Peter Lang, 2008).
[3] The literature cites Keith Hart's first use of the term, in 'Informal Income: Opportunities and Urban Employment in Ghana,' *Journal of Modern African Studies*, 11, 1 (1973): 161–78. See Sabyasachi Battacharya and Jan Lucassen, 'Introduction: Informalisation in History,' and Frederick Cooper, 'African Labour History,' in Jan Lucassen, ed. *Global Labour History: 1–19 and 110–12* respectively.
[4] John D. French, 'The Labouring and Middle-Class Peoples of Latin America and the Caribbean: Historical Trajectories and New Research Directions,' in Lucassen, ed. *Global Labour History: 325–6.*

everyday reality [for women] has tended to consist of a series of exhausting duties – both those involved in earning a living and those that relate to caring for family and children.'[5] Caroline Gatrell argues that idealized, essentialist narratives of the 'good mother' and 'natural womanhood', combine to obfuscate the real work women do to maintain a pregnancy, deliver a healthy infant, and then nurse and care for that child.[6] Looking after children is hard and important work. When women stay home because they or their children are too sick, the sources we are trained to read do not treat that work as an investment in the household economy, but rather as absenteeism from formal sector work. The whole concept of absenteeism needs to be fundamentally rethought.

Taking insights articulated in the 1970s as her touchstone, Wilma Dunaway argues that false analytical divides between production and reproduction and between formal and informal economic sectors, obscure or erase important areas of women's work and suggest separation of categories when worker experiences reveal integration and cross-cutting.[7] The gift economy, or the 'economy of favors' as Janet MacGaffey calls it, underscores Frederick Cooper's point that 'Labour is untidy and claims on people often outweigh claims on wages'.[8] Networking and efforts to build relationships across a spectrum from aspirations of balanced reciprocity to pointedly acknowledged unequal exchange are common in households, neighbourhoods, and workplaces. For the cashew workers lending, borrowing and repaying in cash and kind were essential practices for families, particularly for those with limited access to material resources. Long term investments in unpaid labour and services among family members or colleagues comprised important strategies to stake claims in insecure arenas.[9] Those investments might be understood as part of the household, gift or informal economies, but again they may be done daily by the same person, and simply experienced as a day's work.

---

[5] Andrei Sorolov, 'The Drama of the Russian Working Class and New Perspectives, for Labour History in Russia,' in Lucassen, ed. *Global Labour History*: 442–3.

[6] Caroline Gatrell, *Embodying Women's Work* (New York: McGraw Hill, 2008): 51–75.

[7] Dunaway and colleagues draw on a large bibliography, but the introductory touchstones are from the foundational work of Lourdes Beneria, Terence Hopkins and Immanuel Wallerstein. Beneria, 'Reproduction, Production and the Sexual Division of Labour', *Cambridge Journal of Economics*, 3 (1979): 203–25; Terence Hopkins and Immanuel Wallerstein, 'Patterns of Development of the Modern World-System', *Review of the Fernand Braudel Center*, 1 (2) 1977: 11–145; Wilma Dunaway, ed. *Gendered Commodity Chains: Seeking Women's Work and Households in Global Production* (Stanford: Stanford University Press, 2014).

[8] Cooper, 'Labour History', 91–111; Janet MacGaffey 'New Forms of Remuneration for Labour in Congo- Kinshasa's Economy of Favours,' in Sabyasachi and Lucassen, eds. *Workers in the Informal Sector*: 141–60

[9] MacGaffey, 'New Forms of Remuneration', 152–8.

Enduring notions about households and who heads them are Euro-centric and androcentric. Agrarian and urban households formed around collaborating networks of women and siblings were durable. They should not be seen simply as a short-term contingency.[10] In light of such evidence, Evelyn Blackwood proposed that 'The assumption that at base most households are nuclear and headed by men would be replaced by the assumption that households are groups of kin operating in a variety of cross-cutting relations, one of which may be the conjugal relation'.[11] In short, Blackwood suggests decentring a conjugal house-hold core and an anticipated male head to allow analytical space for varied and durable cross-cutting relations people like Mátchiuassane Boa, her mother and nephew successfully forged in the Limpopo. In southern Africa urban women might elect to live *amancebado* for male companionship and protection, but without expectations of support. Such social groupings should not be made invisible or treated as residual, exceptional, or contingent, but rather as households on an equal footing with any other households.[12]

Along similar lines, the notion of breadwinner has embedded a some-times untested image of a male earning a wage and then sharing that wage with the so-called 'dependents' in his household – dependents assumed to be women, children, the sick and elderly.[13] That image of a male breadwinner further connotes assumptions about employment, government and claims for social benefits that did not hold for colo-nized people in many parts of the world.[14] Where formal sector wages have lost significant value, work by so-called household dependents to leverage formal sector wages into something a family can live on has become essential. Social capital and relationships of reciprocity, giving, receiving, repaying and accumulating favors are central to families' quotidian economic lives. That is particularly true for poor people and people who have to cope with economic uncertainty.[15]

Finally, although the women's narratives underscored the cultural tenet of respect for adult male authority, and the authority of one's in-laws, many of the women experienced violence, neglect or abuse from precisely those people. When that was the case, women turned to others for support – perhaps to the men in their mother's lineage or to a sympathetic *hahán* or older sibling. Men and women held different forms of knowledge, developed different forms of authority and expe-rienced and conveyed their lived history differently. Many women's

[10] Ana Loforte, *Genero e Poder*; Blackwood 'Women Headed Households'.
[11] Blackwood 'Women Headed Households', 56.
[12] Preston-Whyte, 'Women Migrants and Marriage', 166–7.
[13] Naoko Otobe, *Resource Guide on Gender Issues in Employment and Labour Market Policies: Working Towards Women's Economic Empowerment and Gender Equality* (Geneva: ILO, 2014); 82–3; Lindsay, *Working with Gender*.
[14] Cooper,' Labour History,' 111–16.
[15] Bénard da Costa, *O Preço de Sombra*; Rodrigues, *O Trabalho Dignifica*; Cooper,' Labour History,' 91–111; MacGaffey, 'New Forms of Remuneration,' 141–60; Tripp, *Changing the Rules*.

experience with male authority was traumatic. Some women did not fit easily into cultural understandings of what it meant to be respectable. But here we see that women with children of the house and *mulheres sem donos*, crafted narratives of new respectability that honored their shifting experience and knowledge.

History and memory: Narrating a new respectability

The colonial administration typically viewed urban African women as a problem, and women working at Cajú Industrial as troublesome. They were suspect in the urban African community as a whole, in part because they were disproportionately divorced, widowed, separated or single. Factory work, particularly in the dirty, smelly, difficult sectors of Tarana, was poorly understood outside the factory. It was neither sought after nor prestigious. Women who worked in the city's factories did not step into an established narrative of respectability and positive attributes, but over time they forged their own. The qualities their narratives underscored were strength, responsibility, endurance, independence, and commitment. Tarana women's narratives embraced the very independence that others found suspect. They clearly stated a determination to earn a salary at the factory so as not to be dependent upon or to 'chase down' men. The ethic of 'working well' among factory colleagues was scripted throughout the narratives. Although every work place had *zaunzwanas*, rumour-mongers and trouble makers, most of the narratives underscored 'working well' to get through and be sure everyone could go home and be paid.[16]

Here we touch again on women's words because their aspirations were embedded in what they claimed to value. Not surprisingly, goals and values differed somewhat by age cohort and status. Those who were doing well tended to be more expansive in their statements than the very poor. Clearly older women looking back on their lives, and ahead for their children's children had different perspectives than the young women who were still in the thick of very demanding lives surrounded by nurslings and toddlers, or the youngest women who, although poor, still aspired to play. In a conflation of the familiar 'young people nowadays' complaint, and the discourse of what 'doesn't happen anymore,' older women complained: 'In the past our mothers were very good. They stayed suffering in their households to take care of the children. This doesn't happen anymore!'[17] Angelina Sitoe complained, 'In the past women respected themselves and other women's husbands, but it is not like that today'.[18] Joana Uaichele alleged: 'Today when you give

[16] OT Christina Jossias Pelembe, 17 May 1993; Maria Celeste Chavane, 2 June 1993; Julieta Mulungu, 20 May 1993; Emera Mahochi, 2 June 1993; Carolina Sigaugue, 24 May 1993.
[17] OT, Regina Nhantumbe, 26 May 1993.
[18] OT, Angelina Sitoe, 7 June 1993.

birth to a child you do not give birth to a heart, just a body'.[19] Despite their complaints, many women worked at Cajú as a direct result of their decision to stop suffering in their households, many lived with 'other women's' husbands and some also shared Uaichele's disappointment with their children.

Younger women and local women, for whom a classic *lobolo* and *machamba* marriage had never been a probable option, put more stock in picking up the hoe of the city, building a home and raising a family on one's own: 'Many women rent and many own, but it is a good thing for someone to have a house. Build little by little.'[20] Home ownership and security was a major theme. The home could be very modest but if it was yours, it was secure. 'When the *chitiki* money came to me I bought poles and zinc sheets to build a little shanty, just enough to hide my head.' [21] The youngest women valued something nice to wear and a good time on payday, building a home of their own could wait a bit.[22]

Although many women of Cajú had notoriously bad luck with men and marriage, they still largely valued the qualities of a good wife and mother and aspired to household collaboration among men and women. That was not unusual. Scholars of the colonial era have broadly found that Mozambicans valued complementary roles in the sexual division of labour and social reciprocity among family members.[23] Men strongly resisted their wives entering waged labour because that compromised the amount and quality of labour and service women could render their conjugal households. In Carolina Manelele's case, her husband and his family failed to support her excellent hard work, but husbands and lineages usually appreciated and supported women who 'worked well' in their *machambas* and other income generating initiatives. Women who worked for wages still identified largely as mothers and wives. They generally did not view themselves as compromising their households because of their jobs. They viewed their wage labour pay as adding value to the household unit.

Many absent migrant husbands chose not to interfere with their wives' management of household resources if things were going well.[24] Gendered negotiations of household resources were often framed in terms of mutual respect and personal dignity, and were important aspects of marriage. Despite the commitment to mutual respect, male authority was important and it was 'dangerous' for women to challenge it openly.[25] Economic and social changes always shaped the pathways of household negotiations and contestations.

---

[19] OT, Joana Uaichele, 12 July 1993.
[20] OT, Rosalina Tembe, 19 May 1993.
[21] OT, Ofélia Manana Mbebe, 4 June 1993.
[22] OT, Helena Chemane, 26 May 1993; Elisa Tovela, 28 May 1993; Isabel Runga, 27 May 1993.
[23] Chilundo, *Os Camponeses*, 351–2; Loforte, 'Migrantes,' 63; Fialho Feliciano, *Antropologia Económica*, 436ff.
[24] Loforte, 'Migrantes,' 63.
[25] Chilundo, *Os Camponeses*, 351–2.

Harmonious households, safe and sturdy homes, healthy children supported by hoe labour, and standing as dignified adults in one's community remained the goals.

We continue to neglect centrally important, complex phenomena and processes because the sources we use do not understand, see or value them. We value written text, newspapers over songs and conversations. Furthermore, we have not yet fully developed the tools to analyse many complex practices and processes. Women's practices and processes are most likely to be missed or misrepresented by observers and analysts both today and in the past.[26] Following James Scott's observations on how states codified and rearranged processes, relationships and even places in metrics that enabled them to 'see' and thus tally, tax, record and manipulate them, the documents and narratives reveal the extent to which women and their essential contributions were invisible in plain sight. In Lourenço Marques and many other colonial cities, what Scott calls 'ordered spaces' barely extended beyond the tip of the state's nose. The orderly cement city was projected over the much larger *bairros* that surrounded it.

Prioritizing the formal wage and export economy over the much larger, more fluid and complex household, gift and informal economies that the state chose to dismiss as disorder gave a very skewed incomplete view of the production of goods and services in the municipality.[27] Colonial sources often ignored vast indigenous economies or described them as disorder to the point of chaos. The better description was actually fluid, dynamic, and complex.[28] Finally, because women and children dominated the household, gift and informal sectors, they were inadequately drawn into the dominant metrics. They were under-counted, under-measured, uncounted, unmeasured, and often illegal and unlicensed. The narratives that emerge from the recollections of ordinary and poor women make it impossible to overlook these connections and insist that we grapple with their complexity and importance.

In sum, this book does a great deal more than simply present compelling and neglected perspectives on urban industrial labour and migrant life in the late colonial era. By centering women's experiences and their interpretations in Mozambique's leading late colonial industry, it connects the larger cashew economy, and its role in household, gift, informal, and formal sectors. It reveals extensive and acknowledged wage and price fraud in the industry in the 1960s and 1970s. It suggests advantages where disadvantages have been assumed, connects parental and family relationships and forms despite discourses that remove men from paternity, stigmatize women for maternity, value

[26] Feierman, 'Creation of Invisible Histories;' Bradford, 'Women, Gender.'
[27] Henri Bergson in White, *Political Analysis:* 211.
[28] Patrick Chabal spearheaded the recognition of disorder as order with, *Africa Works: Disorder as Political Instrument* (Oxford: James Currey, 1999).

an absent legal spouse and devalue a present common-law partner. It contrasts assumptions around 'industrial man' with the experiences of 'industrial woman.' It concludes that, particularly when it comes to industrial women workers in Lourenço Marques, what the government perceived as disorder may well have been an important order, despite the fact that, for the colonial state and municipality, it was unanticipated, unacknowledged and unwelcome.

Epilogue
Mozambique's Cashew Economy, 1975 to 2014

This study explored Mozambique's rise from 1945 to 1975 to become the world's largest combined producer of raw and processed cashew nuts, contributing around 40 per cent of global production in the peak years of the early 1970s. It emphasized four points regarding the cashew economy. First, there is much more to the cashew economy than simply the exportation of raw and processed nuts to global markets. The household, gift and informal components of cashew food and drink are fundamental and under-appreciated. Second, women play an essential role throughout the value chain in the cashew economy, and their roles are eclipsed if analysts do not explicitly probe gender relations. Third, prices and wages matter a great deal, but analysts pay insufficient attention to the value producers and workers actually receive when their product or labour is commoditized. Finally, the choices men and women make to grow, eat, give, distill, brew or sell cashew nuts and apples, and their decisions about whether to seek work and stay working at cashew shelling factories are complex and strongly shaped by the broader context of their lives.

Mozambique's experience with cashew production and processing over the four decades since independence has drawn international attention. Analysts seek to explain how and why the country slid from global dominance in the 1970s to the present position of producing around 2 per cent of global cashew exports. Many scholars, including those already cited, cover those changes in great detail.[1] The epilogue

---

[1] Introduction, notes 23 and 25 and Chapter 1, note 1. Multiple publications by Hanlon, Pitcher, Pereira Leite, McMillan, Cramer, and Kanji et al. provide details and context. Hanlon: weekly news and analysis web postings: http://www.open.ac.uk/technology/mozambique/ Accessed 1 May 2015. *Peace without Profit*, 'Power without Responsibility', and with Teresa Smart, 'From Disaster to Export Model', in *Do Bicycles Equal Development in Mozambique?* (Woodbridge/Rochester, NY: James Currey 2008): 36–50. Joana Pereira Leite's 'Guerra do Cajú,' details India's continuing role and suggests the overlay between the so-called India Lobby and the World Bank. Nazneen Kanji and her team consistently ask how changes in cashew shelling impact women and families: Carin Vijfhuizen, Carla Braga, Luis Artur and Nazneen Kanji, *Gender, Markets and Livelihoods in the Context of Globalisation; A Study of the Cashew Sector in Mozambique, January 2002 – June 2004* (IIED, 2004) http://pubs.iied.org/G01275.html?k=Gender%20Markets%20 and%20Livelihoods Accessed 4 May 2015. [hereafter Vijfhuizen et al., *Gender, Markets*]. Pitcher's 'The cashew controversy' in *Transforming Mozambique* references key documents and the range of political positions and issues. Christopher Cramer, et al. provide a telling overview of the rural economy in twenty-first century Central and Northern Mozambique that underscores

briefly sketches the main lines of change, and assesses the extent to which contemporary analysts overcome or replicate the challenges identified above for the colonial era literature. [2] I do not know how the narrators experienced the industry's fluctuations after the close of our project. Most of them probably had the same experiences as described by Nazneen Kanji and her colleagues below. They lost their jobs and dispersed.

The changes since independence fall roughly into four periods. The first period is the era of Frelimo's centralized economic control, with nationalized industries and government sponsored labour organization. By the 1980s the national economy was increasingly hobbled by the growing insurgency. The second period is the run up to and aftermath of the 1992 Rome Peace Accord that ended the insurgency and established the preconditions for rebuilding of infrastructure and resumption of trade and agriculture. That period coincided with Frelimo's commitment to multiparty democracy and engagement with International Financial Institutions for credit and economic liberalization and the privatization of previously nationalized sectors of the economy. In the third period, the mid-1990s to the turn of the century, the World Bank pressured the Frelimo government to revise its policy decisions regarding tariff protection of the newly privatized national cashew shelling economy. That period ended with the collapse of world cashew prices and bankruptcy and closing of large cashew processing plants throughout Mozambique. The final period covers the first generation of twenty-first century efforts to reorganize the cashew export and processing sector, largely through smaller scale shelling initiatives mainly clustered in the most densely concentrated cashew producing areas in northern Mozambique, but with some efforts in southern Mozambique.

In the second decade of the twenty-first century Mozambique remains among the world's ten poorest nations.[3] That is an improvement from its position as dead last prior to the Rome Peace Accord, but in light of a decade of 7 per cent and higher growth rates, the ranking reveals that poverty endures and complex inequities have actually increased.[4] Single, widowed and divorced women with children remain a dispro-

---

[contd] critical context, Christopher Cramer, Carlos Oya and John Sender, 'Lifting the Blinkers: A New View of Power, Diversity and Poverty in Rural Labour Markets,' *Journal of Modern African Studies*, 46, 3 (2008): 361–392 [hereafter Cramer et al. 'New View'].

[2] Works that replicate some of the problems mentioned here include Matthias Krause and Friedrich Kaufmann, 'Industrial Policy in Mozambique,' *DIE Discussion Paper*, 10/ 2011 (Bonn: Deutsches Institut für Entwicklungspolitik, 2011); M. Ataman Aksoy and Fehrettin Yagci, 'Mozambique Cashew Reforms Revisited,' in M. Ataman Aksoy, ed. *African Agricultural Reforms: The Role of Consensus & Institutions* (Washington: World Bank, 2012): 177 –217 [hereafter, Aksoy and Yagci in Aksoy, 'Mozambique Cashew Reforms']; Julian Boys 'Jobs, Votes and Legitimacy: The Political Economy of the Mozambican Cashew Processing Industry's Revival,' *Forum for Development Studies*, 41, 1 (2014): 23–52.

[3] http://hdr.undp.org/en/content/human-development-index-hdi Accessed 4 May 2015.

[4] Cramer et al. 'New View,' 364.

portionately large population among low-wage workers and the poorest of the poor.[5] If poverty alleviation is a core concern we need research that takes fuller account of gendered perspectives.

The decline of Mozambique's cashew economy: Weather and war

Many analysts focus on prices, non-price supports, currencies, credit, tax policy, measurements of efficiency, competition, markets and the sizes of small and medium enterprises. Understanding the nature and interplay of these factors is essential and complex. If, however, the larger point is to connect these measurable aspects with the behavior of the majority of people involved in the cashew economy they must be deeply embedded in the socio-economic and cultural context. Unfortunately, many analysts simply mention what they call 'the weather' and 'wartime conditions,' in their discussions of prices, policies, producers and processors. Weather and war are absolutely fundamental to any appreciation of Mozambique's cashew economy after 1975, and their disproportionately harsh impact on women and children should not be diminished. We necessarily begin with weather.

Over these decades, drought, flooding, golf ball size hailstones, and cyclone winds of more than 100 miles per hour repeatedly struck with historically unprecedented force and destruction. That continues to the present, and the statistics are staggering.[6] As illustrated throughout this study, Mozambicans have long experienced cyclical drought and flooding. They developed culturally appropriate food security and coping strategies, many of which involved courting social relationships they could count on in times of stress. Drought was often deadly in the early twentieth century when limited transportation infrastructure frustrated efforts to get relief supplies to the afflicted in time to avoid starvation. In the late colonial era, state and private relief supplies sent along the more fully developed transportation and communication networks in most cases lowered the death toll from drought, flood and windstorms.

In 1981 Mozambique's most devastating drought of the twentieth century struck when wartime insecurity complicated both relief efforts and refugee flight. 4,750,000 Mozambicans were affected by that drought and at least a hundred thousand perished. The so-called apocalypse drought struck the whole region in 1991, putting millions at risk of starvation, but peace initiatives supported relief efforts that diminished the death toll.[7] Subsequent significant droughts struck

---

[5] Vijfhuizen et al., *Gender, Markets*.

[6] Mozambique – Disaster Statistics – Data related to human and economic losses from disasters that have occurred between 1980 and 2010. http://www.preventionweb.net/english/countries/statistics/?cid=117 Accessed 4 May 2015.

[7] Ruth Ansah Ayisi, 'Mozambique: Drought and Desperation,' *Africa Report*, 37, 3 (1992): 33–5.

different regions of Mozambique in 2002, 2005 and 2007. Drought had clear implications for all agricultural production including the cashew harvest. Mature cashew trees are resistant to drought, so families count on them for food security, but seedlings and saplings often succumb to drought stress. People with access to producing trees make different choices about eating or selling their harvest depending on their circumstances. Some sell raw nuts for cash while others avoid starvation by eating their gathered crops. [8]

Less than two years after independence, the Limpopo and Incomati River floods displaced 150,000 people. Those floods were of historic proportions in 1977, but the subsequent floods of 1991 in the South and 2000 in Central Mozambique broke all previous records and took the lives of at least 800 people, and displaced hundreds of thousands. Families lost their homes, seedlings, saplings, planted fields, cattle and small stock. Food security hinged on international aid and any fruits and nuts that survived the deluge. Flooding in 2004 and 2007 similarly displaced hundreds of thousands, but thanks to lessons learned and greater preparedness fewer lives were lost. Between December 2014 and late February 2015, flooding in northern and central Mozambique killed 159 and displaced 160,000 people, and a killer cholera epidemic struck in its wake.[9] The last weather challenge most closely related to the cashew economy is wind damage. Many millions of cashew saplings and seedlings were destroyed by seasonal cyclone winds over this period. In 2008 the winds from Cyclone Jokwe, one of the less damaging storms of these decades, destroyed at least 2 million trees in Nampula Province alone.[10]

By all measures Mozambique's weather since independence took an enormous toll. Between 1980 and 2010, the great majority of people killed by weather related conditions died from drought. Drought caused around 50 million dollars in economic damage. Flooding affected about a third of the population, killed about 1 per cent of those affected, but caused much more economic damage. Droughts were deadly but floods were twelve times more damaging to the economy. Weather related damage overall for three of these four decades amounted to over 800 million dollars. Floods alone did more than 500 million dollars in damage between 1980 and 2010. These are major losses for one of the world's poorest countries. Women comprise a majority of Southern Mozambique's farmers and the majority of the population living in absolute poverty.

War was even more deadly and disruptive than weather. The scale and impact of Mozambique's 16 years of armed conflict was enormous

[8] António Sefane, 'Devido à irregularidade das chuvas, espectro de fome paira sobre o sul de Inhambane,' *Notícias* (12 Março 2005): 2.
[9] Agência de Informação de Moçambique [AIM], *AIM Reports*, 499–501, 6 Jan. 2015 – 24 Feb. 2015.
[10] 'Mozambique: Cashew Nut Harvest to Exceed 85,000 Tonnes,' 4 April 2008, http://allafrica. com/stories/200804040518.html Accessed 4 May 2015

and its legacy is evident to the present. At least 1.5 million Mozambicans fled into international refuge, another four million were internally displaced, and millions more were affected. The cashew orchard was not literally uprooted but the people who planted, tended and harvested it were. By conservative estimates, between one and three million people died in the conflict. People who were displaced or fled to international refuge were vulnerable to malnutrition, epidemics and opportunistic diseases that strike the weak. Women and girls were pressed into the insurgency as carriers and forced to comply with sexual services and domestic work. They were less likely to be armed and when the insurgency ended they were less likely to be compensated and benefit from rehabilitation services.[11]

Schools, clinics, infrastructure and places of employment were explicitly targeted for destruction. In many areas a generation of children lost an opportunity to attend school. Education correlates with acquisition of skills and uneducated people fall disproportionately into the deepest poverty.[12] War damage and disruption cost at least 18 billion dollars in lost productivity between 1980 and 1997. In 1996, four years after the Rome Peace Accord, 90 per cent of the population still lived in poverty, and of that group 60 per cent lived in absolute poverty. The country was still laced with unexploded and unmapped anti-personnel mines.[13] The Mozambique Rural Labour Market Survey [MRLS] conducted in 2002–2003 in the provinces of Manica, Zambezia and Nampula revealed great diversity within the rural population, and broadly documented social differentiation and pockets of continuing abject poverty.[14]

In short, weather and war matter a great deal. From 1975 to 2014, millions of Mozambicans worked hard just to keep themselves and their families safe and alive. The cashew economy, along with the rest of the agricultural economy, was ravaged along with government services, warehouses, markets and transportation infrastructure. Weather and war undermined the health of the national cashew orchard and efforts to revive and expand it. The orchard continues to age into limited production faster than it has been successfully replanted.

Producers, processors and struggles around policy, 1975 to 2014

Although statistics and estimates of Mozambique's export of raw and processed cashew nuts differ somewhat depending upon the source, most show the quite steady upward curve in thousands of

[11] Sam Barnes, *Humanitarian Aid and Coordination during War and Peace in Mozambique, 1985–1995* (Uppsala: Nordiska Afrikainstitute in cooperation with SIDA, 1998).
[12] Cramer et al., 'New View,' 368, 380 –87.
[13] Penvenne, 'Tapestry of Conflict,' 254–7.
[14] Cramer et al., 'New View,' 368, 382–387.

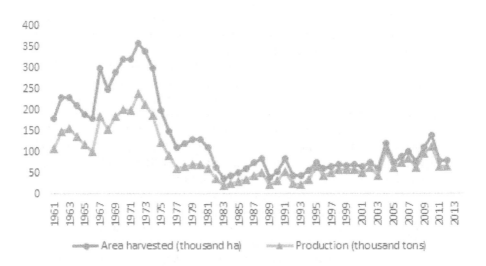

Graph 6 Trend in Area and Production of Raw Cashew Nuts, 1961–2013[16]
(Source: Cashew Handbook 2014, *Global Perspective*, An initiative of CommodityIndia.com in association with African Cashew Alliance. www.cashewinfo.com Fig. 2.23, p. 37.)

tons of raw and processed cashew exports between 1961 and 1973. Mozambique reached its peak national and global cashew production with the harvest of 1972–1973. The Portuguese military coup of 1974 marked the beginning of an exodus of Mozambique's Portuguese and South Asian residents. Prior to independence, they dominated the purchase, transport and marketing of cashew nuts for export and processing, the administrative and technical cadres of the processing industry and the cashew plantation sector. Joana Pereira Leite entitled her analysis of the many ways Indian traders and cashew importers contended with Mozambicans for nuts and market share in the post-independence period, 'The Cashew War'.[15] Some of these businessmen, planters and entrepreneurs remained in Mozambique after independence, but many left and returned only in the era of privatization and liberalization. Cashew production from the Portuguese and internationally owned plantations in Southern Mozambique was small in comparison with that of thousands of small holders, but it was increasingly important in central and northern Mozambique.

Frelimo nationalized the cashew processing industry after independence, partly in response to personnel and capital flight. Frelimo emphasized the value added by kernel production over the export of

---

[15] Pereira Leite, 'Guerra de Cajú,' 311–328.
[16] *Cashew Handbook 2014, Global Perspective*, An initiative of CommodityIndia.com in association with African Cashew Alliance. www.cashewinfo.com Fig. 2.23, p. 37.

raw nuts. The government prohibited the export of raw cashews until the national processing industry was fully supplied. It facilitated transportation and worked with labour unions to support industrial production. Frelimo instituted maternity leave, sick leave, on-site childcare and medical care – all benefits the labour force greatly appreciated. Given the overall economic and transport disruption after the coup in 1974, production levels in the early independence era were impressive. However, drought, war and shortages took an increasing toll. Between 1974 and 1984 kernel processing dropped by two thirds, and then limped along at the lower levels for the rest of the war years.[17] Most of the men and women in the nationalized cashew labour force were kept on, but their hours were diminished and they experienced increased war violence and food shortages.

In the 1990s, with international support, Mozambican refugees and displaced persons began to return to their fields and trees, but peace proved a necessary but insufficient factor for a robust recovery. Returning farmers could not tend and harvest cashew trees in areas that had been mined. The parts and expertise to repair and recover production, infrastructure, storage facilities, markets and transport for the cashew processing industry were largely unavailable or insufficient. Mozambique was deeply in debt, its currency was in flux and many national and international stakeholders contended with Mozambican nationals for advantageous investment opportunities and policy decisions in the wake of war.[18]

The World Bank debacle

After the Rome Peace Accord in 1992 the promise of stability and the hope for a return to regular agricultural production led some Mozambicans to imagine that, despite a generation's loss of market share and the neglect and aging of the national cashew orchard, the country could somehow tap back into cashew shelling and regain some of the record prosperity experienced at the twilight of the colonial era. Some Mozambican and international entrepreneurs invested in the privatization of the large scale cashew shelling factories, assuming that government policy would support their investment while they tried to refurbish their newly acquired plants. They viewed a revived shelling industry as deserving of protection.

India's enormous cashew processing industry was chronically short of raw nuts and strongly encouraged raw nut export over cashew kernel processing in Mozambique.[19] India could more than double

---

[17] Chapter 1, Graph of Kernel Production, 1974–1984, 101.
[18] See note 1 above, Hanlon, Pitcher, McMillan, Cramer, Boys, Krause and Kaufmann all detail the debates around the World Bank's confrontation with Frelimo over cashew exports.
[19] Pereira Leite, 'Guerra de Cajú,' 311–328.

the purchase prices for cashews if it wanted to encourage the sale of raw nuts and discourage their processing in Mozambique.[20] In the mid-1990s the World Bank leaned on the Mozambican government to change its policy regarding raw cashew nut exports and tariffs to favor raw nut exports, implicitly exports to India. Mozambique faced the World Bank's threat that its debt would not be restructured or its credit renewed unless it sharply reduced tariffs on the export of raw cashew nuts. The government felt it had no choice but to concede the World Bank demands, despite strong opposing national sentiment. They cut the tariff in half, but never imposed the even lower level insisted upon by the Bank.

Mozambique's cashew shelling industry confronted many challenges: contention around tax policy, expensive and tight credit, deferred factory maintenance, essential upgrades, and enduring disruption from wartime damage, floods, drought and windstorms. The factor that broke the camel's back was the 40 per cent drop in the global price of cashews in 2000–2001. At that point fourteen of the sixteen newly privatized processing plants closed and 90 per cent of cashew workers lost their jobs. Mozambicans and foreigners who invested in reviving the country's large industrial shelling plants lost their money and their factories closed. Thousands of women and men who had dozens if not scores of years of work experience in the factories also lost their livelihoods and the whole matter was covered in international news. The World Bank emerged as something of a bully-boy.[21]

World Bank funded consultants argued that it was in the best interests of farmers who grew, harvested and sold cashews to allow them to be exported for processing in India without any tax or quota protection for the national processing industry. They assumed an export tariff would directly undercut the price the producer would receive for the product. They somehow assumed that the benefits of such a plan would accrue to the small farmers who provided 90 per cent of the cashews marketed in Mozambique. They failed to take into account that the traders who purchased raw cashews from small farmers provided the sole market for the farmers' cashews and discounted the legal price by more than half in anticipation of lesser quality nuts. Furthermore traders paid most farmers either in trade goods or debt reduction. Economists who computed real producer price apparently did not know what or how small farmers were actually paid.[22] The fact that World

[20] Bessa Ribeiro, 'Sistema mundial,' 196–97, citing *Economia de Moçambique*, Vol. 10, No. 11 (1968): 6–11, 21; Parente and Neto, 'A Agro-Indústria de Cajú,' 37–8.
[21] This controversy was covered extensively at the time by Mozambique News Agency [AIM]; MediaFAX, AfricaAction and Joseph Hanlon's web postings at http://www.open.ac.uk/technology/mozambique/ Accessed 4 May 2015. See also Boys, 'Jobs, Votes;' Kanji et al. 'Cashing in on Cashews,' 76, 79–82.
[22] Historically and to the present negotiations around price basically ignore the producer. They took place starting with the rural trader and went up the chain from there. Bessa Ribeiro, 'Sistema mundial,' 196–8.

Bank consultants failed to anticipate that the benefits of their proposals would not accrue to small scale producers suggests how distant they were from the women, men and children they aggregated simply as producers. It subsequently became clear that South Asian merchants and middlemen benefitted disproportionately from the initial price increase.

The consultants also apparently failed to anticipate the implications of directly exposing farmers to price fluctuations or that India would soon act in its own interest and lower the price it offered for raw cashews.[23] In 2002 Kekobad Patel, the then Chairman of Associação Industrial de Cajú [AICAJU], Mozambique's Cashew Industry Association representing those who had invested in rebuilding the processing industry, attributed the 40 per cent drop in world prices for raw cashew nuts to India's dominant role at the time as the sole market for raw cashew nuts. Without competition from Mozambique's processing plants India could pay what it wished.[24]

Clearly the tensions among the government, cashew processors, cashew exporters and the farmers who brought their cashews to market were nothing new. Each thought the other was a privileged or favored sector, and each struggled for advantage. India remained the giant in the regional and global shelling market. Analysts did not fully consider the complexities of Mozambican household income-generating strategies. The World Bank consultants at least considered India's history of competition with Mozambique for supplies of raw cashews.[25] Analyst Joseph Hanlon expressed his views on the World Bank's pressure to liberalize Mozambique's economy when he titled his book and article: 'Power without Responsibility' and *Peace without Profit.* [26]

Representatives of Mozambique's cashew processors and the World Bank still hold contending interpretations of the facts and implications of what the World Bank calls the reforms of the mid-1990s. In 2002 Kekobad Patel reminded everyone that the:

> World Bank argued that liberalisation would promote competition, which would lead to greater production. They predicted that within five years the cashew orchard would expand to produce 80–90,000 tonnes of nuts a year. Peasant producers would supposedly receive higher prices for their nuts, although some jobs might be lost in the factories, those workers could earn good money by growing their own cashews. None of this has happened.[27]

A decade later, World Bank economists claimed: 'While the reforms resulted in higher producer prices and an increase in output, lack of

[23] Kanji et al., 'Trade Liberalisation,' 5.
[24] AIM, 'Mozambique: World Bank Urged to Pay for Rescue of Cashew Industry,' AllAfrica, 1 October 2002. http://allafrica.com/stories/200012070001.html Accessed 4 May 2015.
[25] See footnote 1 above.
[26] Hanlon, 'Power without Responsibility' and *Peace without Profit.*
[27] AIM Maputo, 'World Bank Urged to Pay for Rescue of Cashew Industry,' http://allafrica.com/stories/200012070001.html Accessed 4 May 2015.

consensus on the specifics of the reforms and associated non-price support arrangements created a situation in which the sector was not able to withstand international price shocks that ultimately led to a collapse of both the processing industry and cashew production.'[28] While AICAJU attributed responsibility and accountability for wrong-headed policies to the World Bank, the World Bank attributed the collapse of processing and cashew production to a lack of consensus.

Throughout the war Mozambican cashew production was stagnant and shrinking, but in many other parts of the world it was growing exponentially. Brazil, Vietnam, and Ivory Coast contended for market share with India. In the changed global context it would have been difficult to recover the wartime loss of market share in any case, but in the mid-1990s Mozambicans felt sabotaged by World Bank interference in their efforts to privatize and revitalize what had been one of the nation's signature enterprises. In one of their first experiments with so-called free-market capitalism, Mozambicans who had invested in the industry's potential lost their capital. A decade later World Bank officials are still defending their actions.[29]

Cashew initiatives since 2000: North and south

The late twentieth-century move to liberalization and privatization broadly undercut workers in most aspects of the cashew industry, but cashew production and export overall has improved since the collapse of 2000 to 2001.[30] In the late 1990s the government reorganized technical support for the cashew economy through the Instituto de Fomento do Cajú [INCAJU]. Its charge was to renovate and enhance the national cashew orchard, promote the trade, processing and development of cashew nut, fruit and nut liquid markets. Both workers and industry business people have organized to promote their interests. The cashew workers union, Sindicato Nacional de Trabalhadores de Indústria do Cajú [SINTIC] is underfunded and has lost influence with liberalization.[31] The emergence of new business groups, such as AICAJU and the Agribusiness Industries Association [AIA] reflect broader public and private support, coordination and leveraging to enhance production, quality and equity throughout the industry. The record is somewhat checkered, and the situations in northern and southern Mozambique differ significantly. Women are no longer the majority labour force, and many of the changes

---

[28] M. A. Aksoy, and F. Yagci, 'Mozambique Cashew Reforms Revisited,' *Policy Research Working Paper* 5939 (Washington, DC: World Bank, 2012) is a preliminary version of Aksoy and Yagci in Aksoy, 'Mozambique Cashew Reforms.' Much of the material overlaps. [hereafter Aksoy and Yagci 'Mozambique Cashew Reforms'].

[29] Aksoy and Yagci 'Mozambique Cashew Reforms.'

[30] Kanji et al., 'Cashing in on Cashew Nuts.'

[31] Cramer et al., 'New View,' 377, 380.

have not served their interests in comparison with the immediate post-independence situation.[32]

The industry's shift to locate processing closer to the large northern cashew orchards began prior to independence. The processing plant in Angoche had the most promising new machinery at the time. Follow up by Kanji et al. showed that when the Angoche factory closed its skilled workforce faced limited options. The workers and the people who depended upon their wages basically became impoverished.[33] Nampula (formerly Mozambique District) is now the heart of the country's most productive cashew orchard and the location of most processing initiatives. TechnoServe, a US-based non-profit organization that says its mission is to 'provide business solutions to poverty' has received a lot of good press, some if it self-generated.[34] TechnoServe recruited local businessmen and invested in orchard enhancement and small scale shelling factories with financing support from the United States Agency for International Development [USAID]. It also subsidized private business support for quality control and marketing. Some of the small plants have made headway with improved coordination, credit, lobbying and marketing, including the development of a specific brand of high quality Mozambican cashew called Zambique. Not surprisingly, the wealthiest farmers with the most trees have succeeded in expanding their cashew orchard and improving stock and output.[35] They have capital to invest and can absorb the risk if the seedlings are destroyed. Between half and 70 per cent of farmers with cashew trees are either poor or very poor, and are not immediately benefitting from these initiatives.[36]

Although prices and production fluctuated a good deal since 2000, the 2007 to 2008 crop exceeded the 85,000 ton target by 10,000 tons, with a third sold raw, a third processed in factories and a third processed and sold in the informal sector.[37] Women are employed in the new northern plants, but they have not competed successfully with men in plants that use the smaller hand cutting machines. Women find work in peeling and sorting, but now men also seek work in these areas. Although the TechnoServe supported factory Miranda-Cajú in Nampula has a good reputation, the benefits do not match those that women experienced immediately after independence in the state owned plants. Miranda-Cajú is exceptional in that it provides a good space for childcare, free daily food for the workers, access to health care

[32] Nazneen Kanji, Carin Vijfhuizen, Carla Braga and Luis Artur have produced a solid record of research on gender and livelihoods around the Mozambican cashew economy, as per their works cited here and those available through the IIED and elsewhere.

[33] Vijfhuizen et al., *Gender, Markets*.

[34] http://www.technoserve.org/about-us Accessed 15 February 2015.

[35] TechnoServe, 'Cashew Industry Brings New Prosperity to Mozambican Communiites,' 2009. www.technoserve.org/files/downloads/cashewmoz Accessed 15 February 2015.

[36] Boys, 'Jobs, Votes,' 44–46; TechnoServe, 'Cashew Industry.'

[37] Hanlon, 'Mozambique,' *131*, 12 June 2008.

and paid holidays. But even working long hours the women do not earn the legal non-agricultural minimum wage.[38]

Olam International began investing in larger scale cashew processing in northern Mozambique at the turn of the century. Its Nampula plant employed four thousand at peak periods, 90 per cent of them women. Processing contracts were initially on a monthly basis and also paid below the legal non-agricultural minimum wage.[39] When Olam pushed to switch to piecework in 2011, the workers realized most of them would earn even less so they went on strike to recoup a monthly minimum.[40] Like the women of Tarana, they realized the piecework quota would be set so high that only highly experienced workers could hope to attain it daily – thus once again what was framed as a bonus was a serious compromise. Mediations failed, and with weak trade unions and global competition, employers in Mozambique have a great deal of power over the workforce in Mozambique.[41] In 2012 Olam opened a new cashew shelling plant in Ivory Coast. With a 30,000 metric ton shelling capacity it will be the largest plant in Africa, and 60 per cent of its labour force will also be comprised of women.[42]

Throughout Mozambique smaller shelling plants have developed satellite processing. The satellites are anchored in piecework pricing.[43] In these areas employers benefit from unpaid, non-contract labour when women bring in their female relatives and children to help complete their quotas.[44] In Nampula's matrilineal households women have greater access to and control over land and trees than in the patrilineal south, but have not benefitted as much as men from outreach regarding interventions to improve cashew yields. Research by Vijfhuizen et al. reveals that women have lost out incrementally. [45]

Cashew export values have risen fairly steadily from the turn of the century low points. By 2011 raw and processed cashews combined comprised Mozambique's sixth most important export commodity. The growth took place largely in small rural plants, mostly in Northern Mozambique. Although 9,000 jobs were created and 18 factories were in production, there was little overlap between the thousands who lost their jobs in the countries large older plants and the thousands working in 2011. Cashew workers still earn less than the legal minimum wage

---

[38] Kanji et al., 'Cashing in on Cashew Nuts,'90–92.

[39] Kanji et al., 'Cashing in on Cashew Nuts,' 95; TechnoServe, 'Cashew Industry.'

[40] Joseph Hanlon, 'Mozambique' 182, News Reports, 11 July 2011.

[41] Cramer et al. 'New View,' 380, 386, 389; Nazneen Kanji, 'Corporate Responsibility and Women's Employment: The Cashew Nut Case,' *Perspectives on Corporate Responsibility for Environment and Development*, 2 (March 2004).

[42] African Cashew Alliance, 'New Factory Opens as Cashew Season Starts in West Africa,' 17 April 2012. http://www.africancashewalliance.com/en/news-and-info/newsletter/new-factories-open-cashew-season-starts-west-africa Accessed 15 February 2015.

[43] Boys, 'Jobs, Votes,' 44–46; Cramer et al. 'New View,' on piecework and Vijfhuizen et al. *Gender, Markets*, on expansion of satellites.

[44] Cramer et al, 'New View,' 371–72.

[45] Vijfhuizen, et al., *Gender, Markets*.

for non-agricultural work, and with some notable exceptions, the benefits and conditions for women in particular remain poor.[46]

When the southern factories closed, the pathways that women forged
from the 1950s to the 1970s largely disappeared. By 2001 more than
8,500 cashew workers lost their jobs and retirees lost their pensions.[47]
No doubt a termination payment helped in the short run, but no compa-
rable jobs opened up. Several scholars have followed southern cashew
shellers: Nazneen Kanji's team in Maputo area and Gaza and Fernando
Ribeiro Bessa's study of the smaller scale Manjacaze cashew workforce. Ribeiro Bessa provided evidence of Tharani's conclusion that
hand shelling produced more whole nuts that fetch the highest prices.
With the steep drop in overall cashew prices at the turn of the century,
however, Manjacaze's old plant had to lay off workers. Three quarters of
the women laid off returned to their *machambas* and 15 per cent went
into informal commerce. Some left for Maputo, but in Bessa Ribeiro's
case those who left had education and connections. Theirs was quite
a different pattern from the cashew shellers of the fifties and sixties.[48]

In the aftermath of the large urban factory closings Kanji's team
found two patterns. First, families who had always consumed,
exchanged and sold nuts and cashew based alcoholic drinks in the
informal economy did so more often.[49] They shifted investment from
wage work to household and informal work. Young people sell plastic
sealed packets of independently processed cashews on street corners
and outside the city's main tourist spots. In that way, the household,
gift and informal economy absorbed some of the product and labour
that was formerly invested in the formal sector. Second, skilled shellers
from Tarana joined a revived satellite program that amounted to a
re-cottagization of cashew processing. Some southern shellers in the
new satellites bought nuts directly from farmers, but most did not have
enough capital to do that. Instead, as was the case in the early 1950s,
women received supplies of nuts from former factory managers. They
gathered on street corners to process the nuts and returned the shelled
product to their suppliers at the fixed piece price.

The southern satellite production met resistance because it was
untaxed, unlicensed and fueled the informal economy. The north satellites were linked to the shelling plants and so fueled the formal sector.
The northern nuts also fetch a higher price than southern nuts, but in
both the north and south, most workers and small-scale producers still
do not receive the legal minimums for their work or product.[50] Taking
into account global business practices in the cashew industry, Nazneen

[46] Kanji, et al. 'Cashing in on Cashews,' 88–91.
[47] Panafrican News Agency, 'Cashew Workers Unemployed,' 20 January 2001.
[48] Bessa Ribeiro, 'Sistema mundial,' 515, 527.
[49] This paragraph draws on Nazneen Kanji, James McGregor, Cecilia Tacoli, *Understanding Market Based Livelihoods in a Globalizing World – Combining Approaches and Methods* (London: IIED, 2004): 14–16.
[50] Hanlon, 'Mozambique,' 131, 12 June 2008; Vijfhuizen et al., *Gender, Markets.*

Kanji is concerned that we may see a 'race to the bottom,' because the usual incentives for corporate responsibility, such as strong civil society, labour unions and public sector vigilance, are largely absent.[51] Kanji's team consistently interrogates how new patterns impact women as producers, sellers, and contract or waged workers.

Gender, markets and complex contexts

The most compelling analyses of the cashew economy from the 1940s to the present attend to and appropriately sustain connections among the many aspects of the cashew economy from household consumption to processed exports, the key roles women played in the value chain, the importance of the actual value of the payment people receive for a product or as compensation for labour and the choices producers and workers make to get the best value and the most control over their product or labour. Unfortunately many studies do not sustain these connections.

Studies still refer to workers, producers, processors, farmers, traders, and the labour force. The words women, gender, men and children are essentially and in most cases literally absent.[52] Yet men and women have quite different social and cultural obligations that shape their experiences in all of these categories. As with Parente and Neto analysts still note what they call high levels of absenteeism, between 30 and 50 per cent, and attribute it to '...preventable diseases like malaria.' [53] Women miss work because they care for children who suffer disproportionately from malaria. Malaria is absolutely not a preventable disease for most Mozambicans, and it is only curable if you get a sick person to high quality health care within twenty-four hours from the onset of symptoms. That is beyond the reach of many Mozambicans. Waiting even another six hours for treatment of a sick child can result in death. [54] Mozambique's health systems are inadequate, particularly for the poor. Kanji et al have demonstrated the value and necessity of paying attention to gender.

Second, interest in the formal sector of the cashew economy, industrial processing and raw nut exporting, continues to eclipse a very substantial component of the cashew economy outside that sector. Aksoy and Yagci found that farmers in Nampula, the most cashew rich province, did not market around a third of their cashew harvest. In the southern regions of Gaza and Inhambane farmers retained 71 and

[51] Kanji heads the Sustainable Agriculture and Rural Livelihoods Programme at the IIED, 'Corporate Responsibility.' 1, 4.
[52] This is largely the case with Klause and Kaufmann, Boys, Aksoy and Yagci.
[53] Boys, 'Votes, Jobs,' 45, citing Krause and Kaufmann (2011): 41.
[54] 'Preventable and Curable but still killing 800,000 every year,' UNICEF Press Release on World Malaria Day, 5 April 2011, http://www.unicef.org/media/media_58351.html Accessed 15 February 2015.

86 per cent respectively, thus more than two thirds of the southern crop did not make it to market.[55] They also noted, without further comment, that in 1996 the price of groundnuts in Gaza and Inhambane had increased so much since the end of the war that people could not afford to eat them. They ate their cashews instead.[56] The fact that rural people were eating a seasonal cash crop because they could not afford the usual year round staples like groundnuts revealed the extent of food shortage. We must pay attention to the entire cashew economy. Cashew nuts and drinks have always played an important role in informal markets. Krause and Kaufmann confirm that the vast majority of Mozambicans do not work in the formal sector, but rather in informal small and medium enterprises that comprise more then 98 per cent of all enterprises and employ more than 40 per cent of all workers, yet the interface of informal and export markets remain under analysed.[57]

Finally, governmental and institutional support for the national cashew processing industry and the cashew economy overall remains relatively underfunded and weak. At one level, the formation and collaboration of INCAJU, AICAJU and AIA are hopeful.[58] The continuing weakness of labour unions, especially in the increasingly rural production sites, however, is not auspicious.[59] The labour force in the new cashew shelling plants does not earn the legal agricultural work minimum wage, let alone the legal industrial work minimum wage. Employers get away with paying people below the legal minimums, but because everyone does it, no one makes much of it.[60]

Christopher Cramer's emphasis on the need for a big picture economic vision backed up by the power and the will to take control and make the vision happen combines well with Vijfhuizen, Kanji, Artur, and Braga's consistent gendered, regional and grounded studies. As argued throughout this work, social complexity and regional diversity are important. If scholars follow the experiences of ordinary women from their households through to industrial processing, the economy looks quite different. The vast majority of Mozambicans are ordinary and poor, and at least half of them are women. Any successful vision for economic growth must engage them and the challenges they face.

[55] Aksoy and Yagci in Aksoy, 'Cashew Reforms,' 197.
[56] Aksoy and Yagci in Aksoy, 'Cashew Reforms,' 231.
[57] Krause and Kaufmann, 'Industrial Policy in Mozambique,' 2, 15, 34.
[58] Boys, 'Votes, Jobs,' 44–6.
[59] Cramer et al., 'New View,' 377, 380, 386.
[60] Cramer et al., 'New View,' 371–2, 374.

Sources and Bibliography

Oral History – Narrators

All narrators from the oral history project at Cajú Industrial de Moçambique were taped at the Chamanculo factory unless otherwise noted. Colonial era names are used for the Districts and Provinces. All narratives were taped and deposited at Arquívo Histórico de Moçambique. Narrators are listed by date of testimony, name, date and place of birth. Instances where age and birthplace are clearly wrong or are uncertain are noted. Not all discrepancies had documentation.

Date of Testimony	*Date of Birth*	*District, Province of Birth*
17 May 1993		
Amélia Mubussele Chiconela	b. 1939	Bilene Macia, Gaza
Celeste Júlio Guambe	b. 1940	Inharrime, Inhambane [Inh]
Leia Papilo Nhavene	b. 1937	Chidenguele, Gaza
Cristina Jossias Pelembe	b. 1942	Xai Xai, Gaza
Cristina Duzenta Cuambe	b. 1952	Inharrime, Inh
19 May 1993		
Rosalina Alberto Tembe	b. 1934	Lourenço Marques [LM], LM
Helena Fazenda Muzimba	b. 1942	Magude, LM
Joana Alberto Chivangue	b. 1939	Maxixe, Inh
20 May 1993		
Carlota Samuel Cubay	b. 1941	Chokwe, Gaza
Joana Tinga Chilaule	b. 1951	Morrumbene, Inh
Albertina Utana	b. 1939	Bela Vista, Maputo
Julieta Mulungu	b. 1939	Moamba, LM
Elena Samo Honwana	ca. 1930	Marracuene, LM
21 May 1993		
Raquelina João Machava	b. 1939	Panda, Inh
Felizarda Servião Bila	b. 1940	Panda, Inh
Laura Nhachunha Tsombe	b. 1945	Chibuto, Gaza

Joana Raci Bambi Nhacumbi	b. 1942	Morrumbene, Inh
Cacilda Gulene Fumo	ca. 1940	LM, LM
Joana Uaichele	b. 1940	Vilanculos, Inh
24 May 1993		
Marta José Cuco	b. 1938	Chonguene, Gaza
Carolina Manuel Sigaugue	b. 1938	Chokwe, Gaza
Joana Massacaira	b. 1938	Manhiça, Maputo
Rabeca Notiço	b. 1943	Chidenguele, Gaza
Eugénia Salamandze	b. 1934	Morrumbene, Inh
26 May 1993		
Saquina Maela Malassanhane	b. 1943	Machava, LM
Cristina Mavila Miambu	b. 1939	Boane, LM
Regina Ofiço Nhantumbo	b. 1943	Chidenguele, Inh
Amélia Manene Chavanguane	b. 1937	Morrumbene, Inh
Amélia Manhiquete	b. 1944	Zavala, Inh
Celeste Marcos Mpendane	b. 1944	Zavala, Inh
Helena Chemane	b. 1953	Chidenguele, Inh
Elena Faustinho Machava	b. 1943	Machava, LM
27 May 1993		
Maria Argentina Nhasinde	b. 1952	Zavala, Inh
Amélia Samuel Muzima	ca. 1950	Uncertain
Marta Nhamave	b. 1947	Chidenguele, Gaza
Rita Famisse Novela	b. 1940	Zavala, Inh (uncertain)
Isabel Rungo	b. 1952	Morrumbene, Inh
Balbina Tinga	b. 1941	Maxixe, Inh
Otília Manuel Zucuela	b. 1937	LM, LM
Matilde Chilengue	ca. 1940	Uncertain
28 May 1993		
Amélia Malenguana	b. 1948	Zavala, Inh
Maria Rosa Xavier Sitoe	b. 1946	LM, LM
Matilde Mussongue Chiduza	b. 1944	Manhiça, LM
Lídia Maluzana Chabana	b. 1935	Manhiça, LM
Elisa Vasco Tovela,	b. 1954	Matutuine, Maputo
Percina Tembe	uncertain	LM, LM
31 May 1993		
Helena Malema Lissinga	b. 1939	LM, LM
Avelina Bene Manjane	b. 1936	Muchopes, Inh
Carolina Rafael Cau	b. 1949	Uncertain
Angelica Nequisse Pacute	b. 1941	Uncertain
Adelaide Nelson Nhabangue	b. 1954	Chidenguele, Gaza
Cristina José Machava	b. 1942	Boane, LM
Marta Elisa Jorge Honwana	b. 1940	Manhiça, LM
2 June 1993		
Emera Mahochi	b. 1923	Inharrime, Inh
Rosa Joaquim Tembe	b. 1929	LM, LM
Isabel Genlane Zandamela	b. 1918	Zavala, Inh

Lina Mitlavane Chivambo	b. 1913	Inhaca, Maputo
Cina Mulhovo	b. 1913	Bilene, Gaza
Carlota Cumbe	b. 1930	Inharrime, Inh
Cecilia Chichavo	b. 1910	Inharrime, Inh
Lezi Tsacalate Bene	b. 1918	Manhiça, LM
Marta Nharemuane Cossa	b. 1927	Manhiça, LM
Rosa Macahiane	b. 1931	Uncertain
Catarina Motiça	b. 1924	Homoine, Inh
Amélia Manhinhana Dengo	b. 1922	Chidenguele, Gaza
Maria Celeste Chavane	b. 1937	Magoanine, Maputo
Melita Tete	b. 1938	Chonguene, Gaza

3 June 1993

Maria Cuambane Nhantumbo	ca. 1920s	Manjacaze, Gaza
Serafina Langa	ca. 1920s	Homoine, Inh
Ester Tafula	b. 1925	Morrumbene, Inh

4 June 1993

Ofélia Manana Mbebe	b. 1922	LM, LM
Elina Chivavale Mulungu	ca. 1930s	LM, LM
Angelica Guamba	b. 1937	Guambe Pequeno, Inh
Virginia Massingue	b. 1944	Uncertain
Cristina Muzamane	b. 1910	Zavala, Inh
Rosalina Mundlouo	ca. 1920s	Uncertain
Carolina Cossa	b. 1926	Bilene, Gaza
Carolina Mundao Manelele	b. 1932	Manhiça, LM
Isabel Muianga	b. 1912	Chidenguele, Gaza
Carolina Mate	ca. 1920s	Uncertain

7 June 1993

Jalane Machava Elmia	b. 1932	Bela Vista, Maputo
Cacilda Hobjuana	b. 1936	LM, LM
Angelina Sitoe	b. 1932	Chibuto, Gaza
Marta Vilanculo	ca. 1920s	Bilene, Gaza
Rozalina Saize	b. 1928	Zavala, Inh
Salmina Cuma	b. 1925	Moamba, LM

9 June 1994

Rosta Munguambe Muianga	b. 1927	Panda, Inh
Caferina Malunguane Maletsuane	b. 1936	Panda, Inh
Percina Muianga	ca. 1920s	Maniça, LM
Catarina Tafula	b. 1910	Massinga, Inh
Marta Cau	ca. 1920s	Muchope, Inh
Amélia Pedro Macaiene	b. 1934	Bilene, Gaza
Felizmenta Namboro	b. 1918	Homoine, Inh

10 June 1993

Catarina Marta Chipendzo	b. 1927	Morrumbene, Inh
Percina Arone Mungumbe	b. 1920	Chidongele, Gaza
Rosa Macohuane Cau	b. 1931	Uncertain

Cecília Ofiço Maculuve	b. 1942	Zavala, Inh
Clemência Uassiliane Mavila	b. 1942	Zavala, Inh
Helena Chicico Chissaque	b. 1940	Zavala, Inh
Amélia Nhavotso	b. 1945	Panda, Inh

Cajú Industrial de Moçambique, Chamanculo Follow-up Narration

12 July 1993
Rosalina Alberto Tembe
Raquelina João Machava
Joana Massacaira
Joana Uaichele
Joana Tinga
13 July 1993
Adelaide Nelson Nhabangue
Percina Tembe
Maria Rosa Xavier Sitoe
Celeste Marcos Mpendane
Amélia Samuel Muzima
Balbina Tinga
Saquina Maela Malassanhane
Amélia Manhiquete
Carlos Maundla
19 July 1993
Cacilda Hobjuana
Felizmenta Namboro
Salmina Cuma
Marta Cau

Cajú Industrial de Moçambique, Machava Factory

26 and 29 June 1993

Luís Guila Muhale	b. 1936	LM, LM

Cajú Industrial de Moçambique, Machava Factory

9 July 1993

Marta Moiana	b. 1949	Matola, LM
Pedro Ananas Mucovele Timba	b. 1941	Machava, LM
Luis Guila Muhale	follow-up narration	

Sociedade Agrícola de Tabacos, Polana

1 July 1993

Nóa Nhamosso	b. 1931	Inhambane
Adelina Matinela	unknown	LM, LM
André Nhaca	ca. 1927	LM, LM

Sociedade Agrícola de Tabacos Taped at Home in Chamanculo Neighbourhood

2 July 1993

| Mariana Macuacua | b. 1932 | Moamba, LM |

Interviews Taped with Women at Home in Chamanculo Neighbourhood

5 July 1993

| Ermelinda Mpfumo | b. 1932 | LM, LM |
| Cecília Boane | b. 1938 | Boane, LM |

Oral Testimony Maputo 1977

The below were selected from a much larger collection of oral testimony I taped between May and November 1977 in the Port, Railways and Municipality of Maputo, Maputo Mozambique. These tapes were deposited in the Centro de Estudos Africanos, UEM in 1984.

Joaquim da Costa	15 and 16 June 1977	Portos e Caminhos de Ferro de Moçambqiue, [PCFM] Maputo
Roberto Tembe	15 and 16 June 1977	PCFM, Maputo
Amélia Alfredo Muiane	13 Sept. 1977	Câmara Municipal de Maputo
Lídia Felizmina Tembe	12 Nov. 1977	Maternidade de Matola, Matola
Magomane Pequenino	15 July 1977	Câmara Municipal de Maputo

Archives

US consular material was acquired through the Freedom of Information Act and is available at Boston University's African Studies Library. The Administração de Conselho de Lourenço Marques [ACLM] archives were the most fruitful for this study, but were completely uncatalogued and stored in an attic. I left carbon copies of all my notes on those files at the Center for African Studies, UEM. The documents were eventually transferred to the AHM, but I have no idea if or how they have been catalogued.

Administração de Conselho de Lourenço Marques
Miscellaneous files, uncatalogued, 1940–1970,
Uncatalogued Red Boxes [R / Cx] Lettered by author, 1947 to 1967
Arquivo Histórico de Moçambique
Secretaria de Negócios Indígenas, uncatalogued files from ACLM
Inspecção dos Serviços Administrativos e dos Negócios Indígenas [ISANI]
United States Department of State, Washington, DC.
American Consul General, Lourenço Marques, Mozambique [USACLM]
Annual Labour Reports, 1950–1961, Annual Economic Reports, 1950–1963, and diverse reports related to employment, 1950–1963. Bound at African Studies Library Boston University.
USACLM, Annual Labour and Economic Reports, 1964–1974, and diverse
Correspondence and reports. Bound at African Studies Library Boston University.

Unpublished Documents, Reports and Theses

Arnfred, Signe. 'Estudo da Situação Social das Mulheres Trabalhadoras na Cidade de Maputo.' *Sintese* [Synopsis of research conducted by the OMM as the basis of their Report on the Social Situation of Women Workers in the City of Maputo] 1982.
___. 'Reflections on Family Forms and Gender Policy in Mozambique.' unpublished typescript, 1990.
Binford, Martha Butler. 'Stalemate: A Study of Cultural Dynamics.' PhD Thesis. East Lansing: Michigan State University, 1971.
Caifaz, Adriana Cândida Biosse de. 'O Xitique, a Mulher e a Economia Familiar nas Zonas Urbanas: O Caso da Cidade de Maputo, 1992–2002.' Têse de Licenciatura. Maputo: UEM, 2005.
Castel-Branco, Nuno. 'An investigation into the Political Economy of Industrial Policy: The Case of Mozambique.' PhD Thesis. London: University of London, 2001.

Castelo, Cláudia Sofia Orvalho da Silva. 'Passagens Para a África Portuguesa: O Povoamento de Angola e Moçambique com Naturais da Metrópole (c. 1920–1974).' PhD Thesis. Lisbon: Universidade de Lisboa, Instituto de Ciências Sociais, 2005.

Chilundo, Arlindo Gonçalo. 'The Economic and Social Impact of the Rail and Road Transportation Systems in the Colonial District of Moçambique (1900–1961).' PhD Thesis. Minneapolis: University of Minnesota, 1995.

Comissão Provincial de Nutrição de Moçambique. *Inquérito nutritional e alimental a 262 operários indígenas da Fabrica de Cimentos da Matola e suas famílias.* Lourenço Marques, unpublished typescript, 1960.

Covane, Luís António. 'Migrant Labour and Agriculture in Southern Mozambique with Special Reference to the Lower Limpopo Valley, 1920–1992.' PhD Thesis. London: Institute of Commonwealth Studies, 1996.

___. 'The Impact of Migrant Labour on Agriculture in Southern Mozambique, 1920–1964.' unpublished paper, n.d.

Domingos, Nuno Miguel Rodrigues. 'Football in Colonial Lourenço Marques, Bodily Practices and Social Rituals.' PhD Thesis. London: University of London, 2009.

Feliciano, José Fialho. 'Antropologia Económica dos Thonga do Sul de Moçambique.' PhD Thesis. Lisbon: Universidade Técnica de Lisboa, 1989.

Flegg, Hilary. 'Age Structure in Urban Africans in Lourenço Marques.' PhD Thesis. Johannesburg: University of the Witwatersrand, 1961.

Frates, L. Lloys. 'Memory of Place, The Place of Memory: Women's Narrations of Late Colonial Lourenço Marques.' PhD Thesis. Los Angeles: University of California at Los Angeles, 2002.

Gengenbach, Heidi. 'Where Women Make History: Pots, Stories, Tattoos, and other Gendered Accounts of Community and Change in Magude District, Mozambique c. 1800 to the present.' PhD Thesis. Minneapolis: University of Minnesota, 1999.

Harries, Patrick. 'Labour Migration from Mozambique to South Africa: With Special Reference to the Delagoa Bay Hinterland.' PhD Thesis. London: University of London, 1982.

Hedges, David. 'Modernização da Cultura de Algodão na Agricultura Moçambicana, 1945 1974.' Unpublished paper. Maputo, UEM, 2004.

___. 'Protection, Finance and Integration in Colonial Mozambique, 1920–1974.' Unpublished paper. Bergen, Norway 1998.

___. 'Transition and Reform, 1957–1966/67: Contradictory Perspectives for Colonial Defence and Development.' Unpublished paper. Maputo, UEM, 1993.

Helgesson, Alf. 'Church, State and People in Mozambique: An Historical Study with special emphasis on Methodist Developments in the Inhambane Region', PhD Thesis. Uppsala: Faculty of Theology, Uppsala University, 1994.

Mandlate, José Cláudio. 'A Companhia do Buzi em Transição: Uma Abordamento de Mão de Obra e da Estrutura de Produção Agrícola da Empresa, 1961–1991.' Têse de Licenciatura. Maputo, UEM, 2004.

___. 'Moçambique, Décadas de 1960–1970: Reforma da Legislação Laborale e sua Implementação: Um Estudo de Caso Recrutamento de Mão de Obra Africana pela Companhia do Buzi.' Unpublished paper. Maputo, UEM, 2004.

Manuense, Hermínia. *Contribution à l'Étude de la Famille Ouvriére à Maputo*. PhD Thesis. Paris: École des Hautes Études en Sciences Sociales, 1989.

Momplê, Lília Maria Clara Carriére. 'Relatório Sintese de Sector Social – Ano 1966.' Junta dos Bairros e Casas Populares. December 1966. Unpublished report from the Archive of Ministério de Coordinação da Acção Ambiental in Maputo.

Murray, Martin. 'Crime Talk: Alarmist Fantasies and Youthful Imaginaries in the 'New' South Africa.' Unpublished paper. Boston: African Studies Association Annual Meeting, November 2003.

Negrão, José. 'One Hundred Years of African Rural Family Economy: The Zambezi Delta in Retrospective Analysis,' PhD Lund: Univ. of Lund, 1995.

Neves [Tembe], Joel Mauricio das. 'Economy, Society, and Labor Migration in Central Mozambique, c.1930–1965: A Case Study of Manica Province.' PhD Thesis. London: School of Oriental and African Studies, University of London, 1998.

Neves, Olga Iglésias. 'Em Defesa da Causa Africana: Intervenção do Grêmio Africano na Sociedade de Lourenço Marques, 1908–1938.' Master's Thesis. Lisbon: Universidade Nova de Lisboa, 1989.

Penvenne, Jeanne Marie. 'African Oral History – Rethinking Oralcy – Ways of Knowing and Telling Truths.' Teaching module of five lectures with bibliography. Maputo, UEM, 2006.

Pereira Leite, Joana, H. I. M. P. 'La Formation de l'Economie Coloniale au Mozambique: Pacte Coloniale et Industrialization. Du Colonialism Portugaise aux Réscaux Informels du Sujétion Marchande, 1870–1974.' Doctorate. Paris: École des Hautes Études en Sciences Sociales, 1989.

Ribeiro, Fernando Bessa. 'Sistema Mundial: Manjacaze e Fábricas de Cajú: uma Etnografia das Dinâmicas do Capitalismo em Moçambique.' PhD Thesis. Vila Real: Universidade de Trás-os-Montes e Alto Douro, 2004.

Schaedel, Martin. 'The Growth and Consolidation of a Mozambican Proletariat in the Last Phase of Colonial Rule.' Excerpt translated by Gottfried Wellmer and edited by David Hedges. *'Eingenborenen-Arbeit': Formen der Ausbeutung unter der Portugiesischen Kolonialherrschaft in Mosambik*. Cologne: Pahl-Rugenstein, 1984.

Souto, Amélia Neves de. 'A Administração Colonial Portuguesa em Moçambique no Período de Marcello Caetano (1968–1974):

Mecanismos e Relações de Poder.' PhD Thesis. Lisbon: Universidade Nova de Lisboa, 2003.

___. 'As Reformas Coloniais Portuguesas na Década de 1960s e o Seu Impacto em Moçambique.' Unpublished paper. Maputo, UEM, 1993.

Young, Sherilynn J. 'Changes in Diet and Production in Southern Mozambique, 1855–1960.' Unpublished paper. Edinburgh, African Studies Association, 1976.

___. 'What Have They Done With The Rain? – 20th Century Transformations in Southern Mozambique with Particular Reference to Rain Prayers.' Unpublished paper. Baltimore, African Studies Association, 1978.

___. 'Women in Transition: Southern Mozambique, 1875–1976.' Unpublished paper. St. Paul, Minnesota, Conference on the History of Women, 1977.

Press

Newspapers, Periodicals and Government Statistics Surveyed

Amaro D. Guerreiro's *Bibliografia Sobre a Economia Portuguesa* indexed newspapers and periodicals by topic for the period 1948/9–1971. Vols. 1–23. Lisbon: Instituto Superior de Economia e Gestão, Universidade Técnica de Lisboa, 1948/9–1971). This book draws particularly on articles about *cajú* from the following: *Journal de Comércio, Lourenço Marques Guardian, Notícias* [Lourenço Marques], *Império, Diário, Diário da Manha, Ultramar, O Século, Gazeta do Agricultor, Indústria de Moçambique, Notícias de Beira, Boletim da Câmara Comércio de Lourenço Marques* and *Actualidade Económico*. Only the most substantive pieces and series are included in the bibliography by author.

The periodicals and papers below were surveyed more systematically:

Agência de Informação de Moçambique [AIM], AIM Reports, 1997–2005
Anais da Câmara Municipal de Lourenço Marques, 1950–1954.
Arquivo, 1987–1996.
Boletim da Associação Comercial de Lourenço Marques, 1965–1975.
Boletim Municipal [Lourenço Marques], 1967–
Brado Africano, 1945–1974.
Diário, 1951–1973.
Estatística Industrial, Lourenço Marques, Imprensa Nacional, 1947–1971.
Estudos Moçambicanos, 1980–2002.
Indústria de Moçambique, 1968–1975.
Império: Revista Mensal Ilustrada, 1951–1956.
Jornal de Comércio, 1948–1973.
Não Vamos Esquecer, 1983.

Notícias, 1948–1974, 1992–1993, 2004–2005.
Outras Vozes, WLSA, 2002–2008.
Tempo, 1970–1974.

Published Documents

Junta de Investigação d'Ultramar. 'Inquérito Habitacional Realizado no Bairro da Munhuana.' *Estudos de Ciências Políticas e Sociais*. No. 72 Lisbon: Junta de Instituto Superior de Ciências Sociais e Política Ultramarina, 1964.

Moçambique. Direcção Provincial dos Serviços de Estatística. 'Inquérito as rendas e as outras características das habitações arrendas na cidade de Lourenço Marques em 1961–1962.' *Estudo 1* [*Supplemento ao Boletim Mensal de Estatística*]. 3 March 1962.

___. *Recenseamento Agrícola de Moçambique*. [Vol. 9 Inhambane, Vol. 10 Gaza, Vol. 11 Lourenço Marques] Lourenço Marques: Imprensa Nacional de Moçambique, 1965–1966.

Moçambique. Direcção dos Serviços de Saúde e Assistência. *Relatório*, Lourenço Marques: Direcção dos Serviços de Saúde e Assistência, 1956.

Moçambique. *Estatísticas Industriais / Estatística Industrial*, [Title and Department varies]. Lourenço Marques: Imprensa Nacional de Moçambique, 1947–1973.

Moçambique. Instituto Nacional de Estatística, Direcção Provincial dos Serviços de Estatística. *IV Recenseamento Geral da População, 1970. Vol. I, Distrito de Lourenço Marques*. Lourenço Marques: Imprensa Nacional, 1973.

Moçambique. Ministério de Saúde. Direcção Nacional de Medicina Preventiva. *Bebidas Alcoolicas Tradicionais – Algumas Considerações e Resultados Preliminares de um Estudo Bibliográfico e Laboratorial*. Maputo: Ministério de Saude, 1979.

Moçambique. Repartição Técnica de Estatística. *Anuário Estatístico*, 1947/8–1973, Lourenço Marques: Imprensa Nacional, 1948–1974.

___. *Censo da População em 1940*. Lourenço Marques: Imprensa Nacional, 1944.

___. *Recenseamento Geral da População em 1950, III: População Não Civilizada*. Lourenço Marques: Imprensa Nacional, 1955.

___. *Recenseamento Geral da População na Província de Moçambique, 1960. Vol. I Distrito de Lourenço Marques*. Lourenço Marques: Imprensa Nacional, 1961.

Tristão de Bettencourt, José. *Relatório do Governador Geral de Moçambique: Respeitante ao Período de 20 Março de 1940 á 31 de Dezembro, 1942*. Lisbon: Imprensa Nacional, 1945.

Published Books, Articles, Essays in Edited Collections

Abreu, Alcinda António. 'A familia, a mulher e os direitos em Moçambique.' In *Eu Mulher em Moçambique*. Coord. Ana Elsa de Santana Afonso, 113–23. Maputo: Comissão Nacional UNESCO em Moçambique e Associação dos Escritores Moçambicanos, 1994.

Afonso, Ana Elsa de Santana. Coord. *Eu Mulher em Moçambique*. Maputo: Comissão Nacional UNESCO em Moçambique e Associação dos Escritores Moçambicanos, 1994.

Aksoy, M. Ataman and Fehrettin Yagci. 'Mozambique Cashew Reforms Revisited'. In *African Agricultural Reforms: The Role of Consensus & Institutions*, edited by M. Ataman Aksoy, 177–217. Washington, DC: World Bank, 2012.

___. 'Mozambique Cashew Reforms Revisited.' *Policy Research Working Paper*. 5939. Washington, DC: World Bank, 2012.

Alden, Chris. *Mozambique and Construction of the New African State: from Negotiations to Nation Building*. New York: Palgrave Macmillan, 2001.

Alexandre, Valentim. 'The Colonial Empire.' In *Modern Portugal*, edited by António Costa Pinto, 41–59. Palo Alto, CA: The Society for the Promotion of Science and Scholarship, 1998.

Allina, Eric. *Slavery by any other name: African Life under Company Rule in Mozambique*. Charlottesville: University of Virginia Press, 2012.

Allman, Jean, Susan Geiger and Musisi Nakanyike, eds, *Women and African Colonial Histories*. Bloomington: Indiana University Press, 2002.

Allman, Jean and Victoria Tashjian. *I will not eat stone: A Woman's History of Colonial Asante*. Portsmouth: Heinemann, 2000.

Ambler, Charles. 'Alcohol, Racial Segregation, and Popular Politics in Northern Rhodesia.' *JAH* 31 (1990): 295–313.

Ambler, Charles and Jonathan Crush, eds, *Liquor and Labor in Southern Africa*. Athens: Ohio University Press, 1992.

Anderson, David and Richard Rathbone, eds, *Africa's Urban Past*. Portsmouth: Heinemann, 2000.

Arnfred, Signe. 'Conceptualizing Gender.' *Feminist Research Centre in Aarlborg Working Paper* 28, Kopicentralen: Aalborg University, 1994.

___. *Sexuality and Gender Politics in Mozambique: Rethinking Gender in Africa*. Woodbridge/Rochester, NY: James Currey, 2011.

Ayisi, Ruth Ansah. 'Mozambique: Drought and Desperation.' *Africa Report* 37, 3 (1992): 33–5.

Baptista, João do Amparo. *O Cajueiro em Moçambique: Série de Artigos Publicados no 'Diário' de Lourenço Marques*. Lourenço Marques: Tipografia Diário, 1959.

___. *Mocambique: Provincia Portuguesa de Ontem e Hoje*. Vila Nova de Famalicão: Centro Gráfico, 1962.

Barbosa, Ernesto Casimiro Neves Santos. *A Radiofusão em Moçambique:*

o Caso do Rádio Clube de Moçambique, 1932–1974. Maputo: Promédia, 2000.

Barnes, Teresa A. *'We Women Worked so Hard: ' Gender, Urbanization and Social Reproduction in Colonial Harare, Zimbabwe, 1930–1956.* Portsmouth: Heinemann, 1999.

Barnes, Terri and Everjoyce Win. *To Live a Better Life: An Oral History of Women in the City of Harare, 1930–1970.* Harare: Baobab Books, 1992.

Barnes, Sam. *Humanitarian Aid and Coordination during War and Peace in Mozambique, 1985–1995.* Uppsala: Nordiska Afrikainstitute in cooperation with SIDA, 1998.

Barrett, Jane, Aneene Dawber, Barbara Klugman, Ingrid Obery, Jennifer Shindler Joanne Yawich. *Vukani Makhosikazi: South African Women Speak.* London: Catholic Institute for International Relations, 1985.

Bastos, Susana Pereira. 'Indian Transnationalisms in Colonial and Postcolonial Mozambique.' *Stichproben; Wiener Zeitschrift für Kritische Afrikastudien* 8 (2005): 277–306.

Battacharya, Sabyasachi and Jan Lucassen. 'Introduction: Informalisation in History.' In *Workers in the Informal Sector: Studies in Labour History, 1800–2000,* edited by Sabyasachi Battacharya and Jan Lucassen, 1–10. New Delhi: Macmillan India Ltd, 2005.

Bay, Edna. ed. *Women and Work in Africa.* Boulder: Westview, 1982.

Bénard da Costa, Ana. 'Famílias na Periferia de Luanda e Maputo: História e Precursos nas Estratégias Actuais.' In *'Lusofonia' em África: História, Democracia e Integração Africana,* edited by Teresa Cruz e Silva, Manuel G. M. Araújo and Carlos Cardoso, 79–94. Dakar: CODESRIA, 2005.

___. *O Preço da Sombra: Sobrevivência e Reprodução Social entre Famílias de Maputo.* Lisbon: Livros Horizonte, 2007.

Bénard da Costa, Ana and Adriano Bisa. 'Home Space as a Social Construct.' *Home Space Ethnographic Report.* http: //homespace.dk/tl_files/uploads/publications/Summaries/HomeSpace_Ethnographic_english_summary_text.pdf Accessed 4 March 2015.

Beneria, Lourdes. 'Reproduction, Production and the Sexual Division of Labour.' *Cambridge Journal of Economics* 3 (1979): 203–25.

Berger, Iris. '"Beasts of Burden" Revisited: Interpretations of Women and Gender in Southern African Societies.' In *Paths toward the Past: African Historical Essays in Honor of Jan Vansina,* edited by R. W. Harms, J. C. Miller, D. S. Newbury and M. D. Wagner, 123–41. Atlanta: African Studies Association Press, 1994.

___. *Threads of Solidarity: Women in South African Industry, 1900–1980.* Bloomington: Indiana University Press, 1992.

Berger, Iris and E. Frances White, eds, *Women in Sub-Saharan Africa: Restoring Women to History.* Bloomington: Indiana University Press, 1999.

Bilale, Cecilia Castanheira. *Mulher Migrante na Cidade de Maputo.* Maputo: Centro de Estudos de População, UEM, 2007.

Birmingham, David. *Frontline Nationalism in Angola and Mozambique.* London: James Currey, 1992.

Birmingham, David and Phyllis Martin, eds, *History of Central Africa: The Contemporary Years, 1965–1995.* London: Longman, 1998.

Bishop, Herbert L. 'Recent Works on the Ba-Ronga.' *London Quarterly Review* 108, 6 [4th Series] (1907): 74–86.

Blackwood, Evelyn. 'Women Headed Households in Agrarian Societes: Not Just a Passing Phase.' In *Gender at Work in Economic Life,* edited by Gracia Clark, 41–59. New York: Rowman & Little Field, 2003.

Bohannan, Laura. 'Shakespeare in the Bush.' *Natural History* 75, 7 (1966): 28–33.

Boléo, José de Oliveira. 'Geografia das Cidades: Lourenço Marques.' *Boletim da Sociedade de Geografia de Lisboa* 63 [Series 5–6] (1945): 217–27.

Bonner, Philip. '"Desireable or Undesireable Basotho Women?" Liquor, Prostitution and the Migration of Basotho Women to the Rand, 1920–1945.' In *Women and Gender in Southern Africa to 1945,* edited by Cheryl Walker, 221–50. Cape Town: David Philip, 1990.

Boserup, Ester. *Women's Role in Economic Development.* New York: St. Martin's Press, 1970.

Bowen, Merle. *State against the Peasantry: Rural Struggles in Colonial and Postcolonial Mozambique.* Charlottesville: University of Virginia Press, 2000.

Bowen, Eleanore Smith [Laura Bohannan]. *Return to Laughter: An Anthropological Novel.* Garden City: Doubleday Anchor, 1964.

Boys, Julian. 'Jobs, Votes and Legitimacy: The Political Economy of the Mozambican Cashew Processing Industry's Revival.' *Forum for Development Studies* 41, 1 (2014): 23–52.

Bozzoli, Belinda, ed. *Class, Community and Conflict: South African Perspectives.* Johannesburg: Ravan Press, 1987.

Bozzoli, Belinda with Mmantho Nkotsoe. *Women of Phokeng: Consciousness, Life Strategy and Migrancy in South Africa, 1900 –1983.* Portsmouth: Heinemann, 1993.

Bradford, Helen. 'Women, Gender and Colonialism: Rethinking the History of the British Cape Colony and its Frontier Zones, c. 1806–70.' *JAH* 37 (1996): 351–370.

Burrill, Emily S., Richard L. Roberts, and Elizabeth Thornberry, eds, *Domestic Violence and the Law in Colonial and Postcolonial Africa.* Athens, Ohio: Ohio University Press, 2010.

Buur, Lars. 'Xiconhoca: Mozambique's Ubiquitous Post-Independence Traitor.' In *Traitors: Suspicion, Intimacy and the Ethics of State-Building,* edited by Sharika Thiranagama and Tobias Kelly, 24–47. Philadelphia: University of Pennsylvania Press, 2009.

Cahen, Michel. 'Corporatisme et Colonialisme – Approche du Cas

Mozambicain, 1933–1979.' [Part I, 'Une Genése difficile, um Mouvement Squelettique,' Part II, 'Crise et Survivance du Corporatisme Colonial 1960–1979.'] *Cahiers d'Etudes Africaines* 92 (1983): 383–417 and 93 (1984): 5–24.

___. 'O Fundo ISANI do Arquivo Histórico de Moçambique: Uma Fonte Importante da História Contemporânea do Colonialismo Português.' *Arquivo* 7 (1990): 63–82.

___. 'L'État Nouveau et la Diversification Religieuse au Mozambique, 1930–1974.' [Part I 'Le Résistible Essor de la Portugalisation Catholique (1930–1961),' Part II, 'La Portugalisation Désespérée (1959–1974).'] *Cahiers d'Etudes Africaines* 158 (2000): 309–50 and 159 (2000): 551–91.

Cahen, Michel, ed. *'Vilas' et 'Cidades' Borges e Villes en Afrique Lusophone.* Paris: Editions L'Harmattan, 1989.

Cann, John P. *Counterinsurgency in Africa: The Portuguese Way of War, 1961–1974.* Westport: Greenwood Press, 1998.

Capela, José. *A Burguêsia Mercantíl do Porto e as Colónias (1834–1909).* Porto: Afrontamento, 1975.

___. *O Álcool na Colonização do Sul do Save, 1860–1920.* Maputo: Edição do Autor, 1995.

___. *O Vinho para o Preto: Notas e Textos Sôbre a Exportação do Vinho para África.* Porto: Afrontamento, 1973.

Carton, Benedict. *Blood from Your Children: The Colonial Origins of Generational Conflict in South Africa.* Charlottesville: University of Virginia, 2000.

Carvalho, Mário de. *A Agricultura Tradicional de Moçambique: A Distribuição Geográfica das Culturas e sua Relação com o Meio.* Lourenço Marques: Missão de Inquérito Agricola em Moçambique, 1969.

Casimiro, Isabel. *'Paz na Terra, Guerra em Casa': Feminismo e Organizações de Mulheres em Moçambique.* Maputo: Promédia, 2004.

___. 'Situação Legal da Mulher perante o Direito a Alimentos.' In *Eu Mulher em Moçambique.* Coord. Ana Elsa de Santana Afonso, 147–72. Maputo: Comissão Nacional UNESCO em Moçambique e Associação dos Escritores Moçambicanos, 1994.

Castelo, Cláudia. *Passagens para África: O Povoamento de Angola e Moçambique com Naturais da Metrópole (1920–1974).* Porto: Afrontamento, 2007.

Castelo, Cláudia, Omar Ribeiro Tomaz, Sebastião Nascimento and Teresa Cruz e Silva, eds, *Os Outros da Colonização: Ensaios sobre Tardo-colonialismo em Moçambique.* Lisbon: Imprensa de Ciências Sociais, 2012.

Chabal, Patrick and Jean-Luc Daloz. *Africa Works: Disorder as Political Instrument.* Oxford: James Currey, 1999.

Chakrabarty, Dipesh. 'Postcoloniality and the Artifice of History: Who Speaks for Indian Pasts?' In *A Subaltern Studies Reader, 1986–1995.* edited by Ranajit Guha, 263–93. Minneapolis, University of Minnesota Press. 1997.

Chatterjee, Partha. 'The Nation and Its Women.' In *A Subaltern Studies Reader, 1986–1995.* edited by Ranajit Guha, 240–62. Minneapolis, University of Minnesota Press. 1997.

Chilundo, Arlindo. *Os Camponeses e os Caminhos de Ferro e Estradas em Nampula (1900–1961).* Maputo: Promédia, 2001.

Chiziane, Paulina. *Niketche: Uma Historia de Poligamia [Romance].* Lisbon: Caminho, 2002.

Clarence-Smith, William Gervase. *The Third Portuguese Empire 1825–1975: A Study in Economic Imperialism.* Manchester: Manchester University Press, 1985.

Clark, Gracia. *Onions are my Husband: Survival and Accumulation by West African Market Women.* Chicago: University of Chicago Press, 1994.

Clark, Gracia, ed. *Gender at Work in Economic Life.* New York: Rowman & Little Field, 2003.

Cooper, Barbara M. *Marriage in Maradi: Gender and Culture in a Hausa Society in Niger, 1900–1989.* Portsmouth: Heinemann, 1997.

___. 'Oral Sources and the Challenge of African History.' In *Writing African History.* edited by John Edward Philips, 191–215. Rochester, NY: University of Rochester Press, 2005.

Cooper, Frederick. *Africa since 1940: The Past of the Present.* New York: Cambridge University Press, 2002.

___. 'African Labor History.' In *Global Labour History: A State of the Art.* edited by Jan Lucassen, 91–116. New York: Peter Lang, 2008.

___. 'Back to Work: Categories, Boundaries and Connections in the Study of Labour.' In *Racializing Class, Classifying Race: Labour and Difference in Britain, the USA and Africa,* edited by Peter Alexander and Rick Halpern, 213–35. New York: St. Martin's Press, 2000.

___. 'Industrial Man Goes to Africa.' In *Men and Masculinities in Modern Africa,* edited by Lisa Lindsay and Stephen F. Miescher, 128–37. Portsmouth: Heinemann, 2003.

Coplan, David. *In Township Tonight! South Africa's Black City Music and Theatre.* London: Longman, 1985.

___. *Songs of the Adventurers.* [Videorecording produced and directed by Gei Zantzinger] Devault, PA: Constant Springs Productions, 1987.

Coquery-Vidrovitch, Catherine. 'The Process of Urbanization in Africa: From the Origins to the Beginning of Independence.' *ASR* 34 (1991): 1–98.

___. 'Urban Cultures: Relevance and Context.' In *Urbanization and African Cultures,* edited by Toyin Falola and Steven J. Salm, 17–22. Durham: Carolina Academic Press, 2005.

Correia, A.B. Ramalho. *A Industrialização da Castanha de Cajú: O Cajueiro e os seus Produtos.* Lourenço Marques: Edição Serviços de Economia e Estatística Geral da Província de Moçambique, 1963.

Costa, Parcídio. 'A Indústria de Moçambique no Limiar da Década de '70.' *Indústria de Moçambique* 4, 7 (1971): 201–10.

Coullie, Judith Lütge. 'The Power to Name the Real: The Politics of Worker Testimony in South Africa.' *Research in African Literatures* 28, 2 (1997): 132–44.

Covane, Luis António. *O Trabalho Migratório e a Agricultura no Sul de Moçambique (1920–1992)*. Maputo: Promédia, 2001.

Cramer, Christopher. 'Can Africa Industrialize by Processing Primary Commodities? The Case of Mozambican Cashew Nuts.' *World Development* 27, 7 (1999): 1247–66.

Cramer, Christopher, Carlos Oya and John Sender. 'Lifting the Blinkers: A New View of Power, Diversity and Poverty in Rural Labour Markets.' *Journal of Modern African Studies* 46, 3 (2008): 361–92.

Crush, Jonathan and Bruce Frayne, eds, *Surviving on the Move: Migration, Poverty and Development in Southern Africa*. Cape Town: Idasa Publishing House, 2010.

Crush, Jonathan, Alan H. Jeeves and David Yudelman. *South Africa's Labor Empire: A History of Black Migrancy to the Gold Mines*. Boulder: Westview Press, 1991.

Cruz e Silva, Teresa. *Protestant Churches and the Formation of Political Consciousness in Southern Mozambique (1930–1974)*. [Introduction by David Hedges, edited by Didier Péclard] Basel: P. Schlettwein Publishing, 2001.

Darch, Colin. 'Trabalho Migratório na África Austral: Um Apontamento Crítico sobre a Literatura Existente, Análise Bibliográfica.' *Estudos Moçambicanos* 3 (1981): 81–96.

Derluguian, Georgi, 'The Social Origins of Good and Bad Governance: Reinterpreting the 1968 Schism in FRELIMO.' In *Sure Road? Nationalisms in Angola, Guinea-Bissau and Mozambique*, edited by Eric Morier-Genoud, 79–101. Boston: Brill, 2012.

de Vletter, Fion. 'Labour Migration to South Africa: The Lifeblood for Southern Mozambique'. In *On Borders: Perspectives on International Migration in Southern Africa*, edited by David A. McDonald, 46–70. New York: St. Martin's Press, 2000.

___. *Migration and Development in Mozambique: Poverty, Inequality and Survival*. [Migration Policy Series No. 43] Cape Town: Southern African Migration Project, 2006.

___. *Sons of Mozambique: Mozambican Miners and Post-Apartheid South Africa*. [Migration Policy Series No. 8] Cape Town: Southern African Migration Project, 1998.

Diamond, Stanley and Fred G. Burke, eds, *The Transformation of East Africa: Studies in Political Anthropology*. New York: Basic Books, 1966.

Dicionário do Estudante, Dicionário Português. Porto: Porto Editora, 1980.

Dominguez, Carlos. *Com o Mundo na Cabeça – Homenagem ás Mulheres de Moçambique*. Figueira da Foz: Associação do Centro Cultural de Matalana, 1997.

Duffy, James. *A Question of Slavery*. Cambridge: Harvard University Press, 1967.

___. *Portuguese Africa.* Cambridge: Harvard University Press, 1959.

Dunaway, Wilma, ed. *Gendered Commodity Chains: Seeking Women's Work and Households in Global Production.* Stanford: Stanford University Press, 2014.

Earthy, Emily Dora. *Valenge Women: The Social and Economic Life of the Valenge Women of Portuguese East Africa, an Ethnographic Study.* London: Oxford University Press, 1933.

Eckert, Andreas and Adam Jones. 'Historical Writing about Everyday Life.' *Journal of African Cultural Studies* 5, 1 (2002): 5–16.

Elkins, Caroline and Susan Pederson, eds, *Settler Colonialism in the Twentieth Century: Projects, Practices and Legacies.* New York: Routledge, 2005.

Enes, António. *Moçambique: Relatório apresentado ao Governo* [4ª edição, fac-similada pela de 1946] Lisbon: Imprensa Nacional, Agência-Geral do Ultramar,1971.

Epprecht, Marc. 'Domesticity and Piety in Colonial Lesotho: the Private Politics of Basotho Women's Pious Associations.' *JSAS* 19, 2 (1993): 202–25.

Feierman, Steven. 'Colonizers, Scholars and the Creation of Invisible Histories.' In *Beyond the Cultural Turn: New Directions in the Study of Society and Culture*, edited by Victoria E. Bonnell and Lynn Hunt, 182–216. Berkeley: University of California Press, 1999.

Ferguson, James. 'Mobile Workers, Modernist Narratives: A Critique of the Historiography of Transition on the Zambian Copperbelt.' *JSAS* Part I, 16, 3 (1990): 385–412 and Part II, 16, 4 (1990): 603–21.

Fialho Feliciano, José. *Antropologia Económica dos Thonga do Sul de Moçambique.* Maputo: Arquivo Histórico de Moçambique, 1998.

Filimão, Estévão J. 'Imagem da Mulher nas Canções da Música Urbana na Beira, 1975–1989: Contribuição ao Estudo das Literaturas Marginais.' In *Eu Mulher em Moçambique.* Coord. Ana Elsa de Santana Afonso, 125–45. Maputo: Comissão Nacional UNESCO em Moçambique e Associação dos Escritores Moçambicanos, 1994.

Finnegan, William. *A Complicated War: The Harrowing of Mozambique.* Berkeley: University of California, 1992.

First, Ruth. *Black Gold: The Mozambican Miner, Proletarian and Peasant.* [Pictures by Moira Forjaz. Worksongs and Interviews Recorded by Alpheus Mangezi]. New York: St. Martins Press, 1983.

Flegg, Hilary and W. Lutz. 'Report on an African Demographic Survey.' *Journal of Social Research* [South Africa] 10 (1959): 1–24.

Frelimo. *Xiconhoca o Inímigo.* Maputo: Edição do Departamento de Trabalho Ideológico, 1979.

French, John D. 'The Laboring and Middle-Class Peoples of Latin America and the Caribbean: Historical Trajectories and New Research Directions.' In *Global Labour History: A State of the Art*, edited by Jan Lucassen, 289–334. New York: Peter Lang, 2008.

Freund, Bill. *The African City: A History.* New York: Cambridge University Press, 2007.

Gaitskell, Deborah. 'Devout Domesticity? A Century of African Women's Christianity in South Africa.' In *Women and Gender in Southern Africa to 1945*, edited by Cherryl Walker, 251–72. Cape Town: David Phillip, 1990.

___. 'Review of Deborah James.' *Journal of Religion in Africa* 32, 2 (2002): 256–61.

___. '"Wailing for Purity": Prayer Unions, African Mothers and Adolescent Daughters, 1920–1940.' In *Industrialisation and Social Change in South Africa*, edited by Shula Marks and Richard Rathbone, 338–57. London: Longman, 1982.

Gaitskell, Deborah, comp. 'Special Issue on Women in Southern Africa.' *JSAS* 10 (1983).

Galli, Rosemary. 'Household Surveys of Women in Urban Mozambique: A Statistical Overview.' *Africa Update* 1, 3 (1994): unpaginated.

Gama, Curado da. *Era uma Vez...Moçambique.* Lisbon: Quimera, 2004.

___. *Moçambique de Outros Tempos.* Lisbon: Quimera, 2006.

Gatrell, Caroline. *Embodying Women's Work.* New York: McGraw Hill, 2008.

Geiger, Susan. 'What's So Feminist About Doing Women's Oral History?' In *Expanding the Boundaries of Women's History: Essays on Women in the Third World*, edited by Cheryl Johnson Odim and Margaret Strobel, 305–18. Bloomington: Indiana University Press, 1992.

___. 'Women and Gender in African Studies.' *ASR* 42, 3 (1999): 21–33.

___. 'Women's Life Histories: Method and Content.' *Signs* 22, 2 (1986): 334–51.

Gengenbach, Heidi. *Binding Memories: Women as Makers and Tellers of History in Magude Mozambique.* [Gutenberg-e electronic book] New York: Columbia University Press, 2005.

___. 'Boundaries of Beauty: Tattooed Secrets of Women's History in Magude District, Southern Mozambique.' *Journal of Women's History* 14, 4 (2003): 106–37.

___. 'I'll Bury You in the Border!' Women's Land Struggles in Post-War Facazisse (Magude District), Mozambique.' *JSAS* 24, 1 (1998): 7–36.

___. 'Naming the Past in a 'Scattered' Land: Memory and the Powers of Women's Naming Practices in Southern Mozambique.' IJAHS 33, 3 (2000): 523–42.

___. 'Truth-Telling and the Politics of Women's Life History Research in Africa: A Reply to Kirk Hoppe.' *IJAHS* 27, 3 (1994): 619–27.

___. '"What My Heart Wanted" Gendered Stories of Early Colonial Encounters in Southern Mozambique.' In *Women and African Colonial Histories*, edited by Jean Allman, Susan Geiger and Musisi Nakanyike, 19–47. Bloomington: Indiana University Press, 2002.

Gersony, Robert. *Summary of Mozambican Refugee Accounts of Principally*

Conflict-Related Experience in Mozambique. Washington, D. C.: Department of State, 1988.

Getecha, Ciru and Jesimen Chipika. *Zimbabwe Women's Voices.* [Photographs by Margaret Waller and David Gombera]. Harare: Zimbabwe Women's Resource Centre and Network, 1995.

Gordon, Suzanne. *A Talent for Tomorrow: Life Stories of South African Servants.* Johannesburg: Ravan Press, 1985.

Grier, Beverly. 'Child Labor and Africanist Scholarship: A Critical Overview.' *ASR* 47, 2 (2004): 1–25

___. *Invisible Hands: Child Labor and the State in Colonial Zimbabwe.* Portsmouth: Heinemann, 2006.

Griesel, Hanlie, *Sibambene: The Voices of Women at Mboza.* [Field assistance Ellen Manquele, Design and Layout by Roselyn Wilson], Johannesburg: Ravan Press, 1987.

Guedes, Amâncio d'Alpoim. 'The Caniços of Mozambique.' In *Shelter in Africa*, edited by Paul Oliver, 200–09. NewYork: Praeger, 1971.

Guha, Ranajit, ed. *A Subaltern Studies Reader, 1986–1995.* Minneapolis: University of Minnesota Press,1997.

Gunner, Elizabeth. 'Songs of Innocence and Experience: Women as Composers and Performers of *Izibongo*, Zulu Praise Poetry.' *Research in African Literatures* 10 (1979): 239–67.

Guyer, Jane. 'Household and Community in African Studies.' *ASR* 24 (1981): 87–137.

Guyer, Jane and Pauline Peters. 'Conceptualizing the Household: Issues of Theory and Policy in Africa.' *Development and Change* 18 (1987): 197–213.

Hall, Margaret and Tom Young. *Confronting Leviathan: Mozambique Since Independence.* Athens: Ohio University Press, 1997.

Hall, Tarquinio. 'Entrevista com Sr. Engr. Gomes e Sousa.' *Império* 4 (August 1951): 16.

Hance, W. A. and I. S. van Dongen.'Lourenço Marques in Delagoa Bay.' *Economic Geography* 33 (1957): 238–56.

Hanlon, Joseph. *Mozambique: Will Growing Economic Divisions Provoke Violence in Mozambique?* Berne: Swiss Peace Foundation, 2000.

___. *Peace without Profit: How the IMF Blocks Rebuilding in Mozambique.* Oxford: The International African Institute in association with James Currey, 1996.

___. 'Power without Responsibility: The World Bank and Mozambican Cashew Nuts.' *ROAPE* 27, 83 (2000): 29–45.

Hanlon, Joseph and Teresa Smart. *Do Bicycles Equal Development?* Woodbridge/Rochester, NY: James Currey, 2008.

Hansen, Karen Tranberg. 'Body Politics: Sexuality, Gender and Domestic Service in Zambia.' *Journal of Women's History* 2 (Spring 1990): 120–42.

___. *Distant Companions: Servants and Employers in Zambia, 1900–1985.* Ithaca: Cornell University Press, 1989.

___. 'Gender and Housing: the Case of Domestic Service in Lusaka, Zambia.' *Africa* 62, 2 (1992): 248–65.

Hansen, Karen Tranberg, ed. *African Encounters with Domesticity*. New Brunswick NJ: Rutgers University Press, 1992.

Hansen, Karen Tranberg and Mariken Vaa. 'Introduction.' In *Reconsidering Informality: Perspectives from Urban Africa*, edited by Karen Tranberg Hansen and Mariken Vaa, 7–24. Uppsala: Nordiska Afrikainstitut, 2002.

Haram, Liv. '"Prostitutes" or Modern Women: Negotiating Respectability in Northern Tanzania.' In *Re-thinking Sexualities in Africa*, edited by Signe Arnfred, 211–29. Uppsala: Nordiska Afrikainstitutet, 2004.

Harries, Patrick. '"A Forgotten Corner of the Transvaal: " Reconstructing the History of a Relocated Community through Oral History and Song.' In *Class, Community and Conflict: South African Perspectives*, edited by Belinda Bozzoli, 93–134. Johannesburg: Ravan, 1987.

___. 'Kinship, Ideology and the Nature of Pre-colonial Labour Migration: Labour Migration from the Delagoa Bay Hinterland to South Africa up to 1895.' In *Industrialisation and Social Change in South Africa: African Class Formation, Culture and Consciousness, 1870–1930*, edited by Shula Marks and Richard Rathbone, 142–66. London: Longman, 1982.

___. 'Slavery, Social Incorporation and Surplus Extraction: The Nature of Free and Unfree Labour in South-East Africa.' *JAH* 22 (1981): 309–30.

___. *Work, Culture and Identities: Migrant Laborers in Mozambique and South Africa, 1860–1910*. Portsmouth: Heinemann, 1994.

Harris, Marvin. 'Labour Emigration Among the Moçambique Thonga: A Reply to Sr. Rita-Ferreira.' *Africa* 30 (1960): 243–5.

___. 'Labour Emigration Among the Moçambique Thonga: Culture and Political Factors.' *Africa* 29 (1959): 50–66.

___. Race, Conflict and Reform in Mozambique.' In *The Transformation of East Africa: Studies in Political Anthropology*, edited by Stanley Diamond and Fred G. Burke, 511–35. New York: Basic Books, 1966.

Hart, Keith. 'Informal Income: Opportunities and Urban Employment in Ghana.' *Journal of Modern African Studies* 11, 1 (1973): 161–78.

Hay, Margaret Jean and Marcia Wright, eds, *African Women and the Law: Historical Perspectives*. Boston: African Studies Center, 1982.

Hedges, David. coord. *História de Moçambique: Moçambique no Auge do Colonialismo, 1930–1961*. Maputo: Livraria Universitária, 1999–2000.

Henriksen, Thomas. *Revolution and Counterrevolution: Mozambique's War of Independence 1964–1974*. Westport: Greenwood, 1983.

Hermele, Kenneth. *Land Struggles and Social Differentiation in Southern Mozambique: A Case Study of Chokwé, Limpopo, 1950–1987*. [Research Report, 82] Uppsala: Scandinavian Institute of African Studies, 1988.

Herrick, Allison Butler and staff of the American University, eds, *Area Handbook for Mozambique*. Washington, DC: US Government Printing Office, 1969.

Hodgson, Dorothy L. and Sheryl A. McCurdy, eds, *'Wicked' Women and the Reconfiguration of Gender in Africa*. Portsmouth: Heinemann, 2001.

Hofmeyr, Isabel. *'We Spend Our Years as a Tale That is Told': Oral Historical Narrative in a South African Chiefdom*. Portsmouth: Heinemann, 1993.

Honwana, Raúl. *O Algodão e o Ouro*. Maputo: Associação dos Escritores Moçambicanos,1995.

Honwana, Raúl Bernardo Manuel. *The Life History of Raúl Honwana: an Insider View of Mozambique from Colonialism to Independence, 1905– 1975*. Boulder: Lynne Rienner, 1988.

Hopkins, Terence and Immanuel Wallerstein. 'Patterns of Development of the Modern World-System.' *Review of the Fernand Braudel Center* 1, 2 (1977): 11–145.

Hume, Cameron. *Ending Mozambique's War: The Role of Mediation and Good Offices*. Washington, DC: United States Institute of Peace Press, 1994.

Hunt, Nancy Rose. 'Introduction.' *Gender & History* 8, 3 (1996): 323–37.

___. 'Placing Women's History and Locating Gender.' *Social History* 14 (1989): 359–79.

Iliffe, John. *The African Poor: A History*. New York: Cambridge University Press, 1987.

International Labour Organization [ILO]. *Women and Poverty in Mozambique: A Synthesis of a study on Feminization of Poverty in Mozambique*. Geneva: ILO Office, 2001.

Isaacman, Allen. 'Colonial Mozambique, an Inside View: The Life History of Raúl Honwana.' *Cahiers d'Etudes Africaines* 38, 1(1988): 59–88.

___. *Cotton is the Mother of Poverty: Peasants, Work and Rural Struggle in Colonial Mozambique, 1938–1961*. Portsmouth: Heinemann, 1996.

Isaacman, Allen and Barbara Isaacman. *From Colonialism to Revolution, 1900–1982*. Boulder: Westview, 1983.

Isaacman, Allen and Richard Roberts, eds, *Cotton Colonialism and Social History in Sub-Saharan Africa*. Portsmouth: Heinemann, 1995.

Jhabvala, R. 'Labour Markets, Labor Movements and Gender in Developing Nations.' *International Encyclopedia of the Social and Behavioral Sciences*. London: Elsevier Science Ltd, 2001: 8185–91.

James, Deborah. *Songs of the Women Migrants: Performance and Identity in South Africa*. Edinburgh: Edinburgh University Press, 1999.

Jeater, Diana. *Marriage, Perversion and Power: the Construction of Moral Discourse in Southern Rhodesia (Zimbabwe) 1890–1930*. New York: Oxford, 1993.

___. 'No Place for a Woman: Gwelo Town, Southern Rhodesia, 1894– 1920.' *JSAS* 26, 1 (2000): 29–42.

Jeeves, Alan H. *Migrant Labour in South Africa's Mining Economy: The*

Struggle for the Gold Mines' Labour Supply, 1890–1920. Kingston: McGill University Press, 1985.

Jeeves, Alan H. and Jonathan Crush, eds, *White Farms-Black Labor: The State and Agrarian Change in Southern Africa, 1910*–1950. Portsmouth: Heinemann, 1991.

Jeeves, Alan H. and David Yudelman. *South Africa's Labor Empire: a History of Black Migrancy to the Gold Mines*. Boulder: Westview Press, 1991.

Johnson, Hazel and Henry Bernstein with Raul Hernan Ampuero and Ben Crow. *Third World Lives of Struggle*. London: Heinemann, 1982.

Johnson, Phyllis and David Martin, eds, *Frontline Southern Africa: Destructive Engagement*. New York: Four Walls Eight Windows, 1988.

Jone, Claúdio. 'Press and Democratic Transition in Mozambique, 1990 –2000.' *Les Nouveaux Cahiers de l'IFAS / IFAS Working Paper Series*. Johannesburg: Institut Français d'Afrique du Sud, 2005.

Junod, Henri. *The Life of a South African Tribe*. New York: University Books Inc. 1962.

Kanji, Nazneen. 'Corporate Responsibility and Women's Employment: The Cashew Nut Case.' *Perspectives on Corporate Responsibility for Environment and Development* 2 (2004).

Kanji, Nazneen, Carin Vijfhuizen, Carla Braga, and Luis Artur. 'Cashing in on cashew nuts: women producers and factory workers in Mozambique.' In *Chains of Fortune: Linking Women Producers and Workers with Global Markets*, edited by Marilyn Carr, 75–101. London: Commonwealth Secretariat, 2004.

___. Liberalisation, Gender and Livelihoods: the cashew nut case *Working Paper 1* (English) Mozambique Phase 1: The North, January–December 2002. London: IIED, Maputo: UEM, 2003.

___. Liberalisation, Gender and Livelihoods: the cashew nut case *Working Paper 1* (English) Mozambique Phase 2: The South, January–December 2003. London: IIED, Maputo: UEM, 2003.

___. 'Trade Liberalisation, Gender and Livelihoods: the Mozambique Cashew Nut Case,' Paper prepared for the XI World Congress of Rural Sociology, Working Group 8: From Peasant Agronomy to Capitalist / Industrial Agriculture. Trondheim, Norway, 2004.

Kanji, Nazneen, James McGregor, Cecilia Tacoli. *Understading Market Based Livelihoods in a Globalizing World – Combining Approaches and Methods*. London: IIED, 2004.

Krause, Matthias and Friedrich Kaufmann. 'Industrial Policy in Mozambique.' *DIE Discussion Paper* 10. Bonn: Deutsches Institut für Entwicklungspolitik, 2011.

Lachartre, Brigitte. *Enjeux Urbaines au Mozambique: de Lourenço Marques á Maputo*. Paris: Karthala, 2000.

Lains e Silva, Helder.'O Alargamento do Mercado Mundial Corresponde a uma Ofensiva da União Indiana para Eliminar a Concorrência da Africa,' *Gazeta do Agricultor* 14, 162 (1962): 10–12.

___. *Paracer sôbre a Industrialização da Castanha de Cajú em Moçambique.* Lisbon: Missão de Estudos Agrónomicos do Ultramar, n. d.

Lee, Rebekah. *African Women and Apartheid: Migration and Settlement in Urban South Africa.* London: I. B. Tauris Publishers, 2009.

Lindberg, Anna. *Experience and Identity: A Historical Account of Class, Caste and Gender among the Cashew Workers of Kerala, 1930–2000.* Lund: Studia Historica Lundensia, 2001.

___. *Modernization and Effeminization in India: Kerala Cashew Workers since 1930.* Copenhagen: Nordic Institute of Asian Studies Press, 2005.

Lindsay, Lisa. *Working with Gender: Wage Labor and Social Change in South-western Nigeria.* Portsmouth: Heinemann, 2003.

Lindsay, Lisa and Stephan F. Miescher, eds, *Men and Masculinities in Modern Africa.* Portsmouth: Heinemann, 2003.

Lobato, Alexandre. 'Do Conhecimento da Baia a Criação do Município.' *Boletim Municipal* 2 (1968): 9–20.

___. *Lourenço Marques, Xilunguíne: Biografia da Cidade, I– A Parte Antiga.* Lisbon: Agência-Geral do Ultramar,1970.

___. 'Lourenço Marques, Xilunguíne: Pequena Monografia da Cidade.' *Boletim Municipal* 3 (1968): 7–19.

Lobato, Alexandre e Parcídio Costa. *Moçambique na Actualidade, 1973.* Lourenço Marques: Imprensa Nacional de Moçambique,1974.

Loforte, Ana Maria. 'A Persistência dos Valores 'Tradicionais' nas Comunidades Urbanas e a Etnicidade.' *Trabalhos de Arqueologia e Antropologia* 6 (1989): 21–8.

___. *Género e Poder entre os Tsonga de Moçambique.* Maputo: Promédia, 2000.

___. 'Migrantes e Sua Relação com o Meio Rural.' *Trabalhos de Arqueologia e Antropologia* 4, (1987): 55–69.

Longmore, Laura. *The Dispossed: A Study of the Sex-life of Bantu Women in Urban Areas in and around Johannesburg.* London: Jonathan Cape, 1959.

Lonsdale, John. 'Agency in Tight Corners: Narrative and Initiative in African History.' *Journal of African Cultural Studies* 13 (2000): 5–16.

Lopes, Armando Jorge, Salvador Júlio Sitoe, and Paulino José Nhamuende. *Moçambicanismos: para um Léxico de Usos do Português Moçambicano.* Maputo: Livraria Universitária, 2002.

Loureiro, João. *Memórias de Lourenço Marques: Uma Visão do Passado da Cidade de Maputo.* Lisbon: Maisimagem-Comunicação Global, 2003.

Lubkemann, Stephen C. 'The Transformation of Transnationality among Mozambican Migrants in South Africa.' *Canadian Journal of African Studies* 34, 1 (2000): 41–64.

Lucassen, Jan. ed. *Global Labour History: A State of the Art.* New York: Peter Lang, 2008.

Lyne, Robert Nunez. *Mozambique: Its Agricultural Development.* London: T. Fisher Unwin, 1913.

Macango, Lorenzo. 'Um Antropólogo Norte-Americano no 'Mundo que o Português Criou': Relações de Raça no Brazil e Moçambique segundo Marvin Harris.' *Lusotopie* (1999): 143–61.

Machiana, Emídio. *A Revista 'Tempo' e a Revolução Moçambicana: da Mobilização Popular ao Problema da Crítica na Informação, 1974–1977.* Maputo: Promédia, 2002.

MacGaffey, Janet. 'New Forms of Remuneration for Labour in Congo-Kinshasa's Economy of Favours.' In *Workers in the Informal Sector: Studies in Labour History. 1800–2000,* edited by Sabyasachi Battacharya and Jan Lucassen, 141–60. New Delhi: Macmillan India Ltd. 2005.

MacQueen, Norrie. *The Decolonization of Portuguese Africa: Metropolitan Revolution and the Dissolution of Empire.* New York: Longman, 1997.

Magaia, Albino [With Photographs by Ricardo Rangel]. 'Prostituição, Tráfico Sexual Mata a Fome.' *Tempo* 211 (1974): 18–25.

Magaia, Lina. *Dumba Nengue, Run for your life: Peasant Tales of Tragedy in Mozambique.* Trenton, NJ: Africa World Press, 1988.

___. *Recordações da Vovó Marta.* Maputo: JV Editores, 2010.

Maier, Karl. *Conspicuous Destruction: War, Famine and the Reform Process in Mozambique.* New York: Human Rights Watch, 1992.

Manghezi, Alpheus. 'A Mulher e o Trabalho: Entrevistas.' *Estudos Mozambicanos* 3 (1981): 45–56.

___. 'Interviews with Mozambican Peasant Women.' In *Third World Lives of Struggle,* edited by Hazel Johnson and Henry Bernstein with Raul Hernan Ampuero and Ben Crow, 164–72. London: Heinemann, 1982.

___. 'Ku Thekela: Estratégias de Sôbre-Vivência Contra a Fome no Sul de Moçambique.' *Estudos Moçambicanos* 4 (1983): 19–40.

___. *Macassane, Uma Cooperativa de Mulheres Velhas no Sul de Moçambique: Entrevistas e Canções Recolhidas por Alpheus Manghezi.* Maputo: Arquivo Histórico de Moçambique, 2003.

___. 'O Trabalho Forçado por quem o Viveu.' *Estudos Moçambicanos* 2 (1981): 27–36.

___. *Trabalho Forçado e Cultura Obrigatória do Algodão: O Colonato do Limpopo e o Reassentamento Pós-Independência c. 1895–1981.* Maputo: Arquivo Histórico de Moçambique, 2003.

Manning, Carrie. *Politics of Peace in Mozambique's Post Conflict Democratization, 1992–2000.* Westport: Praeger, 2002.

Manuense, Hermínia. 'Contribuição ao Estudo da Mulher Operária no Maputo: o Caso de Cajú.' In *Eu Mulher em Moçambique,* Coord. Ana Elsa de Santana Afonso, 39–59. Maputo: Comissão Nacional UNESCO em Moçambique e Associação dos Escritores Moçambicanos, 1994.

Marks, Shula. 'Patriotism, Patriarchy and Purity: Natal and the Politics of Zulu Ethnic Consciousness.' In *The Creation of Tribalism in Southern Africa.* edited by Leroy Vail, 215–40. Berkeley: University of California Press, 1989.

Marks, Shula and Richard Rathbone, eds, *Industrialization and Social Change in Southern Africa*. London: Longman, 1982.

Mateus, Dalila Cabrita. *A PIDE/DGS na Guerra Colonial: 1961–1974*. Lisbon: Terramar, 2004.

Matusse, Hilário. 'Bairros de Maputo: Chamanculo, Memórias de um Bairro.' *Tempo* 682 (1983): 22–28.

___. 'Mafalala: Fronteira entre a Cidade e o Subúrbio.' *Tempo* Part I, 685 (1983): 14–19 and Part II, 686 (1983): 24–29.

Maylam, Paul. 'Explaining the Apartheid City: 20 Years of South African Urban Historiography.' *JSAS* 21, 1 (1995): 19–38.

Maylam, Paul and Iain Edwards, eds, *The People's City: African Life in Twentieth-Century Durban*. Portsmouth: Heinemann, 1996.

McMillan, Margaret, Dani Rodrik, Karen Horn Welch. 'When Economic Reform Goes Wrong: Cashews in Mozambique.' *Faculty Research Working Paper*. Cambridge: Kennedy School of Government, Harvard University, 2002.

Medeiros, Eduardo. *Bebidas Moçambicanas de Fábrico Caseiro*. Maputo: Arquivo Histórico de Moçambique, 1998.

Mendes, Maria Clara. 'A rede urbana em Moçambique.' *Livro de Homenagem a Orlando Ribeiro*. Lisbon: Centro de Estudos Geográficos, 1988: Vol 2, 609–17.

___. 'Maputo Antes da Independência: Geografia de uma Cidade Colonial.' *Memórias do Instituto de Investigação Científica Tropical*. Segunda Série, 68. Lisbon: Instituto de Investigação Científica Tropical, 1985.

Mendonça, Fátima. 'Dos Confrontos Ideológicos na Imprensa em Moçambique,' In *Os Outros da Colonização: Ensaios sobre Tardo-colonialismo em Moçambique*. edited by Cláudia Castelo, Omar Ribeiro Tomaz, Sebastião Nascimento and Teresa Cruz e Silva, 193–220. Lisbon: Imprensa de Ciências Sociais, 2012.

Miranda, António. 'African Cashews: Stimulating an Entrepreneurial Approach.' *New Agriculturist* http: //www.new-agri.co.uk/06–5/focuson/focuson6.html Accessed 4 May 2015.

Mitchell, Hilary Flegg. *Aspects of Urbanization and Age Structure in Lourenço Marques, 1957*. [Communication 11] Lusaka: University of Zambia, Institute for African Studies, 1975.

Monteiro, José Firmo de Sousa. *Relatório sobre o Resgate dos Machongos de Sul do Save: Referente á 31 de Dezembeo 1951*. Lourenço Marques: Imprensa Nacional, 1953. [Same Title and Author for Subsequent Dates 31 Dec. 1953, 31 Dec. 1957 and 31 Dec. 1959].

___. *Resgate dos Machongos do Sul do Save, Um Caso Típico: Primeiras Jornadas de Engenharia de Moçambique*. Lourenço Marques: Empresa Moderna, 1965.

Moodie, T. Dunbar with Vivienne Ndatshe. *Going for Gold: Men, Mines and Migration*. Berkeley: University of California Press, 1994.

Morais, João Sousa. *Maputo: Património da Estrutura e Forma Urbana: Topologia do Lugar*. Lisbon: Livros Horizonte, 2001.

Morier-Genoud, Eric, ed. *Sure Road? Nationalisms in Angola, Guinea-Bissau and Mozambique.* Boston: Brill, 2012.

Morier-Genoud, Eric and Michel Cahen, eds, *Imperial Migrations: Colonial Communities and Diaspora in the Portuguese World.* New York: Palgrave Macmillan, 2012.

Morton, David. 'Chamanculo in Reeds, Wood, Zinc & Concrete.' *Slum Lab – Made in Africa, Sustainable Living Urban Model.* 9 (2014): 43–6.

Muianga, Aldino. *Meledina (ou a História duma Prostituta).* Maputo: Ndjira, 2004.

Negrão, José. *Cem Anos de Economia da Família Rural Africana.* Maputo: Texto Editores, 2005.

Newitt, Malyn. *A History of Mozambique.* Bloomington: Indiana University Press, 1995.

___. 'The Late Colonial State in Portuguese Africa.' *Itinerário* 23 (1999): 110–22.

Odim, Cheryl Johnson and Margaret Strobel, eds, *Expanding the Boundaries of Women's History: Essays on Women in the Third.* Bloomington: Indiana University Press, 1992.

O'Laughlin, Bridget. 'Class and the Customary: The Ambiguous Legacy of the *Indigenato* in Mozambique.' *African Affairs* 99 (2000): 5–42.

___. 'Proletarianisation, Agency and Changing Rural Livelihoods: Forced Labour and Resistance in Colonial Mozambique.' *JSAS* 28, 3 (2002): 511–30.

Oliver, Paul, ed. *Shelter in Africa.* NewYork: Praeger, 1971.

Opello, Walter C. 'Pluralism and Elite Conflict in an Independence Movement: FRELIMO in the 1960s.' *JSAS* 2, 1 (1975): 66–82.

Otobe, Naoka. *Resource Guide on Gender Issues in Employment and Labour Market Policies: Working Towards Women's Economic Empowerment and Gender Equality.* Geneva: ILO, 2014.

Paulo, Margarida, Carmeliza Rosário, Inge Tvedten. *'Xiculungo': Social Relations of Urban Poverty in Maputo, Mozambique.* [CMI Report 2007: 13] Bergen: Chr. Michelsen Institute, 2007.

___. *'Xiculungo' Revisited: Assessing the Implications of PARPA II in Maputo, 2007–2010.* [CMI Report. 2011: 1] Bergen: Chr. Michelsen Institute, 2011.

Parente, José Ismar and Alfredo Lopes Neto. A Agro-Indústria do Cajú em Moçambique. [*Comunicação* 79] Lourenço Marques: Instituto de Investigação Agronómica de Moçambique, 1973.

Penvenne, Jeanne Marie. *African Workers and Colonial Racism: Mozambican Strategies for Survival in Lourenço Marques, Mozambique, 1877–1962.* Portsmouth: Heinemann, 1995.

___. 'A Tapestry of Conflict: Mozambique 1960–1995.' In *History of Central Africa: The Contemporary Years*, edited by David Birmingham and Phyllis Martin, 230–66. London: Longman, 1998.

___. 'Elsa Joubert's Poppie Nongena.' In *African Novels in the Classroom*, edited by Margaret Jean Hay, 153–66. Boulder: Lynne Rienner, 2000.

___. 'Fotografando Lourenço Marques: A Cidade e os seus Habitantes de 1960 á 1975.' In *Os Outros da Colonização: Ensaios sobre Tardo-colonialismo em Moçambique*, edited by Cláudia Castelo, Omar Ribeiro Tomaz, Sebastião Nascimento e Teresa Cruz e Silva, 173–91. Lisbon: Imprensa de Ciências Sociais, 2012.

___. 'Gender Studies, Area Studies, and the New History, with Special Reference to Africa.' In *Curricular Crossings: Women's Studies and Area Studies – A Web Anthology for the College Classroom* (2000) http://www3.amherst.edu/~mrhunt/womencrossing/penvenne.html Accessed 3 March 2015.

___. 'Settling Against the Tide: The Layered Contradictions of Twentieth Century Portuguese Settlement in Mozambique.' In *Settler Colonialism in the Twentieth Century: Projects, Practices, Legacies*, edited by Caroline Elkins and Susan Pedersen, 79–94. New York: Routledge, 2005.

___. 'Two Tales of a City – Lourenço Marques, 1945–1975.' *Portuguese Studies Review* 19, 1/2 (2011): 249–69.

___. *Trabalhadores de Lourenço Marques, 1870–1974.* [Estudos, 9] Maputo: Arquivo Histórico de Moçambique, 1993.

___. '"We are all Portuguese!" Challenging the Political Economy of Assimilation, Lourenço Marques, 1870 to 1933.' In *The Creation of Tribalism in Southern Africa*, edited by Leroy Vail, 255–88. Berkeley: University of California, 1989.

Penvenne, Jeanne Marie and Bento Sitoe. 'Power, Poets and the People: Mozambican Voices Interpreting History.' *Social Dynamics* 26, 2 (2000): 55–6.

Pereira de Lima, Alfredo. *Edifícios Históricos de Lourenço Marques.* Lourenço Marques: Livraria Académica, 1966.

___. *História dos Caminhos de Ferro de Moçambique.* Lourenço Marques: Administração do Porto e dos Caminhos de Ferro de Moçambique, 1971.

___. *O Palácio Municipal de Lourenço Marques.* Lourenço Marques: Livraria Académica, 1967.

___. 'Para um Estudo da Evolução Urbana de Lourenço Marques.' *Boletim Municipal* 7 (1967): 7–16.

___. *Pedras que já não Falam.* Lourenço Marques: Impresso Tipografia Notícias Moçambique, 1972.

Pereira Leite, Joana. 'A Economia do Cajú em Moçambique e as Relações com a Índia: dos Anos 20 ao Fim da Època Colonial.' In *Ensaios de Homenagem a Francisco Pereira de Moura*, edited by Instituto Superior de Economia e Gestão, 631–653. Lisbon: Instituto Superior de Economia e Gestão, Universidade Técnicade Lisboa, 1995.

___. 'A Guerra do Cajú e as Relações Moçambique – Índia na Época Pós-colonial.' *Lusotopie* (2000): 294–332.

___. 'Colonialismo e Industrialização em Moçambique: Pacto Colonial, Dinamização das Exportações e 'Import-substitution.' *Ler Historia* 24 (1993): 53–70.

Pereira Leite, Joana and Nicole Khouri. *Os Ismailis de Moçambique: Vida Económica no Tempo Colonial.* Lisbon: Edições Colibri, 2012.

Personal Narratives Group. *Interpreting Women's Lives: Feminist Theory and Personal Narratives.* Bloomington: Indiana University Press, 1989.

Pfeiffer, James. 'African Independent Churches in Mozambique: Healing the Afflictions of Inequality.' *Medical Anthropology Quarterly* 16, 2 (2002): 176–99.

___. 'Money, Modernity and Morality, Traditional Healing and the Expansion of the Holy Spirit in Mozambique.' In *Borders and Healers: Brokering Therapeutic Resources in Southeast Africa,* edited by Tracy J. Luedke and Harry G. West, 81–100. Bloomington: Indiana University Press, 2006.

Pinsky, Barry. *The Urban Problematic in Mozambique: Initial Post-Independence Responses, 1975–1980.* Toronto: Centre for Urban and Community Studies, 1982.

Pinto, António Costa, ed. *Modern Portugal.* Palo Alto, CA: The Society for the Promotion of Science and Scholarship, 1998.

Pitcher, M. Anne. *Transforming Mozambique: The Business of Politics, 1975–2000.* Cambridge: Cambridge University Press, 2002.

Pitcher, M. Anne and Scott Kloeck-Jenson. 'Men, Women, Memory and Rights to Natural Resources in Zambezi Province.' In *Strategic Women, Gainful Men: Gender, Land and Natural Resources in Different Rural Contexts in Mozambique,* edited by Rachel Waterhouse and Carin Vijfhuizen, 125–52. Maputo: UEM and Action Aid, 2001.

Preston-Whyte, Eleanor. 'Women Migrants and Marriage.' In *Essays on African Marriage in Southern Africa,* edited by Eileen Jensen Krige and John L. Comaroff, 158–73. Cape Town: Juta & Company Ltd., 1981.

Rangel, Ricardo. *Pão Nossa de Cada Noite.* [Texts by Calane da Silva: José Craveirinha, José Luís Cabaço, Luís Bernando Honwana, Nelson Saúte and Rui Nogar] Maputo: Marimbique, 2005.

Redding, Sean. *Sorcery and Sovereignty: Taxation, Power and Rebellion in South Africa, 1880–1963.* Athens: Ohio University Press, 2006.

___. 'South African Women and Migration in Umtata, Transkei 1880–1935.' In *Courtyards, Markets and City Streets, Urban Women in Africa,* edited by Kathleen E. Sheldon, 31–46. Boulder: Westview Press, 1996.

Reynolds, Pamela. *Dance Civet Cat: Child Labour in the Zambezi Valley.* Athens: Ohio University Press. 1991.

Ribeiro, Fatima and António Sopa, Coord. *140 Anos de Imprensa em Moçambique: Estudos e Relatos.* Maputo: Associação Moçambicana da Língua Portuguesa, 1996.

Ribeiro, Margarida Calafate. *África no Feminino: As Mulheres Portuguesas e a Guerra Colonial.* Porto: Afrontamento, 2007.

Rita-Ferreira, António. 'A Oscilação do Trabalhador Africano entre o Meio Rural e o Meio Urbano.' *Indústria de Moçambique* 2 (1969): 96–9.

___. 'Esboço Sociológico do Grupo de Povoações: Meu, Homoíne, Moçambique.' *Boletim da Sociedade de Estudos de Moçambique.* 26 (1957): 75–180.

___. *Evolução de Mão de Obra e das Remunerações no Sector Privado em Moçambique desde 1950 á 1970: Análise da Situação Cambial de Moçambique.* Lourenço Marques: Comissão Coordenadora do Trabalho de Análise de Situação Cambial da Provincia de Moçambique, 1971.

___. 'Labour Emigration among the Moçambique Thonga: Comments on Marvin Harris's Reply.' *Africa* 31 (1961): 75–7.

___. 'Labour Emigration among the Moçambique Thonga: Comments on a Study by Marvin Harris.' *Africa* 30 (1960): 141–52.

___. *O Movimento Migratório de Trabalhadores entre Moçambique e a Africa do Sul.* Lisbon: Junta de Investigações do Ultramar, Centro de Estudos Políticos e Sociais, 1963.

___. 'Os Africanos de Lourenço Marques.' *Memórias do Instituto de Investigação Científica de Moçambique.* [Ciências Humanas, 9 Ser. C] Lourenço Marques: Instituto de Investigação Científica de Moçambique, 1967–1968.

Roberts, Richard. 'History and Memory: The Power of Statist Narratives.' *IJAHS* 33 (2000): 513–22.

Robertson, Claire C. *Trouble Showed the Way: Women, Men and Trade in the Nairobi Area, 1980–1990.* Bloomington: Indiana University Press, 1997.

Rocha, Aurélio. *Associativismo e Nativismo em Moçambique: Contribuição para o Estudo das Origens do Nacionalismo Moçambicano (1900–1940).* Maputo: Promédia, 2002.

Rodrigues, Cristina Udelsmann. *O Trabalho Dignifica o Homem: Estratégias de Sobrevivência em Luanda.* Lisbon: Edições Colibri, 2006.

Rodrigues Júnior, José. *Transportes de Moçambique.* Lisbon: Editorial Ultramar, 1956.

___. *Voz dos Colonos de Moçambique (Inquérito).* Lourenço Marques: Tipografia Notícias, 1945.

Roesch, Otto. 'Migrant Labour and Forced Rice Production in Southern Mozambique: The Colonial Peasantry of the Lower Limpopo Valley.' *JSAS* 17, 2 (1991): 239–70.

Roque da Silveira, Nuno. *Lourenço Marques: Acerto de Contas com o Passado, 1951–1965.* Lisbon: Edições Calibri, 2011.

Saevfors, Ingemar. *Maxaquene: a Comprehensive Account of the First Urban Upgrading Experience in New Mozambique.* New York: UNESCO, 1986.

Santos, Norberto Teixeira. 'Avaliação Nutricional da População Infantil Bantu (0–5 Anos) de uma Zona Suburbana da Cidade de Lourenço Marques.' *Revista Ciências Medicinas* 17 [Ser. B Lourenço Marques] Lourenço Marques: Tipografia Académica, 1975.

Santos Oliveira, Teresa dos. 'Recordações sobre Lourenço Marques, 1930–1950.' *Arquívo* 2 (1987): 85–108.

Sapire, Hilary and Jo Beall. 'Introduction: Urban Change and Urban Studies in Southern Africa.' *JSAS* 21 (1995): 3–17.

Saul, John. *Recolonization and Resistance: Southern Africa in the 1990s.* Trenton: Africa World Press, 1993.

Saúte, Alda Romão. *O Intercâmbio entre os Moçambicanos e as Missões Cristãs e a Educação em Moçambique.* Maputo: Promédia, 2005.

Saúte, Nelson. *Moçambique: A Oitava Côr do Arco-íris.* Madrid: Agência Española de Cooperación Internacional, 1998.

___. *Os Habitantes da Memória: Entrevistas com Escritores Moçambicanos.* Praia-Mindelo: Embaixada de Portugal, 1998.

Schmidt, Elizabeth. *Peasants, Traders, and Wives: Shona women in the history of Zimbabwe, 1870–1939.* Portsmouth: Heinemann, 1992.

Scott, James C. *Seeing Like a State: How Certain Schemes to Improve the Human Condition have Failed.* New Haven: Yale University Press, 1998.

Sheldon, Kathleen. 'Crêches, *Titias* and Mothers: Working Women and Child Care in Mozambique.' In *African Encounters with Domesticity.* edited by Karen Tranberg Hansen, 290–309. New Brunswick: Rutgers University Press, 1992.

___. 'Machambas in the City: Urban Women and Agricultural Work in Mozambique.' *Lusotopie* (1999): 121–140.

___. 'Markets and Gardens: Placing Women in the History of Urban Mozambique.' *Canadian Journal of African Studies* 37, 2/3 (2003): 358–95.

___. *Pounders of Grain: A History of Women, Work and Politics in Mozambique.* Portsmouth: Heinemann, 2002.

___. 'Women and Revolution in Mozambique: A Luta Continua.' In *Women and Revolution in Africa, Asia and the New World,* edited by Mary Ann Tétreault, 33–61. Columbia: University of South Carolina Press, 1994.

___. 'Writing about Women: Approaches to a Gendered Perspective in African History.' In *Writing African History,* edited by John Edward Philips, 465–89. Rochester: University of Rochester, 2005.

Sheldon, Kathleen, ed. *Courtyards, Markets, City Streets: Urban Women in Africa.* Boulder: Westview Press, 1996.

Shetler, Jan Bender. *Imagining Serengeti: A History of Landscape Memory in Tanzania from Earliest Times to the Present.* Athens: Ohio University Press, 2007.

___. 'The Gendered Spaces of Historical Knowledge: Women's Knowledge and Extraordinary Women in the Serengeti District, Tanzania.' IJAHS 36, 2 (2003): 283–307.

Silva, Maria da Conceição Tavares Lourenço da. 'As Missões Católicas Femininas.' *Estudos de Ciências Políticas e Sociais* 37 (1960): 49–77.

Silva, Terezinha da. 'A Journey of an Old Woman.' In *Photos: Women from Finland and Mozambique / Fotos Mulheres de Moçambique e da Finlândia,* edited by Magi Viljanen and Rui Assubuji, unpaginated.

Maputo: Embassy of Finland, 2005.

Sithole, Ndabaningi. *Frelimo Militant: The Story of Ingwane from Mozambique, an Ordinary, Yet Extraordinary, Man, Awakened.* Nairobi: Transafrica, 1977.

Sitoe, Bento. *Dicionário Changana-Português.* Maputo: Instituto Nacional do Desenvolvimento da Educação, 1996.

___. 'Translation: Languages and Cultures in Contrast.' *Discussion Papers in the African Humanities, 9,* Boston: African Studies Center, Boston University, 1990.

___. *Zabela: My Wasted Life.* [Translated by Renato Matusse] Harare: Baobab Books, 1996.

Sitoe, Bento with Narciso Mahumana and Pércida Langa, *Dicionário Ronga-Português.* Maputo: Prometra/Ciprometra, 2008.

Smith, Allen. 'The Peoples of Southern Mozambique: An Historical Survey.' *JAH* 14 (1973): 565–80.

Soares, Paulo Ribeiro. 'O Cajú e o Regime de Propriadades no Mossuril entre 1930 e 1950.' *Arquivo* 4 (1988): 91–104.

Sopa, António, Maria das Neves and Maria Deolinda Chamango. *Sebastião Langa: Retratos de uma vida.* [Photograph Selection and Research] Maputo: Arquivo Histórico de Moçambique, 2001.

Sorolov, Andrei. 'The Drama of the Russian Working Class and New Perspectives for Labour History in Russia.' In *Global Labour History: A State of the Art.* edited by Jan Lucassen, 397–452. New York: Peter Lang, 2008.

Souto, Amélia Neves de. *Caetano e o Ocaso do 'Império': Administração e Guerra Colonial em Moçambique Durante o Marcelismo (1968–1974).* Porto: Afrontamento, 2007.

___. 'Media in Mozambique.' *Africa Review of Books* 1, 2 (2005).

Spence, C. F. *Economic Survey of the Colony of Moçambique (Portuguese East Africa).* Lourenço Marques: Lourenço Marques Guardian, 1943.

___. *The Portuguese Colony of Mozambique: An Economic Survey.* Cape Town: A.A. Balkema, 1951.

Stedman-Jones, Gareth. *Outcast London: a Study in the Relationship between Classes in Victorian Society.* New York: Pantheon, 1971.

Steward, J. E., W. Ncube and K.C. Dengu-Zvigbo. *Standing at the Crossroads, WLSA and the Rights Dilemma: Which way do we go?* Harare: WLSA, 1997/ 1998.

Stichter, Sharon. *Migrant Labor.* New York: Cambridge University Press, 1985.

Swai, Elinami Veraeli. *Beyond Women's Empowerment in Africa: Exploring Dislocation and Agency.* New York: Palgrave Macmillan, 2010.

Tembe, Eulália. 'The Significance of Widowhood for Women.' *Outras Vozes Suplemento do Boletim* 8 (2004): 36–8.

Tornimbeni, Corrado. 'Migrant Workers and State Boundaries: Reflections on the Transnational Debate from the Colonial Past in Mozambique.' *Lusotopie* (2004): 107–20.

Tripp, Aili Mari. *Changing the Rules: The Politics of Liberalization and the Urban Informal Economy in Tanzania*. Berkeley: University of California Press, 1997.

Urdang, Stephanie. *And Still They Dance: Women, War and the Struggle for Change in Mozambique*. New York: Monthly Review Press, 1989.

___. 'Rural Transformation and Peasant Women in Mozambique.' *Research Working Paper* 40 [World Employment Programme, WEP, 10] Geneva: ILO, 1986.

Vail, Leroy and Landeg White. *Capitalism and Colonialism in Mozambique: A Study of Quelimane District*. Minneapolis: University of Minnesota, 1980.

___. 'Forms of Resistance: Songs and Perceptions of Power in Colonial Africa.' *American Historical Review* 88 (1983): 883–91.

___. *Power and the Praise Poem, Southern African Voices in History*. Charlottesville: University of Virginia, 1991.

Valá, Salim Crimpton. *A Problemática da Posse da Terra na Região Agrária de Chókwé (1954–1955)*. Maputo: Promédia, 2003.

Van Onselen, Charles. *Chibaro: African Mine Labour in Southern Rhodesia, 1900–1930*. London: Pluto Press, 1976.

___. *The Seed is Mine: The Life of Kas Main, a South African Sharecropper, 1894–1985*. New York: Hill and Wang, 1996.

Vaughan, Megan. 'Which Family? Problems in the Reconstruction of the History of the Family as an Economic and Cultural Unit.' *JAH* 24 (1983): 275–83.

Viegas, Joaquim, 'Problemas Agrícolas em Moçambique: A Castanha de Cajú: Mecanização Indústrial e a sua Influência na Estrutura Economica de Moçambique,' *Império*, (March /April1952): 9, 85–8.

Vieira, Carlos Alberto. *The City of Lourenço Marques Guide*. Johannesburg: Cape Times, Limited, 1956.

___. *Recordações de Lourenço Marques*. [Photographs by Carlos Alberto Vieira, Text by Ana Paula Lemos, Coordinated by Joaquim Carlos Vieira] Lisbon: Alétheia Editores, 2005.

Vijfhuizen, Carin. *'The People You Live With': Gender Identities and Social Practices; Beliefs and Power in the Livelihoods of Ndau Women and Men in a Village with an Irrigation Scheme in Zimbabwe*. Wageningen: Grafisch Service Centrum van Gils B.V., 1998.

Vijfhuizen, Carin, Carla Braga, Luis Artur and Nazneen Kanji. *Gender, Markets and Livelihoods in the Context of Globalisation; A Study of the Cashew Sector in Mozambique, January 2002 – June 2004*. London: IIED, 2004.

Viljanen, Magi and Rui Assubuji. *Photos: Women from Finland and Mozambique – Fotos: Mulheres de Moçambique e da Finlândia*. Maputo: Embassy of Finland, 2005.

Vines, Alex. 'Renamo's Rise and Decline: The Politics of Reintegration in Mozambique.' *International Peacekeeping* 20, 3 (2013): 375–93.

Waterhouse, Rachel and Carin Vijfhuizen, eds, *Strategic Women, Gainful*

Men: Gender, Land and Natural Resources in Different Rural Contexts in Mozambique. Maputo: UEM and Action Aid, 2001.

Walker, Cherryl, ed. *Women and Gender in Southern Africa to 1945*. Cape Town: David Philip, 1990.

White, Louise G. *Political Analysis: Technique and Practice*. Belmont: Wadsworth Publishing Co. 1994.

White, Luise. *Speaking With Vampires: Rumor and History in Colonial Africa*. Berkeley: University of California Press, 2000.

White, Luise, Stephan F. Miescher, David William Cohen, eds, *African Words, African Voices: Critical Practices in Oral History*. Bloomington: Indiana University Press, 2001.

Wilson, Francis. *Labour in the South African Gold Mines 1911–1969*. Cambridge: Cambridge University Press, 1972.

Women and the Law in Southern Africa. 'Some Reflections on the Working of the Assistance Centres for Victims of Domestic Violence, 2000–2003.' *Outras Vozes: Suplemento do Boletim* 8 (August 2004): 1–7.

___. 'WLSA Mozambique – Research on Violence against Women.' *Outras Vozes: Suplemento do Boletim* 8 (August 2004): 8–11.

World Bank and Ministry of Agriculture, Mozambique. 'Cashew Production and Marketing among Smallholders in Mozambique: a Gender-Differentiated Analysis Based on Household Survey Data.' *Discussion paper 1* Maputo: Ministry of Agriculture, 1998.

Young, Sherilynn J. 'Fertility and Famine: Women's Agricultural History in Southern Mozambique.' In *The Roots of Rural Poverty in Central and Southern Africa*. edited by Robin Palmer and Neil Parsons, 67–81. Berkeley: University of California Press, 1977.

Yudelman, David and Alan Jeeves. 'New Labour Frontiers for Old: Black Migrants to the South African Gold Mines, 1920–1985.' *JSAS* 13 (1986): 101–24.

Zamparoni, Valdemir. 'Copos e Corpos: A Disciplinização do Prazer em Terras Coloniais.' *Travessias: Revista de Ciencias Sociais e Humanas em Lingua Portuguesa* 4/5 (2004): 119–37.

___. *De Escravo a Cozinheiro: Colonialismo e Racismo em Moçambique*. Salvador: Universidade Federal da Bahia, 2007.

___. 'Lourenço Marques: Espaço Urbano, Espaço Branco?' In *Actas do Colóquio 'Construção e Ensino da História de África*, 89–109. Lisbon: Comissão Nacional para as Comemorações dos Descobrimentos Portugueses, 1995.

Zeleza, Paul Tiyambe. 'Gender Biases in African Historiography.' In *Engendering African Social Sciences*, edited by Ayesha M. Imam, Amina Mama, Fatou Sow, 81–115. Dakar: CODESRIA Book Series, 1997.

Zimba, Benigna. *Mulheres Invisíveis: O Género e as Políticas Comerciais no Sul do Moçambique, 1720–1830*. Maputo: Promédia, 2003.

Index

abandonment, 121–122, 137, 143, 207; *abandonar*, 20; men on, 14; migration and, 89, 146; in song, 171, 173–175

absenteeism, 38, 43, 61, 104; drinking and, 109n113; family rituals and, 207, 211; illness and, 158–159, 201; *Malalanyana* and, 107–108; Parente and Neto on, 116–119, 155, 230

absolute poverty, 220–221. *See also poverty*

abuse, 121–122, 153; of children, 138, 144–146, 149, 157, 202; from families, 145, 149, 212; migration and, 89; sexual, 85, 115, 149, 195n72; from supervisors, 35, 114. *See also domestic violence*

Acção Social (social services), 158, 200–201

Administração de Conselho de Lourenço Marques (ACLM), 17n35, 106–107, 109–111; conscript labour and, 128; records of, 114, 117

Administrative Post of Munhuana (PAM), 108

administrative reports, 61

administrative staff, 19, 23–24, 193

adult status, 84, 123, 131–132

adultery, 179, 207

African elites, 8, 57, 59–60, 197; *mestiços*, 182–184, 206; middle class, 59

age cohorts, 20, 213

agency, 4, 130, 171; of narrators, 24, 26, 34; social, 38, 200; of workers, 95, 119

'Agostinho' (song), 171–175, 187, 204

Agribusiness Industries Association (AIA), 226, 231

agricultores (model farmer), 138–141

agricultural products, 43–44, 51, 62–63, 68; drought and, 220; in north, 71

Agricultural Research Project, 49

agriculture, 4, 19, 132, 218; cashew economy and, 43, 221; census, 51; colonial, 128; commercial, 44, 49–51, 133; drought and, 220; in *machongos*, 84; men in, 191; planting season, 119; soil fertility, 137; three-tiered mixed, 50; traditional, 49; urban, 161; as women's task, 123. *See also cashew orchards; family farmers; machambas*

Agro-industry of Cashews in Mozambique, 75, 77

agronomy, 11

aguardente, 45, 56n72, 79

Aksoy, M. Ataman, 230

alcoholic drinks, 12, 35, 43, 55–62, 162; *aguardente*, 45, 56n72, 79; beer, 55, 57–59, 134, 209; distillation of, 45, 47–48, 55–60, 217. *See also brewing; cashew drinks*

alcoholism, 87n22; drunkenness, 42–43, 56–57, 60, 195

allergy to cashew dust, 94–95, 105

amancebado (common-law marriage), 20, 148–149, 156, 175; advantages of, 3; colonial law on, 38; in urban areas, 180, 196, 202–206, 212. *See also family forms*

amapaka famine (1922), 133

amêndoa. See cashew kernels

Anacardiaceae (cashew family), 94

anacardic acid, 47, 88, 93–95

Anacardium occidentale (cashew plant), 34–35, 45–48, 94–95

androcentrism, 3, 141, 154, 184, 212

Angoche, 227; Companhia Colonial de Angoche, 66, 69, 71

Angola, 4, 7

Lightning Source UK Ltd.
Milton Keynes UK
UKHW021644050821
388196UK00002B/66